# Pacific Literatures as World Literature

## Literatures as World Literature

Can the literature of a specific country, author, or genre be used to approach the elusive concept of "world literature"? **Literatures as World Literature** takes a novel approach to world literature by analyzing specific constellations—according to language, nation, form, or theme—of literary texts and authors in their own world-literary dimensions.

World literature is obviously so vast that any view of it cannot help but be partial; the question then becomes how to reduce the complex task of understanding and describing world literature. Most treatments of world literature so far either have been theoretical and thus abstract, or else have made broad use of exemplary texts from a variety of languages and epochs. The majority of critical work, the filling in of what has been traced, lies ahead of us. **Literatures as World Literature** fills in the devilish details by allowing scholars to move outward from their own areas of specialization, fostering scholarly writing that approaches more closely the polyphonic, multiperspectival nature of world literature.

Series Editor:
Thomas O. Beebee

Editorial Board:
Eduardo Coutinho, Federal University of Rio de Janeiro, Brazil
Hsinya Huang, National Sun-yat Sen University, Taiwan
Meg Samuelson, University of Adelaide, Australia
Ken Seigneurie, Simon Fraser University, Canada
Galin Tihanov, Queen Mary University of London, UK
Mads Rosendahl Thomsen, Aarhus University, Denmark

Volumes in the Series
*German Literature as World Literature*, edited by Thomas O. Beebee
*Roberto Bolaño as World Literature*, edited by Nicholas Birns and Juan E. De Castro
*Crime Fiction as World Literature*, edited by David Damrosch, Theo D'haen and Louise Nilsson
*Danish Literature as World Literature*, edited by Dan Ringgaard and Mads Rosendahl Thomsen
*From Paris to Tlön: Surrealism as World Literature*, by Delia Ungureanu
*American Literature as World Literature*, edited by Jeffrey R. Di Leo

*Romanian Literature as World Literature*, edited by Mircea Martin, Christian Moraru, and Andrei Terian
*Brazilian Literature as World Literature*, edited by Eduardo F. Coutinho
*Dutch and Flemish Literature as World Literature*, edited by Theo D'haen
*Afropolitan Literature as World Literature*, edited by James Hodapp
*Francophone Literature as World Literature*, edited by Christian Moraru, Nicole Simek, and Bertrand Westphal
*Bulgarian Literature as World Literature*, edited by Mihaela P. Harper and Dimitar Kambourov
*Philosophy as World Literature*, edited by Jeffrey R. Di Leo
*Turkish Literature as World Literature*, edited by Burcu Alkan and Çimen Günay-Erkol
*Elena Ferrante as World Literature*, by Stiliana Milkova
*Multilingual Literature as World Literature*, edited by Jane Hiddleston and Wen-chin Ouyang
*Persian Literature as World Literature*, edited by Mostafa Abedinifard, Omid Azadibougar, and Amirhossein Vafa
*Mexican Literature as World Literature*, edited by Ignacio M. Sánchez Prado
*Beyond English: World Literature and India*, by Bhavya Tiwari
*Graphic Novels and Comics as World Literature*, edited by James Hodapp
*African Literatures as World Literature*, edited by Alexander Fyfe and Madhu Krishnan
*Feminism as World Literature*, edited by Robin Truth Goodman
*Polish Literature as World Literature*, edited by Piotr Florczyk and K. A. Wisniewski
*Taiwanese Literature as World Literature*, edited by Pei-yin Lin and Wen-chi Li
*Pacific Literatures as World Literature*, edited by Hsinya Huang and Chia-hua Yvonne Lin
*Central American Literature as World Literature*, edited by Sophie Esch (forthcoming)
*Hungarian Literature as World Literature*, edited by Péter Hajdu and Zoltán Z. Varga (forthcoming)
*Kazuo Ishiguro as World Literature*, by Chris Holmes (forthcoming)

# Pacific Literatures as World Literature

Edited by Hsinya Huang and
Chia-hua Lin

BLOOMSBURY ACADEMIC
NEW YORK • LONDON • OXFORD • NEW DELHI • SYDNEY

BLOOMSBURY ACADEMIC
Bloomsbury Publishing Inc
1385 Broadway, New York, NY 10018, USA
50 Bedford Square, London, WC1B 3DP, UK
29 Earlsfort Terrace, Dublin 2, Ireland

BLOOMSBURY, BLOOMSBURY ACADEMIC and the Diana logo are trademarks of Bloomsbury Publishing Plc

First published in the United States of America 2023
Paperback edition published in 2024

Volume Editor's Part of the Work © Hsinya Huang and Chia-hua Lin, 2023
Each chapter © Contributors, 2023

Cover design by Simon Levy

All rights reserved. No part of this publication may be reproduced or transmitted in any form or by any means, electronic or mechanical, including photocopying, recording, or any information storage or retrieval system, without prior permission in writing from the publishers.

Bloomsbury Publishing Inc does not have any control over, or responsibility for, any third-party websites referred to or in this book. All internet addresses given in this book were correct at the time of going to press. The author and publisher regret any inconvenience caused if addresses have changed or sites have ceased to exist, but can accept no responsibility for any such changes.

Library of Congress Cataloging-in-Publication Data
Names: Huang, Hsinya, editor. | Lin, Chia-hua (Chia-hua Yvonne) editor.
Title: Pacific literatures as world literature / edited by Hsinya Huang and Chia-hua Lin.
Description: New York : Bloomsbury Academic, 2023. | Series: Literatures as world literature | Includes bibliographical references. |
Summary: "Examines trans-Pacific poets and writers to suggest a different way of understanding Oceanic literature and its place in world literature"– Provided by publisher.
Identifiers: LCCN 2022047152 (print) | LCCN 2022047153 (ebook) | ISBN 9781501389320 (hardback) | ISBN 9781501389368 (paperback) | ISBN 9781501389337 (ebook) | ISBN 9781501389344 (pdf) | ISBN 9781501389351 (ebook other)
Subjects: LCSH: Pacific Island poetry–History and criticism. | Pacific Island literature–History and criticism. | LCGFT: Literary criticism. | Essays.
Classification: LCC PN849.O26 P26 2023 (print) | LCC PN849.O26 (ebook) | DDC 809–dc23/eng/20230120
LC record available at https://lccn.loc.gov/2022047152
LC ebook record available at https://lccn.loc.gov/2022047153

| ISBN: | HB: | 978-1-5013-8932-0 |
|---|---|---|
| | PB: | 978-1-5013-8936-8 |
| | ePDF: | 978-1-5013-8934-4 |
| | eBook: | 978-1-5013-8933-7 |

Series: Literatures as World Literature

Typeset by Integra Software Services Pvt. Ltd.

To find out more about our authors and books visit www.bloomsbury.com and sign up for our newsletters.

# Contents

List of Figures   ix
Foreword: A Writer's Ocean   x

Introduction   *Hsinya Huang and Chia-hua Lin*   1

Part 1   Colonialism: The Pacific Ocean

1. The Wilkes Expedition (1838–1842) and the Formation of a US Empire of Bases in the Pacific   *John R. Eperjesi*   21
2. Epeli Hauʻofa's Pronouns   *Paul Lyons*   35
3. Mountains of Taiwan, Japanese Colonization, and Western Science   *Chia-li Kao*   51
4. Demilitarization and Decolonization in CHamoru Literature from Guåhan (Guam)   *Craig Santos Perez*   67

Part 2   Indigenous Resistance to Colonialism

5. Decolonizing Guam with Poetry: "Everyday Objects with Mission" in Craig Santos Perez's Poetry   *Anna Erzsebet Szucs*   85
6. Remapping Mānoa Valley in Hawaiian Literature   *Chia-hua Lin*   101
7. Planetary Boundaries, Planetary Imaginary: Homing Pacific Eco-poetry   *Hsinya Huang*   117
8. The Ecological Vision of the Ainu Reflected in Their Oral Tradition   *Hitoshi Oshima*   135

Part 3   Ocean and Ecology

9. Becoming Oceania: Toward a Planetary Ecopoetics or Reframing the Pacific Rim   *Rob Wilson*   147
10. Island Imaginations, Bioregionalism, and the Environmental Humanities   *Kathryn Yalan Chang*   163

11  Decolonizing Oceanic Realms: Voices from Australia Pacific  *Iris Ralph*  183

12  Whale as Cosmos: Multispecies Ethnography and Contemporary Indigenous Cosmopolitics  *Joni Adamson*  195

Notes on Contributors  211
Index  215

# Figures

6.1 "Mānoa Valley" by Albert Wendt — 104
6.2 Mural on the Pillars — 109
6.3 Wood carving at Ka Papa Lo'i O Kānewai — 110
6.4 Picture of the irrigation system — 112
6.5 People working in the lo'i kalo — 113

# Foreword: A Writer's Ocean

As a writer, publishing one short story every two weeks is not difficult for me. What makes it hard, however, is that I live on an island in the West Pacific. I am constantly lured by the ocean. For example, I dive and fish, patrol the mountains, and look for the timber for the *tatala* (Tao canoe).[1] I also practice our island people's knowledge of flora and fauna and immerse myself in night voyaging. Through many nights, I row the tatala and catch flying fish until dawn. Oftentimes, I converse with the elders about the ways of our island and time flies by. It is nearly impossible for me to focus on writing, so sometimes I simply quit. Now, reflecting on these experiences, I realized it was all my faulty thinking. It was truly wrong for me to try to conform to the ways of thinking, the grammar, and the writing method of the mainstream culture. In trying to be conformative, my writing became out of tune, incongruous, and irrelevant. It was also the case that as I gained higher mastery of my Indigenous language, it hindered the progress of my already-bad Mandarin writing. My writing does not fit into the syntax and structure of the mainstream "Han Chinese composition." Besides, I wrote things irrelevant to the dominant values, but as I cared too much about how the mainstream culture felt, the fault was mine.

\* \* \*

So today, the worldview I endeavor to put forth is that of "the universe of a small island," which is marginalized by the mainstream culture. I realize that we live on "different planets." Reflecting on my previous writing experience with this new insight, I confess that I have wrongly viewed writing as more complicated than it needs to be.

---

[1] Editors' note: *Tatala* is an assembled canoe of Tao people. It is closely related to the fishing tradition of the Tao people, especially to the flying fish culture. As Hsiang-hua Wang suggests, "the tatala boat is an essential tool of production for every family or clan" (n.p.). Karen Kan-Lun Tu also points out that tatala is important not only to the daily lives of the Tao people but also to Tao people's ethnic identity (63). Tatala is also closely related to Tao people's traditional knowledge on trees, canoe building, and navigation. The embellishment on tatala manifests both Tao aesthetics and their cosmology. In Wang's words, "tatala represents the accumulation of wisdom passed down from the people's forefathers" (n.p.). Consequently, tatala is a significant symbol of Tao people's resilience in the form of passing down the traditional knowledge. Before the flying fish season (from February to June) of 2022, Syaman Rapongan built a tatala with his son, Ranpogan, celebrating the intergenerational continuity of traditional knowledge. The building of tatala is an act of resurgence of the Tao people, through which they "[reconnect] with land, culture, and community" (Elliott 67). For more information regarding Syaman Rapongan's literature and Tao canoe and navigation, refer to Huang's comparative article on "Performing Archipelagic Identities in Bill Reid, Robert Sullivan, and Syaman Rapongan."

    As a self-identified "Oceanic litterateur," I honestly have not given much thought to the substantial meaning of any of my book titles. I still remember that when I took the mandatory Chinese composition class in my freshman year in 1980, the professor gave almost all the students B+ or higher grades, but he gave me a C. The professor wrote his comments in red: "I don't understand what you are writing about." My autobiographical fiction *Eyes of the Sky* (2012) commences with a long narrative of a giant jackfish. As I submitted my manuscripts to the publisher, my editor asked me to change the jackfish into a human narrator; that is, the story must be told from a first-person human I. My thought then was: "since we live on different planets, why do I have to follow the perspectives of 'your' literature"? We live on different planets, and thus we hold different worldviews. I am writing the literature of my home island *Pongso no Tao* (Orchid Island/Lanyu), where fishes, the sky, winds, clouds, rain, ocean and tides, the sun, and the moons should be the core of our stories/literature. Our life is oriented toward an entirely different worldview. For instance, Tao people live by the "night count," in which the moon is measured. Our everyday life and activities are regulated by this calendar. In this calendar, each night/moon has its own name, hence the plural "moons." Whereas in the mainstream literature, there are cities, streets, and alleys, here are ocean, tides, and a multitude of playful fishes in our life and literature.

    Therefore, I declare again that I was raised to speak my Indigenous language, not Mandarin. My Indigenous language allows me to understand the primeval oceanic sentiment while Mandarin allows me to understand world literature and Chinese/Sinophone literature. I realize that my Mandarin writing is flawed, but my literature is my love story with the ocean. I submerge myself in the world of salt water and waves. Only when I am in the ocean, and when I feel the elegance of my body in it, do I gain deep understanding of the oceanic literature of my people. My body is not as strong and fit as it was back in the days, but I still immerse myself in the embrace of the ocean. I enjoy submerging myself in the tenderness of the sea.

    The writers discussed in this volume also write from and for different societies and through their writings and what they write about reveal different worldviews. Together they forge a beautiful constellation that will help us to navigate the infinite world of Oceania.

Syaman Ranpongan<br>
Translated by Chia-hua Lin

# Works Cited

Elliott, Michael. "Resurgence: The Drive for Renewed Engagement and Reciprocity in the Turn Away from the State." *Canadian Journal of Political Science*, vol. 51, no. 1, 2018, pp. 61–81.

Huang, Hsinya. "Performing Archipelagic Identities in Bill Reid, Robert Sullivan, and Syaman Rapongan." *Archipelagic American Studies: Decontinentalizing the Study of American Culture*, edited by Michelle Ann Stephens, and Brian Russell Roberts. Duke UP, 2017, pp. 281–301.

Tu, Karen Kan-Lun. *Wa and Tatala: The Transformation of Indigenous Canoes on Yap and Orchid Island*. 2017. The Australian National University, PhD dissertation.

Wang, Hsiang-Hua. "The Tao People's Tatala Boats on Lanyu" Ethnobotany in Taiwan, http://tk.agron.ntu.edu.tw/ethnobot/TATALA/tatala.htm. Accessed May 24, 2022.

# Introduction

### Hsinya Huang and Chia-hua Lin

As the site where life first formed, a crucial element of the climate, and an abundant but a fragile resource, the ocean is of vital importance to our planet. The Pacific has the largest and deepest of the world's ocean basin. Not only has it contributed to the world economy, but it also provides extensive fishing grounds, sea transportation, and food resources as well as oil, gas, and minerals to advance human civilization. Trade across the Pacific between the Americas and Pacific countries has surpassed that across the Atlantic between the Americas and Europe since 1970s. Diverse trans-oceanic, historical, economic, and cultural relations link peoples, cultures, ecological systems, and political territories within this immense water. It is a vast expanse of water that not only reaches the continents of Asia, Australia, and the Americas but also houses "a sea of islands" (between 25,000 to 30,000 islands). Precisely because of this vastness, its past and present remain susceptible to demarcations of imperial and colonial powers, and its future is intimately connected with our common planetary belonging. This volume employs the Pacific as a concept, method, and contact zone to conjure transpacific poets and writers whose work enacts "forces of becoming oceanic" (Wilson, "Becoming Oceania" 24). By suggesting a different mode of understanding, viewing, and sensing the world, we aim to "re-world" the Pacific as central to sustaining planetary well-being and envisioning solidarity across lands and waters. As Rob Wilson puts it brilliantly, the Pacific signifies "a bioregional site of coalitional *promise* as much as a danger zone of antagonistic *peril*" ("Oceania as Peril" 261). To explore the significance of the Pacific as a site of both "promise" and "peril," this volume examines the flows of powers, cultures, ideas, and practices across the Pacific. It illuminates how these flows across the Pacific, involving Asia, the Americas, Pacific Islands, and Australia, have been harnessed for politics of domination and resistance.

The authors of this volume reorient the Pacific to bring to the fore the lived experiences of the Pacific in a multitude of texts which reflect geo and aqua significance and relevance. Oceanic perspectives are accentuated to remap contacts and exchanges beyond the confines of continental territorial claims. Through in-depth readings of imaginaries, visuals, and narratives, they explore the significance of Pacific literature and re-world it into world literature by transcending and transforming national boundaries into planetary belonging. They ask in what way re-worlding Pacific literature invokes a paradigm shift in reading, interpreting, and understanding world literature. Other issues investigated include the ways in which the mixture of discourses, imaginaries, and practices perform Pacific cultures and politics; how Indigenous collaborations reveal both the complicity and resistance of the Pacific populations to colonial powers; how the contact and exchange among islands and between islands and continents impact the cultural distinctions of the populations and communities as well as their continuance; how to conceptualize next steps of decolonial (island) studies. By bringing together critical works of poets, scholars, and activists based in North America, Japan, Taiwan, Korea, Europe, Hawai'i, and Guåhan/Guam, this volume decenters continental/land poetics as such via long-standing transpacific ties, re-worlding Pacific literature as world literature.

## Worlding and Re-worlding: Indigenous and Oceanic Connectivity of the Pacific

The idea of "worlding" was first introduced by Gayatri Spivak to postcolonial cultural studies, where she explores how the project of Imperialism has violently put together the episteme that appropriates and contains colonial subject as Europe's other. What is at stake, as Spivak postulates, is a "worlding," the re-inscription of a cartography that presupposes an "uninscribed earth" and thereby transforms native lands into the colonized space (247). Subsequently, for the last two decades, such worlding projects as Rob Wilson and Christophier Leigh Connery's (2007) have emerged as postcolonial "re-worlding" effort and advanced a field of cultural studies, which recognizes difference in the homogenizing world and brings forth "critical and generative response to Western hegemony" and its static model of the globe (ix). Spivak's postcolonial invocation of "worlding" predominantly challenges the archives of British Empire as a way of cultural containment. In a similar vein but from different critical angles and locales, Wilson alongside other postcolonial and cultural critics such as Arif Dirlik remaps the world by revisioning postcolonial theories and transnationalisms in contemporary age of globalization to forge postcolonial creation and resistance to global capital ("Afterword" 212).

Wilson and Dirlik focus on Asia Pacific as "space of cultural production" (1995), exhibiting Asia/Pacific nuances in postcolonial studies since Edward Said's *Orientalism* (1978). Their critical stance challenges the idea of the "*Pacific Rim*" as "unsatisfactory because it focuses too exclusively on the edges of the region, leaving out of the picture what is inside, which historically played an important part in the formation of the region" (59; italics original). In her recent work *Ocean Passages*, Erin Suzuki likewise pinpoints the controversy and limitation of the concept of Pacific Rim: "while imperialist imaginings of the Pacific had posited the region as a boundless expanse filled with territory to be claimed, Pacific Rim discourse, by its very naming, delimits the possibilities of territorial expansion" (12). The critical scholarship in Asia Pacific and Pacific Rim studies postulates how the transpacific approach could be enriched by looking at rising Asia Pacific economies and migrancy of peoples, ideas, cultures, and goods across and around the Pacific. Nevertheless, this version of treating Asia Pacific as a unique space of cultural production over what they name the Pacific as the "American Lake" runs a risk of absorbing the more fluid and dynamic transcultural exchanges and oceanic movements from Indigenous Pacific. Pivoting on the "Asia-Pacific" formulation, circulated and fortified by global capitalism, Western modernity, and military strategies, transpacific cultural critics do not capture experiences and innovations from Indigenous Pacific or what is in Epeli Hauʻofa's trope of "Oceania" as "a sea of islands." The pervasive omission of Indigenous subjects in contemporary transpacific knowledge production entails our efforts to integrate the transpacific with Indigenous advocacy to re-world alternative ways of knowing, sensing, and thinking, and in so doing, to reframe and enrich our perceptions of the world.

Indeed, Setsu Shigematsu and Keith Camacho (2010) contend that the Asia Pacific paradigm, while useful for analyzing transpacific networks of powers, makes invisible the multiplicity of Pacific Islanders' contributions. By the same token, Amy Kuʻuleialoha Stillman, Vicente Diaz, J. Kēhaulani Kauanui, and others have indicated that the contemporary formulations of the transpacific studies have largely excluded Indigenous histories, cultures, and communities as well as the legacies of settler colonialism and struggles for decolonization within the Indigenous Pacific (qtd. in Espiritu 484). This power imbalance treats the Pacific Ocean as a site of imperial and colonial dominance, theorizing the Pacific only as a "geopolitical production of the U.S. Empire" (ibid. 485).

To rectify this discursive slant, our task conceptualizes the Pacific as a critical site of relationality and intersectionality, where we examine Indigenous Pacific vis-à-vis the transpacific to elucidate the linked structures of imperial and colonial dominance. The Indigenous postulations of the Pacific constitute an important aspect of our (re-)worlding project as we put forth some sort of "radical otherness that cannot be dismissed or assimilated to national belonging paradigms" (Suzuki, "Transpacific" 355). In *Postcolonial Pacific Writing* (2005), Michelle Keown calls attention to the omission of the Pacific Islands, which are subsumed by labels such as "the Asia Pacific region" (8–9). Paul Sharrad opens his book *Albert Wendt and Pacific Literature* (2003) by stressing the ways Pacific writers respond to "the demand of postcolonial theory (and of its critics) for cultural and historical specificity" and yet are paradoxically excluded from the largely "Afrocentric concerns of postcolonial diaspora in the transatlantic metropolises that still dominate anglophone publishing" (32). Paul Lyons's *American Pacificism* continues to revise colonial discourses about the Pacific by conjuring oceanic imaginaries, which have been traditionally ignored in comparative and world literary studies. Hauʻofa's paradigm-shifting figure for the Pacific coalition-building is called "Oceania," detailed in Rob Wilson's and Paul Lyon's chapters in this volume. Wilson, a bridge-builder who has mobilized transpacific connections, and the author of *Reimagining the American Pacific*, reinscribes the Pacific into his creative writing in addition to his scholarship, and the result is a brilliant transpacific poetry collection *When the Nikita Moon Rose* (2021).

This volume draws on a narrative and critical frame that is big and inclusive enough to transcend borderlands and "borderwaters" (Roberts 1) and, in so doing, reveal the deep stories of oceanic connectivity, in which the Pacific is history. These deep stories of oceanic ties and flows fashion identities, imaginaries, practices, and discourses that weave together intra-Pacific, transnational, and trans-Indigenous cultural production. As such, they take us to embark on a transborder journey, "navigating beyond the violent divisions / of national and maritime borders, beyond / the scarred latitudes and longitudes / of empire, to navigate the cartography / of our most expansive legends / and deepest routes," in the poetic rendition of Craig Santos Perez, one of this volume's authors ("The Fifth Map").

## (Re)Imagining the Pacific: Indigenous Resistance and Decolonial Insights

This volume mobilizes a reimagination of the Pacific beyond the Euro-American/continent-centered framework by unfolding "what is inside." Activating and taking inspiration from transnational cultural studies of (re-)worlding, it argues for the centrality of the Pacific within the disciplinary practices of comparative and world literature. As an ongoing historical process, worlding cannot be understood in abstract or theoretical terms alone but involves vibrant everyday practices conveyed through the Pacific (oceanic) imaginaries and narratives. We trace the modes and mores of imperialism and colonialism across the Pacific, emphasizing the encounters and crossroads where transformation or counter discourses and practices take place.

(Re-)worlding Pacific literature is to push its definition and understanding beyond the scope of a regional literature by problematizing the relationship between literature and locality. Landmark writing such as Teresia Teaiwa's (2006, 2017, 2021) and Epeli Hau'ofa's (2008) has probed into the pathways of the Indigenous Pacific and the trajectories of diaspora and migrancy and brought to the forefront a rich "Oceana's library," knowledge that Indigenous Pacific populations possess (Subramani, "The Oceanic Imaginang" 151). Precisely, Hau'ofa, a well-known Tongan and Fijian scholar, points out in his pathbreaking chapter, "Our Sea of Islands," Pacific islands have long been imagined as far off and isolated and thus economically dependent on the powerful nations (29). As Hau'ofa suggests, in this conceptualization of the Pacific, "the small island states and territories of the Pacific, that is, all of Polynesia and Micronesia, are too small, too poorly endowed with resources, and too isolated from the centers of economic growth for their inhabitants ever to be able to rise above their present condition of dependence on the largesse of wealthy nations" (29). To counter this Eurocentric perspective, Hau'ofa elaborates on how mutual dependence and reciprocity have always been a significant aspect of Oceanian cultures (36). He challenges us to move beyond the belittling Western perception and to conceptualize the Pacific as "sea of Islands" (31). In this view, we see the ocean as not separating and dividing but connecting the Pacific Islands. Hau'ofa's idea is fundamental to this volume's reading of Pacific literature as world literature, for it pushes us to acknowledge and appreciate the largess and richness of the Pacific communities and cultures.[1]

Likewise, in her poem, "AmneSIA," Teresia Teaiwa pinpoints how the Pacific discourse should transcend the "Rim" and derives her imaginaries specifically from oceanic and islanding environments:

> who's gonna give a damn if they don't/can't remember
> that the whole of the donut is filled with coconuts
> they're after all american pie in the east
> and some kind of zen in the west
> east and west are of course relative
> the rim of our basin
> is overflowing with kava
> but the basin of their rim
> is empty
>
> (*Sweat and Salt Water* 69)

Instead of "the hole in the doughnut" (36), an empty space, a famous metaphor Hauʻofa employs to sarcastically reflect on the colonial Pacific, Teaiwa's poem fills this space with coconuts, a significant plant in many Pacific islanders' cultures. By stating that "the basin of their [Westerners'] rim / is empty" while "the rim of our [Pacific Islanders'] basin / is overflowing with kava," she opens a world of the Pacific bounty and beauty, a world of relationality and reciprocity, by subverting the discourse of the colonial binary dyad of Pacific rim and basin. Through innovative imaginaries deeply rooted in their oceanic and islanding experiences, both poets exemplify how Pacific literature performs cultures and practices, subversive to the Eurocentric and continental ways of conceptualizing and understanding the world.

Hauʻofa and Teaiwa's imaginaries elucidate contemporary politics of decolonial investigations by delinking modernity and colonial matrix of power from the perspectives of the Pacific (transpacific and Oceania). To view the Pacific anew requires such radical delinking of coloniality and modernity. Central to this volume is thus an attempt to re-world Indigenous Pacific and islanding perspectives into our understanding of world literature and in so doing establish a "decolonial genealogy," to borrow Lisa Yoneyama's words (2017).

Based on Foucauldian concept of genealogy, Yoneyama stresses the significance of a "conjunctive critique of the transpacific as a critical methodology by which to consider alternatives to transwar, interimperial, Cold War formations" (472). As she states, a decolonial genealogy works to "clarify the specific geohistoric conditions" under which

---

[1] For book-length cultural and knowledge production of the Pacific/Oceania, refer to Wendt (1980, 1995), Subramani (1985), Sharrad (2003), Hereniko and Wilson (1999), Hattori (2004), Teaiwa (2021), Webb and Nandan (2007), Keown (2007), Kauanui (2008), Diaz (2010), Camacho (2012), Banivanua Mar (2016), Flores and Kihleng (2019).

the Pacific has been constituted as "an object of knowledge or nonknowledge" (472). While joining forces in delineating "a decolonial genealogy," our project scales up the temporality and spatiality of the transpacific by conjuring works from diverse locales and approaches. We aim to examine how transnational and trans-Indigenous studies across the Pacific meet and in their common endeavors and actions challenge and resist the Euro-American/continental dominance of the Pacific.

Indeed, as in the twenty-first century, the powers of the United States continue to dominate the ocean, complicated by the rise of China in the midst, inclusiveness and convergence become crucial in any discursive formation so that any genealogical inquiry into the Pacific entails the potential synergies of Indigenous resistance and decolonial thought of the transpacific. The US strategies to expand are shown not only in the Pacific pivot of cultural, military, and economic policy but also in the development of a transpacific partnership. This partnership brings together a dozen countries—not including China—in a trade pact whose aim is to increase its influence. That pact signals how the transpacific, up to now an academic term, has reached mass consciousness.[2] Pivoting on a decolonial genealogy converging Indigenous Pacific and the transpacific, we ask what kind of newness can be perceived and what has compelled us into a common enterprise of re-worlding the Pacific in the world literature. What new sensibilities and awareness can be raised as we pull together a "de-colonial genealogy" to confront the legacies of structural violence arising from imperial and colonial hegemony in the Pacific?

However, Yoneyama like many others seems to bypass the important work of Indigenous Pacific in dismantling various forms of colonialism. For instance, as she comments, the vast areas of Asia and the Pacific Islands that were formerly colonized or occupied by the Japanese Empire were only reorganized and then mobilized to secure the US geopolitical ascendancy (472). This view risks some oversights about intra-Pacific coloniality, a non-Western power dominating the region—traditionally regarded as an "American Lake," including Japanese imperialism and militarism on Guam/Guåhan and Taiwan before and during the Second World War. The concept of decoloniality has been construed within Western epistemology and yet its application needs to recognize multiple forms of coloniality of knowledge and sensing and to realize how coloniality has affected "epistemology (the principles and assumptions that regulate knowing) and aesthetics (the principles and assumptions that regulate taste and subjectivity)" (Mignolo x). A part of this volume such as Perez's chapter, "Demilitarization and Decolonization in CHamoru Poetry from Guåhan (Guam)," addresses colonial structural power imminent in the Pacific through discourse, cartography, and institutional power.

To read Pacific literature as world literature, this volume dismisses any convenient package regarding the Pacific. With chapters that investigate literature from the Pacific

---

[2] For some critical delineations of other relevant concepts such as transnationalism, trans-Indigenous, and transpacific, see Allen (2012), Sakai and Yoo (2012), Huang et al. (2012, 2018), Nguyen and Hoskins (2014), Suzuki (2014, 2021), Yoneyama (2016, 2017), and Keown et al. (2018).

Northwest Coast, Native America, Pacific Islands such as Guåhan, Marshall Islands, Hawaiʻi, Aotearoa/New Zealand, Tonga, Fiji, Samoa, Solomons, Taiwan, Okinawa, and Japan, the contributors of this volume challenge the unthinking acceptance of such terms as "Asia Pacific" and "Pacific Rim" and clarify the hidden power relationships and hegemonic oppression that manifest in ideological constructions of the region. The retrieval or recovery of hidden or buried stories can only be made possible by a critical frame which is inclusive and an attitude and awareness which is relational, intersectional, and convergent. Tracey Banivanua Mar anticipates the myriad ways in which a critical focus on connectivity, circuits, and networks may "continue to extend our knowledge of such, often hidden, histories" ("Author's Response" 459–60). For Banivanua Mar, decolonization is "a concept that has been configured by Indigenous and colonized peoples as an elemental and intergenerational process—a stateless and maneuverable site of independence and sovereignty" (461–62). The sovereignty of nation-states, settlers' nations, or territories should not be privileged over that of peoples (*Decolonisation and the Pacific* 8). By exploring the dialectics between decolonization and the Pacific, the authors of this volume along with Banivanua Mar endeavor to build a new language for decolonial genealogy and through mutual care and reciprocity to imagine, re-world, reclaim, and heal in the aftermath of imperialism, militarism, and colonialism in the Pacific. The struggle for our common planetary future, as Candace Fujikane asserts, "calls for a profound epistemological shift" (3).

## Pacific Literature as World Literature: Conceptual Framework

In his book, *What Is World Literature?*, David Damrosch states that world literature "encompass[es] all literary works that circulate beyond their culture of origin" (4). Damrosch further clarifies that "a work only has an *effective* life as world literature whenever, and wherever, it is actively present within a literary system beyond that of its original culture" (4; emphasis added). This vision of world literature propels us to rethink being in relation beyond the nationalist and imperialist matrix. "[H]ow are we, artists, critics, poets, and humanists, to embark on a radical rebuilding of our epistemologies" beyond national and international borders (Moraru n.p.)?

This volume examines the "*effective* life" of the literary works and their presence within and beyond the transpacific context. The authors based on diverse locales across the globe bring forth culture-specific reading to produce non-Eurocentric epistemologies. Indigenous ecopoetics, for example, requires a non-Eurocentric, non hierarchical, and non-anthropocentric way of reading. Referring to Indigenous Pacific ecopoetics, Craig Santos Perez underscores the idea of interconnection and interrelatedness of humans and the nonhuman world as well as the importance of knowing the Indigenous histories of the Pacific. As he continues, native writers employ oceanic imaginaries to conceive the planet as sites of healing, co-belonging, resistance, and mutual care ("Teaching" n.p.). It is precisely the idea of interconnection and relatedness that Pacific literary works convey by traveling beyond their cultures of origin to be read as world literature. In his influential article, "The Oceanic Imaginary," Subramani pinpoints a relationship between the rootedness of Indigenous Pacific Islanders and the worldliness of their works; namely, with their roots firmly in Oceania, scholars and writers can receive and reciprocate freely forms and styles of world literatures (152). He calls for a regional literature to "allow Oceanic imaginations to reach beyond narrow ethnicities and national boundaries in order to draw from a wider range of sources" (152). This volume goes beyond a nation-state-centered reading and advocates fluid oceanic imaginaries as a means of resistance to colonial hegemonic oppression and demarcation. As Subramani argues, "the site of most *effective* resistance, of course, is literary production itself" (157; emphasis added).

The conceptual framework of this volume is historical, interdisciplinary, interregional, and global, which enables readers to understand and evaluate the diversity of relations that have connected the peoples, cultures, multispecies, and ecosystems of the Pacific with the rest of the world. It introduces new modes of research such as multispecies ethnography, and practices such as ecopoetics and Indigenous cosmopolitics, as well as language and metaphors with which to imagine life in "Oceania." It provides valuable insights into the history and development of humanity and ecological vision in the Pacific. Its exploration of cultural perspectives of nature and more-than-human beings reveals the interrelation between ecological consciousness/vision, myths, and world literature.

Our project involves several layers of meaning and significance. First, to redress the oversights of world literature centralized in Western countries and unified by the medium of English as a vehicle of expression, we employ a decolonial methodology to evoke a "palimpsestic history of the region that drew attention to its multiple histories of colonization and migration" (Suzuki, *Ocean Passages* 13–14). The valuable insights into the history and development of humanity and ecological vision in the Pacific's contribute to the development of a collective effort of comparative studies of literature, covering a broad and grounded range of research themes. The re-worlding reveals the experience of "counter-conversion" as a reversal and turn away from Euro-American codes of nation-state boundaries, "developmentalist framework of global dependency and neocolonial entanglement in modern worlding" that stresses Native Pacific "smallness and belittlement" (Wilson, *Be Always Converting* 121). All such hegemonic and colonial imposition of nationhood and borders could be turned over and cast away through "counter vision of Pacific place-making and history-shaping" (130). As Wilson contends, transpacific authors and culture makers figure the regenerations of "native attitude taking place across the contemporary Pacific otherwise and elsewhere" (120). Collectively they forge a "counter-conversion," "re-worlding" the Pacific through their "counter-visions and counter-memories" (119–20). To this, we would add that it is furthermore a "counter-conversion" from the continental to the insular, from land to sea, and from the anthropocentrism to interconnectedness of humans and more-than-human beings in the Pacific. These islanding perspectives generate actions and communities, as Hauʻofa figures it, to fight colonial belittlement and enclosure by enlarging the world from the global segregations to planetary co-belongings.

Furthermore, our idea of bringing the Indigenous peoples to the center is inspired by the trans-Indigenous methodology developed by Chadwick Allen. Reflecting on transnational studies of Native American literature, Chadwick Allen proposes that trans-Indigenous research methodology requires us to go beyond the national borders drawn by the colonial powers (2). Allen suggests in *Trans-Indigenous* that "projects arranged by settler nation-state, by geographical or geopolitical region, or by hemisphere, while often advocated for their progressive potential, can be viewed as problematic within indigenous-focused paradigms" (xii). In this, we envision a common ground for comparison which is at once transnational and trans-Indigenous. We challenge the divisions and borders set up by nation-states and bring oceanic imaginaries to the core of re-mapping world literature. We create dialogues that are "center-to-center-to-center, indigenous-to-indigenous-to-indigenous" ("A Transnational Native American Studies?" 8). We urge critics and scholars to "place Indigenous histories and politics, cultures and worldviews, and multiple realities at their vital center" (*Trans-Indigenous*, xvi). We, however, also seek to push the limit of the trans-Indigenous research methodology by proposing dialogues not just between Indigenous peoples but also among Indigenous peoples, minorities, and colonial settlers.

By exploring the dynamic relationship between Indigenous people and (neo) colonial powers and voicing out against the oppressive structures, this volume envisions a center-to-center dialogue between Pacific inhabitants and the imperial and colonial powers. We bring together voices that call for the recognition of the humanity of the Pacific. Our conceptual framework does not only identify the Pacific space as a site of colonial encounters but utilizes it as a methodology which, as Erin Suzuki puts it, "confront[s] us with a radical otherness that cannot be easily assimilated to dominant paradigms of national belonging" ("Transpacific" 355). Suzuki cautions that when we bring forth the silenced voices, we must also deliberate on ways that the discourse itself may alternately invoke or erase the Indigenous histories of the region (356). This volume confronts its reader with disruptions, rupture, and erasure that emerge from violent Pacific histories of colonialism and imperialism.

To sum up, our volume moves beyond the hegemonic concept of the Pacific to reevaluate the transpacific in conjunction with Oceania where the living conditions and cultural and ethnic diversity of the Pacific Island nations sustain to fight against ongoing colonial erasure. The Pacific is not an abstract geopolitical idea but represents multiple sites and relational communities and heritages, in which Indigenous Pacific, transpacific, Asia-America, and Australia Pacific meet and render transnational/transcultural dynamics and dialogue possible.

## Structuring the Volume

The volume comprises twelve chapters evenly divided into three parts that are respectively titled "Colonialism: The Pacific Ocean," "Indigenous Resilience to Colonialism," and "Ocean and Ecology." The chapters in the first part engage and, to some extent, push back against the imperial and colonial imagination and dominance of the Pacific. They examine the dynamic power relationships that underlay the discourse and conceptualization of the Pacific, inquiring into the roles that imperialism, militarization, and colonialism have played in the construction of the contemporary Pacific. They explore the issues surrounding imperialism, (neo)colonialism, and militarism and examine how the idea of the Pacific is constructed in the dynamic colonial relationships.

In the first chapter, "The Wilkes Expedition (1838–1842) and the Formation of a US Empire of Bases in the Pacific," John R. Eperjesi brings attention to the history of the origins of the US empire of bases in the Pacific. Tracing back to 1838, Eperjesi argues that "[t]he mission of the Wilkes Expedition (Ex.) was to provide charts for whalers, sealers, and China traders, thus, to expand the imagined boundaries of Jacksonian America deep into Oceania." Analyzing the history of US imperialism and militarism in the Pacific, Eperjesi explains that "oceanic peoples that did not align with or got in the way of the spatial imperatives of a militarized American Pacific were internally or externally excluded, made exceptional, deprived of civil and human rights, forced into schools designed to erase cultural identity, or forced into service work for military or tourist industries." The Wilkes Expedition was a foundational moment in the formation of the US empire through the American Pacific archive in general and the hydrographic survey in particular. Eperjesi lays bare the strategies of an emergent military empire that slowly insinuated itself across the Pacific, uprooting and rerouting oceanic peoples in the process. His critique of the Wilkes Expedition is a move toward decolonization through demilitarization and represents "decolonizing movements in Oceania struggling for dignity, economic justice, political independence and/or cultural recognition."

In Chapter 2, "Epeli Hauʻofa's Pronouns," Paul Lyons stresses the Pacific Islanders' own stories and myths by celebrating Epeli Hauʻofa's influential narratives. Hauʻofa's oceanic polemics is subsequently deployed through succinct analyses of three writers—Juliana Spahr, Craig Santos Perez, and Kathy Jetñil-Kijiner. Lyons's insights unveil Hauʻofa's use of pronouns as a way of foregrounding "the call and sound of plural possessives." Throughout Hauʻofa's work, these pronouns constitute sites for "engaging challenges facing the region." Lyons reads Hauʻofa's narration as a way that shows "how possessive pronouns resonates with issues relating to possession and dispossession in the multiple senses of the word." Hauʻofa's spirit not only keeps appearing and returning in contemporary Pacific creative and discursive works, but it also yields a powerful trope for a new "Oceania," which is a new form, according to Lyon, to counter the power of colonialism and to advocate for the networking and alliance of peoples who live in and love Oceania. We would like to dedicate this volume to Lyons, our beloved and well-respected colleague, mentor, and one of the pioneers in Pacific Island Studies, who unfortunately passed away in 2018. Lyons generously sent us his work in 2015 but sadly we were not able to publish it before he left us. He is tremendously missed by all his colleagues, and we are honored that we can include his legacy in this volume. We would also like to express our heartfelt gratitude to Monica Lyons, Lyons's partner, for generously granting us the permission to publish his work and for her help in proofreading it. Mahalo nui loa.

Chapter 3, "Mountains of Taiwan, Japanese Colonization, and Western Science" by Chia-li Kao, turns to Taiwan's unique colonial history. Drawing on Kano Tadao's (1906-1945) *With Mountains, Cloud and Savages: Travel in the Mountains of Taiwan* (1941), Kao examines the intricate relationship among colonial landscape, Japanese imperialism, and Western science. The chapter considers Kano's depiction of mountains in colonial Taiwan to explore the ways in which Japanese nationalist and imperialist approach to science has affected the mapping of the island's landscape. Having been considered to be an accomplice of Japanese imperial expansion, however, Kano's writing also transcends the colonial ideology of depreciating the island and elevates Taiwan's mountains to the high aesthetic appreciation by referencing to the famous Japanese poet Bashō's aesthetic concept of "sabi." Kano's writing, as Kao contends, becomes a precursor of contemporary Taiwanese nature writing.

Picking up from where Hau'ofa and Lyons left off, Craig Santos Perez shoulders over the distinct heritage of decolonizing the Pacific. In Chapter 4, "Demilitarization and Decolonization in CHamoru Poetry from Guåhan (Guam)," he examines a selection of poetry by CHamoru authors from Guåhan (Guam) that addresses the themes of demilitarization and decolonization. Guåhan is the southernmost island of the Marianas archipelago and the largest and most populated island in the western Pacific region known as Micronesia. Guåhan has been an "unincorporated territory" of the US since 1898, and the Department of Defense currently occupies 30 percent of the island's landmass with military bases. Through his close reading of the texts by CHamoru poets, Perez discusses how their poetry reveals the environmental injustice and land dispossession caused by militarism, advocates for demilitarization, and articulates a decolonial vision of land stewardship. Perez investigates how CHamoru poetry enters the public sphere as literary activism and testimony in support of CHamoru self-determination and sovereignty. A prolific poet and activist from Guam and currently based in Hawai'i, Perez calls attention to the negative effects of colonialism and militarization on his homeland and in the Pacific through his decolonial poetics and aesthetics. He reminds his readers of the mistreatment of his people, the special "unincorporated" status of Guam, and the land that is taken over by the US Army. His poetry and poetics as well as his scholarly work reveal the life circumstances of the island communities and respond to, as well as critique, the colonial conditions of Guam.

Chapter 5 reads Perez's poetry from a different angel of cultural materialism. In "Decolonizing Guam with Poetry: 'Everyday Objects with Mission' in Craig Santos Perez's Poetry," Anna Erzsebet Szucs looks at everyday objects mentioned in Perez's poetry and seeks to unfold the "mission" these objects have. "Everyday objects" relate to the everyday life, history, and culture of the Indigenous people of Guam. Szucs argues that ordinary objects, which have significance in Pacific culture, are deliberately placed in Perez's poems. They convey the message of resistance and decolonial protest and pursuit of survival and can be considered as representations of activism. Chapter 5 ushers in the second part of this volume, "Indigenous Resilience to Colonialism." In addition to "Decolonizing Guam with Poetry," there are three other chapters that examine Pacific Islanders' resistance to colonialism and their resilience in the face of colonial oppression. Deviant from Western epistemology and the idea of Indigenous peoples as victims, these chapters foreground the significance of Indigenous knowledges, traditions, cultures, kinship, and worldviews, gesturing toward decolonial resurgence of the Indigenous peoples. They bring Indigenous epistemologies and cosmologies to the center and, in doing so, explore the opportunities and possibilities of a decolonial revival in research and methodology by reading and re-worlding the Pacific literature.

In Chapter 6, "Remapping of Mānoa Valley in Hawaiian Literature," Chia-hua Lin examines Kānaka Maoli's resilience in their remembering and honoring their genealogical link to the 'āina (land). As a result of the deeply problematic Western mapping practices and ideologies, the landscape of Hawai'i as well as the lifeways and foodways of Kānaka Maoli has been dramatically altered since the arrival of the White settlers. Despite the devastation of colonization, Kānaka Maoli continue to survive and strive against the oppression, exploitation, and degradation inflicted by the settlers. Lin first discusses the problematics of Western mapping practice and the anthropocentric and capitalist ideologies that lie behind Western cartography. She then moves on to investigate how Kānaka Maoli confront the Western mapping with their worldview and ways of knowing. Lin draws examples from poems by Albert Wendt and Brandy Nālani Mcdougall alongside the community practice at Ka Papa Lo'i O Kānewai, a restored lo'i kalo (water taro field) near the University of Hawai'i at Mānoa. Engaging poetry and praxis in a dynamic dialogue, Lin explores how Kānaka Maoli claim their presence, demonstrate their resilience, and resist the Western ideologies through their way of mapping the 'āina and wai (water).

In Chapter 7, "Planetary Boundaries, Planetary Imaginaries: Homing Pacific Eco-poetry," Hsinya Huang examines Pacific eco-poetry of "homing in" to represent the unique Indigenous experience of islands as ecosystems that are dynamic and interconnected. Drawing on poetry by Kathy Jetñil-Kijiner of Marshall Islands, Huang investigates Indigenous homing experiences in conjunction with the violent history of nuclear militarism in the Pacific. Addressing the "slow violence" of nuclear radiations and enforced dislocation, Jetñil-Kijiner's poetry testifies the drastic changes of Indigenous Pacific in lands and waters. Not only does her poetry lay bare the colonial trajectory in Oceania, but it stresses the islanding poetics as activism, through which Jetñil-Kijiner enables decolonial contestation and voice. Reading Jetñil-Kijiner's poetry as a distinct example of Indigenous resistance, this chapter also brings in broader implications for comparative studies of world literature, environmental humanities, and Native and Pacific studies in the Anthropocene.

Chapter 8, Hitoshi Oshima's "The Ecological Vision of the Ainu Reflected in Their Oral Tradition," uses the preface of Yukie Chiri's anthology of the Ainu divine songs to examine the ways that the Ainu, the Indigenous people of the northern islands of the Japanese Archipelago, conceive Nature as divine and animals, plants, artifacts as well as humans are all sacred. Under the Japanese colonization, the Ainu have gone through a cultural genocide. Oshima's chapter aims to recover the Ainu ecological vision as a pathway to decolonial revival. The Ainu ecology is based on the vision of the world as a place of sympathy and antipathy between humans and other beings. The notion of death and life as a cycle constitutes a significant part of their ecology. Celebrating Indigenous worldviews, Oshima re-worlds the Pacific into Indigenous cosmos of relations and intersections among all the beings and things.

Part Three of this collection, "Ocean and Ecology," focuses on the dynamics between ocean and ecologies and opens with Rob Wilson's critical delineation of "interconnected Pacific as a planetary bioregion," his forging of "ocean-based ecopoetics." While the four chapters in this part examine the myriad issues surrounding the discourse of the Anthropocene (in which human beings become, on a global scale, a major force and impact on Earth's geology and ecosystems), they also amply demonstrate localized perceptions of the environment and human-nature relationship. Indeed, in recent years, issues surrounding the ecological world in the Pacific region have sparked intriguing and provocative discussions. Such research celebrates the networking and coalition of peoples and a shared value of the Pacific environment and ecologies, which becomes crucial to contemporary scholarships of the humanities for the environment.

Chapter 9, Rob Wilson's "Becoming Oceania: Toward a Planetary Ecopoetics or Reframing the Pacific Rim," problematizes the Pacific Ocean or the "Pacific Rim" as the site of global-capitalist political economy and instead moves toward a vision of "becoming Oceania," projected as "a site of transpacific, cross-border, and transnational solidarity in the forging of a transpacific ecopoetics." Wilson reminds us that the Pacific Ocean as "ocean commons" has been threatened from the Bikini atoll nuclear testing during the Cold War era down to the latest nuclear disaster in Fukushima Japan in 2011 in terms of its "water, ground, and air of local dwelling." He persuasively encourages scholars to frame the shared oceanic horizon to help "build up tactics and affects of ecological solidarity and modes of co-dwelling" and to regard "the interconnected Pacific as a planetary bioregion." Wilson reads a wide range of texts through this lens, including Epeli Hau'ofa, Brandy Nālani McDougall, Craig Santos Perez, and Juliana Spahr, as well as the earlier American writer Jack Kerouac. He advocates forging ocean-based ecopoetics and moving toward "planetary belonging, ecological confederation, peace, and trans-racial solidarity."

Chapter 10, Kathryn Yalan Chang's "Island Imaginations, Bioregionalism, and the Environmental Humanities," traces the history of how the Eighth Naphtha Cracker Project in Taiwan was proposed in 2006 and finally ceased in 2011. Based on *Wetlands, Petrochemicals, and Imagining an Island* (2011), coedited by two Taiwanese writers Sheng Wu and Mingyi Wu, Chang advocates an alternative imagination of Taiwan's future during the anti-Kuokuang campaign. Through critical lens of environmental humanities, Chang examines how communities and NGOs successfully halt Changhua County's Eighth Naphtha Cracker Project, a project that would have damaged land, air, and water and threatened the endangered pink dolphin.

Based on a similar ecocritical ground, Chapter 11, "Decolonizing Oceanic Realms: Voices from Australia Pacific" by Iris Ralph turns to global south and examines literature from Australia Pacific. Ralph addresses oceanic imaginaries which haunt Ray Lawler's *Summer of the Seventeenth Doll*, an Australian play that cannot be discussed without at least some reference to the nefarious practice of blackbirding in the Pacific. Timothy Winton's novel, *Shallows*, relates to oceanic imaginaries, too, in the context of commercial and industrial whale slaughter in the borderwaters between the Pacific and Indian Ocean.

Throughout the nineteenth and twentieth centuries, the modern whaling industry has wiped out or subsumed sustainable human-cetacean cultures. In the last chapter, Chapter 12, "Whale as Cosmos: Multispecies Ethnography and Contemporary Indigenous Cosmopolitics," Joni Adamson explores how events staged around whale as commons and cosmos offer insights into the activities of Indigenous, ethnic minority, and civil society groups who organize a movement that has been described as "Indigenous cosmopolitics." While exploring the relevance of this movement for ecocriticism, Adamson also examines the emergence of new modes of research being referred to as "multispecies ethnography" by scholars who study humans within the "cosmos" of their entanglements with other kinds of living beings. Adamson's "Whale as Cosmos" considers both "Indigenous cosmopolitics" and "multispecies ethnography" in Niki Caro's 2002 film *Whale Rider*, based on Maori writer Whiti Ihimaera's acclaimed novel *The Whale Rider*, alongside Linda Hogan's *People of the Whale* of Pacific Northwest. She argues that these transpacific works demand an "activist event" that "draws attention to the political and artistic ways" not only "for human rights" but "for the protection of 'Mother Earth' as an entire 'cosmos' of relations." Rereading the Indigenous transformational characters for the ways they inspire new research methodology, she urges audiences and readers to "re-vision the planet as a cosmos of multispecies communities existing in intimate, entangled relations."

## Coda

The singular geopolitical category of the "Pacific," as Alice Te Punga Somerville among others observes, is a historically Euro-American concept (2015, 2018). The development of the concept and discourse of the "Pacific," in other words, goes hand in hand with the rise of imperial powers and becomes a tool for colonization and exploitation of not only the abundant marine resources but also the cultures, heritages, and peoples who have inhabited this water for thousands of years. A significant part of our volume investigates these international forms of empire, laying bare the worlding projects of colonization, militarization, and assimilation. Transpacific militarization connects the territorial legacies of the nineteenth-century imperialism to the capital-driven neocolonial projects of the twentieth and twenty-first centuries. As Hsuan L. Hsu observes, while the US neocolonial dominance over Asia has been supported "by the US bases on Pacific islands," the ongoing militarization of the Pacific region has made the histories of Asian and Pacific Island communities "inextricable" from one another (282). The complex dynamics of diaspora and exile, dispossession and displacement, have informed the specificity of the space which comprises the so-called American Pacific.

Much resistance to such contemporary forms of empire is taking place in the Pacific "re-worlding" dynamics of cultural production and site-based field experiences. This volume takes on a resistant and decolonial agenda to examine the dynamic and shifting relationships between empire, Indigenous, and immigrant communities in the Pacific, and to propose Indigenous literatures in the transpacific context to be engaged in their geopolitical complexity. The second part of the volume, in particular, foregrounds the Indigenous agency which is set on the move by fighting the military and imperial superstructures. The connections established at the level of grass roots mobilized by international colonial forms may work "not only to reify existing colonial or imperial networks, but to forge alternative political and cultural coalitions," to borrow Suzuki's decolonial vocabulary (*Ocean Passage* 113).

Finally, we revisit the Pacific as a site of ecological perils and opportunities. Through the in-depth analysis of literatures about waters and lands of the Pacific, this volume appeals to those who concern about the environmental challenges that create unbearable living conditions for all marine life and threaten precious ecosystems. The impacts of climate change and the environmental crisis faced by the globe are most profound but practically invisible. Since islands surrounded by oceans account for nearly 1/6 of the Earth's total land area, and the ocean takes up around 70 percent of the surface of the Earth, island/ocean ecology as explored in this volume is intimately bound up with the health and thus the well-being and future flourishing of the planet. Hau'ofa notes that there is a "world of difference" between figurations of Oceania in Indigenous cosmologies and colonial representations of the Pacific as small, remote, sparsely populated "islands in a far sea" (32). Western conceptions of the Pacific as "empty space" or the "hole in the doughnut" underpins Cold War geopolitics, as Britain, France and the United States selected nuclear testing sites remote from their own metropolitan centers but located within their own colonial or semicolonial spheres of influence (31). By contrast, the Indigenous people understand their waters and lands as part of a "universe" comprising not just land surfaces but "the surrounding ocean … the underworld with its fire-controlling and earth-shaking denizens, and the heavens above with their hierarchies of powerful gods and named stars and constellations" (31).

We critique the colonial mindset and worldview based on the metaphor of the island as an isolated and closed laboratory (ecosystem) and the Pacific as a timeless space. By retrieving the long-standing traditions, cultures, and practices of the Pacific Indigenous communities, we offer fresh oceanic perspectives and weave them into the interconnected web of planetary ecologies, counteracting the environmental degradation caused by imperialism, colonialism, globalization, and modernity. Bringing together scholars, poets, and activists from North America, East Asia, Europe, and Pacific Islands, the volume reframes Pacific literature in the context of world literature, interlocking three themes central to the study of the world literature: imperialism, colonialism and militarism; Indigenous resistance and resilience; and ocean and ecology. It is the first volume from East Asia to bring together scholarship on works by Pacific-based poets and writers with a specific purpose of global circulation and reception of Pacific literature.

This is a long-overdue project, initiated by Rob Wilson, in the summer of 2009, when he team-taught a summer seminar with Chadwick Allen at National Sun Yat-sen University in Taiwan on Pacific cultural production, counter-conversion, and the ecological framework of "Oceania." Paul Lyons passed in the process of preparing the manuscripts for publication. In his memory, we continue to make it happen despite wars, pandemics, and other adversities, which we have faced with strength. Amid all the chaos, there are intersections, relations, care, and solidarities across and beyond the Pacific. For our volume, Syaman Rapongan, a prominent Indigenous writer from Orchid Island (or *Pongso no Tao*), puts together a foreword to celebrate literature that manifests practices of "navigating the infinite world of Oceania." The relational and reciprocal approaches come to us as resonant Pacific heartbeats. Throughout the volume, the critical juxtaposition of the transpacific and oceanic works shifts the angle of references and, as it does, opens a new pathway to understanding and sensing the world, one in which we imagine more equitable comparisons and networks. The valuable lessons the Pacific has to offer should not be delivered in the forms of theoretical abstraction but in those of vigorous connectivity and reckoning of transformation to come.

## Works Cited

Allen, Chadwick. *Trans-Indigenous: Methodologies for Global Native Literary Studies.* U of Minnesota P, 2012.

———. "A Transnational Native American Studies? Why Not Studies That Are Trans-Indigenous?" *Journal of Transnational American Studies*, vol. 4, no. 1, 2012, n.p.

Banivanua Mar, Tracey. "Author's Response: Transcendent Mobilities." *Journal of Pacific History*, vol. 51, no. 4, 2016, pp. 459–62.

———. *Decolonisation and the Pacific: Indigenous Globalisation and the Ends of Empire.* Cambridge UP, 2016.

Camacho, Keith L. *Cultures of Commemoration: The Politics of War, Memory, and History in the Mariana Islands.* U of Hawai'i P, 2012.

Damrosch, David. *What Is World Literature?* Princeton UP, 2003.

Diaz, Vicente M. *Repositioning the Missionary: Rewriting the Histories of Colonialism, Native Catholicism, and Indigeneity in Guam.* U of Hawai'i P, 2010.

Diaz, Vicente M., and J. Kēhaulani Kauanui. "Native Pacific Cultural Studies on the Edge." *The Contemporary Pacific*, vol. 13, no. 2, 2001, p. 315.

Espiritu, Yến Lê. "Critical Refugee Studies and Native Pacific Studies: A Transpacific Critique." *American Quarterly*, vol. 69, no. 3, 2017, pp. 483–90.

Flores, Evelyn and Emelihter Kihleng, eds. *Indigenous Literatures from Micronesia.* U of Hawai'i P, 2019.

Fujikane, Candace. *Mapping Abundance for a Planetary Future: Kanaka Maoli and Critical Settler Cartographies in Hawai'i.* Duke UP, 2021.

Hattori, Anne Perez. *Colonial Dis-Ease: US Navy Health Policies and the Chamorros of Guam, 1898–1941.* U of Hawai'i P, 2004.

Hau'ofa, Epeli. *We Are the Ocean: Selected Works.* U Hawai'i P, 2008.

Hereniko, Vilsoni, and Rob Wilson, eds. *Inside Out: Literature, Cultural Politics, and Identity in the New Pacific.* Rowman & Littlefield Publishers, 1999.

Hsu, Hsuan L. "Guahan (Guam), Literary Emergence, and the American Pacific in *Homebase* and *from Unincorporated Territory*." *American Literary History*, vol. 24, no. 2, 2012, pp. 281–307.

Huang, Hsinya, Philip Deloria, Laura Furlan, and John Gamber. "Introduction." Special Forum on "Charting Transnational Native American Studies: Aesthetics, Politics, and Identity." *Journal of Transnational American Studies*, vol. 4, no. 1, 2012, pp. 1–15.

Huang, Hsinya, Rob Wilson, and Alice Te Punga Somerville. "A Collaborative Review of *Trans-Indigenous: Methodologies for Global Native Literary Studies*." *Verge: Studies in Global Asias*, vol. 4, no. 2, 2018, pp. 81–105.

Kauanui, J. Kēhaulani. *Hawaiian Blood: Colonialism and the Politics of Sovereignty and Indigeneity*. Duke UP, 2008.

Keown, Michelle. *Pacific Islands Writing: The Postcolonial Literatures of Aotearoa/New Zealand and Oceania*. Oxford UP, 2007.

———. *Postcolonial Pacific Writing: Representations of the Body*. Routledge, 2005.

———. "War and Redemption: Militarism, Religion and Anti-Colonialism in Pacific Literature." *Anglo-American Imperialism and the Pacific: Discourses of Encounter*, edited by Michelle Keown, Andrew Taylor, and Mandy Treagus. Routledge, 2018, pp. 25–48.

Keown, Michelle, Andrew Taylor, and Mandy Treagus, eds. *Anglo-American Imperialism and the Pacific: Discourses of Encounter*. Routledge, 2018.

Mignolo, Walter D. *The Politics of Decolonial Investigations (On Decoloniality)*. Duke UP, 2021.

Moraru, Christian. "'World,' 'Globe,' 'Planet': Comparative Literature, Planetary Studies, and Cultural Debt after the Global Turn." *The 2014–2015 ACLA Report on the State of the Discipline of Comparative Literature*. Dec. 3, 2014, https://stateofthediscipline.acla.org/entry/%E2%80%9Cworld%E2%80%9D-%E2%80%9Cglobe%E2%80%9D-%E2%80%9Cplanet%E2%80%9D-comparative-literature-planetary-studies-and-cultural-debt-after. Accessed Feb. 25, 2022.

Nguyen, Viet Thanh, and Janet Hoskins, eds. *Transpacific Studies: Framing an Emerging Field*. U of Hawai'i P, 2014.

Perez, Craig Santos. "The Fifth Map: For Hsinya." *Dialogist*. https://dialogist.org/v4i2-craig-santos-perez.

———. "Teaching Ecopoetry in a Time of Climate Change." *The Georgia Review*, 2020. https://thegeorgiareview.com/posts/teaching-ecopoetry-in-a-time-of-climate-change/. Accessed Feb. 25, 2022.

Roberts, Brian Russell. *Borderwaters: Amid the Archipelagic States of America*. Duke UP, 2021.

Said, Edward. *Orientalism*. Pantheon Books, 1978.

Sakai, Naoki, and Hyon Joo Yoo, eds. *The Trans-Pacific Imagination: Rethinking Boundary, Culture, and Society*. World Scientific, 2012.

Sharrad, Paul, ed. *Albert Wendt and Pacific Literature: Circling the Void*. Manchester UP, 2003.

Shigematsu, Setsu, and Keith L. Camacho, "Introduction: Militarized Currents, Decolonizing Futures." *Militarized Currents: Toward a Decolonized Future in Asia and the Pacific*, edited by Setsu Shigematsu and Keith L. Camacho, U of Minnesota P, 2010, pp. xv–xlviii.

Spivak, Gayatri Chakravorty. "The Rani of Sirmur: An Essay in Reading the Archives." *History and Theory*, vol. 24, no. 3, 1985, pp. 247–72.

Subramani. "The Oceanic Imaginary." *The Contemporary Pacific*, vol. 13, no. 1, 2001, pp. 149–62.

———. *South Pacific Literature: From Myth to Fabulation*. U of the South Pacific, 1985.

Suzuki, Erin. *Ocean Passage: Navigating Pacific Islander and Asian American Literatures*. Temple UP, 2021.

Suzuki, Erin. "Transpacific." *Routledge Companion to Asian American and Pacific Literatures*, edited by Rachel Lee. Routledge, 2014, pp. 352–64.

Te Punga Somerville, Alice. "Searching for the Trans-Indigenous. [Review of Trans-Indigenous: Methodologies for Global Native Literary Studies by Chadwick Allen]." *Verge: Studies in Global Asias*, vol. 4, no. 2, 2018, pp. 96–105.

———. "Unpacking Our Libraries: Landlocked, Waterlogged, and Expansive Bookshelves." *American Quarterly*, vol. 67, no. 3, 2015, pp. 645–52.

Teaiwa, Teresia K. "Charting Pacific (Studies) Waters: Evidence of Teaching and Learning." *The Contemporary Pacific*, vol. 29, no. 2, 2017, pp. 265–82.

———. "On Analogies: Rethinking the Pacific in a Global Context." *The Contemporary Pacific*, vol. 18, no. 1, 2006, pp. 71–88.

———. *Sweat and Salt Water: Selected Works*. U of Hawai'i P, 2021.

Webb, Jen, and Kavita Nandan. *Writing the Pacific: An Anthology*. Institute of Pacific Studies, 2007.

Wendt, Albert. *Lali: A Pacific Anthology*. Longman Publishing, 1980.

———. *Nuanua: Pacific Writing in English Since 1980*. U of Hawai'i P, 1995.

Wilson, Rob. "Afterword: Worlding as Future Tactic." *The Worlding Project: Doing Cultural Studies in the Era of Globalization*, edited by Rob Wilson and Christopher Leigh Connery, North Atlantic Books, 2007, pp. 209–23.

———. *Be Always Converting, Be Always Converted: An American Poetics*. Harvard UP, 2009.

———. "Becoming Oceania: Ecopoetics and the Planetary Pacific Rim, or 'Walking on Water Wasn't Built in a Day.'" *Shifting Grounds: Cultural Tectonics along the Pacific Rim*, edited by Bridgette Glaser and Jutta Ernst. West Publishing House, 2020, pp. 23–39.

———. "Oceania as Peril and Promise towards Theorizing a Worlded Vision of Transpacific Ecopoetics." *Oceanic Archives, Indigenous Epistemologies, and Transpacific American Studies*, edited by Yuan Shu, Otto Heim, and Kendall Johnson, Hong Kong UP, 2019, pp. 261–82.

———. *Reimagining the American Pacific from South Pacific to Bamboo Ridge and Beyond*. Duke UP, 2000.

———. "Seven Poetic Constellations of Asia/Pacific World-Making: Reflections on the Diasporic Life and Organic-Intellectual Work of Arif Dirlik." *Inter-Asia Cultural Studies*, vol. 22, no. 4, 2021, pp. 512–20.

———. *When the Nikita Moon Rose*. https://www.academia.edu/990550/When_the_Nikita_Moon_Rose_serial_poem. Accessed May 30, 2022.

Wilson, Rob, and Arif Dirlik, eds. *Asia/Pacific as Space of Cultural Production*. Duke UP, 1995.

Wilson, Rob, and Christopher Leigh Connery. *The Worlding Project: Doing Cultural Studies in the Era of Globalization*. North Atlantic Books, 2007.

Yoneyama, Lisa. *Cold War Ruins: Transpacific Critique of American Justice and Japanese War Crimes*. Duke UP, 2016.

———. "Toward a Decolonial Genealogy of the Transpacific." *American Quarterly*, vol. 69, no. 3, 2017, pp. 471–82.

Part One

# Colonialism: The Pacific Ocean

# 1

# The Wilkes Expedition (1838–1842) and the Formation of a US Empire of Bases in the Pacific

John R. Eperjesi

> *The fundamental tenet of all military geography is that every feature of the visible world possesses actual or potential military significance.*
> —Myung Mi Kim, *Commons*

During the long 1890s, the United States seized colonies in the Pacific as business and political leaders struggled to find a way out of the post-bellum economic crises that were repeatedly shocking American society, crises which were increasingly taking the form of open class warfare. Between 1881 and 1905 there were more than 37,000 labor strikes in the United States (Gage, n.p.). During this volatile period, socialism and anti-imperialism emerged as legitimate political discourses and active social movements that offered alternatives to visions of the Pacific as a militarized American lake.

To counter the growing popularity of socialism and anti-imperialism and thus contain this explosive historical conjuncture, state intellectuals and captains of industry, working through an emergent mass media, managed to shift the defining question of the period from capital versus labor to a question of the home market versus overseas markets. A capitalist utopia in which new markets solved the crisis of domestic overproduction, thus dissolving class conflict, became the hegemonic discourse through which economic questions were discussed and debated. Making a series of exceptions to its founding anti-empire rhetoric, the United States colonized Guåhan/Guam, Hawaiʻi, the Philippines, and Sāmoa, projecting that these "stepping stones" would secure commercial circulation, keep a rising Japanese empire in check, provide access to the mythical China market, and thus help resolve the crisis of overproduction. Viewed from the perspective of the United States Navy, these colonies all possessed potential strategic military value. This potential was relentlessly developed as the militarization of the Pacific quickly accelerated so that by 1945, 44 percent of all US military bases were located in the region (Calder 14). Chalmers Johnson, a

---

An earlier version of the article, "Basing the Pacific: Exceptional Spaces of the Wilkes Exploring Expedition, 1838–1842," was published in *Amerasia Journal*, vol. 37, no. 3, 2011, pp. 1–17.

This chapter is dedicated to the memory of my friend and mentor Paul Lyons (1958–2018).

former cold warrior and Japan specialist-turned critic of imperialism, argued that the fundamental unit of the US empire is "not the colony, [but] the military base" ("Our Military Empire"). The United States currently operates around 800 foreign military bases, although no one, not even the Pentagon, knows the exact size of this large and shadowy empire (Vine).

What are the origins of the US empire of bases in the Pacific? It is tempting to assume that this empire materialized suddenly during the 1890s, but such a periodization, while orderly, is a little too neat. The military basing of the Pacific was gradual and began much earlier in the nineteenth century, one important and unacknowledged origin of which was the United States Exploring Expedition, also known as the Ex. Ex. or Wilkes Expedition, named after its commanding officer, Navy Lieutenant Charles Wilkes.[1] The mission of the Wilkes Expedition, which began in 1838 and concluded in 1842, was to provide charts for whalers, sealers, and China traders, thus to expand the imagined boundaries of Jacksonian America deep into the Pacific. Over these 4 years, the Expedition surveyed 280 Pacific islands and created 180 charts, some of which were used up through the Second World War (Philbrick xix).

The Wilkes Expedition, the largest expedition by a Western nation ever sent to sea at one time, was an empire-building and islander-hating (and at times islander-loving) adventure that involved the burning of villages, slaughtering of natives, grave robbing, and stealing of artifacts, all in the name of scientific progress. One of the most important contributions of the Expedition to a rapidly expanding United States was a vast archive of detailed ethnographic knowledge organized around broad questions concerning the origins of man and the hierarchy of races. The Expedition condensed and significantly advanced the racializing project of mid-nineteenth-century American ethnography, an important and often overlooked link between philology and modern anthropology. Expedition ethnologists, who were not in methodological or ideological harmony and ultimately arrived at very different answers to the broad questions mentioned above, nevertheless tended to frame encounters with Pacific Islanders through stereotypes of the "savage" Indian and "docile" slave. Summarizing the impact of the Expedition in relation to the history of US expansionism, Barry Alan Joyce writes, "By applying American images of savagery to world cultures, American scientists and explorers helped construct the foundation for an American racial *weltanschauung* that contributed to the implementation of manifest destiny in this period and laid the ideological foundations for future American imperialism" (10).

Studies of the Expedition have provided valuable critiques of the scientific cataloging of racial and ethnic others, yet there has not been as much critical attention directed at the representations of oceanic space by Wilkes and his team of scientists and artists. The identity of the other is often discussed apart from the space of the other, perhaps because culture is more interesting than the science of water or hydrography. Yet hydrographic representations of oceanic space have deeply and at times disastrously

---

[1] US military expansion into the Pacific could be said to begin with Captain David Porter who in 1812 claimed Nuka Hiva in the Marquesas for the United States (Dudden 15).

impacted oceanic cultures. Wilkes's obsessive, micrological surveying practices generated an immense amount of hydrographic data that delivered representational precision, both mathematical and artistic, to fantasies of a future commercial empire in the Pacific. In the process of generating these data, the scientific and artistic crew of the Expedition marked off several exceptional, or in Wilkes's words "singular," harbors in the Pacific—Pago Pago in Sāmoa, the Pearl River in Hawaiʻi, and Juan de Fuca (the outlet for Puget Sound) in the Pacific Northwest. Wilkes evaluates and catalogs these local places in terms of their "potential military significance" to apply the suggestive martial mimicry of Korean American poet Myung Mi Kim (32). Like the spatial story theorized by Michel de Certeau, hydrography functions as a "prediction and a promise of success at the beginning of battles, contracts, or conquests" (124). These singular deepwater harbors slowly evolved from being objects of scientific knowledge within a discourse of what Mary Louise Pratt terms "anti-conquest" into a constellation of military bases that have supported US imperialist expansion in the region from the Philippine-American War through the Cold War and from the Obama administration's "Asia-Pacific Pivot" to the current Biden administration's "New Cold War" with China.

## On Hydrography

In 1838, a naval squadron composed of six vessels, including war sloops, departed from the Norfolk Naval Yard in Virginia. In official instructions to Wilkes, Secretary of the Navy James K. Paulding wrote:

> The United States government, having in view the important interests of our commerce embarked in the whale-fisheries, and other adventures in the great Southern Ocean, by an Act of the 18th of May, 1836, authorized an Expedition to be fitted out for the purpose of surveying and exploring that sea, as well as to determine the existence of all doubtful islands and shoals, as to discover and accurately fix the position of those that lie in or near the track of our vessels in that quarter, and may have escaped the observation of scientific navigators.
> (qtd. in Wilkes vol. 1, xxv)

As Paul Lyons notes, Paulding believed the United States needed "a more permanent military presence in Oceania" (60).

While Pacific Islanders had navigated between islands for thousands of years, up through the 1760s, Pacific crossings by Europeans moved along the well-known sea-lanes of the Spanish galleons sailing from the South American continent to the Mariana and Philippine archipelagoes (Fernandez-Arnesto 50, 299; Philbrick 290). With improvements in the chronometer and the discovery of a cure for scurvy, ships began to venture into uncharted areas. James Cook's three exploring expeditions may have triggered the scientific invasion of the Pacific, but the search for remote seal rookeries and the pursuit of the nomadic sperm whale moved American vessels into areas never reached by Cook (Philbrick 303). Ships' captains had previously relied on hand-drawn maps that failed to make note of hundreds of small islands, shoals, and sharp coral reefs. The mostly unmapped, reef-strewn Fiji Islands, for example, were thought to be so dangerous that ships headed there could not purchase insurance (Philbrick 12–13).

While American studies scholars have addressed the relationship between land surveying and westward expansion, little attention has been paid to the science of hydrography and the role of this spatial practice in creating stability and security for an emergent US empire in Asia and the Pacific. Hydrography, in the form of charts and surveys, enables military and commercial vessels to control and move with precision through an area, much as a topographic chart does in relation to land. Hydrography involves the measurement and description, or what Pratt terms "global resemanticizing," of the physical features of bodies of water, the seabed, and littoral land areas (42). Joyce notes that Wilkes had a "fanatical desire to chart every nook and cranny of ... dangerous islands" (123). Wilkes was a representative "seeing-man" whose "imperial eyes look out and possess" (Pratt 18). To the dismay of his publisher who was expecting an exotic adventure narrative, Wilkes's *Narrative of the U.S. Exploring Expedition* is packed with dry, mind-numbing data calculating the direction and speed of currents and winds, the temperature of water at various depths, the air temperature at different times, the height and fall of waves, and high and low tides. Wilkes's obsessive, micrological practices of measuring, recording, triangulating, calculating, fixing, collecting, collating, sounding, and accumulating helped build a totalizing "American Pacific archive" (Lyons 76). This American Pacific archive also included verbal and visual representations of hills, mountains, volcanoes, lagoons, coastlines, harbors, or any prominent geographic feature that could aid in fixing a ship's position. Expedition artists James Drayton and Alfred Agate used the recently invented *camera lucida* to project images that could be traced and then engraved, delivering an unprecedented level of mimesis and scientific authority to their representations of Oceania.

As the Expedition moved across the Pacific after rounding Cape Horn, Wilkes surveyed hundreds of uncharted islands, reefs, lagoons, and atolls in and around the archipelagos and islands of Tuamotu, Sāmoa, and Fiji before heading north to the Hawaiian Islands. Prior to the Expedition's departure, Wilkes developed a novel system for quickly surveying islands. Vessels would be divided up and positioned along the shore of an island and then begin firing their guns in rapid succession. By noting the time between the gun's flash and report, the officers were able to calculate the distance between the vessels. In his study of the Expedition, Nathaniel Philbrick sardonically notes, "What effect this day-long display of firepower had on the island's native populations can only be guessed" (119). Vessels worked their way around the island while officers used sextants to measure angles between the vessels and fixed points on shore, gradually covering the island in a trigonometric web. Philbrick points out that "[t]he system brought a new level of speed and accuracy to the survey of the Pacific" (20).

The hydrographic survey, with its strange combination of brute firepower and tenacious math, created order out of apparent oceanic chaos; it fragmented in the process of collating. Hydrography, in other words, "founds spaces" (de Certeau 123). One site where jagged surfaces, destructive currents, and powerful winds combine with particular ferocity is at the entrance to harbors. The scientific corps of the Expedition surveyed, and thus helped secure, deepwater harbors—the Pearl River in Hawai'i, the bays of San Francisco, and Juan de Fuca—that would evolve into material supports for the Americanization and militarization of the Pacific. Amy Ku'uleialoha-Stillman reveals:

> As trade expanded, military security concerns intensified. Maintaining access to deep-water harbors was not simply a matter of protecting the financial interests of those who profited from trade activities. Deep-water harbors were also necessary to establishing military might, and to keeping the military expansion and aggression of others in check.
>
> (250–51)

## Exceptional Harbors

One important deepwater harbor in the history of the US basing of the Pacific was located at Pago Pago in Eastern Sāmoa. The Expedition reached Pago Pago in 1839. At the time, the Samoan archipelago was a busy crossroads for traders and whalers, but the reefs were poorly charted in European terms. Wilkes singled out the harbor of Pago Pago on the island of Tutuila for special attention. An enframing gaze posits Tutuila as geographically contained, symmetrical, and separate from Western Sāmoa: "The island of Tutuila is high, broken, and of volcanic appearance. It is seventeen miles long, and its greatest width is five miles. The harbor of Pago-Pago penetrates into the centre, and almost divides the island in two parts" (Wilkes vol. 2, 74). Wilkes then shifts registers as his focus moves from the island in general to the particular, from the geographic to the poetic: "The harbor of Pago-Pago is one of the most singular in all the Polynesian isles" (vol. 2, 75). In the *Narrative*, this statement appears beneath a drawing by Wilkes of a harborscape dominated by two massive American vessels lying at anchor around which a scattering of much smaller and blurry native canoes are clustered. Wilkes's hydrographic representations of Pago Pago erase Samoans from the scene, rendering them residual, small, and indistinct, an instance of imperial "textual apartheid that separates landscape from people, accounts of inhabitants from accounts of their habitats" (Pratt 61). The drawing supports the discursive containment that isolates Pago Pago from the rest of the Samoan archipelago, a part separate and separable from the whole.

Elaborating on the singularity of Pago Pago, Wilkes writes,

> It is the last place on which one would look for a place of shelter. The coast near it is particularly rugged, and has no appearance of indentations, and the entrance being narrow, is not easily observed. Its shape has been compared to a variety of articles; that which it most nearly resembles is a retort; it is surrounded on all sides by inaccessible mural precipices, from eight hundred to one thousand feet in height.
>
> (vol. 2, 75)

Steep cliffs frame the harbor, making it a "natural" fortress. For Wilkes, Pago Pago was valuable because it "is not easily observed." This statement makes sense in terms of naval language games that isolate, evaluate, and organize places in terms of their strategic value, whether actual or potential, and then code this strategic value as embedded in nature. Surveys and drawings of Pago Pago make this local place visible in order to appreciate the fact that in reality it is "not easily observed."

As the nineteenth century progressed, the scramble for the Pacific intensified. The strategic importance of Pago Pago increased in the context of inter-imperialist rivalry between Britain, Germany, and the United States. Before departing from the Samoan archipelago, Wilkes signed a commercial and diplomatic treaty with the principal chiefs of Sāmoa, as he did in Tahiti and Fiji, for as Joyce notes, "the United States government sought the same commercial and legal rights and privileges granted previously to English and French consuls" (70). In 1872, another treaty was signed giving United States permission to build a coaling station at Pago Pago. In 1898, US designs on Pago Pago intensified after the United States colonized Guåhan and the Philippines and annexed Wake Island. Captain Alfred Thayer Mahan, the naval historian and state intellectual whose immensely popular and influential books on the role of sea power in history were carefully studied by people like Theodore Roosevelt, created the theoretical context in which the plan to administer Pago Pago was articulated. Mahan was serving on the Naval War Board where he asserted that the location of Pago Pago was "so suitable in case of operations in that quarter, that … political possession of the whole island in which the port is, or at least of ground sufficient for fortifications, is desirable" (qtd. in Chappell 220–22). Mahan believed, "Coaling stations were more important than colonies for the maintenance of the world navy" (Connery 186). American Sāmoa was administered by the US Navy and used as a military base from the beginning of the century until 1951 when the island was transferred to the Department of the Interior.

While it might appear that Wilkes thought the harbor at Pago Pago was the jewel of the Pacific, he deployed the same euphoric rhetoric when describing the Pearl River in Hawai'i, San Francisco, and Juan de Fuca. When surveying the Pearl River, Wilkes noted that if not for the dead coral reef blocking the entrance to the harbor, it would afford the "best and most capacious harbour in the Pacific" (qtd. in Philbrick 242). Of San Francisco, Wilkes wrote, "It boasts the finest harbour in the world" (vol. 4, 168). Looking out over Juan de Fuca, Wilkes gushed, "Nothing can exceed the beauty of these waters, and their safety: not a shoal exists within the Straits of San Juan de Fuca, Admiralty Inlet, Puget Sound, or Hood's Canal, that can in any way interrupt their navigation by a seventy-four gun ship" (vol. 4, 325–26). This euphoric image of a "seventy-four gun ship" cruising the sublime waters of the Pacific Northwest, of a floating military machine in the garden, has been elided by interpretations of the American nineteenth century transfixed by Fredric Jackson Turner's frontier thesis. Wilkes's martial fantasies became reality in Hawai'i in 1887 when the Navy began to lease Pearl Harbor as a naval base, and in 1891, when a Naval Station was established in Puget Sound. In 1940, the Hunters Point Naval Shipyard was constructed in San Francisco.

The official goal of the Wilkes Expedition was to produce knowledge, not enlarge the territory of the United States. In his instructions to Wilkes, Navy Secretary Paulding wrote: "You will neither interfere, nor permit any wanton interference with the customs, habits, manners or prejudices of the natives of such countries or islands as you may visit" (qtd. in Wilkes vol. 1, xxix). Wilkes and crew drew attention to the negative impact Europeans had on the Indigenous populations of Hawai'i, Sāmoa, and Tahiti, groups the scientists and artists idealized for their physical beauty, strength, and intelligence. These Pacific sites, which were thickly populated by Western missionary and commercial interests, were places where members of the Expedition felt most secure and could move around freely as they collected data and conducted surveys. Sites lacking a thick Western presence, such as the Tuamotus and Fiji, were places where the Expedition encountered the strongest opposition to exploration and were thus viewed as being inhabited by dangerous savages. When the Expedition approached the Tuamotus, what Europeans described as a treacherous chain of atolls in French Polynesia known in the nineteenth century as the Dangerous Islands or Dangerous Archipelago, and attempted to survey Reao, the native inhabitants would not allow surveying boats to land on shore. After several failed attempts at landing, Wilkes fired mustard seed at the islanders to clear the beach, making explicit the violent linkage between power and knowledge. In Fiji, cultural conflicts over the rights of salvage led to an explosive conflict between Fijians and Expedition members that ended when Wilkes decided to burn two villages on Malolo Island, grimly affirming Walter Benjamin's seventh thesis on the philosophy of history: "There is no document of civilization which is not at the same time a document of barbarism" (Joyce 46, 104–09; Benjamin 256).

The Secretary of the Navy declared: "The Expedition is not for conquest, but discovery. Its objects are all peaceful; they are to extend the empire of commerce and science; to diminish the hazards of the ocean, and point out to future navigators a course by which they may avoid dangers and find safety" (qtd. in Wilkes vol. 1, xxix). While surveys of Pacific islands and archipelagos were primarily in the service of trade, surveys of the Pacific Northwest were directed toward territorial conquest. In his autobiography, Wilkes reflects on his first encounter with the Columbia River area: "As I viewed the territory as entirely neutral as to our rights as well as theirs, although fully satisfied it was to be full part and parcel of our country" (Wilkes et al. 505). Joyce notes that "the chief object of his [Wilkes's] visit to California was to obtain and report accurate information in regard to the bay of San Francisco to the government at Washington, with a view of future acquisition" (14). The Expedition charted 800 miles of Pacific coastline, surveying littoral areas of Oregon and California decades before the interior of the continent was mapped. During the first half of the nineteenth century, in addition to the venture into Oceania, there was an equally important errand into prized ports along the coastline, from San Diego in the south to Juan de Fuca in the north.

One important contribution of the Expedition to imperial cartography at this time was in the form of data that made visible and concrete the abstract linkages connecting strategic deepwater harbors in Oceania to those along the Pacific Coast. The basing of the Pacific was not sudden but gradual, for as Jonathan Kamakawiwoʻole Osorio argues, colonialism works not only through the "naked seizure of lands and governments, but through a slow, insinuating invasion of people, ideas, institutions" (3). The spatial practice of hydrography conducted by the Expedition was a founding moment in the slow insinuation of proto-colonialism and militarism that led to the formation of a US empire of bases in the Pacific. The hydrographic survey, a panoptic instrument deployed by an expansionist US state apparatus, projected Mahanian mastery over oceans, rivers, lagoons, and strategic littoral spaces and in the process worked to separate Native Americans and Native Pacific Islanders from their homelands and home waters. Hydrography subjected the large, richly complex, fluid worlds of Oceania to an instrumentalization of space or what Max Horkheimer and Theodor Adorno in their critique of instrumental reason describe as a "mathesis universalis" in which the "multiplicity of forms is reduced to position and arrangement, history to fact, things to matter" (7). As Chris Connery comments, "We are still living in the Mahanian period" (183).

## Oceanic Multitude

Mahanian command of the oceanic worked to separate Pacific Islanders and coastal Native Americans from ancestral lands and waters. Describing the importance of the sea to Pacific Islanders, Paul D'Arcy writes: "The waters of the Pacific were cultural seascapes rich in symbolic meaning, crowded with navigational markers, symbols of tenure, fishing and surfing sites, and reminders of gods and spirits in the form of maritime familiars and sites of their exploits" (168–69). From an Indigenous perspective, the basing of the Pacific transformed familiar seascapes into unfamiliar territories; historically deep rituals, passages, and memories were blocked by a rebuilt physical environment. Osorio has created a deterritorializing countermemory of Pearl Harbor which returns this place to its Hawaiian name, "Puʻuloa," erased and forgotten by the militarized territorialization of Oʻahu and the Pearl River area:

> Puʻuloa has become unfamiliar terrain to us, much like the language of our elders and for some of the same reasons. The terrain itself is altered: streams have been interdicted and redirected by culverts and ditches, springs have disappeared, whole ecosystems that fed the once rich Ewa coastline have been strangled or neutered, and, in any case, many Hawaiians, unless they join the armed services or the large corps of civilian workers at Pearl Harbor, generally find the place forbidding.
> (4)

Osario's countermemorial recalls a local place, Puʻuloa, that was destroyed by a "slow insinuating invasion" long before the bombing of Pearl Harbor in 1941.

From a perspective plotted inside Oceania, another destructive effect of the positivistic will to hydrographic precision and panoptic order has been the image of the Pacific as made up of small, strategically located, isolated islands, little dots separated by vast expanses of water. From the bird's-eye view of imperial cartography, movement between islands by Pacific Islanders disappears and becomes historically invisible and unimportant. The imperialist imaginary of the American Pacific archive, while packed with hydrographic insights, created blindness to histories of Oceania from below as constellating a monumental space of travel, exchange, communication, and reciprocity. Outlining the "situated knowledge" eclipsed by foreign knowledges of the Pacific, Margaret Jolly imagines "lying low in a canoe, looking up at the heavens, scanning the horizon for signs of land, and navigating powerful seas with the embodied visual, aural, olfactory, and kinesthetic knowledge passed down through generations of Pacific navigators" ("Imagining Oceania" 509). For Native Pacific scholars, artists, and activists, Oceania is mobilized as a critical and poetic counternarrative to the reified image of the Pacific projected by the "mathesis universalis" of a Euro-American imperial cartography that cut the Pacific into "administrative units of study that bore no resemblance to voyaging spheres" (D'Arcy 5). Oceania is more than a geographical description; it is a decolonizing prescription for a "unifying regional identity" (Wood 347). One of the starting points for this identity involves deconstructing administrative imperial cartography by imagining "lying low in a canoe, looking up at the heavens."

"What the map cuts," de Certeau writes, "the story cuts across" (129). Opposition to the cartography of "belittlement and Oceania's interiorization of myths and metaphors of smallness and dependency," to borrow the words of Subramani, draws inspiration from the visionary spatial stories of the late Tongan anthropologist/novelist/artist Epeli Hau'ofa (154). Narrating the production of regional space by seafaring Pacific Islanders, Hau'ofa observes:

> Theirs was a large world in which peoples and cultures moved and mingled, unhindered by boundaries of the kind erected much later by imperial powers. From one island to another they sailed to trade and to marry, thereby expanding social networks for greater flows of wealth. They traveled to visit relatives in a wide variety of natural and cultural surroundings, to quench their thirst for adventure, and even to fight and dominate.
>
> (33)

Oceanic counternarratives work to restore affective and material connections between Native Pacific Islanders and the land and sea, connections repressed by the histories of Euro-American colonialism and militarism in the region. Yet these repressed connections are making a profound return. "The land and sea constitute our genealogies," Vicente Diaz and J. Kēhaulani Kauanui write, "and, not surprisingly, they lie at the heart of the varied movements to restore native sovereignty and self-determination" (319). At the same time, one does not want to essentialize the relationship between Pacific Islanders and the ocean. In a critical reading of Hau'ofa, Jolly comments, "Inspiring as his vision is, it tends to celebrate a particular subject position, that of a 'world traveler.' It echoes the particulars of his own life history ... Such celebrations of ancient voyages seem to meld with the experience of contemporary migration" ("On the Edge?" 422).

Jolly reminds readers, "There is a big difference between living in the interior of a large, mountainous island and living in archipelagos of smaller islands or on coral atolls" (423).

Oceania is not a flat or homogenous space and the name Pacific Islander does not describe a uniform or internally consistent subject group. The concept of and proleptic hope for Oceania situates discrepant histories of resistance and accommodation in a comparative framework through which regional solidarity can be imagined and struggled over. Resistance to the militarization and basing of the Pacific has historically assumed many forms and levels of intensity, ranging from the overt to the covert, from the political to the cultural, from armed combat to legal maneuvering, from struggles for independence to petitions for greater inclusion within the US empire. To take one example of the former, in 1898, after 327 years of colonization by the Spanish, Filipino nationalists passionately fought for independence against the United States. The United States fought a bloody war to suppress Filipino independence and when the official war ended in 1902, an unofficial guerrilla movement opposing colonization continued for another decade.

Eastern Sāmoa, on the other hand, was relatively calm until the 1920s when a protest movement emerged against Navy rule. The protests, known as "Mau," were not for political independence but for greater cultural recognition by the United States and a more responsible naval presence (Chappell 218). JoAnna Poblete-Cross contends that American Samoans had "complicated forms of affiliation with the United States. Since the beginning of relations with the U.S., American Samoans have emphasized the protection and preservation of their culture, land, and ways of life" (504). Poblete-Cross further writes, "Since the U.S. government had very little interest in American Sāmoa until World War II, and only limited involvement after that, American Samoans have not felt the direct and obvious impact of U.S. colonialism in their daily lives" (506). The prophet of American sea power, Alfred Thayer Mahan, may have anticipated the general contours of twentieth-century American Pacific history, yet he overestimated the particular strategic naval importance of Pago Pago. Eastern Sāmoa has not had to confront or negotiate the massive military, economic, or tourist flows that have violently reshaped Guåhan, Hawai'i, the Marshall Islands, and the Philippines.

Plantation owners and missionaries prepared the way for the colonization of Hawai'i, which was relatively peaceful compared to the high number of casualties during the Philippine-American War. As the Mau movement was emerging in Eastern Sāmoa, Kamehameha Schools in Hawai'i were instructing Native Hawaiian men on "how to assimilate into and embrace American culture" (McGregor 218). A popular, widespread struggle for cultural recognition did not appear in Hawai'i until the Native Hawaiian Cultural and Political Renaissance of the 1970s, which, as Davianna Pomaika'i McGregor notes, "restored the significance and practice of the Native Hawaiian language, culture, religion, healing arts, fighting arts, navigational arts, and political sovereignty" (221). The Hawaiian sovereignty movement is currently working through questions of whether to move toward political independence, toward political recognition within the framework of statehood, or in some other direction, questions also being struggled over by decolonization movements in Guåhan and Eastern Sāmoa.

The United Nations counts Guåhan as one of the world's sixteen remaining colonies or "non-self-governing territories." As Michael Lujan Bevacqua points out, after September 11, "Guam has been a magnet for military activity and buildup" (33). Chamorro delegations to the UN have been calling upon the United States to decolonize the island, yet the United States "refuses to respect, or even accept openly or publicly, that the island and its people have any right to decolonization" (34–35). Keith L. Camacho and Laurel A. Monnig provide a wide historical frame for understanding the issue of decolonization in Guåhan which reveals that "Chamorro movements pushed for an end to military rule and called for recognition of civil rights as early as 1901 in the form of a petition signed by a group of Chamorro political elites" (150). Unending military buildup on hyper-militarized islands such as "USS Guam"—the $8 billion Marine Corps Base Camp Blaz was activated in 2020—continues to reproduce a vision of Oceania as the "still colonized 'fourth world'" (Perez 11; Diaz and Kauanui 323; Wilson 11).

This Oceanic multitude of uneven and staggered resistance movements must be kept in focus when narrating the devastating history of US imperialism in the region. This history reveals that Oceanic peoples that did not align with or got in the way of the spatial imperatives of a militarized American Pacific were internally or externally excluded, made exceptional, deprived of civil and human rights, forced into schools designed to erase cultural identity, or forced into service work for military or tourist industries. Those who openly fought against colonization were tortured and incarcerated in strategic hamlets, internment camps, reservations, or simply killed. With the basing of the Pacific, Native Pacific Islanders and the Indigenous populations of the Pacific Northwest became outsiders in their home islands, archipelagos, atolls, and coastal areas. March 7, 2021, commemorated 75 years of Bikini Islanders' displacement from their homes as a result of the nuclear colonization of the Marshall Islands during the Cold War. Bikini Islanders, who are currently spread throughout the Marshall Islands, have filed suits against the US government involving the cleanup and resettlement of Bikini. Yet as Teresia K. Teaiwa notes, "Bikini Islander settlements have been troubled by environmental, social, economic, political, physical, and emotional considerations" (18). And yet the basing of the Pacific has also given rise to a region-wide anti-base movement that is working to make connections and alliances between local social movement groups in Hawai'i, Okinawa, the Philippines, South Korea, and the Mariana Islands.

The Wilkes Expedition was a foundational moment in the formation of a US empire of bases in the Pacific. The American Pacific archive in general, and the hydrographic survey in particular, helped create security and stability for an emergent military empire that slowly insinuated itself across the Pacific, uprooting and rerouting Oceanic peoples in the process. This critique of the Wilkes Expedition is a move toward deimperialization, which Kuan-Hsing Chen argues is necessary to counter the reproduction of imperialism and colonialism in the present (x). US imperialist expansion in Asia and the Pacific continues to spread both spatially and temporally through an empire of bases that, as Johnson argued, "perpetuates Cold War structures, even without the Cold War's justification" (5). This is a critical moment in Oceania, as the Biden administration has begun to justify a "New Cold War" with China, thus amplifying the disastrous military buildup and war maneuvering instigated by Obama's "Asia-Pacific Pivot." Rather than providing support for a New Cold War, the US empire of bases in the Pacific should be demilitarized and repurposed to help fight the climate emergency, which is the immediate and long-term threat to the peoples and places of Oceania and the planet.

## Works Cited

Benjamin, Walter. *Illuminations*, edited by Hannah Arendt, Shocken Books, 1968.

Bevacqua, Michael Lujan. "The Exceptional Life and Death of a Chamorro Soldier: Tracing the Militarization of Desire in Guam, USA." *Militarized Currents: Towards a Decolonized Future in Asia and the Pacific*, edited by Setsu Shigematsu and Keith L. Camacho, U of Minnesota P, 2010, pp. 33–62.

Calder, Kent E. *Embattled Garrisons: Comparative Base Politics and American Globalism*. Princeton UP, 2007.

Camacho, Keith L., and Laurel A. Monnig. "Uncomfortable Fatigues: Chamorro Soldiers, Gendered Identities, and the Question of Decolonization in Guam." *Militarized Currents: Towards a Decolonized Future in Asia and the Pacific*, edited by Setsu Shigematsu and Keith L. Camacho, U of Minnesota P, 2010, pp. 147–80.

Chappell, David A. "The Forgotten Mau: Anti-Navy Protest in American Samoa, 1920–1935." *Pacific Historical Review*, vol. 69, 2000, pp. 217–60.

Chen, Kuan-Hsing. *Asia as Method toward Deimperialization*. Duke UP, 2010.

Connery, Chris L. "Ideologies of Land and Sea: Alfred Thayer Mahan, Carl Schmitt, and the Shaping of Global Myth Elements." *Boundary 2*, vol. 28, no. 2, 2001, pp. 173–201.

D'Arcy, Paul. *The People of the Sea: Environment, Identity, and History in Oceania*. U of Hawai'i P, 2006.

de Certeau, Michel. *The Practice of Everyday Life*. U of California P, 2002.

Diaz, Vicente M., and J. Kehaulani Kauanui. "Native Pacific Cultural Studies on the Edge." *The Contemporary Pacific*, vol.13, no. 2, 2001, pp. 315–42.

Dudden, Arthur P. *The American Pacific: From the Old China Trade to the Present*. Oxford UP, 1994.

Fernandez-Armesto, Felipe. *Pathfinders: A Global History of Exploration*. W.W. Norton, 2006.

Gage, Beverly. *The Day Wall Street Exploded: A Story of America in Its First Age of Terror*. Oxford UP, 2010.

Hau'ofa, Epeli. *We Are the Ocean*. U of Hawai'i P, 2008.

Horkheimer, Max, and Theodor W. Adorno. *Dialectic of Enlightenment*. Continuum, 1993.

Johnson, Chalmers. *Blowback: The Costs and Consequences of American Empire*. Holt, 2000.

———. "Chalmers Johnson on Our Military Empire." *Tom Dispatch*, Mar. 21, 2006, https://tomdispatch.com/tomdispatch-interview-chalmers-johnson-on-our-military-empire/. Accessed Oct. 25, 2021.

Jolly, Margaret. "Imagining Oceania: Indigenous and Foreign Representations of a Sea of Islands." *The Contemporary Pacific*, vol. 19, no. 2, 2007, pp. 508–45.

Jolly, Margaret. "On the Edge? Deserts, Oceans, Islands." *The Contemporary Pacific*, vol. 13, no. 2, 2001, pp. 417–66.
Joyce, Barry Alan. *The Shaping of American Ethnography: The Wilkes Expedition, 1838–1842*. U of Nebraska Press, 2001.
Kim, Myung Mi. *Commons*. U of California P, 2002.
Lyons, Paul. *American Pacificism: Oceania in the U.S. Imagination*. Routledge, 2006.
McGregor, Davianna Pomaikaʻi. "Engaging Hawaiians in the Expansion of the U.S. Empire." *Journal of Asian American Studies* vol. 7, no. 3, 2004, pp. 209–22.
Osorio, Jonathan Kay Kamakawiwoʻole. *Dismembering Lahui: A History of the Hawaiian Nation to 1887*. U of Hawaiʻi P, 2002.
Perez, Craig Santos. *from unincorporated territory [hacha]*. Omnidawn, 2008.
Philbrick, Nathaniel. *Sea of Glory: America's Voyage of Discovery: The Exploring Expedition*. Penguin, 2003.
Poblete-Cross, JoAnna. "Bridging Indigenous and Immigrant Struggles: A Case Study." *American Quarterly*, vol. 62, no. 3, 2010, pp. 501–22.
Pratt, Mary Louise. *Imperial Eyes: Travel Writing and Transculturation*. Routledge, 1992.
Stillman, Amy Kuʻuleialoha. "Pacific-ing Asian Pacific American History." *Journal of American Studies*, vol. 7, no. 3, 2004, pp. 241–70.
Subramani. "The Oceanic Imaginary." *The Contemporary Pacific*, vol. 13, no. 1, 2001, pp. 149–62.
Teaiwa, Teresia K. "bikinis and other s/pacific n/oceans." *Militarized Currents: Towards a Decolonized Future in Asia and the Pacific*, edited by Setsu Shigematsu and Keith L. Camacho, U of Minnesota P, 2010, pp. 15–32.
Turse, Nick. "America's Empire of Bases 2.0." *The Nation*, Jan. 10, 2011, https://www.thenation.com/article/archive/americas-empire-bases-20/. Accessed Sept. 23, 2021.
Vine, David. *The United States of War: A Global History of America's Conflicts: From Columbus to the Islamic State*. U of California P, 2020.
Wilkes, Charles. *Narrative of the United States Exploring Expedition: Vol 1–5*. G.P. Putnam & Co, 1856.
Wilkes, Charles et al., eds. *Autobiography of Rear Admiral Charles Wilkes, U.S. Navy, 1798–1877*. Naval History Division, 1978.
Wilson, Rob. "Towards an Ecopoetics of Oceania." Keynote Address, 21st Annual University of Hawaiʻi School of Pacific & Asian Studies Graduate Conference. Mar. 10, 2010.
Wood, Houston. "Cultural Studies for Oceania." *The Contemporary Pacific*, vol. 15, no. 2, 2003, pp. 340–74.

# 2

# Epeli Hauʻofa's Pronouns

Paul Lyons

*Would I lie if I said* there's a house
where no pronouns are kept.
—Craig Santos Perez, *from unincorporated territory* [saina]
*Only we can make our region real.*
—Teresia K. Teaiwa, "Specifying Pacific Studies"

## Pronominal Turns

Epeli Hauʻofa's essays have achieved a field-defining status in Pacific studies, providing language and metaphors with which to imagine everyday life in the region that Hauʻofa and other Pacific writer-scholars redefined as "Oceania." Among the essays' remarkable qualities are their handlings—subtly modified to meet the occasion of each essay—of plural possessive pronouns in relation to regional identity, cultural memory, and the *Moana Nui* (Pacific Ocean, Oceania). With the wisdom of one legendary for building relations throughout Oceania and beyond, Hauʻofa shows how possessive pronouns resonate with issues relating to possession and dispossession in the multiple senses of these words. These extend from the colonialist meanings of possession as related to maps and territories (places claimed as "our overseas possessions") to the physical senses, which, as Vicente M. Diaz argues in reading Hauʻofa's works, include ways of smelling (bodily smells, smells of islands [334]) as indexes to memory-complexes, to various states of being possessed or visited by spirits.[1] Hauʻofa claimed that "Our Sea of Islands" was written "with an aim of exorcising a particularly nasty ghost, the ghost of belittlement" (qtd. in White, "Foreword" xiv). In "Toward a New Oceania," Albert Wendt likewise argued that Oceania "must try to exorcise [bad] *aitu* [spirits] both

---

[1] On the "polemics of possession" as this refers to a constituent part of colonial narratives over time see Rolena Adorno's reading of the Spanish tradition. Vicente Diaz, responding to Hauʻofa's call to "devise other methods" for doing history ("Pasts" 457), notes how an Oceanian history of the olfactory senses suggests ways to "augment if not supplement" a historiography overly reliant on the textual and visual (326). Mahalo to Richard Hamasaki for commenting on this essay.

old and modern" (73). At the same time, Hauʻofa expresses, in the Preface to *We Are the Ocean: Selected Works*, his "gratitude to the ancient spirits of Hawaiʻi who always welcome me to their land and shower me with inspiration and aloha" (xxi).

What a diverse region can be "said to possess" that is "not abundant elsewhere," as Wole Soyinka elaborates in *Of Africa*, extends beyond "resources, touristic landscapes, strategic locations"; it includes "dynamic possessions—ways of perceiving, responding, adapting, or … structures of human relationships" (vii). With a similarly rich appreciation of cultural possessions and spirits as complex inheritances turning in time and space, Hauʻofa marks the centrality of plural possessive pronouns to contemporary Oceanian thought in the titles of several essays—*Our Crowded Islands* (1977), "The Future of Our Past" (1985), "Our Sea of Islands" (1993), "The Ocean in Us" (1997), "Our Places Within" (2003).[2] The centrality of plural possessive pronouns—related to an Oceanic prioritizing of collective over individualistic approaches to questions about rights—is pronounced as well in the crescendos rising out of repetitions of pronouns in crucial passages.

The most cited of these passages, the conclusion to "Our Sea of Islands," well illustrates the qualities with which Hauʻofa's pronouns often seem to shimmer as they rotate, affording a variety of entrance points into what is imagined as "our" ancient inheritance. While Hauʻofa maintains that the sea cannot be "ours" in a strictly possessive sense, a shared recognition of being *of* the *Moana Nui* (of the Ocean that "we are" and that is "in us"), as it has sustained life, belief, and structured culture and history, is rendered back to Oceanians in his essays as a form of self-possession. If his "our" contains an immanent "human" call to a world historically interconnected by oceanic movements, it is nonetheless a variegated universal that calls differently to particular audiences. Phrases such as "all of us in Oceania today, whether Indigenous *or otherwise*, can truly assert that the sea is our single common heritage" and "the sea is our pathway to each other and *everyone else*" (*We Are the Ocean* 54, 58, emphasis added) at once mark boundaries and assert the possibility of shared historically and affectively based commitments. In such ways, Hauʻofa invites diversely positioned audiences to participate in approaching the region's complex histories of possession and dispossession, inclusion and exclusion, as well as to reflect upon their respective responsibilities in relation to current movements toward repossession across an expanded conception of Oceania.

> Oceania is vast, Oceania is expanding, Oceania is hospitable and generous, Oceania is humanity rising from the depths of brine and regions of fire deeper still, Oceania is us. We are the sea, we are the ocean, we must wake up to this ancient truth and together use it to overturn all hegemonic views that aim ultimately to confine us again, physically and psychologically, in the tiny spaces that we have resisted

---

[2] "Our Sea of Islands," "The Ocean in Us," and "Our Places Within: Foundations for a Creative Oceania" are collected in *We Are the Ocean*.

accepting as our sole appointed places and from which we have recently liberated ourselves. We must not allow anyone to belittle us, and take away our freedom.
(*We Are the Ocean* 39)

My sense is that much of what has made Hauʻofa's "Our Sea of Islands" "the most visionary piece ever to emerge in Pacific Studies" (Teaiwa "L[o]osing" 346) for a spectrum of critics who hear his injunction ("we must wake up") differently *moves about* in the plural possessive pronouns of such passages. Hauʻofa at once invites hearers to slot themselves into the noun position—without fixing the identity of the noun for which the plural possessive pronouns stand in—while rendering back suggestions that "we" will never hear the call and sound of plural possessives in the same way.[3] This is to suggest that Hauʻofa achieves a mobile and multi-phonic poetics of pronominal usage that is deeply informed by Pacific oratory and storytelling and a warm Oceanic spirit.

Hauʻofa turns away from plural possessive pronouns that function to prevent the region's peoples from realizing historical connections or crossed and mutual "possessions" of each other (Dening 132, see also Mishra and Smith). The latter are in Oceanian archives and oral histories and can be seen as prefiguring alternative futures. Ethnically exclusivist pronouns—whether those of other-than-Oceanians or people he "claim[s]" as his "own" (*We Are the Ocean* 29)—are seen as dispossessing Oceanian peoples materially and existentially. Hauʻofa elaborates instead a contemporary Oceanian philosophical ethics according to which "we must not allow anyone to belittle us" (39) flowers into *we must not belittle anyone else*. It flows from this that in his version of Oceanian ethics one must not harm or appropriate other people's lands, fisheries, languages, or cultural possessions (stories, dances, practices, images, and so forth). For Hauʻofa, to imagine a stronger Oceanian "our" is not to dispossess (or categorically bar from participation) a "them," American, Asian, or otherwise.[4] However, the notion that an Oceanian "our" is "hospitable"—however much this is enacted through Hauʻofa's own interpersonal warmth and openness—does seem to require committed consideration of Oceanian conceptions of guest/host relationships. It would seem to require as well considerations of how an "our" works in relation to genders and sexualities, a question that suggests how abstract inclusivities might cover over specific inequalities. For instance, in her review of *A New Oceania*, a collection of

---

[3] For an alternative scene of reading involving pronouns see Deborah Madsen, who describes Vine Deloria's skillful deployment of pronouns to mark and counter the senses in which the noun they stand in for—"Indian"—has come to signify lack.

[4] While long appreciating Hauʻofa's care to avoid "racialized exclusions of the dominant forms of Hegelian ocean-making," Rob Wilson questions the tendency in Hauʻofa toward an "en toto" equation of mainland Asian thought with neoliberal capitalism (Wilson, *Be Always Converting* 130). This forecloses Pacific and Asian linkages that would "move beyond" regional frameworks toward a "more capacious vision of alternative belonging [and] ecological confederation" (Wilson, "Toward an Ecopoetics of Oceania" 2). Wilson models his own version of "shaping into prefigurative realization, another transnational and transcultural Asia/Pacific region" in which Polynesian gods are "*co-present* at the event of world globalization" (*Be Always Converting* 139, 142).

responses to "Our Sea of Islands," Teaiwa suggests ways in which bracketing gender in a discussion of an "our" functions to hide problems facing women in Oceanian society ("Review" 216).

Hauʻofa specifically engages ways in which minding the entrance points of plural possessives may be a matter of survival for peoples struggling against inundating versions of an occupying, imperial *we*. In the so-called post-independence era, there are "those of us who must focus on strengthening their ancestral cultures in their struggles against seemingly overwhelming forces in order to regain their lost sovereignty" (*We Are the Ocean* 42). Despite his conviction that the nation-state form, a strictly colonial creation in Oceania, functions neo-colonially, often with the complicity of Indigenous elites, he repeatedly affirms Indigenous struggles to repossess lands, seas, and culture within the available schema. The regional "ours" that he envisions nests within, and remains supplemental to, other on-the-ground engaged forms of "ours." As he states this, the "our" of "regional identity … is something additional to the other identities we already have, or will develop in the future, something that should serve to enrich our other selves" (*We Are the Ocean* 42). This "our" could thus be counted on to support Nona Beamer's appeal to the US government:

> Give heed to our voices. We have extended aloha to you, and you seek to extinguish our very being. Respect us; be aware that we were once a sovereign international nation. We are descendants of a mighty civilization and deserve to be listened to in our own homeland.
>
> (qtd. in Beamer 16)

In short, in acknowledging diverse political realities, imperatives, and ways of being and belonging in Oceania, Hauʻofa preserves both the multiplicities and the singularities of positionalities across bioregional time, and he encourages conversations among those committed to self-determination and cultural continuity for Oceanian peoples, which cannot be thought outside of a "philosophy of reverence" for the natural world ("Pasts to Remember" 468).

In "Our Sea of Islands," notably, an aspect of affective connections—including connections extended to those with whom one expects to disagree—precedes any argumentation. Hauʻofa anticipates that his essay will disturb people who have "dedicated their lives" to Oceania, people for whom he holds nonetheless "the greatest respect and affection, and always will" (*We Are the Ocean* 27). Although the occasion of the essay's delivery is an academic meeting—a rolling out of "new perspectives" (*We Are the Ocean* 30) with politico-philosophical-material implications first to academics in Pacific studies and later to colleagues at the University of the South Pacific—"Our Sea of Islands" sounds through its multiple tonal registers like it is addressed both to and beyond the academic audience. Its "we" refers not only to academics but also to Indigenous Pacific leaders, to artists, to students, to those who must "wake up" to the destructiveness of developmental views of Oceania, and to those who have settled and become part of Oceanian cultures. Its "we" refers as well to "similar people elsewhere" who might share the "common task of protecting the seas" (*We Are the Ocean* 55) and to the "we" of those "ordinary people" and mobile Oceanians to whose experience the essay gives expression.

Hau'ofa's pronominal poetics involve what might appear to be programmed inconsistencies by which he leads the reader through seemingly opposite positions in order to show their non-contradictions while also suggesting the epistemological violence of collapsing positionalities and temporalities into each other. His poetics thus stand against colonial oppositions of indigeneity/modernity, purity/hybridity, tradition/inauthenticity, and realism/myth. As Damon Salesa states in "The Pacific in Indigenous Time," "indigenous Pacific ways, histories, languages stand not in opposition to other great forces at work in the present—postcolonialism, development, globalisation, commercialization—but are articulate with them, as well as with a deep and resonant past" (31). Within a page, Hau'ofa asserts that those who love Oceania can claim it because "this mother has a big heart ... [and] adopts anyone who loves her" (*We Are the Ocean* 34–5) and supports the idea:

> Alliances are already being forged by an increasing number of Islanders with the tangata whenua of Aotearoa and will inevitably be forged with the Native Hawaiians. It is not inconceivable that if Polynesians ever get together, their two largest homelands will be reclaimed in one form or another.
> (*We Are the Ocean* 35)

In the first view, living in and loving Oceania makes one Oceanian (*We Are the Ocean* 51); in the latter, pan-Polynesian sovereignties present as alternatives to conventional nationalisms, which Hau'ofa sees as connected to a "new world order" in which states effect the work of a transnational corporate order. The first posits Oceanian kinship systems—in the sense that one's lines of affiliation are coextensive with the movements of one's relatives and kin—as alternatives to either ethnic nationalism or the kind of "cosmopolitan patriotism" that Anthony Appiah formulates and as suturing the gaps between homeland and home(s) within a new mobile liberal subjectivity. At the same time, Hau'ofa recognizes as Islanders non-Indigenous peoples of the islands, in particular indo-Fijians but implicitly all settlers who are committed to Oceania. In contrast, an Indigenous Fijian regime compelled to enact a "racist constitution" (*We Are the Ocean* 82), acting out of a sense of "ethnic absolutism," Hau'ofa suggests, ethically replicates the logic it elsewhere contests and turns from aspects of its own history.[5] For Hau'ofa, being anti-"ethnic absolutism" and pro-Indigenous is not a contradiction. The relation of "routes" and "roots" in Hau'ofa is likewise treated non-dialectically, as non-contradictions, through a centering of principles of reciprocity. These are the "core of all Pacific cultures" and most immediately visible within "families and kin groups" who continue the "ancient" mobility of their ancestors in their settlement of the Pacific

---

[5] See James Clifford on Hau'ofa's sense of regret of "a lost opportunity to ... inhabit, attentively, the contradictions of different historical dynamics" (207).

region: "For everything homeland relatives receive, they reciprocate with goods they themselves produce, by maintaining ancestral roots and lands" (*We Are the Ocean* 36).

Through maintaining such an interconnected series of non-contradictions, Hau'ofa approaches what are often volatile political situations, or situations involving various kinds of displacement, with a calming authority. This might be attributed to the stately, optative manner of extending pronouns that recalls Oceanian forms of problem-solving. The essay itself has aspects of oration, conversation, storytelling, or the quality of a "brilliant and attentive teacher" whose shifts in register can be likened to "attending to individual students' needs" (Bal 492).

One might surmise as well that Hau'ofa uses plural possessive pronouns in ways, inflected by Polynesian language, that will be heard differently by different audiences. Some pronouns are used in the form of an "address" to his audience; others are used in the form of statements that include identities of the listeners in the words "we" and "our." It is well to remember that in English "our" is one word, with a limited number of semantic functions; in Polynesian languages "our" must first be marked possessive and then joined to a pronoun that carries number. This is seen, for example, in *ōlelo Hawai'i* (Hawaiian language) in the phrases "ko kākou" (possessive plural, inclusive of everyone present, including the speaker); "ko kāua" (our, the two of us); "ka māua" (belonging to us two, exclusive; not belonging to others); and "ka mākou" (belonging to all of us, plural; but not to them, others). A pronoun that in English would be one word might, heard in a Polynesian key, refer to "you and me" or "all of us who are present at the time of this utterance" or "all who are of a particular group" or a specific number, or, in certain forms, us but not them. "All of us," when uttered in a roomful of Pacific Historians, might refer to the historians in the room, the Oceanians for whom thinking in Pacific time is seen to be crucial, or others who attempt to locate themselves within Pacific history. Pacific pronouns are marked in ways that indicate proximity and direction, establishing the relationship between the speaker and the listeners much more precisely and appropriately, and they rely on specific markers (with the singular possessives "his" and "her") to differentiate gender. They might be inflected by irony, humor, or humility as well. My sense, given the turns in Hau'ofa's pronominal poetics, and his facility in six Pacific languages (he considered English as one of them), is that he includes such valences to call to parts of his audiences without disconnecting them from others. As a master orator, storyteller, and ethical philosopher, and as a writer whose sense of humor remained "intact" (*We Are the Ocean* 107), Hau'ofa recognizes that language and narrative are important for what one wants to say and for how affective connections are forged.

## Pronouns and (Dis)possession in Oceania

*Once I mentioned to an islander that I thought of naming my book* Our Hawaii. *He flared up at once, "You don't think it's your Hawaii, do you?"*
—Erna Fergusson, *Our Hawaii*

*Guam is one of [our] most curious possessions. Guam is no longer "Guam."*
—Craig Santos Perez, *from unincorporated territory* [hacha]

Echoes of "Our Sea of Islands" resound across Oceania. They are found in expressions of Native Pacific lines of affiliation (including intellectual and literary genealogies), in consciously Island-centered projects like Aiko Yamashiro's and Noelani Goodyear-Kaʻōpua's "We are Islanders," in policy documents such as "Our Sea of Islands—Our Livelihoods—Our Oceania: a Framework for Pacific Oceanscape" (2010) (cited in the Palau Declaration), and in the Moana Nui Statement (2011), which reads in part: "We, the people of *Moana Nui*, connected by the currents of our ocean home ... choose cooperative transpacific dialogue between and amongst the peoples of the Pacific, rooted in traditional cultural practices and wisdom."[6] Echoing Hauʻofa, Yamashiro and Goodyear-Kaʻōpua argue that Natives and settlers committed to "the value of Hawaiʻi," when "locked in a gaze" toward the continental United States, "tend to see our islands, our unique cultural knowledges, and even ourselves as small, inconsequential, disempowered, and inferior" (2).[7] In this section I briefly reflect on three poets—two Indigenous and one non-Indigenous—who reference Hauʻofa in their work, drawing out aspects of his thought that he does not discuss explicitly so that his work keeps returning and gathering meanings. Their pronouns, like Hauʻofa's, function critically as linguistic sites for engaging challenges that face Oceania.

In one strand of his multilayered poetic trilogy—*from unincorporated territory [hacha]* (2008); *from unincorporated territory [saina]* (2010); *from unincorporated territory [gumaʻ]* [2014])—Chamorro poet Craig Santos Perez highlights what might be called dispossessed or dispossessive plural pronouns. In a section from *[saina]*, he describes how "Hauʻofa draws our attention to an oceania, préoceania, and transoceania surrounding islands, below the waves, and in the sky—a deeper geography and mythology" (62). Quoting Hauʻofa, Perez brackets the pronouns in Hauʻofa's passages—the pronominals that in the original text function to join Oceanians to each other, to the Oceania region, and to the Oceanian cosmos. This bracketing implies that Oceanian connections are zeroed in on and cancelled out by colonial and neocolonial regimes:

> [Our] universe comprised not only land surfaces but also the surrounding ocean as far as [we] could traverse and exploit it, the underworld with its fire-controlling

---

[6] In her discussion of Asian and Pacific activisms as affiliated "methods" of critiquing empire, Candace Fujikane details the relation of this paragraph from *Moana Nui* to Hauʻofa. Moana Nui meets at the same time as APEC, as the World Social Forum meets at the same time as the annual World Economic Summit in Davos, to express an antithetical vision. Words like "transpacific" in this hearing are directly meant to (re)turn their meanings toward a Pacific-centered vision and thus away from those implied by the Trans-Pacific Partnership (TPP), whose "transpacific" elides Oceanians.

[7] Cf. Hauʻofa: "As individual, colonially created, tiny countries acting alone, we could indeed ... disappear into the black hole of a gigantic Pan-Pacific doughnut" (*We Are the Ocean* 42). The "we" in Yamashiro and Goodyear-Kaʻōpua refers to "ʻōiwi [Hawaiians] and settlers who have benefited from the Hawaiian Renaissance ... [who] see so many unfulfilled promises and obligations to the Hawaiian people and nation" (3). The collection explores the question, "How do we ally in meaningful ways, and what will 'solidarity' actually require?" (8).

and earth-shaking denizens, and the heavens above with their hierarchies of powerful gods and named stars and constellations that [we] could count on to guide [our] way across the seas.

(qtd. in 63–64; brackets added by Perez)

The brackets orthographically convey the violence and sadness that constitute the gap between the Oceania that Hauʻofa (and Perez) summons up for repossession, and the Guåhan (Guam) caught in the cross-hairs of the ecological, military, cultural, and economic sightings of the United States and other imperial forces. Perez presents plural possessive pronouns as fenced off, captured, caged, zoned for ownership. The nouns they stand in for are denied access or title; their forests, seabed minerals, arable lands, and ocean views are parceled out. Their lands are used as decontamination sites. Perez cuts up documents, makes footnotes of testimony from hearings, and draws lines through passages while leaving them legible. A footnote describing how "toxic chemicals have snaked into our—" (107) is snapped off. In these contexts, the poet's questions stream together with a ghostly absence of question marks: "*what is our story* / who will listen to these stories / i have told what stories / have you listened to will tell those stories" (107). Of the voyage out he writes: "[we] cross with only these possessions ... [we] / carry our stories overseas to the place called 'voice' / and call / to know our allowance of water" (126).

In the low islands, including the atolls of the Marshall Islands, the sense of being inundated is more literal; as performance-artist Kathy Jetñil-Kijiner's "Tell Them" performs, that a "them" be brought to care about the stories of an "us" is an urgent matter.[8] Although the poem implies that the ignorance and lack of concern on the part of the continental "them" has catastrophic consequences for the Marshallese "we," the speaker has not given up hope that if the "them" knew better it might be recruited to show genuine care, alter its conduct, and even press for governmental reductions of fossil fuels. The pronouns of the poem are amplified by the figure of "friends," who are interposed as a necessary mediator between the "we" and the "them" in the afterlife of the poem's own performance. In the absence of a possible face-to-face between "we" and "them," friends who accept the injunction to "tell them"—who stand in as pronouns for nouns—may in turn swell the ranks of needed advocates. The speaker begins with the words, "I prepared a package/for my friends in the states" (70). It is full of island creations, earrings, and a woven basket, inside of which the speaker leaves a message (the remainder of the poem) in which she requests that her friends display the Marshallese gifts and turn any questions they receive about them into a teaching moment: "you tell them / they're from the Marshall Islands / show them where it is on a map / tell them we are a proud people" (70–71).

---

[8] Kathy Jetñil-Kijiner recently spoke on behalf of civil society at the UN Climate Leader's Summit, in particular about the impacts of climate change on Pacific Islanders. She concluded with a performance of her poem "Dear Matafele Peinem." Videos of her performing poetry can be accessed at https://jkijiner.wordpress.com.

Wearing Marshall Islands creations in the continental United States is represented in "Tell Them" as an everyday, activist act. The poem proceeds as a series of statements that the friends are to communicate to "them" about who the Marshallese are, their diversity, and their determination not to be forced into leaving the atolls by rising seas: "tell them about the water / how we have seen it rising/flooding across our cemeteries"; "we are the ocean / terrifying and regal in its power"; "tell them what it's like / to see the entire ocean level with the land"; most importantly, tell them "that we are nothing without our islands" (71–72). The speaker does not specify whether the "friends" who receive her gifts are Marshallese, but many might be, as one-third of all Marshallese now live in the United States. Whether through displacement or processes of "world enlargement" (*We Are the Ocean* 30), they now live among the "them" in what Hauʻofa calls "the lands of diaspora" (*We Are the Ocean* 57).

Given the ongoing movements of settlers into Oceania, the concept of an inclusive "our" *in* Oceania is mediated by histories of displacement and dispossession. Juliana Spahr stands out among poets/essayists who have taken on the challenge of writing about settler ambivalences through the use of plural possessive pronouns. Her work engages senses in which plural possessive pronouns can appear to mark "dispossession" both in the way that Judith Butler and Athena Athanasiou consider one existential meaning of "dispossession" to be the sensation by which, in recognizing difference, the (colonial) subject experiences a distancing from sovereign authority, and in seeming to diminish the "places" in which settlers and natives are "allowed" to gather together.[9] Spahr celebrates Hauʻofa as a force of "connect" along a spectrum of Indigenous positions that include the force of "disconnect" (oppositional approaches predicated on binary givens). While she does not necessarily disagree with Indigenous Oceanians who argue for "disconnect[ion]" in the fight against (neo)colonialisms, she raises the questions of how a settler can participate politically and poetically in an Oceanian "our" without an invitation and of what accepting that hospitality might involve.[10]

In "Gathering: Palolo Stream," a poem from *Fuck-You-Aloha-I-Love-You* (2001), Spahr most directly addresses the prepositioned dynamics of the pronoun "we" in a settler-colonial state. (Elsewhere in the collection she writes: "I am meditating on the word we / like we all are all of the time" [47]). "Gathering: Palolo Stream" sets out

---

[9] Butler and Athanasiou differentiate this sense of "dispossession" categorically from that experienced through colonization, in which Indigenous peoples are dispossessed of land, customary forms of governance, and language.

[10] In "Connected Disconnection in Pacific Multicultural Literature," Spahr emphasizes the co-presence of different languages within Pacific poems, as these are correlative with the co-presence of different positionalities in Pacific "contact zones." Spahr suggests that the site of "connection" (the co-presence of languages within one poem) marks as well the site of disconnection (differential power dynamics at work in standard English, creole, and languages minoritized within the world republic of letters) and the challenges facing "projects to reclaim violated boundaries" (79). On the polemics of pronouns for the settler see also Susan Schultz's answer to the question she poses herself: "What pronoun(s) will you use in writing about EuroAmerican poets?" which concludes, "as I write, I notice the pronouns shifting from us to them, from they to we, and will honor their divergences from a stable subjectivity by permitting them their pronominal diasporas" (13).

a premise that the poem will test: "A place allows certain things/and certain of we of a specific/place have certain rights" (19). The "certain of we" that "on paper" (26) has "certain rights" in this case are Native Hawaiians, who are "allow[ed]" customary gathering rights by the state, which in many instances are abrogated by private landowners ("certain of us who are owning / place") who block access to the stream. However, for the speaker, the conditions that establish such protective "entitlements"—and reference the whole system of Hawaiian entitlements—mark boundaries of possession/ dispossession in several directions. As disposed as a certain "we" might be to support Native gathering rights, for the speaker the idea that the "we" has only certain rights extends metaphorically into areas of human relations and intellectual boundaries as well and raises questions about whether there is effectively any "we" at all. That a "certain of we" has gathering rights seems to suggest that another "certain of we" does not have them, and that, given the premises on which the "rights" are "allowed," there might be other less visible things in "place" that the leftover "certain of we" (the majority settlers) should not be allowed.

The word "allows," in the first instance referring to juridical "rights" guaranteed by the occupier's law, seems to refer as well to the whole system of enunciated and unenunciated allowances, tacitly accepted, including the proprieties of what to say when and in what place. Through this word as well as through the plural pronominal "we" in the phrase "we the people," Spahr points to state-authored fictions that allow different people and entities such as corporations, developers, educational institutions, and the military, exceptional rights. The law thereby remains a machine for the pseudo-protection of "certain rights" and the large-scale dispossession and displacement of Native peoples. Spahr's poem thus performs not only the numbingly absurd fact that native access to land must be granted by those who have stolen it but also to the fact that in many cases where a request for access is granted, the permission then runs up against the uneven compliance of private landowners, who can define adjacent land use and thereby refuse access to the granted native access land. Stretches of the stream banks are now paved over or littered with "busted television[s]" (22). Spahr leaves the reader with a strong sense of the historical divisions perpetuated by the state—often implicit in the unstated rules of what a place "allows"—that prevent people from gathering (politically assembling) against the system: "Certain of we have rights and / these rights are written so that / there is a possible keeping, a / keeping away, that denies / gathering" (3).

## The Quality of "Our" Survival

*Why, they even tried to dispossess us of our dislike of being dispossessed! And I'll tell you something else—if we don't resist, pretty soon they'll succeed! These are the days of dispossession, the season of homelessness, the time of evictions. We'll be dispossessed of the very brains in our heads!*

—Ralph Ellison, *Invisible Man*

Few in Oceania achieve the authority and comprehensive vision requisite to turning the words "we" or "our" as Hau'ofa does, as if he had gathered different audiences around a metaphorical talanoa.[11] Even when Hau'ofa's primary audience is marked by the occasions for which they were written, or by cues within the essay, it is done in ways that acknowledge and welcome the diversity of "we"s convened within an "our." Geoff White catches Hau'ofa's connective magic in asking, somewhat rhetorically: "How could someone who devoted himself to building a sense of community of and for Pacific Islanders, challenging the often suffocating presence of foreign practices, evoke such a sense of warmth, kindness, and connection?" (9). Hau'ofa himself expressed the desire to remain "intellectually and emotionally close to the ground" ("A Promise of Renewal" 52) and was listened to in Oceania as a "chief of knowledge" (Winduo 114) who captured the ways in which the "universe of Oceanian mores" (*We Are the Ocean* 38) remained crucial to the ability of Oceanians "to survive reasonably well" (*We Are the Ocean* 29) in the global system. Outside of what he considered Oceania, he has become *the* Oceanian prophet of blue reason, an Oceanian José Marti, an "Our Epeli" who erects "mental barriers" against global capital, espouses globalization-from-below, and authorizes the view that the Ocean might function as "our" (humanity's) commons.

While Hau'ofa's texts do embrace a view of "our relationship with our Earth" in terms of a planetary "our," and while he shares a vision of a totality characterized by "a world of people connected to each other" (*We Are the Ocean* 50), his pronouns ask readers to not let out of their view either the priority that Hau'ofa gives to the "practical struggle for survival" of "ordinary" Oceanians (*We Are the Ocean* 87) or the deliberativeness with which his frameworks, metaphors, and aesthetics are Pacific-centering. Hau'ofa's world-building hope that "Oceania is humanity rising from the depths of brine and regions of fire still deeper" (*We Are the Ocean* 39), for instance, references deep cosmological "time" and Pele's fire rising from the seabed to form volcanic islands. Likewise, if Hau'ofa is to be read as an "ecologist," ecology should not be separated from his approach to an Oceanian philosophical ethics in which "culture and nature are inseparable" (*We Are the Ocean* 56). For Hau'ofa "the removal of a people from their ancestral, natural surrounding" and the destruction of their lands by "mining, deforestation ... and the like" are of a piece with "the destruction of age-old rhythms of cyclical dramas that lock together familiar time, motion, and space." As Craig Santos Perez writes, "when land is / caged [we] / —of theft—[i sihek] / are caged within / [our] disappearance" (*[guma']* 71). To destroy land, pollute seas, or forcibly relocate peoples is on the order of destroying "all of a nation's libraries, archives, museums, monuments, historic buildings, and all its books and other documents" ("Pasts" 468–69). The holism often remarked in Hau'ofa's work becomes, in these contexts, inseparable from an activist Oceanian ethos, which expresses that "we must tie history and culture to empirical reality and practical action" (*We Are the Ocean* 55). The works both describe holism and are holistic: statements in the essays

---

[11] See Halapua on talanoa as an Oceanian philosophy of relationship-building and problem-solving.

on ecology or cross-cultural exchange are not detachable from grassroots activism, and they lose their force without this complementary work.

An Oceania without Oceanians or without others "who love her" would not be an Oceania in the terms Hauʻofa elaborates but rather a vast haunted and polluted sea, one zoned into dumps, sweat shops, and military outposts. This is the kind of future Hauʻofa saw under construction in the "Asia Pacific" by organizations "creating … a new set of relationships that excludes us totally" (*We Are the Ocean* 47) and that refused genuine polemic. "In APEC we do not exist" (*We Are the Ocean* 46), he wrote. This was in part because no Pacific Island Nations were represented in Asia-Pacific Economic Cooperation APEC, but mostly it was because within APEC's vision of "economic cooperation" the world of Islanders and island cultures were understood to be literally expendable and because the neoliberal philosophy that frames rights as belonging in the first instance to persons, and then frames corporations as persons, so completely contrasts with Oceanian beliefs in collective rights. In this sense, the "our" in "our sea of islands" rises up from the seabed against the pushdown logic of a "theirs"; for Hauʻofa "we cannot afford to ignore our exclusion because what is involved here is our very survival" (*We Are the Ocean* 34). Thus he satirizes the developmental discourses under which Islanders are recurrently "urged" to participate in their own dispossession in order to support the economic, scientific, military, pedagogical, and geopolitical gains of powerful nations. This participation is for the "good of humanity," as the US government described nuclear testing. Hauʻofa responds:

> Modern society is generating and accumulating vast quantities of waste matter that must in the near future be disposed of where there will be the least resistance. It may well be that for the survival of the human species in the next millennium we in Oceania will be urged, in the way the people of Banaba and Bikini were urged, to give up our lands and seas.
>
> (*We Are the Ocean* 46)

The "use" of Pacific islands has been a litany of human rights and ecological abuses, systematically unreported, at least in the United States by organizations like the *New York Times*, as Beverly Keever documents in *News Zero: The New York Times and the Bomb*. Bikini Islanders were relocated for "atomic tests that [putatively] would benefit all mankind" (*We Are the Ocean* 47). "It may well be," Hauʻofa writes, satirizing both the emotionally uninvolved language of those who plan and execute such decisions concerning others, and the escalating rhetorics of urgency by which "for the good of mankind" becomes for "the survival of the human species." That Islanders were and are being "urged" to "give up" the *Moana Nui* that they were and are being asked to let the *Moana Nui* be used as the world's dump reflects the argument that disasters (economic, ecological, militaristic) create the conditions for corporate or exceptional state solutions to be introduced in ways that lead to "accumulation through dispossession" and that regard impacted human subjects as the waste of modernity (see DeLoughrey 124; Butler and Athanasiou 12),

On at least one of many levels, then, Hau'ofa's essays can be read as part of a growing body of Indigenous "survivance" narratives.[12] Against the forces that see Islanders and Island cultures as disposable, and against the forces that are buying up the natural resources both above and below the islands and seas of Oceania, Hau'ofa posits Indigenous innovation, microeconomic circuits of barter, and regional interdependence, along with a deep and elemental identification with the *Moana Nui*:

> A common identity that would help us to act together for the advancement of our collective interests, including the protection of the ocean for the general good, is necessary for the quality of our survival in the so-called Pacific Century, when, as we are told, important developments in the global economy will concentrate in the huge regions that encircle us.
>
> (*We Are the Ocean* 42)

An Oceania not progressively unified and without its own strong and creative resistance cultures would not be able to confront the issues of "the Pacific Century," including the issue of the term "Pacific Century." Officials who use this term typically have only been able to see the region as a theater in which Oceanians play at best bit parts. Despite Hau'ofa's hopes for him, President Obama, born and raised in Hawai'i, seemed as ill-disposed as his predecessors were to give Oceanian people agential or more than nonderivative roles in the future they imagine for the Asia Pacific region. In "Remarks to the Australian Parliament," for instance, Obama claimed that

> our new focus on this region reflects a fundamental truth—the United States has been, and always will be, a Pacific nation. Asian immigrants helped build America. [...] From the bombing of Darwin to the liberation of Pacific islands, from the rice paddies of Southeast Asia to a cold Korea Peninsula, generations of Americans have served here, and died here—so democracies could take root; so economic miracles could lift hundreds of millions to prosperity.

In an effort against such grandiose teleological narratives as the speech by Obama, Hau'ofa in "Pasts to Remember" and "Our Place Within" sharply distinguishes between "ours" and "theirs" (perhaps here echoing the Polynesian pronouns *mākou* [ours, plural exclusive] and *lākou* [theirs, plural]). He uses these words as a drum refrain that resonates through all of the scales of his composition: "non-oceanians may construct and interpret our pasts or our present, but they are their constructions and interpretations, not ours. Theirs may be excellent and very instructive, but we must rely much more on ours" ("Pasts to Remember" 457). He continues, "Let others do their reconstructions of our pasts; we have dialogue with them, and form alliances with some.

---

[12] Anishinaabe writer and scholar Gerald Vizenor describes "survivance" as, among many other things, an "active sense of presence over absence"; an "active resistance and repudiation of dominance, obtrusive themes of tragedy, nihilism, and victimry"; and an affirmation of a consciousness (natural reason) based on the "incontestable presence that arises from experiences in the natural world" (11).

But we must have our histories—our roots and identities—that are our own distinctive creations" ("Pasts to Remember" 459). "On matters of cultural creativity," he writes, echoing the Black Arts Movement, "we must be self-assessed by our own standards of evaluation" (*We Are the Ocean* 86).[13] The work of the Oceania Center for the Arts materializes a space apart from "our" formal institutions, which hold "non-essential" any academic or creative work that does not articulate itself with externally generated terms of globalization. The center performs an alternative, autonomy-seeking logic that aims to allow its participants to make something that is "unmistakably ours," to dance and paint the "place within" of the "our" in a Pacific way.

Hau'ofa's "our" breathes from the (grass) roots outward; in the terms of his essays, no genuine alliances between Oceania and its outside (the "region" and its peoples not being coterminous with the world) could be forged without minding those priorities. The openings of his "our," however—its distinctive Oceanian manner of including the listener as the word turns—should encourage reflection on the complex weave of any "our" and of the human responsibilities of being within it. His "our" might be envisioned as a gathering hall, or as a creative home, with various entry points, whose walls are adorned on the inside and outside with carvings imbued with cultural meanings. Or his "our" can be envisioned as a home without walls, vast and exposed to winds, salt-air, vast oceans, and clouds like the islands, continental and volcanic, into which peoples have long entered and moved around by myriad routes, impressing their histories on the lands and seas, and creating ways of interacting with other peoples and of living in high islands and atolls. For Hau'ofa, an Oceanian "our" must respect these histories and the durable values they have given rise to in order to imagine a future in which, joining with those outside the region, a new "we"

> may ... make new sounds, new rhythms, new choreographies, and new songs and verses about how wonderful and terrible the sea is, and how we cannot live without it. We will talk about the good things the oceans have bestowed on us, the damaging things we have done to them, and how we must together try to heal their wounds and protect them forever.
>
> (*We Are the Ocean* 93)

## Works Cited

Adorno, Rolena. *The Polemics of Possession in Spanish American Narrative*. Yale UP, 2007.

Appiah, Anthony. "Cosmopolitan Patriotism." *Critical Inquiry*, vol. 23, no. 2, 1997, pp. 617–39.

Bal, Mieke. "Masterly Maxims." *PMLA*, vol. 129, no. 3, 2014, pp. 491–97.

---

[13] Clifford, referencing the negritude movement of the early 1950s, describes Indigenous movements of 1980s and 1990s as that of the early 1916.

Beamer, Kamanamaikalani. "Tūtū's Aloha 'Āina Grace: Intergenerational Wisdom." *The Value of Hawai'i 2: Ancestral Roots, Oceanic Visions*, edited by Aiko Yamashiro and Noelani Goodyear-Ka'ōpua, Center for Biographical Research, 2014, pp. 11–17.

Butler, Judith and Athena Athanasiou. *Dispossession: The Performative in the Political*. Polity, 2013.

Clifford, James. *Returns: Becoming Indigenous in the Twenty-First Century*. Harvard UP, 2013.

Deloria, Vine. "Aesthetics of Survivance: Literary Theory and Practice." *Survivance: Narratives of Native Presence*, edited by Vine Deloria, U of Nebraska P, 2008, pp. 1–23.

DeLoughrey, Elizabeth. "Heavy Waters: Waste and Atlantic Modernity." *PMLA*, vol. 125, no. 3, 2010, pp. 703–12.

Dening, Greg. "Possessing Tahiti." *Remembrances of Pacific Pasts: An Invitation to Remake History*, edited by Robert Borofsky, U of Hawai'i P, 2000, pp. 112–32.

Diaz, Vicente M. "Sniffing Oceania's behind." *Contemporary Pacific*, vol. 24, no. 2, 2012, pp. 323–44.

Ellison, Ralph. *Invisible Man*. Vintage Books, 1989.

Fergusson, Erna. *Our Hawaii*. Knopf, 1942.

Fujikane, Candace. "Asian American Critique and Moana Nui 2011: Securing a Future beyond Empires, Militarized Capitalism and APEC." *Inter-Asia Cultural Studies*, vol. 13, no. 2, 2012, pp. 189–210.

Halapua, Sitiveni. "Talanoa Process: The Case of Fiji." Paper presented at the East-West Center, Honolulu, Hawai'i, 2000.

Hau'ofa, Epeli. "A Promise of Renewal: An Interview with Epeli Hau'ofa." (with Subramani). *Inside/Out: Literature, Cultural Politics, and Identity in the New Pacific*, edited by Rob Wilson and Vilsoni Hereniko, Rowman & Littlefield, 1999.

———. "Pasts to Remember." *Remembrances of Pacific Pasts: An Invitation to Remake History*, edited by Robert Borofsky, U of Hawai'i P, 2000, pp. 453–71.

———. *We Are the Ocean: Selected Works*. U of Hawai'i P, 2008.

Jetñil-Kijiner, Kathy. "Tell Them." *The Value of Hawai'i 2: Ancestral Roots, Oceanic Visions*. Center for Biographical Research, 2014, pp. 70–72.

Madsen, Deborah, "Writing in the Fourth Person: A Lacanian Reading of Vizenor's Pronouns." *Gerald Vizenor: Texts and Contexts*, edited by A. Robert Lee and Deborah Madsen, U of New Mexico P, 2011, pp. 130–51.

Mishra, Sudesh and Russell Smith. "Editors' Introduction: Minor Histories of the Pacific." *Australian Humanities Review*, vol. 52, 2012, n.p.

*Moana Nui Statement*. Sept. 10, 2014, www.Moananui2011.org. Accessed Dec. 18, 2021.

Obama, Barrack. "Remarks by President Obama to the Australian Parliament." Nov. 11, 2011, www.whitehouse.gov. Accessed Dec. 18, 2021.

Palau Declaration on "The Ocean: Life and Future": Charting a Course to Sustainability. Annex B to the Palau Declaration, available at www.forumsec.org.

Perez, Craig Santos. *from unincorporated territory [hacha]*. Tinfish Press, 2008.

———. *from unincorporated territory [saina]*. Omnidawn, 2010.

———. *from unincorporated territory [guma']*. Omnidawn, 2014.

Salesa, Damon. "The Pacific in Indigenous Time." *Pacific Histories: Ocean, Land, People*, edited by David Armitage and Alison Bashford, Harvard UP, 2014, pp. 31–52.

Schultz, Susan. "Introduction" *Jack London Is Dead: Contemporary Euro-American Poetry in Hawai'i*, Tinfish Press, 2012, pp. 10–19.

Sokinka, Wole. *Of Africa.* Yale UP, 2012.
Spahr, Juliana. "Connected Disconnection and Localized Globalization in Pacific Multi-lingual Literature." *Boundary 2*, vol. 31, no. 3, 2004, pp. 75–100.
———. *Fuck-You-Aloha-I-Love-You.* Wesleyan UP, 2001.
Teaiwa, K. Teresia. "For or before an Asia Pacific Studies Agenda? Specifying Pacific Studies." *Remaking Area Studies: Teaching and Learning across Asia and the Pacific*, edited by Jon Goss and Terrance Wesley-Smith, U of Hawai'i P, 2010, pp. 110–24.
———. "L(o)osing the Edge." *Contemporary Pacific*, vol. 13, no. 2, 2001, pp. 343–57.
———. "Review of *A New Oceania*." *Contemporary Pacific*, vol. 8, no. 1, 1996, pp. 214–17.
Waddell, Eric, Vijay Naidu, and Epeli Hau'ofa, eds. *A New Oceania: Rediscovering Our Sea of Islands.* U of South Pacific P, 1993.
Wendt, Albert. "Toward a New Oceania." *A Pacific Islands Collection*, edited by Richard Hamasaki and Wayne Westlake, *Seaweeds and Constructions 7*, 1983, pp. 71–85.
White, Geoffrey. "Foreword." *We Are the Ocean: Selected Works of Epeli Hau'ofa.* U of Hawai'i P, 2008, pp. ix–xx.
———. "Conjuring Oceania." *Contemporary Pacific*, vol. 22, no. 1, 2010, pp. 108–11.
Wilson, Rob. *Be Always Converting, Be Always Converted.* Harvard UP, 2009.
———. "Toward an Ecopoetics of Oceania: Worlding the Asia-Pacific Region as Space-Time Ecumene." Keynote Address for 21st Annual Conference: "Crosscurrents: New Directions in Pacific and Asian Studies," UH-Mānoa School of Pacific and Asian Studies, March 10, 2010.
Winduo, Steven Edmund. "Chief of Oceania." *Contemporary Pacific*, vol. 22, no. 1, 2010, pp. 114–16.
Yamashiro, Aiko and Noelani Goodyear-Ka'ōpua. "Introduction" *The Value of Hawai'i 2: Ancestral Roots, Oceanic Visions*, Biographical Research Center, U of Hawai'i P, 2014, pp. 1–8.

3

# Mountains of Taiwan, Japanese Colonization, and Western Science

## Chia-li Kao

When Japan acquired Taiwan as its first colony in 1895, searching, collecting, and organizing the knowledge of this tropical island through scientific exploration were crucial concerns of the Japanese imperialist government. Referring to land surveys and census records as examples, scholar Jento Yao argues that modern Japan's colonial base in Taiwan epitomizes Foucault's idea of governmentality.[1] In the year following the signing of the Treaty of Shimonoseki, the National Diet of Japan (国会, Japan's bicameral legislature) subsidized scholars from Tokyo Imperial University to conduct botanical, zoological, mineralogical, and anthropological research of Taiwan's environment and people for the purpose of efficiently managing the new colony (Wu 6; Sakano 228). This growing reservoir of knowledge enabled the imperialist government to fortify its grip on the colony, a grip that included the control of the mountains. The Japanese colonial government coveted the copious natural resources of camphor wood and other timber species in the mountains where many Aboriginal people lived, and it viewed the Taiwanese Aboriginal people as a threat and standing in the way of its acquisition of the mountains. Ironically, the suppression of the Aborigines and the controlling of the mountains also eventually led to the rise of the leisure activity of mountain-climbing in the 1920s, an activity that would be hampered but not ultimately deterred by the Aboriginal uprisings that continued to take place in the 1930s.

The colonization of Taiwan aided Japan in establishing modern, scientific forms and practices of knowledge well before the middle of the twentieth century. Japanese

---

This essay is based on the findings of the research project (MOST 103-2410- H-005- 047-) funded by Taiwan's Ministry of Science and Technology. A longer Chinese version of this essay was published in *Chung Wai Literary Quarterly* (中外文學) in 2016, with the title of "Kano Tadao's Writing about Traveling in the Mountains of Taiwan: Constructing Modern Knowledge and Expressing Aesthetics of 'Nature' during the Japanese Colonial Period" (鹿野忠雄的台灣高山行旅書寫：日治時期「自然」的現代知識建構與美學表現).

[1] As Jento Yao analyzes the land survey and census launched by the Japanese government, it reveals the form of power of that government. Yao argues that the colonial government's requirement for accuracy and details in the land survey and census witnesses Foucault's ideas of knowledge production and biopolitical governmentality.

researchers' academic works in Taiwan, such as conducting fieldworks and organizing disciplinary knowledge, reflected knowledge absorbed from the work of scientists including naturalists who were collecting and recording species of plants and animals in the colonies of the West.[2] Such knowledge deeply influenced Taiwanese people's understanding of local environments and the landscape in the decades after the end of the Second World War. To explicate the intertwined history of the Japanese colonialist venture in Taiwan and the bases of modern knowledge, I will discuss a work of travel writing published in 1941, *With Mountains, Cloud and Savages: Travel in the Mountains of Taiwan* (hereafter referred to as *WMCS*). Written by one of the preeminent Japanese naturalist writers, Tadao Kano (1906–1945), it is a record of Kano's trips to the mountains of colonial Taiwan. First, I analyze the trajectory of how nature knowledge production transferred from the West and Japan to Taiwan in the process of social, academic, and political modernization. Then, I examine how Kano's travel writing and "theological nature," the central concept and idea that is found in Kano's writings, denote ecocentric values and are a precursor of contemporary Taiwanese Nature Writing.

## Tadao Kano, Naturalists, and the Colonial Mountains of Taiwan

Tadao Kano is one of Taiwan's most outstanding naturalists. He held an international reputation among fellow naturalists and other scholars from early on in his career. From childhood, he was enthusiastic about collecting insects, and by the time he was a secondary school student, despite his young age and level of education, he was receiving significant attention from scholars of entomology. In the preface of his most important writing, *WMCS*, Kano wrote about the time when he first saw Dr. Teizō Esaki's collection of species of precious and beautiful insects from Taiwan. It enchanted him so much that he decided to cross the seas between Japan and Taiwan in order to enroll in the newly established Taipei High School (founded in 1925). Kano's high school years in the colony, between 1925 and 1929, connected him to Taiwan for the rest of his life.

Yamasaki Tsukane, the author of Kano's biography, *A Life of Tadao Kano: A Naturalist Who Loved Taiwan* (1992), argues that Kano is an indispensable figure in understanding the natural history of Taiwan because his research reflects not only conventional natural historical research in the areas of entomology, zoology, biogeography, and geology but also research in the areas of cultural anthropology (e.g.,

---

[2] Yonghua Wu is the first major scholar to collect and write about the primary accounts of botanical and zoological explorations of Taiwan published before 1945 by people from the West as well as by the Japanese colonial government. His works are collected in four critical studies: *Forgotten Japanese Zoologists in Taiwan* (1996), *Forgotten Japanese Botanists in Taiwan* (1997), *Plant Hunting in Formosa: A History of Botanical Exploration in Formosa in the Nineteenth Century* (1999), and *Animal Collecting in Formosa: A History of Zoological Exploration in Formosa in the Nineteenth Century* (2001).

ethnography and studies of the prehistory of different tribes of Taiwanese Aborigines). As Yamasaki also writes, Kano made numerous fieldtrips to the mountains of Taiwan, taught himself Aboriginal languages, and learned about Aboriginal culture from the years when he was a high school student. The fieldtrips cultivated Kano's close attachment to the mountains; they also influenced him to pursue biogeography and ethnography as an established naturalist. He taught himself Latin and Greek in order to work with Western-based taxonomies and nomenclature, and he kept in contact with Japanese scholars and naturalists. After he returned to Japan and entered Tokyo Imperial University in 1930, he revisited Taiwan several times to do more research (which was funded by the Japanese government as well as by private patrons). His research on Taiwan's mountains became the basis for his doctoral diploma. He published many groundbreaking essays about Taiwan's mountains including an essay about his discovery of a glacial vestige extending the Wallace Line to Orchid Island.[3]

In understanding all of Kano's naturalist work—his research, travel writing, academic career, mountain-climbing experiences, and so forth—one also must address the role that this work played in Taiwan's colonial history. *WMCS* is a collection of eight articles. Only the final article was a newly finished work in 1941; his professional description of the relationship between Jade Mountain (Niitaka Mountain, 新高山) and the Bunun tribe in this article demonstrates the copious outcome of Kano's cultural and geographic research on Aborigines.[4] The other of seven articles had been previously published (between 1931 and 1932) in *Mountains* (山岳), the official journal of the Japanese Alpine Club. The first six articles record Kano's return to Taiwan in the summer of 1931 to go mountain-climbing. They convey Kano's deep attachment to the mountains, which he had last seen one year earlier (a very long time for Kano). The seventh article is a memoir of Kano's experience of mountain-climbing in the summer (July) of 1927. Published in 1931, at the time when Kano was still in Japan, it is a vivid account of Taiwan's mountains, and a moving recollection of Kano's nostalgia for them, which prompted his return trip in the summer of 1931. Kano writes:

> I had pondered over my act that I am dying to cross the seas to visit the heart of this distant mountain. I observed my frenzy objectively. I came to be aware that Taiwan's mountains, whose attractive, adventurous and colorful scenery is composed of the majestically impressive mountains, primitive forest, and naïve savages, has become the existence of something that now is inseparable to me. This is probably the reason why I am attracted so much to remove all obstacles to come

---

[3] Kano's biography in this paragraph is a summary of Tsukane Yamasaki's book.
[4] Jade Mountain is the highest and the most important mountain in Taiwan. Robert Swinhoe, the British consul, named it Morrison Mountain after W. Morrison, the captain of a commercial ship, *USS Alexander* (Xu 13), and this name is sometimes seen in pre–Second World War documents. When Jade Mountain was measured and found to be higher than Japan's holy mountain, Fuji Mountain, the Meiji Emperor renamed it (in 1897) Niitaka Mountain, which literally means the *new* highest mountain (within the territory of the Japanese Empire) (Numai 24).

here every year before these things ruin. I tried to think of every possible reason in my heart to explain this deeply tied fate.

(*WMCS* 88–89)[5]

The insuppressible yearning for Taiwan's mountains was Kano's primary motivation to travel in the Japanese colony of Taiwan. Although this motivation is never expressly stated—Kano says only that nothing can separate him from Taiwan's mountains—it reflects that he existed in many senses or terms outside of the colonial relationship between Taiwan and Japan during the period of Japanese colonial rule. The time that he spent in Taiwan, and his face-to-face and heart-to-heart communication with the mountains of Taiwan especially, is a testimony to how colonialism never succeeds entirely and how it often produces outcomes that are antithetical to it.

The deep affection and admiration for the beauty of Taiwan's mountains permeates Kano's writing. Ecocritic Bei Liu notes that there are two main scientific traditions in the West that trace back to Ancient Greece: mathematical physics and natural history (31–32). The first emphasizes rationality and treats nature as a mechanical and experimental object that can be controlled, conquered, and reformed. The second represents a different kind of emphasis and a different kind of regard for nature. Knowledge of "the object"—nature—which is gained through direct contact and fieldwork often results in and is motivated by a sincere respect for and even by a reverence for, and humility in the face of, nature. As Liu notes, this respect, reverence, and humility differ from the arrogant attitudes toward nature that characterize much work published in the areas of science (and technology) and form the cornerstones of ecocriticism (Liu 31–32).

## Natural History, Religion, Imperialism, and Scientific Knowledge

Regarded as a predecessor of ecocriticism, Gilbert White's *The Natural History of Selborne* (1789) is one of the most representative and influential texts in the tradition of Western natural history writing. White's description of the Selborne microcosm also reflects his belief in a universe ordered by a higher power (divine Providence). In Donald Worster's eminent scholarly study, *Nature's Economy*, he uses the phrase "science in Arcadia" to argue that White's work had a significant cultural on European society, at a time when the Europe was undergoing industrialization and social disintegration. In particular, as Worster argues, it had an unexpected influence on the emergence of natural history writing and on contemporary environmental theories. White and his successors attempted to replace the modern scientific concept of a detached, purposeless, and mechanical universe with the natural historian's warm, open, pious inquiries about nature (35–36). Worster's argument is useful to the work

---

[5] References originally in Japanese and Chinese are translated by me.

of many ecocritics, who restore "warmth" to cold science, or an attitude toward nature that reflects deep affection for it and the need to be morally responsible to it. As Paul Lawrence Farber notes, White's vision is reflected in the work of two other great eighteenth-century naturalists—Carl Linnaeus and Georges Louis Leclerc, Comte de Buffon—thinkers who described nature as "perfect" and argued that "such perfection reflected God's wisdom and, indeed, proved the existence of a divine Creator" (18). Such ecocritical interpretation of Gilbert White's influence highlights a lost spirit of modern science that needs to be reclaimed nowadays—a spirit that derives from personal contact with and reverence for nature.

Ironically, the Judeo-Christian religious sentiment that characterized natural history writings in the West assisted imperial powers in plundering the world's natural resources. Judeo-Christianity conveniently offered to Western imperial powers a rationale for exploiting nature (as well as people) (Lynn White 9-10). Felix Driver uses the term "geography militant cultures of exploration" to argue that naturalists at this time took on the roles of adventurous accomplices in imperial quests for empirical knowledge about the earth (3). Similarly, as Farber contends, the "greater presence of Europeans worldwide and the potential commercial value of many natural products stimulated systematic collecting on a hitherto unimaginable scale, creating opportunities for naturalist to explore exotic regions" (24). Thus, voyages of exploration gradually became defined as a "state interest," and natural historians and other scientists took on, willingly or by default, colonizer roles (Sörlin 54). Scientific travel became integral to commercial capitalism and military expansion. The East India Company's patronage of scientific research and Captain Cook's collaboration with the Royal Navy in his expeditions are two examples (Sörlin 67-69). Scientific collections and natural science findings not only were the obsessive interest of colonizing nations, but they also served these powers, as they were a catalyst for constructing national consciousness and for competing with other colonial powers for distant colonies.

A belated empire, Japan fully understood the practical and symbolic value of the findings of natural historians—findings by both its own scholars and Western scholars—and the role that these findings could play in a state's ambitious imperial ventures. When naturalist activities became popular among all classes in Europe during the late Victorian period, the Meiji government (1868-1912) was implementing Westernization programs. Both academic and amateur naturalists joined together to produce knowledge for the professional and entertaining needs of different scientific audiences. Such knowledge also contributed to the publication of nature knowledge and history in the forms of popular magazines and science fictions. Japan recognized the value of both serious and popular science literature. Not only was the development of science education and technology viewed as a means of achieving modernity, but the very concept of nature was also used by Japan in the construction of itself as a modern nation and empire. Analyzing two different Japanese pronunciations of the same Chinese character of "nature," Julia Adeney Thomas points out that the Japanese concept of nature refers to a totality or integral state as well as to the physical natural world (174–76).⁶ In Thomas's analysis, this kind of discovery implies a search for the totality of culture and an attempt to structure modern subjectivity in the process of Japan's social and national transformation. Thomas's analysis compares with Hiromi Mizuno's discussion of the development of scientific education in Japan. Mizuno uses the term "scientific nationalism" to refer to the Japanese government's emphasis on science and technology, areas that it saw to be "the most urgent and important assets for the integrity, survival, and progress of the nation" (11). (As Mizuno also notes, this historical legacy continued to influence Japanese society in the postwar period [11–12].) The Japanese government made substantial efforts to import Western science into Japan and to disseminate this science through rigorous education programs and thus modernize and transform Japanese society. Building and extending upon the knowledge that it was importing from the West as well as on the knowledge that its own thinkers were producing in the metropolis, the Japanese government used and depended on the work of natural science thinkers and explorers who were gathering knowledge from the inside of Japan, as well as from its distant colonies. The colonies, especially Taiwan's mountains, were "unknown" to the Japanese colonizers and perceived as "virgin land" in the colonial and academic sense. Taiwan's Chinese bureaucrats prior to its Japanese administrators hesitated to approach the mountains and left behind only a few documents of what they found; nonetheless, these records appealed to the new colonizers for the reason they pointed to the mountains' abundant natural resources. With the purpose to manage the Aborigines in Taiwan's mountains and the mountain's resources, the Japanese colonial administrators began to systematically collect, categorize, and study their new subjects under "the microscope" tools of Western science. These findings and research by natural scientists, natural historians, anthropologists, ethnologists, botanists, zoologists, geologists, and mineralogists were the reservoir of "modern" knowledge about Taiwan's mountains.

## A Naturalist's Travel Experience and His Writing

Kano's writing of Taiwan's mountains reflects his training in Western scientific methods and his knowledge of the Western sciences including the natural sciences. Those epistemologies critically shaped almost every corner of the world where colonization extended to in the nineteenth and twentieth centuries. On the one hand, it goes without saying that Kano's recollections of his fieldtrips and mountain-climbing experiences in colonial Taiwan point to the role that these activities played in the Japanese government's ambitious colonial project to manage (in the Foucauldian sense of governmentality) its colonies through meticulous and accurate surveys, statistics, and taxonomies. On the other hand, to condemn Kano for being only a Japanese colonialist without thoroughly acquainted with his nature writing might result in oversimplifying the complicated

---

⁶ There are two pronunciations of nature in Japanese. First is *jinen*, which connotes naturalness or spontaneous practices. Second is *shizen*, which means environments or nature.

colonial condition in Taiwan and under-recognizing the full legacy of this colonialism in the postwar period. It is undeniable and controversial that the base of so-called modern research on Taiwan's mountains was formed during the Japanese colonial period, and such anthropological, geological, zoological, and botanic knowledge continues to be referred to and taught in postwar Taiwan. Recognizably, it reflects and betrays colonialist legacies and attitudes, but it remains an indispensable information base for contemporary Taiwanese nature writers who might not know so much about the colonial history of Taiwan's natural environments but feel responsible for bringing out the profound essence of these extant environments and elaborating environmental discourse. Kano's work displays not only profuse scientific knowledge but also a deep feeling for Taiwan's mountains. Showing scientific knowledge and love for nature is essential in contemporary Taiwanese nature writing. For that reason, contemporary nature writers like Ke-xian Liu recognize Kano as a pioneer of Taiwanese nature writing.

Kano's scientific background and fieldtrip experiences built up his solid knowledge base about tropical islands. Attracted by enormously rich and varied tropical environments, he traveled Taiwan and Orchid Island several times to conduct biogeographic and ethnographic research that tied those islands to southern China, Indochina, Indonesia, and Australia. Based on his fieldwork, Kano extended the faunal boundary line, Wallace Line, to the ocean between Taiwan and Orchid Island; this was recognized as a great contribution to biogeography. His outstanding natural and cultural knowledge about tropical islands attracted the Japanese government's attention, which finally led to his dispatch to South Seas (*Nan'yō*, 南洋) and his disappearance in North Borneo.

In his travel writing, Kano emphasizes Taiwan's high humidity that is caused by its location in the south sea. Cloud, a mist formed by overflowing water vapor in the tropical sea, exemplifies the unique beauty of Taiwan's mountains. Kano uses various rhetoric and aesthetic linguistic expressions to delineate the seemingly fickle clouds. He wrote:

> I like cloud and have boundless love for cloud in the mountains of Taiwan. Cloud changes mercurially every moment and shows thousands of shapes, whose variation is not restricted to Taiwan particularly. Yet, I think that cloud here can be differentiated from that in the inland because it is produced at the top of soaring high mountains of this island, which is located in the warm south sea.[7] Cloud in Taiwan contains much more abundant water that I have imagined and its flow feels more adhesive than that in the north. The flow sometimes twines around the skin of mountains, drifts away alone, or draws together into something magnificent and beautiful that touches me so much. Sometimes a huge cloud crosses over a mountain ridge and then falls down, which looks just like a waterfall. We call it "cloud fall"; I secretly attributes the cloud's adhesive power to such phenomenon.
>
> (311)

---

[7] In contrast with "overseas land" of colonies, the imperial metropole of the Japanese Empire was called "the inland" during the colonial period.

Kano's observations and depictions of clouds are rational and scientific. He analyzes a cloud's location (e.g., tropical sea, island, and mountains), composition (how much water it contains), properties (adhesive power), movements (e.g., assemble, drift away, flow down, and cloud fall), and the modern terms themselves (the phenomenon of cloud fall). His scientific analysis highlights cloud's warmth, humidity, and adhesiveness, which he attributes to the local specialty of Taiwan as a tropical island. Kano's description is neither just insipid explanation of modern scientific knowledge nor traditional lyric expression of personal affection. Rather, his accurate scientific analysis helps readers profoundly appreciate the unique natural beauty of Taiwan's mountains.

Kano's writing reflects the influence of the body of Western natural history that owes to Gilbert White. This influence is the expression of a feeling of intimacy with the nature that one observes and experiences. Thomas J. Lyon states that the experience of a writer as an "observer-participant" in nature—"the feel of being outdoors, the pleasure of looking closely, and the sense of revelation in small things closely attended to"—is the determining characteristic of nature writing (277). Without the self's infusion into nature or the personal interpretation of nature, this writing becomes insipid. If it only piles up natural history and scientific facts, it cannot touch readers' hearts. As Lynn L. Merrill discloses, the most successful natural history writings are reflective of "an aesthetic science, nature closely examined to enhance the pleasure that an ordinary person takes in" (14). The natural history writer who is powerfully affected through his or her senses by nature can transform the most ordinary natural history essay into a powerfully aesthetic and rhetorical literary creation. As both Lyon and Merrill note, this requires the act of walking into nature, an act that is crucial for the natural history writer who wants to really understand nature. Kano does not get to know Taiwan's mountains and the Aboriginal peoples through colonial discourse, which produces distorted images of the colony. Contacting and sensing nature directly helps him avoid simply repeating colonial discourse.

## Theological Nature and Its Transformation of Colonial Ideology

Kano always pays homage to the mountains of Taiwan in his records of his mountain-climbing trips. For Kano, Taiwan's mountains are filled with spirituality, and their spiritual embodiment is "the god of mountains" (山神), a phrase that Kano often uses. Also, his attitude toward the mountains is one of extreme humility. For example, on one trip, when he found that the weather was getting worse as he was nearing the summit of Southern Jade Mountain, he asked himself: "Did my act of stepping in the virgin mountain enrage the god of mountains? Or, did the god want us to go through a more severe ordeal? So far I could feel that the Heaven was harboring malicious designs to us" (66). On another trip to the Eastern Peak of Jade Mountain, when he reached the summit and saw the incredible scene of heaps of fallen and broken gigantic rocks and trees at the bottom of ravines, he saw the full ferocity and power of the god of the mountains. Similar feelings of astonishment and homage occur when he successfully ascends mountains that are higher than 3,000 meters (10,000 feet): Yudapei Mountain, Dongluan Mountain, and Benxiang Mountain.[8] Kano does not dare to claim credit but instead attributes those achievements to "the blessing given by the god of mountains" (176). On his trips, he admits that human beings' wisdom and their possession of modern knowledge and excellent equipment do not guarantee a safe mountain-climbing trip. He believes that the good or bad mood of the god of the mountains will determine whether a climber will reach the summit without misfortune. In Kano's writings, he does not project a figure of an arrogant colonizer who despises the colonial society because of his or her sense of superiority; instead, he projects the figure of a modest mountain climber submissive to the god of the mountains. Mountains in Taiwan have been claiming people's lives for centuries and they continue to do so nowadays because of mercurial weather and complicated landforms. When he was traveling in the mountains accompanied and helped by Aboriginal guides, Kano had to carefully deal with many unpredictable challenges just as a common mountain climber, not as an authoritative colonizer. Being surrounded by mountains turns him into an ordinary (usually powerless) human standing in front of magnificent mountains. Nature's glories and power of creation and destruction, which a Western naturalist has ascribed to the Creator, thus exert similar theological effects on Kano. Kano's theological beliefs do not mean that he is irrational, superstitious, and lacking in scientific knowledge. Rather, that faith critically complements his scientific knowledge and his skills as a mountain climber, and they help him to modestly and respectfully relate to nature.

In addition to the influence of Western natural history writing that one can see in Kano's descriptions of Taiwan's mountains, there is also the influence of Japanese traditional views of nature, which trace to ancient myth and represent nature as gods and as entities to be worshiped (Ye and Tang 26).[9] (This is why, for example, Shinto shrines are usually built in natural surroundings such as forests.) Both Japanese traditional mythology and Western natural history writing deeply shaped Kano's understanding of and love for Taiwan's mountains. His writings do not reflect the common colonial imagination, under which Taiwan's mountains and its Aboriginal people as "barbaric." They reflect a very different perception, one that sees Taiwan as a sacred land.

The great height of Taiwan's mountains awed the Japanese colonizers, and it has also deterred any covetous human beings' destruction to environments since primitive

---

[8] The records of the first ascents of mountains in the Japanese colonial period only counted the "written" dates and excluded the Aborigines' historical traces. Since the mountains of Taiwan had been different Aborigines' living and hunting areas for hundreds of years, Aborigines should be the first peoples who had reached the summits.

[9] Many natural mythological stories are collected in two important texts of Japanese Classic Literature, *An Account of Ancient Matters* (古事記) and *The Chronicles of Japan* (日本書記). These texts, which also function as Japanese foundation narratives, relate that nature, not a god or a human being, gave birth to Japan.

time. The preserved nature turns the colonial mountains into the uncontaminated, sacred regions, where modern people can find a spiritual and holy reserve to soothe their souls. In Kano's travel writings, he sometimes uses the word "uncivilized" (未開) to describe Taiwan's mountains, but in his writings this does not carry a negative meaning or mean "barbaric." It refers to an immemorial theological and mythological time. When Kano stands on the top of Wulameng Mountain, he expresses: "On this spatially limited apex, the trace of human footprints is nowhere to be found. Only the sun still shines upon this pure realm of gods from the primeval time" (117).[10] Looking at the august and gigantic Mabolasi Mountain, he "[can] think of nothing and only kneel down to worship the eternity" (*WMCS* 118).[11] In Kano's writing, the colonial mountains are not depicted as a place of darkness and of bloodthirsty, head-hunting, barbaric, and horrifying savages. Rather, they are depicted as places where gods reside and the sun everlastingly shines. They represent a pure, pristine, eternal, mystic, bright, and sacred realm. When Kano enters the spectacular forests on Mabolasi Mountain, he is overwhelmed by the beauty of this antique, sacred environment. He writes:

> This primeval forest is spectacular. The trunks of trees are covered with fluffy, silk-like soft green moss. Lichen of Usnea, hanging from branches, look as lonely as immortals. These scenes prove that human beings had never entered this forest since the primeval time. As soon as a visitor steps into this thoroughly plentiful purity, he or she cannot but be affected by the virginity of the forest. The god of Mabolasi Mountain must live in this forest. I straighten up with respect from my heart and take another look at this absolute godly realm. For animals flourish under the god's benevolence, this place is a safe area. Goats, deer, and bears leave the records of their free lives, which can be identified through their disorderly footprints on the ground … However, with their acute senses, they know we have invaded their place and so they vanish without a trace. The solitary black shadow in the forest coldly approaches us.
>
> (252)

In this description of Taiwan's mountains, Kano tells us that the mountains are the dwellings of the gods, and all kinds of animals propagate here under the gods' blessings and protection. The gods, forests, and animals together form a free, comfortable, nature-centered paradise. Outsiders (including Kano himself) are described almost as being transgressors who invade the independently circulating and reproducing natural ecosystems of the mountains. This passage implicitly argues that the mountains were ecologically robust and autonomous before foreigners came to it and excessively exploited the mountains' natural resources, causing enormous environmental

---

[10] Wulameng Mountains in Kano's text is the name of the mountain in the Bunun language; "it also is known by the name of Mabolasi" (Yan 116).

[11] Mabolasi Mountain in Kano's text refers today to Xiuguluan Mountain (Yan 116).

destruction. It also reflects a Japanese aesthetic and theological tradition based on respect for nature. As Weiqu Ye and Yuemei Tang describe this aesthetic and tradition:

> The gods' kindness grows forests on the earth. Human beings benefit from nature; nature is the womb of life, as well as the source of life. Thus, human beings feel especially affectionate with nature. [...] Humans' affection for nature integrates their life with nature. The co-existence between humans and nature is a characteristic of Japanese aesthetics.
>
> (30)

Nature in the Japanese people's perception gives birth to all kinds of life forms, including human beings. To put this differently, nature is regarded as the root of Japanese people and culture, including literature and a distinctive aesthetic. Without understanding the significance of nature, it is impossible for one to understand the core of Japanese culture. Nature in this sense not only contains the theological and mythological implications of the birth of human beings and the earth but also echoes current environmental arguments and appeals. Kano's nature-centered travel writing reflects a sensibility that differs markedly from standard colonial perceptions of and attitudes toward Taiwan's mountains. He does not view these as degenerate hinterlands; he sees them as uncontaminated sources that preserve the seeds of all kinds of life and cultural forms.

## Nature as Aesthetic and Literary Appreciation

A special affection for nature significantly influences the development of Japanese aesthetics and classic literature. Shimada Kinji, one of Japan's founding scholars of comparative literature, points out that *Kokin Wakashū* (古今和歌集), the first imperial anthology of Japanese poetry, and *haikai* (俳諧), a Japanese poetic style established and theorized by Bashō, are two of four representative classic texts that capture the life and thought of ancient Japanese people.[12] In the seasonal poems, collected in *Kokin Wakashū* and thematically divided according to the seasons of spring, summer, fall, and winter, it is easy to observe the significance of how nature deeply impacts the Japanese people's daily lives and initiates their unique aesthetic. Represented by Bashō's renowned travel poetry, *haikai* in particular reflects that nature plays a principal role in the Japanese aesthetic. The sense of "sabi" (さび)—the essential concept of Japanese aesthetics specified by *haikai*—also permeates Kano's travel writings. Named by Kano's wife, the title of *WMCS* suggests that nothing is more solitary than remote mountains

---

[12] The other two texts are *Genji Monogatari* (源氏物語), a masterpiece of Imperial Literature (王朝文学), and *Nō Play* (能劇), a unique style of Japanese drama. The former carefully delineates Japanese women's inner world and the latter demonstrates the Japanese religious view of life and death.

secluded by thick clouds, and such solitude can be broken only by the sound of Bunun people's hunting. In addition, "sabi," the Chinese character that literally means solitude, encompasses various subtle aesthetic ideas that cannot be reduced to the meaning only of solitude; it refers to the nature-oriented relationship between humans and environments.

As the word "with" in the title of *WMCS* suggests, Kano sought to interact with the mountains, and they in turn powerfully affected him. This is to say, the preposition "with" presupposes the traveler's bodily and spiritual engagement in the environment; it carries meanings of communication as well as aesthetic performance and philosophical meditation. We can see this, for example, in the following:

> As we have almost reached the summit of Malijianan Mountain, I sit down on a cold stone and take a rest. It is completely tranquil here, like the primitive ray of the morning sun, inside of which I allow my spirit to swim freely. I temporarily let go myself in the intractable dreamlike instant. In this serene moment, I concentrate my attention; I hear the sound of the wind blowing from the valleys like the earth's breath and the whispering of babblers in the thickets of somewhere. Their sound complements the tranquil surroundings. I have come so far to arrive here! Thinking of it, I find my eyes moisten. My feeling of melancholy during the trip waves along like the wind. I don't dislike it. It is not emotional lingering over my farewell to my beloved city. Instead, it is happiness that I find, as I am closely embraced by the sublimity and pristineness of the mountains.
>
> (*WMCS* 239)

This passage exemplifies the Japanese concept of "sabi." Popularized after Bashō's aesthetic theories, "sabi" refers to the pursuit of the most faithful artistic representation of nature. Eminent Japanese aesthetic scholar Yoshinori Ōnishi traces the etymology of "sabi" and its usage in classic texts, and he defines this word from three perspectives. First, "sabi" indicates solitude, seclusion, desolation, emptiness, serenity, austerity, simplicity, chastity, indifference to fame, and wealth (Ōnishi 241–42). The second linguistic layer of "sabi" connotes the positive values accumulated through temporality such as agedness, antiquity, venerability, and quaintness (ibid. 257–58). The third semantic usage of "sabi," usually in an adjective form, combines previous two definitions to reflect the artistic and philosophic concept of the intrinsic quality of materials (ibid. 277–79). For example, "kami-sabi," composed of "kami" (god) and "sabi" (an adjective form), is a word used by Kano to speak of the essence of the mountains of Taiwan: it carries a complex meaning of mythological divinity, spatial seclusion, temporal venerability, and intrinsic nobility and virtue.

Ōnishi's clear and detailed linguistic analysis of "sabi" greatly helps scholars to understand Kano's travel writing aesthetic. The descriptions of Kano as a traveler sitting down to enjoy the nature of a mountain in Taiwan such as Malijianan Mountain represent the essence of "sabi." The extreme height of the mountains separates them from the worldly clamor and tumult of human activity. They are tranquil in the sense of being distant from places where there is more human activities, and they are ancient in comparison with human life and divine in their essential character. The sounds and movements of the wind and the birds, which would seem to break the mountains' serenity, actually serve to accentuate it. The oxymoronic senses of "sound-in-tranquility" and "motion-in-stillness" express the infinite life rhythms and secrets of nature and characterize Kano's descriptions of the mountains. In his writings, he does not regard nature as something that he stands outside of and observes from the perspective of an outsider. He regards himself to be a component of the natural environment, and he accepts whatever nature bestows upon him. Nature, instead of human beings, centers Kano's travel writing, and "sabi" is the kernel of his aesthetic. According to that fundamental Japanese aesthetic, a traveler, as an art meditator and translator, expresses all essences of "sabi" in words. When the traveler interacts with nature, he or she seems to immerse with surroundings in order to grasp the beauty of nature. However, grasping the beauty of nature does not mean that the traveler has the power to control, explain, or manage nature. He does not assume or act as if he has a leading role in controlling, explaining, and managing nature. Kano's use of "sabi" contrasts with other writers of the time who reflect anthropocentric ideas about nature. The latter express that humans, colonizers in particular, have the right to exploit nature. Kano's writings do not describe Taiwan's mountains from the perspective of "the colonizer," or one who regards nature as something uncivilized, barbaric, and dangerous. Rather, they express the exquisite, unique, and artistic qualities of the mountains: seclusion, serenity, simplicity, antiquity, and divinity.

## Conclusion: Scientific, Theological, and Aesthetic Nature

*WMCS* is an antecedent of contemporary Taiwanese nature writing as well as a natural history record of colonial Taiwan. Kano was attracted to the tropical island of Taiwan when he saw pretty specimens of insects in his youth. Not long afterward, he realized his dream to travel to Taiwan. He came to Taiwan as a student, a mountain climber, and a newly born naturalist scholar. Kano devoted his entire life to academic research, and the Western scientific training that he received in conducting this research was invaluable. The display of abundant scientific knowledge in Kano's writing points to the influence of the Western sciences as well as the controversial role that natural history writing played in the efforts of imperial powers' acquirement and control of territory. However, it did not only function as a tool of imperialism. For its author Kano, direct contact with natural environments helped him cultivate his reverence for nature and avoid a colonizer's arrogance. This reverence was influenced by contemporary Western religious beliefs about nature. Kano, as did many of his Western counterparts, understood nature as something that was divinely ordained and not in the control of humans. Therefore, his travel writing conveys a sense of humility and submission toward nature.

In addition to the influence of Western natural history and Western theological beliefs about nature, *WMCS* also displays Japanese traditional understandings of nature as the origin of life forms. These reinforce Kano's belief that humans should respect nature. In his travel writings, Kano describes Taiwan's mountains as the embodiment of the gods and as the gods' bright, sacred, and vital lodgings. This manifests a set of beliefs different from colonial discourse in which Taiwan's mountains and its Aboriginal people were regarded to be respectively a resource and a barbaric race. Kano's use of Bashō's aesthetic concept of "sabi" in his travel writing reveals his particular affinity for these mountains that are characterized by seclusion, serenity, antiquity, and divinity. Kano's text shows his training in Western science including natural history, his knowledge of Japanese classic views of nature, and his particular appreciation of the "sabi" aesthetic. These naturalist, literary, and artistic influences on Kano's writing together constitute a perspective that differs markedly from dominant colonialist perspectives. Kano's writings about Taiwan's mountains not only circumvent a dominant Japanese colonial ideology, but they also reflect the harmonious relationship possible between humans and nature.

## Works Cited

Driver, Felix. *Geography Militant: Cultures of Exploration and Empire*. Blackwell, 2001.

Farber, Paul Lawrence. *Finding Order in Nature: The Naturalist Tradition from Linnaeus to E. O. Wilson*. The Johns Hopkins UP, 2000.

Kano, Tadao. *With Mountains, Cloud and Savages: Travel in the Mountains of Taiwan* [山と雲と蕃人と：台湾高山紀行]. Bunyūsha [文遊社], 2002.

Liu, Bei. "On the Genealogy of Ecocriticism [論生態批評的生成語境]." *An Introduction to Ecoliterature* [生態文學概論], edited by Tsai Chenhsing, Bookman [書林], 2013, pp. 23–43.

Lyon, Thomas J. "A Taxonomy of Nature Writing." *The Ecocriticism Reader: Landmarks in Literary Ecology*, edited by Cheryll Glotfelty and Harold Fromm, U of Georgia P, 1996, pp. 276–81.

Merrill, Lynn L. *The Romance of Victorian Natural History*. Oxford UP, 1989.

Mizuno, Hiromi. *Science for the Empire: Scientific Nationalism in Modern Japan*. Stanford UP, 2009.

Numai, Tetsutarō. *A History of Mountain Climbing in Taiwan* [台灣登山小史], translated by Wu Yonghua. Morning Star [晨星], 1997.

Ōnishi, Yoshinori. *Yūgen, Aware and Sabi* [幽玄・あはれ・さび]. Shoshi shinsui [書肆心水], 2012.

Sakano, Tōru. *The Imperial Japan and Anthropologists, 1884-1952* [帝国日本と人類学者：一八八四——一九五二年]. Keisō Shobō, 2005.

Shimada, Kinji. *Comparative Literature in Japan* [日本における比較文學]. Kamkang U [淡江大學], 1984.

Sörlin, Sverker. "Ordering the World for Europe: Science as Intelligence and Information as Seen from the Northern Periphery." *Nature and Empire: Science and the Colonial Enterprise*, edited by Roy MacLeod, U of Chicago P, 2000, pp. 53–69.

Thomas, Julia Adeney. *Reconfiguring Modernity: Concepts of Nature in Japanese Political Ideology*. U of California P, 2001.

White, Gilbert. *The Natural of History of Selborne*. Oxford UP, 1993.

White, Lynn Jr. "The Historical Roots of Our Ecologic Crisis." *The Ecocriticism Reader: Landmarks in Literary Ecology*, edited by Cheryll Glotfelty and Harold Fromm, U of Georgia P, 1996, pp. 3–14.

Worster, Donald. *Nature's Economy: A History of Ecological Ideas*. Cambridge UP, 1994.

Wu, Yonghua. *Forgotten Japanese Zoologists in Taiwan* [被遺忘的日籍台灣動物學者]. Morning Star [晨星], 1996.

Xu, Qiongfeng and Fanyu Liu. *History of Mountain Climbing in Taiwan: Chronicle* [臺灣登山史. 紀事]. Construction and Planning Agency, 2013.

Yamasaki, Tsukane. *A Life of Tadao Kano: A Naturalist Who Loved Taiwan* [鹿野忠雄: 台湾に魅せられたナチュラリスト]. Heibonsha [平凡社], 1992.

Yan, Nanjun, trans. *With Mountains, Cloud and Savages: Travel in the Mountains of Taiwan* [山、雲與蕃人——台灣高山紀行]. Yu shan she [玉山社], 2000.

Yao, Jento. "Knowing Taiwan: Knowledge, Power and the Japanese Colonial Governmentality of Taiwan [認識臺灣: 知識、權力與日本在臺之殖民治理性]." *Taiwan: A Radical Quarterly in Social Studies* [臺灣社會研究季刊], vol. 42, 2001, pp. 119–82.

Ye, Weiqu and Yuemei Tang. *The Japanese Aesthetics: "Mono no aware" And "Yūgen"* [物哀與幽玄—日本人的美意識]. Guangxi Normal U [廣西師範大學], 2002.

4

# Demilitarization and Decolonization in CHamoru Literature from Guåhan (Guam)

Craig Santos Perez

CHamoru (also spelled Chamorro or Chamoru) people are the Indigenous peoples of the Mariana archipelago, a fifteen-island chain that extends 500 nautical miles in a north-to-south crescent in the region of the northwest Pacific Ocean known as Micronesia. The island of Guåhan (Guam) is the largest (212 square miles) and southernmost island of the Mariana archipelago. Guåhan can be located at 13 degrees north latitude and 144 degrees east longitude. However, because this island is so small, it often does not appear on many maps of the world. Relatedly, the history and literature of Guåhan have remained invisible on most studies of world literature. To combat this invisibility, this chapter highlights how contemporary CHamoru literature exposes the violent histories of colonialism and militarism and advocates for decolonization and demilitarization. Specifically, I will examine the first text of CHamoru literature to circulate internationally, *Mariquita, a Tragedy of Guam* (1986), by Chris Perez Howard, as well as two poems by respected CHamoru activists, Melvin Won Pat-Borja and Kisha Borja-Quichocho-Calvo.

Around 2000 BC, the people now known as CHamoru sailed in outrigger canoes from the region of Austronesia, arrived to the Marianas, and developed clan-based social networks, a matriarchal society, ancestral spiritual practices, and a sustainable communal economy based on fishing and agriculture. In 1521, Ferdinand Magellan made landfall on Guåhan, which became the first inhabited Pacific Island to become known to Europeans. Spain nominally claimed Guåhan in 1564, establishing its first colony in the Pacific. In the following decades, galleons loaded with silver from Mexico (along with soldiers, merchants, missionaries, government officials, and supplies) embarked from Acapulco and reprovisioned off Guåhan before arriving in the Philippines to trade with Chinese merchants. The Spanish Empire mapped "a great circular loop" around the Pacific with Guåhan as "a sure and useful landmark and stopover" on the transpacific trade route (Rogers 15). In 1668, Spanish authorities officially colonized the island and shortly thereafter initiated the Christian conquest of the Pacific by establishing a mission on Guåhan supported by a colonial government and military. The Catholic authorities renamed the archipelago "las Islas Marianas" (the Mariana Islands), to honor the queen of Spain, María Ana de Austria, who funded the mission. Many CHamorus resisted the conversion efforts, which led to nearly three decades of active conflict known as the Spanish-Chamorro Wars from 1668 to 1695. By the end of the wars, military conquest and foreign diseases had led to massive CHamoru depopulation, and the survivors were subjected to the Spanish ecclesiastical policy of reducción, or the "forced relocation and concentration of the population from rural areas into villages with a garrison and church," to facilitate conversion, acculturation, and taxation (Wiecko).

The Spanish-American War of 1898 ended Spanish control of the Mariana archipelago. After defeat, Spain sold the fourteen northern islands to Germany, and Guåhan became a territory of the United States, along with other former Spanish colonies. The acquisition of these new territories created a controversy within American politics about whether or not they should be incorporated into the nation, and whether full constitutional rights should apply. These questions were taken up by a series of landmark Supreme Court cases, collectively known as the Insular Cases, dating from 1901 to 1922. The court ultimately decided that the rights of the constitution and citizenship did not automatically apply to the new possessions and would instead be determined by Congress. This decision created a new political category, the "unincorporated territory," which meant that a territory like Guåhan could be a possession of the United States without becoming a fully incorporated part of the nation.

From 1898 to 1941, the US Navy administered Guåhan (with a navy captain appointed as the governor) and established schools, hospitals, businesses, and roads. During this era, Guåhan became a strategic location for US military transports traveling between San Francisco, Hawai'i, and the Philippines. In 1914, Japan seized the northern Mariana islands from Germany, forming the "new Japanese frontier in the equatorial Pacific" (Peattie 16). In December 1941, Japan bombed and invaded Guåhan and defeated the US forces, uniting the archipelago under Japanese rule. Guåhan was renamed Omiya Jima, or "Great Shrine Island," and Japanese authorities transformed Guåhan into a strategic base for Japan's vision of a "Co-prosperity Sphere of Greater East Asia." This era was marked by traumatic violence and wartime atrocities against the CHamoru people, including land theft, forced labor, rape, beheadings, massacres, death marches, and concentration camps.

On July 21, 1944, the US military began its invasion of and battle for Guåhan, eventually defeating the Japanese forces and reclaiming the island. During the postwar period, the fourteen northern Mariana islands became part of the United Nations Trust Territory of the Pacific Islands, administered by the United States until the 1970s, when their political status changed to the Commonwealth of the Northern Mariana Islands. Guåhan, on the other hand, remained an unincorporated territory, and its residents became US citizens after the passage of the Organic Act of Guam in 1950, which also established a civilian governor, the government of Guam, the Guam Legislature, and the courts. Throughout the following decades, the United States militarily refurbished Guåhan into an "unsinkable U.S. communications and logistics platform, monitoring satellites and missiles, supporting antisubmarine and B-52 bomber operations, and harboring prepositioning supply ships for rapid deployment strike forces" (Rogers 51–52). Guåhan's location and topography have made it one of the longest continuously colonized places in the world and one of the most important US military outposts in the Asia-Pacific region. As Robert Rogers puts it, Guåhan's strategic value rendered it "far more significant than islands much larger, much less isolated, and much better known" (1).

## The Second World War and *Mariquita, a Tragedy of Guam*

*Mariquita: A Story of Guam*, by Chris Perez Howard, was first published in 1982 by Guåhan-based publisher PPH & Company and republished in 1986 as *Mariquita: A Tragedy of Guam*, by the Institute of Pacific Studies at the University of the South Pacific in Fiji. It was republished again in 2019 by the University of Guam Press, under the title *Mariquita—Revisited*. I will be citing the 1986 version since it has been the most widely circulated, and it was the first CHamoru text to circulate beyond the reef of Guåhan and into the larger literary world.

Perez Howard was born on Guam in 1940 to Maria "Mariquita" Aguon Perez, a CHamoru woman, and Edward Howard, an American naval officer from Indiana. Mariquita and Edward met and fell in love during the US Naval Era on Guam, but their cross-cultural marriage was violently interrupted in 1941, when Japan bombed, invaded, and occupied the island. During the occupation, Edward was sent to Japan as a prisoner of war, and Mariquita was forced to work in the fields and serve a high-ranking Japanese officer. Tragically, Mariquita is murdered toward the end of the occupation, yet her body is never found. After the war, Perez Howard and his father moved to Indiana. Thirty-five years later, the author returned to Guåhan to reconnect with his culture and family, as well as to learn about his mother's life and the circumstances of her death.

Trained as a journalist, Perez Howard conducted archival research and oral interviews, which was funded by a grant from the Guam Insular Arts Council. Additionally, he engaged various archives, as well as historical and cultural texts. Yet he does not bring these elements together in a seamless narrative; instead, *Mariquita* is written, as Paul Sharrad notes, in "varying narrative viewpoints and a curious hybrid of documentary and fictional devices, chatty oral history and written formality, biography, and autobiography" (152). Throughout the book, the reader encounters "strange shifts in generic mode and tone: from lyric dramatization of a fiery temperament against a 'Pacific paradise' backdrop to textbook language of ornithology" (152). Moreover, Perez Howard includes various visual materials throughout *Mariquita*, including photographs, newspaper articles, and government documents. The materiality of *Mariquita* speaks to how assembling materials "compensate for and express the experience of historical loss as existential void" (159). Sharrad suggests that *Mariquita* emerges from "the large central hole of Mariquita's disappearance and works with the less dramatic but equally important gaps in historical memory" (159). *Mariquita* is thus "full of signs that show absence by their residual presence. [...] This is a key element in what makes the writing so difficult for Perez Howard: the speaking silences, present absences of his world" (154). Perez Howard himself addresses the difficulty of this writing when he writes in the preface:

> From the first day of research to the last punctuation it was difficult. I never realized that the history of Guam was so confusing and so often contradictory. To try and decipher the truth from conversation so richly embroidered with imagination was also difficult. But the most difficult was trying to remain emotionally uninvolved when the story was about my mother.
>
> (vi)

Writing from a dwelling space marked by colonial violence and Indigenous absence involves constructing a narrative from fragments of memory and history. Perez Howard, by utilizing multiple discursive modes, as well as various visual materials, builds a narrative of the last years of his mother's life to give structure to her absence, to give voice to her silence, and to get to know and remember her. As he poignantly notes, it was through the research, interviews, and writing of the book that he "began to know her" (v). In addition to storytelling as being a form of cultural connection, it was also a form of colonial and military critique. Toward the end of *Mariquita*, Perez Howard writes: "This book, besides being a tribute to my parents is also for my family and those like them. It is written with the hope that people will know through the life of one girl, the sad history of the occupation of Guam" (89). Moreover, literature is a form of cultural memory. In the dedication page of the novel, Perez Howard situates his work within a longer cultural tradition: "Storytelling was an important feature in the Chamorro culture as it was the way to remember things for years to come" (ii). Perez Howard weaves this into the work of his novel: "It appears that the hardships I have had to face and overcome prepared me to write this book so that my mother and others who suffered the occupation would be remembered" (89).

*Mariquita* begins in 1938, when an 18-year-old Mariquita stands atop Tutujan Hill and looks upon Guåhan's capital, Hagåtña (Agana). She sees the Dulce Nombre de Maria Cathedral, the Government House, the Bank of Guam, the police station, the old Spanish bridge, the Spanish plaza, the power plant, and the Navy Yard. The buildings of Hagåtña provide insight into the legacies of Spanish colonialism and the presence of American colonial rule in Guåhan.

Mariquita grew up in a modern, two-story concrete house in the section of Hagåtña known as Dr. Sargent district, located along the ocean, and named after a surgeon in the US Medical Corps who served on Guam between 1929 and 1931. The top floor contained the bedrooms, while the ground floor consisted of a kitchen, dining area, a small room, and a terrace. Their lot was "attractively landscaped" and the back of the house faced a "special composition of earth, sea and sky" (12). The Perez family was able to afford a modern house because Mariquita's parents were both teachers within the new American education system. Mariquita shared a bedroom with her sister, Carmen, and their room housed many modern objects, including cosmetics, toiletry items, a radio, an old doll, photographs, a sewing table, clothes, shoes, handbags, and even a medal she won for weaving from the American legion. The family preferred to eat and entertain in a separate outdoor structure, which contained laundry and cooking facilities. Mariquita's relative, Aunti Da, lived with the family and preferred to cook outside with the wood fire as opposed to using the new kerosene stove inside. During religious feast days, neighbors gathered at the Perez house to eat, sing, dance, and tell stories. The Perez family continued to speak CHamoru language at home, despite the colonial and "pompous law that only English was to be spoken in school and on the playground as well as in government and at public affairs" (15). The Perez family house was a space of comfort, peace, and culture.

Mariquita's life changes when she meets, falls in love with, and marries Edward Howard, an American sailor stationed on Guam. She moves out of the family home and, with her new husband, rents a small house closer to Apra Harbor, where Edward's ship, the USS *Penguin*, was anchored. After they have their first child, Chris, they move to a larger house in Hagåtña, and Mariquita's cousin moves in with them to help maintain the household. The depiction of this marriage, in the analysis of Robert Tenorio Torres, suggests "an amicable coexistence between the Chamorro and American cultures" (30) because Mariquita and Edward represent "dichotomous cultural entities who will merge through marriage, and create a new culture and a new order for the islands … [Mariquita] symbolizes the Chamorro of the colonial Spanish world, and Edward is the savior symbol who will raise her up from the heaps of colonial subjugation" (31).

Unfortunately, the tragedy would soon impact the newly married couple and their home. First, a powerful typhoon strikes the island in 1940 and damages the Perez family house with its strong winds: "Waves were lapping at the back door, and the outside kitchen had already been sent crashing into the sea" (Perez Howard 41). This typhoon foreshadows the storm of imperial struggle that would begin on December 8, 1941, when the Japanese military bombs the island, targeting military, transportation, communications, and energy facilities. As they hear the bombs exploding nearby, the Perez family abandons their Hagåtña homes and travels to their ranch in the village of Tumon, where they take shelter in a cave. On December 10, Japanese soldiers invade the island and defeat the US military forces. The invading soldiers ransack Mariquita's house, stealing food and possessions. Part of a wall was torn apart for firewood. Her family itself is torn apart when Edward is taken as a prisoner of war and sent to a prison camp in Japan. In the meantime, the Perez family house was used as a Japanese military outpost, and their family was forced to move and live at their ranch full-time. The military destruction and occupation of these two houses are symbolic of the military destruction and occupation of Guåhan.

The Perez family responds to the destruction and eviction from their homes with strength and resilience. They turn to a more modest, sustainable form of life. Their two-room ranch house is made of wood, with a tin roof. Instead of beds, the family slept on mats, which were woven by the women. An open kitchen with a wood fire was attached to the house, reminiscent of the separate structure of their Hagåtña home. The family collected water from rain barrels, made their own soap, and used coconut oil lamps. Tall fruit trees surrounded the house, and the family harvested enough food to survive and to fill the agricultural quota demanded by the Japanese military. Other family ranches, owned by relatives, surrounded their ranch. As the narrator points out: "The Perez family became a loving, working survival unit. This unity was matched by the other families. Together they epitomized the noble character of their Chamorro heritage" (65).

By June 1944, nearly twenty thousand Japanese soldiers had arrived on Guåhan, anticipating a US invasion. During this time, the Kaikuntai, an agricultural unit whose mission was to feed the soldiers, also arrived. CHamoru men from the ranch were taken to work in military labor battalions to help the Japanese military fortify the island. The women were taken to work in the fields to grow and prepare food for the soldiers. Mariquita was assigned to work as a personal servant to the Taicho, a high-ranking officer, at the headquarters of the Kaikuntai in the village of Tai. Mariquita, along with twelve other women, were forced to cook, clean, and launder clothes, as well as massage and wash the officers (even though it is not described in the text, it is likely that the women were also raped). As the US bombing of Guam intensified, the Taicho becomes more and more abusive to Mariquita: "The Taicho took out his sword in anger and struck her with the blunt edge. He scolded and cursed her. Her head began bleeding profusely … Mariquita was ordered to go to the Taicho's quarters and wait there for him" (80). The narrator does not describe the Taicho's quarters, in which Mariquita remained until late that evening. He only reveals: "Mariquita was never seen again" (80). This lack of description represents absence, silence, and trauma.

As Naoto Sudo notes, *Mariquita* is a powerful and emotional critique of Japanese militarism and colonialism. He argues that the portrayal of violence against Mariquita and the CHamoru people "exposes from the viewpoint of the colonized how empty the Japanization of Guam was and the illusory nature of the 'Greater East Asia Co-Prosperity Sphere.'" While anti-Japanese sentiments form major threads of the text, another scholar, Valerie Woodward, points out several moments in the novel when "ruptures caused by race within the production of patriotic colonial subjects"—such as American racism, militarism, and colonialism—raise "serious questions about the value and meaning of US citizenship for the people of Guam" (76–79). Throughout *Mariquita*, Perez Howard offers a profound and emotional critique of Japanese and American imperialism on Guåhan.

While Mariquita itself is a form of decolonial critique, it also led Perez Howard to both reconnect with his Indigenous CHamoru identity and join to the CHamoru self-determination and sovereignty movement. In 1987, Perez Howard wrote an essay, "Thoughts and Confessions of a Chamorro Advocate," which was published in the anthology *Chamorro Self-Determination: The Right of a People I Derechon I Taotao*. Perez Howard opens his essay by admitting that when he returned to Guam in 1979, an active period of Chamorro decolonial and Indigenous activism, he felt like "a stranger in [his] homeland" and that he did not "belong among [his] own people" (125–26). Part of his alienation and identity crisis was caused by his lack of knowledge of cultural history and practices. He confesses: "I became acutely aware of my shortcomings and began to suffer embarrassment. Not only did I not speak the language, I had little knowledge of the island, its history, and culture. Above all else, however, was that I could not remember my mother, through whose identity I called myself Chamorro" (126). It was through researching and writing *Mariquita* that Perez Howard reconnected to his native identity: "Since returning to Guam I have sought information about my Chamorro heritage and, as a result, discovered another identity—my Chamorro self" (vi). Paul Sharrad emphasized this point in his analysis of the novel by showing how it is through the "subaltern retrieval of the bits and pieces that fall outside of official histories [that] the reclamation of Indigenous identity and story can begin" (159).

As he learned more about CHamoru history, culture, and politics, he also realized the harms of American colonialism. He admitted: "What I eventually came to know is that the relationship [between Guåhan and the United States] was one of guardian-toward and not the beautiful marriage of two peoples which I had so superficially held as true" ("Chamorro Advocate" 127). One aspect of the relationship between Guåhan and the United States that shattered Perez Howard's romantic perception was the issue of war reparations. In 1945, the United States passed the Guam Meritorious Claims Act to grant financial relief to residents of Guam whose property had been destroyed as a result of the war or were appropriated by the military. The act did not provide for claims of forced labor, forced march, or internment. In the act's one-year filing period, less than 1,000 claims were filed among a surviving Chamorro population of about 22,000—all of whom suffered varying degrees of atrocities during the war. Without homes, electricity, or mass media, most people simply didn't know they could file claims. According to the Navy's Land and Claims Commission (which oversaw the Guam Claims Act of 1945), the average reparation amount of death claims was about $1,900 dollars (though not all claims were accepted). Plus, the Navy placed fiscal ceilings claims and used a sliding scale. For example, a claim would be issued for $500 if the deceased was 12 years old or younger, with an increase of $500 for each additional year of age up to age 21, and a decrease of $100 per year for each additional year up to age 61, at which age the amount awardable remained at $1,000. Only one maximum death claim was ever paid (Dames 214). Even though not all families or people who suffered war crimes on Guam received reparations, the United States waived, through the 1951 Treaty of Peace with Japan, future wartime claims that could have been made by US citizens and nationals against Japan (Leon Guerrero; Punzalan). In 1952, when Perez Howard was 12 years old, his family received a check from the Federal Government in the amount of $1,528.89—compensation for the death of his mother ("Chamorro Advocate" 129).

Many CHamorros and their advocates felt that the people of Guam were not fairly compensated by the Guam Claims Act of 1945 and that the United States failed to seek compensation from Japan by waiving war claims. To add insult to injury, Guam was not included in any future war claims legislation, such as the War Claims Act of 1948 (as amended and enacted in 1962) and the Micronesian Claims Act of 1971 because Congress believed the people of Guam had already been adequately compensated. Perez Howard learns the history of war reparations, or lack thereof, through his research. As he continued working on his book, Japanese military ships docked in the Naval Station of Guam and offered tours on their vessels. Along with a friend, Perez Howard picketed the ships and carried signs that read: "War Reparations for Guam" (Dames 398). This initial foray into political activism led Perez Howard to volunteer for Senator Cecilia Bamba, who co-sponsored legislation to create a Guam Reparations Commission: "[Perez Howard] volunteered to go with [Bamba] from village to village—sharing the story of his mother, eliciting the stories of others, and assisting with the preliminary survey of potential war claimants. This provided the groundwork for the eventual tiling of legal claims and the introduction of federal legislation to award just compensation" (Dames 292).

Engaging in this work of story filing and listening "raised [his] consciousness as a CHamorro and led [him] to really begin questioning the United States and [his] being an American" (Dames 293). Senator Bamba would become the executive director of the Commission on Self-Determination, and Perez Howard became her administrative assistant. He went on to help found and chair the Organization of People for Indigenous Rights (OPI-R), one of the major Chamorro rights groups to emerge in the 1980s and one of the first nongovernmental and non-administrative groups to represent Guam at the United Nations. Overall, Perez Howard's experience of researching and writing a work of literature led him to not only reconstruct and articulate his Indigenous Chamorro identity, but it also led him to become actively involved in the Chamorro decolonization and sovereignty movement.

## The Military Buildup and CHamoru Poetry

In 2006, the United States and Japan announced a major realignment of US military forces and operations in the Asia-Pacific region. Described as a "Mega-Buildup," it would include the construction of facilities to house and support the transfer of 8,600 marines and their 9,000 dependents from Okinawa to Guam, as well as 7,000 transient Navy personnel, 1,000 Army personnel, and 20,000 foreign workers. Additionally, the buildup would establish an Air and Missile Defense Task Force, a live firing range complex, and the creation of a deep-draft wharf in Apra Harbor for nuclear powered aircraft carriers (Kirk and Natividad).

For proposed military projects, the Department of Defense is required to prepare an environmental impact statement to assess the potential environmental, social, and cultural impacts. The draft environmental impact statement (DEIS) of the military buildup was released in November 2009 and made available online and in print at various locations on Guåhan. The draft of the environmental impact statement was released for download online (www.guambuildupeis.us) and in printed form at the University of Guam Robert F. Kennedy Memorial Library and the Nieves M. Flores Memorial Library on Guam, as well as at the mayor's offices in several villages of Guåhan, including Dededo, Yigo, Agat, Mangilao, and Barrigada. The statement comprised nine volumes and 11,000 pages. Some of the impacts described include limiting access to an area known as Pågat (the richest site of ancient CHamoru artifacts on Guåhan) to build the live firing range complex, eliminating hundreds of acres of jungle rich with medicinal plants to construct permanent military facilities and a camp for foreign laborers, removing more than 70 acres of living coral reef from the ocean floor to build a deep-draft wharf and producing over 8 tons of hazardous waste. The DEIS also noted that the increase in population would increase instances of violence, crime, prostitution, and rape; moreover, it would put an unsustainable stress on affordable housing, social services, education, health care, and utility services such as water, power, and sewage. Residents of Guåhan were given a ninety-day period to read the DEIS in order to submit online commentary or voice their opinions (or "testify") for 3 minutes or less at public hearings held throughout the island. The comment period lasted from November 20, 2009, to February 17, 2010. Comments were accepted online or by mail; additionally, the public could submit oral or written comments during the four public hearings on Guåhan, which were held between January 7 and January 12, 2010, at two public high schools, the University of Guam Field House and the Yigo Gymnasium.

The first DEIS public hearing was held on January 7, 2010, at Southern High School in the village of Santa Rita, which is near the naval base. In fact, the history of Santa Rita began when villagers from the ancient village of Sumay were evicted and relocated so that the US military could make room for the construction of the naval station (Babauta). One person who testified was CHamoru poet Melvin Won Pat-Borja, who was teaching creative writing at Southern High School at the time. Won Pat-Borja was born on Guåhan in 1981. He graduated from Southern High School and then went on to attend the University of Hawaiʻi at Mānoa, where he majored in secondary education. While living in Hawaiʻi, he was introduced to slam poetry and spoken word. He was a member of Hawaiʻi's national slam team, and he won the finals as Grand Slam Champion in 2005. In 2007, he returned to Guåhan and cofounded the Sinangån-ta Youth Movement. In addition to his work as a poet and educator, Won Pat-Borja is also an accomplished hip-hop and rap artist (Pereda).

At the hearing, Won Pat-Borja was representing the organization, We Are Guåhan, which is, according to its website, a "multi-ethnic collective of individuals, families and grassroots organizations" that emerged in November 2009 to "inform and engage our community on the various issues concerning the impending military build up." We Are Guåhan aims to "unite and mobilize our people to *protect and defend* our resources and our culture. We Are Guåhan promotes peaceful, positive and prosperous change for our island."

Instead of reciting talking points for his 3-minute testimony, Won Pat-Borja performed a spoken-word poem titled "No Deal" (though the poem was performed orally, the author sent me a text copy via personal communication. The poem was composed without line breaks, so it appears as prose when I quote it here). "No Deal" opens in a classroom, with the speaker in the poem, a teacher, being asked a question by a student: "Sir, what if we protest and unite as a people, and in the end they just do whatever they want?" At first the teacher is rendered speechless by his student's fear, but then he responds:

> I am not naïve to the reality of the situation, I understand that the federal government has done worse things and gotten away with it, like smallpox blankets, like nuclear testing in the Marshall Islands, like dropping bombs on Vieques, like holding the sovereign queen of Hawaiʻi at gunpoint to sign the annexation.

The teacher draws these transnational connections to expose the abuses of US colonialism and to insist that CHamorus are not alone in this struggle. Won Pat-Borja asserts that CHamorus can find strength in their ancestral claims because "for centuries [CHamorus] have been the guardians and caretakers" of Guåhan. This genealogical insistence dispels the belief that Guåhan is merely, as Won Pat-Borja memorably phrases, "part of a perverse manifest destiny."

Won Pat-Borja suggests that the hopelessness the student feels, mirroring the hopelessness that many residents felt after the DEIS was released, causes some to believe that "the best course of action is to make a deal." However, Won Pat-Borja resists making a deal, thinking of the long-term genealogical effects the military buildup will have on CHamorus: "I cannot go home and look my son in the eyes and tell him that I love him knowing that behind closed doors, I am making a deal, I cannot look at my students and tell them I care about their future if I am making a deal—I am not here to make a deal." While the teacher refuses to make a deal regarding the military buildup, he also points out the fact that many CHamorus have made deals with the military:

> We are loyal servants fighting for your freedom of action, fighting so that you can let the federal government label Guam sovereign US soil and impose the largest military relocation in history. We are so loyal that we enlist more sons and daughters into America's armed services to fight and die than anywhere else in the world. We have paid your ultimate sacrifice time and again.

Not only is Guåhan a strategic location for American military bases, it has also become an invaluable resource for military recruiters. CHamorus have enlisted and died in the US armed forces at some of the highest rates in the nation. During the Vietnam War, Guåhan had one of the highest killed-in-action rates per capita. In 1980, the Department of Defense estimated that 5 percent of Guåhan's population was in the military, which was twelve times the national average. During the Iraq war, most recruitment officers struggled to meet their quotas; however, Guåhan's recruiters excelled: four of the army's twelve most successful recruiters were based in Guåhan (Bevacqua 35). The military is the major employer on Guåhan, and there are three JROTC programs in the public schools, as well as an ROTC program at the University of Guam (ROTC stands for the Reserve Officers' Training Corps, a group of college- and university-based programs to train commissioned officers for the US armed forces; JROTC is the "junior" program for high schools and middle schools). A key reason for recruiting success is economic: 25 percent of the population is defined as poor, and around 40 percent receives food stamps (Kirk and Natividad). Many CHamorus see the military as their only opportunity to gain economic, social, and political capital. Out of the relationship between CHamorus and the military emerged the description of Guåhan as a "recruiter's paradise" (LaPlante).

With these contexts in mind, let us return to Won Pat-Borja's poem-testimony. The speaker of the poem mentions Guåhan's high enlistment rates to show the cruel irony that even though CHamorus sacrifice their lives in the military, Guåhan continues to be exploited by the US military for the sake of its geopolitical ambitions. Won Pat-Borja explores this irony when he asks how the US government can consider CHamorus "Americans" if they "add insult to injury by burdening us with 8,600 marines all of whom Okinawa has lost its patience for, a nuclear aircraft carrier that will cost us a coral reef, over 20,000 foreign workers to make it all happen, and an army ballistic missile system to defend it all" ("No Deal"). In the next moment of the poem, the teacher powerfully proclaims: "The hands of your Presidents are drenched in the blood of our fallen—the same presidents that we are not allowed to vote for." Evoking the Insular Cases, Won Pat-Borja exposes the truth that the entirety of the US constitution does not apply to Guåhan since it is an unincorporated territory. Moreover, the sacrifice of CHamoru soldiers does not change the colonial truth that CHamorus do not have the right to vote for the president who decides their fate. Angered at this injustice, Won Pat-Borja concludes the poem with volcanic rhetoric:

> Let the record show that in the face of oppression and injustice, the people of Guam refuse to live a life absent of liberty, that we refuse to accept anything less than justice, that we refuse to sell Guam to the highest bidder. And should we die fighting your war machine, let your history books show your children the struggle that we fought to find freedom in a country filled with hypocrisy. Let the record show that Guåhan stood up and said, Uncle Sam, sorry, but *No Deal*.

Throughout Won Pat-Borja's passionate testimony, audience members at the public hearing cheered loudly, sometimes muffling his words. As he exclaimed, "No Deal," with strength and conviction, the audience erupted into cheers. Won Pat-Borja's poem offers hope that CHamorus can find the strength to refuse to live under such an unjust and oppressive situation and to continue to protect Guåhan.

Another CHamoru poet and educator, Kisha Borja-Quichocho-Calvo, testified through poetry at the January 9, 2010, hearing in the village of Mangilao. Mangilao is located in central Guam and houses the sacred village of Pågat, which was under threat to become a live firing range complex. Before Borja-Quichocho-Calvo performed her poem, she prefaced it by saying: Protect and defend, our beliefs, our culture, our land, our ocean, and our language. We are supposed to do this all the time, not just some times, all the time. And the military is coming in again and taking these things away from us. We have to stop them from doing this to us again ... I say *No* and *Wake up*.

After her preface, she recites her poem, titled "Re-Occupation Day (a.k.a. 'Liberation Day')," which begins: "Every 21st of July, / the people of Guåhan march in their red, white, and blue, / thanking uncle sam and his men in uniform." On July 21, 1944, the US military returned to Guam and a 3-week battle for the island ensued, which would ultimately end Japanese rule. "Liberation Day" was created a year later. This annual commemoration was seen as a time of rebirth and forgiveness, emphasizing "notions of spiritual salvation, national sacrifice, and cultural obligation" (Camacho 86). The first liberation celebrations resembled Catholic rituals, as opposed to civic or military ceremonies, and the themes of salvation and liberation became intertwined, reflecting the "interconnected nature of spirituality, identity, and nationality in postwar Guam" (89). Liberation Day underwent a shift in the 1950s–1960s when the key commemorative theme became Chamorro loyalty to America, and the actual event became more civic and secular with parades, marching bands, and floats. Young women even competed to become "Liberation Day Queen" by selling fundraising tickets. Over the years, Liberation Day has shaped the collective memory of the Chamorro people. Some scholars believe that the rhetoric of salvation and liberation inscribed by Liberation Day ignited Chamorro "codes of indigenous indebtedness" (Diaz 158), thus partially explaining Chamorro enlistment patterns and "the high levels of public and phatic patriotism, military and civilian loyalty and devotion" (Bevacqua 36). In other words, the Chamorro soldier "willingly and loyally shoulders the indigenous sacrifice" (48) as military service becomes payment toward the Chamorro debt for being liberated in 1944.

Borja-Quichocho-Calvo questions this perceived liberation and re-articulates July 21 as "Re-Occupation Day," suggesting that the US return is merely a continuation of the colonial occupation of Guam that began in 1898. To Borja-Quichocho-Calvo, CHamorus continue to be enslaved "by the SPAM-crazed golden arches / by drafts and recruitments / by 'the land of the free'" ("Re-Occupation Day"). The speaker then begins to name some of the injustices caused by US colonialism: "They took [Sumay] / and used it for their military. / They made us citizens / but denied us the vote. / They stole our language / and made us speak english." The colonial trespasses onto CHamoru language, rights, and land are unforgivable and strongly overturn any perception that America might be the "land of the free."

One of the reasons why this theme of liberation and freedom is still so prevalent on Guam is that these celebratory nationalist narratives are circulated through the colonial education system. As Borja-Quichocho-Calvo states in the poem: "Our history books say that we're free, / that we're making good money from tourism." Instead of repeating these narratives, she disrupts and dispels any hegemonic narrative that would celebrate Guåhan's unincorporated status. The poem culminates as the speaker drives through the village of Tomhom (Tumon), the island's main tourist center:

>  As I drive through Tomhom,
>  my view of the ocean obstructed
>       by the Outrigger and the Hyatt,
>  I think of the stories Tåta used to tell me
>  about the latte stone huts that once lined the ocean
>  and how they were bulldozed
>  to keep up with the times—
>  No trespassing signs now line the ocean.

Latte stone huts are the housing structures that ancestral CHamorus built before Spanish colonialism; in fact, many remains of latte stone huts lie within the confines of Pågat. While Tomhon is currently a "mini-Waikiki" lined with hotels, bars, restaurants, duty-free shopping, and strip clubs, the village was once an important and vibrant center of ancestral CHamoru life. Human and architectural remains are unearthed every time a new hotel or development is built. The "No Trespassing" signs, however, relate to the military fences that figuratively surround the island, from Andersen Air Force base in the north of Guåhan to Naval Station in the South. Thus, the military fence is a constant reminder not only of the prevalence and power of the US military, but it also reminds CHamorus of the fact that a third of their island was taken from them and that they have no access to these ancestral lands (unless, of course, they join the military).

Borja-Quichocho-Calvo's poem ends in a tone of mourning. The penultimate line of the poem is written in CHamoru, and the last line translates it into English: "I taotao-hu trabiha ti man libre. / My people are not free." Just as the title of her poem renames "Liberation Day" as "Re-Occupation Day," the poem itself resignifies liberated CHamorus into still colonized CHamorus by exposing the colonial truths about US imperialism and militarism in Guåhan's history. Borja-Quichocho-Calvo aimed to sway the audience to stand up, shed their patriotism, and say "No" to the military buildup. Poetry became the weapon to pierce through the ideological veil of American exceptionalism. Poetry became political rhetoric in the fight for CHamoru self-determination.

These poetic testimonies stood out from the other public comments because their recitations were more rhythmic and rhetorically compelling. The poetic testimonies were also more personal than some of the testimonies that were more data driven. In all, over 10,000 comments were submitted at the public hearings and through the online portal, a majority of which rejected the military buildup. The activism succeeded in protecting the sacred area Pågat and in both delaying and reducing the military buildup.

Unfortunately, the activism was not able to stop the buildup entirely. As I write this in 2021, the US military is moving forward, though with adjustments to the plan. Now, the number of marines to be transferred from Okinawa to Guåhan is 5,000, and the live firing range complex that was originally proposed for Pågat is being built in an area of northern Guåhan known as Litekyan (Ritidian), which not only is a wildlife refuge, an ancestral CHamoru village with latte stones and burial sites, and a habitat for medicinal plants used by traditional healers, but also is close to the Northern Guam Lens Aquifer, the main source of drinking water for the island. A contract for the live-fire training complex has already been awarded ($78 million to Black Construction), and the clearing of hundreds of acres of limestone forest has begun. Protests are ongoing as CHamorus continue to fight to protect the lands and waters of Guåhan.

## Conclusion

As evident, CHamoru literature is decolonial in the sense that it functions to decolonize hegemonic representations of CHamoru history, culture, and identity, as well as to expose and critique imperialism, militarism, and colonialism. At the same time, CHamoru authors have entered into the public and political realms, enacting a decolonial activism in which literature travels beyond the page and becomes a tool through which to inform and engage the community on political issues, to unite and mobilize different groups, and to rally and inspire people.

This spirit of decolonial literary activism was captured in the aforementioned anthology *Chamorro Self-Determination: The Right of a People / I Derechon i Taotao* (1987). In the preface, the editors Laura Torres Souder and Robert Underwood wrote:

> Inspired by their own heritage and motivated by their own history, today, many Chamorros are articulating issues pertaining to their existence as a people. They articulate, define and seek redress to issues not merely as participants in an American body politic, but as members of an indigenous people whose cultural institutions predate any of the social, economic, and political institutions, which currently hold sway on Guam. This spirit has fueled the movement for Chamorro self-determination, inspired the artistry of the island's creative community, and motivated the quest for the return of stolen lands.

As the editors point out, there is a symbiotic relationship between CHamoru activism and the CHamoru artistic and creative community. In this way, political and social activisms are inextricably linked to literary and aesthetic creation, which in turn works to revitalize Indigenous culture and identity. CHamoru authors are some of the most passionate voices on the island. CHamoru literature has developed alongside the decolonization movement, which began earnestly in the 1980s and 1990s. Literature became a way for CHamorus to articulate cultural pride, expose the crimes of empire, and protect the lands and waters of Guåhan.

## Works Cited

Babauta, Leo. "Santa Rita." *Guampedia*, Oct. 13, 2019, http://www.guampedia.com/santa-rita/. Accessed Mar. 20, 2015.

Bevacqua, Michael Lujan. "The Exceptional Life and Death of a Chamorro Soldier: Tracing the Militarization of Desire in Guam, USA." *Militarized Currents: Toward a Decolonized Future in Asia and the Pacific*, edited by Setsu Shigematsu and Keith L. Camacho, U of Minnesota P, 2010, pp. 33–62.

Borja-Quichocho-Calvo, Kisha. "Re-occupation Day (aka Liberation Day)." *YouTube*, 2010, http://www.youtube.com/watch?v=Fi5yN9ehtZI. Accessed Feb. 24, 2012.

———. "Re-occupation Day (aka Liberation Day)." Written version of the poem provided through personal communication.

Camacho, Keith L. *Cultures of Commemoration: The Politics of War, Memory, and History in the Mariana Islands*. U of Hawaiʻi P, 2011.

Dames, Vivian. "Rethinking the Circle of Belonging: American Citizenship and the Chamorros of Guam." PhD dissertation, Social Work and Political Science, University of Michigan, 2000.

Diaz, Vicente. "Deliberating 'Liberation Day': Identity, History, Memory, and War in Guam." *Perilous Memories: The Asia-Pacific War(s)*, edited by T. Fujitani, Geoffrey M. White and Lisa Yoneyama, Duke UP, 2001, pp. 155–89.

Howard, Chris Perez. *Mariquita: A Tragedy of Guam*. U of the South Pacific P, 1986.

Howard, Chris Perez. "Thoughts and Confessions of a Chamorro Advocate." *Chamorro Self-Determination: The Right of a People I Derechon I Taotao,* edited by Souder-Jaffery and Underwood, Chamorro Studies Association and Micronesian Area Research Center, University of Guam, 1987, pp. 125–26.

LaPlante, Matthew D. "U.S. Territories: A Recruiter's Paradise." *Salt Lake Tribune,* August 5, 2007.

Leon Guerrero, Victoria. "The War Reparations Sage: Why Guam's Survivors Still Await Justice." *Guam War Survivor Story Website,* http://guamwarsurvivorstory.com/. Accessed Mar. 10, 2015.

Pereda, Nathalie. "Melvin Won Pat-Borja." *Guampedia,* Oct. 13, 2019, https://www.guampedia.com/melvin-won-pat-borja/. Accessed Mar. 19, 2021.

Punzalan, Bernard. "Guam World War II War Claims: A Legislative History." *Guampedia,* http://www.guampedia.com/guam-world-war-ii-war-claims-legislative-history/. Accessed Mar. 10, 2015.

Rogers, Robert. *Destiny's Landfall: A History of Guam.* U of Hawai'i P, 1995.

Sharrad, Paul. "Filling in the Blanks: Mariquita, a Hybrid Biography from Guam." *New Literatures Review: Islands Special,* 2011, pp. 149–62.

Souder-Jaffery, Laura and Robert A. Underwood, eds. *Chamorro Self-Determination: The Right of a People I Derechon I Taotao.* Chamorro Studies Association and Micronesian Area Research Center, U of Guam, 1987.

Sudo, Naoto. "Colonial Mirror Images of Micronesia and Japan: Beyond the Tug of War between 'Americanization' and 'Japanization.'" *Postcolonial Text,* vol. 1, no. 1, 2004, http://postcolonial.org/index.php/pct/article/viewArticle/272/773. Accessed Oct. 14, 2014.

Torres, Robert Tenorio. "Post-Colonial and Modern Literature of the Marianas: A Critical Commentary." *Micronesian Journal of the Humanities and Social Sciences,* vol. 3, nos. 1–2, 2004, pp. 26–44.

United States Department of the Navy. "Draft Environmental Impact Statement for Guam and CNMI Military Relocation Available for Public Review." Guam and CNMI Military Relocation Supplemental Environmental Impact Statement (website), U.S. Department of the Navy, http://guambuildupeis.us/. Accessed Mar. 20, 2015.

We Are Guåhan. "About." *We Are Guåhan* (website), http://www.weareguahan.com/about-weareguahan/. Accessed Mar. 20, 2015.

Part Two

# Indigenous Resistance to Colonialism

5

# Decolonizing Guam with Poetry: "Everyday Objects with Mission" in Craig Santos Perez's Poetry

Anna Erzsebet Szucs

## Introduction

Activism and Indigenous literature are often connected and Indigenous authors write as a political act. Craig Santos Perez, poet and activist from Guam, uses his poetry to call attention to the negative effects of colonialism and militarization on his homeland and throughout the Pacific. In his poetry, he constantly reminds his readers of the mistreatment of his people the Chamorros, the special status of his home country (an "unincorporated territory" of the United States) and the disappearing land that is taken over slowly by the US Army. Guam is a strategically important place for the US Navy due to its central location in the Pacific Ocean. However, it is rarely talked about in the media and generally presented as a holiday paradise and not as an important military base it is. It is invisible to the public. Perez, currently living in Hawai'i, looks at his original home from afar and shows his readers the reality of the colonized Guam through poetry. "I started writing poetry after my family migrated from our home(is) land of Guåhan (Guam) to the state of California. Poetry became a way for me to stay connected—to remember where I come from." This connectedness to the land is clearly represented in his poetry. Perez criticizes the US Army that occupies increasingly larger areas of the island of Guam and mistreats the Natives on their own land. His poems can be read as activist texts because they reveal important information about the life circumstances of the author's community and respond to, as well as critique, colonial and postcolonial conditions of the Pacific and Guam. This study looks at everyday objects mentioned in Perez's poetry and seeks to unfold their "mission." "Everyday objects" do not only refer to traditional objects of the Chamorro culture but also they can be examples of modern objects (borrowed from Western culture) that relate to the everyday life of the Indigenous people of Guam. The research analyzes poetry from the poet's ongoing multivolume series titled *from unincorporated territory*, which currently stands at four books: *[hacha], [saina], [guma'],* and *[lukao].*

This chapter was originally published in *Indigenous Research of Land, Self, and Spirit,* edited by Robin Throne, copyright 2020, IGI Global. Reprinted by permission.

## The Power of the Colonized Guam

Ferdinand Magellan was the first European to reach Guam in 1521 and the following three and a half centuries Guam was under Spanish colonization. In 1898, after signing the Treaty of Paris as the end of the Spanish-American War, Guam was transferred to the United States and remained under the US Army's control until 1941 when the Japanese army occupied and renamed it to Omiya-Jima (Holy Shrine Island). After 3 years of occupation by the Japanese army, the US Armed Forces "liberated" Guam on July 21, 1944. Guam's special status, "unincorporated territory," was given in 1950 when US President Harry Truman signed the Organic Act. It stated that Guam could stay a self-governing country, but at the same time it would be dependent on the absolute power of the US Congress, as well as the US armed forces would continue to exercise extensive control (Woodward 69–70).

With the Organic Act, a civilian government was established; however, citizens of Guam are under the control of the Department of Interior and thus, they are not given the full rights of US citizenship (Heim 134). The Office of Insular Affairs defines an unincorporated territory as a "United States insular area in which the United States Congress has determined that only selected parts of the United States Constitution apply" (qtd. in Lai 4). Many criticize the status of being "unincorporated," since, in it, Guam is caught in an enforced colonial bond (Na'puti and Bevacqua 840). In an infamous interview, Lieutenant Colonel Douglas from the US Air Force said: "People on Guam seem to forget that they are a possession, and not an equal partner." Furthermore, he added, directly addressing the people of Guam: "you belong to me and I can do with you as best I please" (Lieutenant Colonel Douglas qtd. in Na'puti and Bevacqua 839–40).

The United States brought considerable changes to the Pacific and Guam since the Second World War. Guam is home to a large US military base that occupies one-third of the island today (Heim 135). Along with the US military came the Trans-Pacific Partnership (TPP) that has an immense influence on international trade and the increasing business transactions on Guam and the neighboring countries (Perez, "Transterritorial Currents" 621). Guam's economy is strongly dependent on tourism, the army, and jobs from the service industry that are related to the military (Hsu 286). US territoriality and colonialism have transformed the Pacific and it has affected all aspects of the everyday lives of the citizens, such as their language, dining, architecture, sport, clothing, and literature (Perez, "Transterritorial Currents" 622).

## Resurrected Connection with Chamorro Land

The land tells the history of colonial times, as the consequences of the US militarism and colonialism all over the Pacific are palpable in the landscapes and the forced dislocations, write Na'puti and Bevacqua (841). Military bases, new ports, countless hotels, and their facilities made Guam's landscape visibly different. Historically, colonization by the Spanish and later the Americans fundamentally shaped the lives of Chamorros (the Native people of Guam) through religious conversions, the institution of new education systems, and cohabitation practices. The cumulative effect was the disconnection of the Chamorros from their land. These influences together lessened their desire to preserve and take care of nature and what nature could provide (Naʻputi and Bevacqua 852). However, when the US military discovered and disrespected historical and cultural artifacts at the new live firing range complex's construction site, which is neighboring the ancient Påågat village, locals finally felt obligated to defend their homeland with its cultural legacy and reconnected with their old values (ibid. 853). The mistreatment of these valuable cultural artifacts was important in reawakening their connection to the land. After reviving newly found old values, people protested and spoke up against the military development as they were fed up with the colonizers and with not being heard. Soon, Pågat became the leading symbol for the people of Guam who wanted to take part in the decision-making on their island (ibid. 853). Pågat is considered a highly endangered historic site in the area. It preserves the remains of the lattes; the stone foundations of buildings and houses from prehistorical times; as well as subterranean freshwater resources, remedial plants, clay pots and dishes, and work tools of the ancient Chamorro people (ibid. 846). Social movements and local activism arose as a reaction to the military buildups, endangered ecology, disappearing culture, and the forgetting of one's history (ibid. 847).

These movements speak up against the US military bases and highlight the negative impacts on their land and their daily lives caused by military actions (Naʻputi & Bevacqua 844). They emphasize the importance of culture and history and deeply care for the environment that surrounds them (ibid. 848). Craig Santos Perez argues that Pacific Islanders are ready to claim back "real and symbolic territories through acts of survival, agency, adaptation, and resilience" (Perez, "Transterritorial Currents" 622). Activists reveal the problems surrounding physical dislocations in their demands and blame the US military for mentally separating indigenes from their cultures. Chamorros are physically removed from their homes to help the expansion of the military base, but at the same time, they are excluded from decision-making about their land (Naʻputi & Bevacqua 842).

## Literature as Resistance

Activism and Indigenous literature are oftentimes linked together. Literary and scholarly works are frequently charged with political messages and Indigenous writers and poets of the Pacific write as a political act. The activism is not simply in the content of the text but also in the *act of writing* itself. These texts are filled with cultural and historical references. Perez explained it precisely in an interview:

> Poetry has always been important parts of political movements, and political movements have always inspired poetry. Poetry can help us articulate our own

politics and interrogate oppressive structures and the language(s) of power. Poetry is a form of empowerment and inspiration. Poetry is a creative act amidst acts of destructive violence. Poetry is an expression of dignity, humanity, resilience, and hope.

("Poet to Poet Interview" n.p.)

Perez plays an active role in activism through his writing. In his poetry, he displays the negative effects that colonialism, militarism, and tourism have had on his home country. The themes of Perez's poetry collections are political and cover a range of topics including history, translation, environmentalism, colonialism, tourism, Indigenous myths, and more. The texts often incorporate maps and quotations from original documents to underscore how colonialism operates through language, explained Perez in an interview ("Poet to Poet Interview"). He also pointed out that the family stories are included and paralleled with historical events in order to address the bigger political-historical picture and show the human side of history and how it has affected his immediate family. His poems reveal, he continued, "the politics of survival, resistance, and resurgence" and for that, he wants to articulate "decolonial politics through poems of protest, critique, and witness" (ibid.).

"The nature of survivance is unmistakable in native stories, natural reason, remembrance, traditions, and customs. The character of survivance creates a sense of native presence over absence, nihility, and victimry," writes Native American Anishinabe writer Gerald Vizenor (1). Indigenous communities can only survive if they resist and reject dominance by adopting and incorporating old traditions and tribal wisdom into their daily lives (11). Recollection and continuation of stories, traditions and customs are crucial for survival. Including myths and old stories in modern, printed literature can be seen as a novel way of resisting domination, persistence to pass on Indigenous knowledge, and a tool of literary activism to the younger generation. There is strength and survivance in everyday objects, too. Just like Native stories, they carry on important cultural knowledge and instigate continuance. Objects that originally appeared in ancient myths and stories are now revived in contemporary literature, including Perez's, to carry messages of activism. They pass on the activist ideas of the poet as they perpetuate and claim "survivance" for the Chamorro culture.

## Everyday Objects with Mission in Craig Santos Perez's Poems

What does "everyday object" mean in the context of this chapter? *Merriam-Webster Dictionary* gives a sufficient interpretation that is applicable to answer this question. An object is "something material that may be perceived by the senses" and "something that when viewed stirs a particular emotion." This chapter analyzes ordinary objects from literary texts by Perez and argues that they carry cultural meanings and "stir" other emotions than the ones generally known and widely accepted. It focuses on the connotative, cultural, and historical meanings of the objects and investigates

Perez's reasons for incorporating them into his writings. Due to the attached cultural significance, stories, histories, and traditions attributed to particular objects, this research does not limit the examination solely to the objects but expands its scope to the everyday life practices that accompany them.

In Pacific Islander principles, there is no discernible distinction between culture and nature. Therefore, it is argued that they can be, and must be, studied together. In nature, on the land and in the ocean, there are natural objects which are regularly depicted to carry cultural significance. Similar to man-made objects, they are often presented in Pacific Islanders' literature, including Perez's works, and since they convey cultural importance, too, they are included in the examination of everyday objects of this paper. When "everyday objects" are mentioned both man-made and natural objects are implicated. Objects in Pacific Islanders' literature have never been purely ordinary—they are heavily charged with cultural and historical significance, and the use of objects in the examined texts takes a step further to activism. The additional meanings come from history, traditions, stories, myths, and legends. The objects are representations as they stand in for activism. Representations convey cultural meaning and often the meanings are constructed by Perez who consciously chooses historically and culturally important objects from his culture. The readings of the texts containing ordinary objects as representations are interpreted as having a "mission." The "mission" that is proposed in this study is political and rooted in Chamorro traditions, cultures, histories, present-day struggles, and the foreseeable future of Guam. It will be disclosed how literary activism is carried out in Perez's poetry through objects and how everyday objects can act as agents to deliver this mission.

Everyday objects can be traditional objects that relate to Chamorro culture. In this instance, the object's importance comes from cultural, historical, or mythological references. They are connected to local everyday life practices that are still often enacted by the community. Some objects are in danger of being forgotten or becoming extinct. In these cases, it is the poet's responsibility to immortalize the object, and the stories and traditions embedded in them, for the future generation. Objects, whether they are man-made or natural, are a big part of who the Chamorro people are as a community. They carry stories that shaped history and are shaping the future of Guam.

## Objects from an Unincorporated Territory

Many authors, including Perez, use code-switching between English and their native language, Michelle Keown discusses. Quoting Gilles Deleuze and Félix Guattari, Keown points out that when a "minor" author uses a "major" language, the language of the controlling group, in their writings, he or she "deterritorializes" the language of the dominant group by permitting the "minor" language to enter the "major" language's system (164). Therefore, the "minor" language "occupies the dominant language," weakens its absolute power, and "[shifts] the parameters of meaning" to the cultural realm of the "minor" writer (ibid.). For Perez, the "minor," oppressed, and occupied group of Guam is his own people, the Chamorros. He utilizes different multiple languages, such as Chamorro, English, Spanish, and Japanese. Chamorro is the native language of Guam and the other three are the languages of the colonizers, historically and in the present day. By using more than one language, Perez recalls the shared past and enhances the significance of the Native language. He incorporates other languages to signal the colonial past and the colonizers' culture to show how together these foreign influences are integrated into Chamorro culture and everyday life (Lai 2). He uses the Chamorro language to dominate the other three. Chamorro readers will feel pride, connectedness, and kinship reading Chamorro texts and foreign readers will have to consult outside sources, such as a dictionary if they want to understand the text entirely. Perez, obtaining the knowledge of the language, takes back the power from the non-Chamorro-speaking readers. Chamorro language is particularly significant as, in the past, to help "culturally assimilate" children to Western culture; it was banned in schools and even the Chamorro-English dictionaries were taken and burned (Hsu 285). Nowadays the language is taught again in public schools and there is a growing common interest in traditional customs and values (ibid. 287). Ordinary objects in literature mentioned in the Chamorro language represent material culture, perform traditions, and carry extra, significant connotations to the literal ones, such as Indigenous concepts and worldviews.

In Perez's poetry, the Chamorro words are sometimes translated into English directly after each word, sometimes a few pages later, and sometimes not translated at all. Due to the unpredictability of the translations, readers must turn the pages back and forth to find the link and translations among particular poems, explains Paul Lai (11). This makes reading complicated but also engaging as it requires much attention which is ideal if the author wants to remind his readers of a particular argument.

An example of translating traditional Chamorro objects, names of food, animals, and heavenly bodies appears in a poem titled "from tidelands." The poem is divided into ten sections and spread out through the book, [Saina], requiring the reader to turn the pages back and forth to follow the sense of the poem. Two parts of the mentioned poem are entirely in Chamorro language first, and thirteen pages later in multiple languages; English, Spanish, Japanese, and Chamorro, blended together (Perez, *from unincorporated territory [Saina]* 67, 83). In the first version of the text, twenty-three Chamorro words can be read, while in the second variant contains only six Chamorro, seven English, six Japanese, and four Spanish words. The first Chamorro version of the poem reads: "puti'on / plåtu / guihan dångkolo / rusåt / kulepbla / katupat / paluman / haggan / higai / guagua' kuadrâo / gue'ha / kuronan potta / tuhong / guagua' antigu / bålas / saligao / hugeten månglo' / henton ulu / guihan dikike' / apåcha / uhang / piña / sinangan'ta" (67), meaning: star, plate, large fish, rose, snake, a traditional rice dish cooked inside a woven pouch made of coconut leaves, bird, green sea turtle, woven palm leaves, square basket to carry fish, fan made from coconut fronds, door wreath, hat, old-fashioned basket, bamboo whip, centipede, windmill, headband woven from coconut leaves, small fish, grasshopper, shrimp, pineapple, our spoken words. All objects and creatures that are referred to in the poem are related to Chamorro traditions or Guam's natural environment. They can be read as representations of activism since they display additional meaning, especially because they appear in both Chamorro and colonial languages. As the readers turn the pages back and forth to read the two parts together, they recognize that while time and history progressed, the Chamorro object and language were colonized and lost their original meanings and disappeared. In this poem, Perez calls attention to the disappearing culture and traditions while replacing Native words with foreign ones. However, he also encourages perseverance with the six untranslatable Chamorro words. The words or phrases that were not changed into other languages are *puti'on* (star), *katupat* (rice pouch), *higai* (woven palm leaves), *guagua' antigu* (basket), *henton ulu* (headband), and *sinangan'ta* (our spoken words) (ibid. 83). They represent ancient knowledge (navigation by stars), traditional customs (rice dish, weaving, basket, headband), and Native language (spoken words). In the poem, all of these objects metaphorically survive colonization; by not being translated, Perez helps to ensure they continue to live on in his poetry.

In other parts of the series, Perez explores the meaning of water, evidently one of the most important elements in *from unincorporated territory*. Hanom (or water) is a reoccurring word and image in all four books. It is often written three times as "hanom hanom hanom," other times only once, sometimes in parentheses, sometimes without, and again other times in italics. Water supports life and it constitutes a large amount of the human body. "[O]ur bodies are sixty percent water" (*from unincorporated territory [Saina]* 129) is a sentence that appears throughout the series and Perez plays with its variations. He "dismantles" the human body and studies its parts: "[our] bones are twenty percent of water" (*from unincorporated territory [guma']* 40), "[our] blood is eighty percent water" (ibid. 9), "our tongues are 70% hånom" (Perez, *from unincorporated territory [lukao]* 39), "our hair is 10% hånom" (ibid. 51), "our skin is 40% hånom" (ibid. 67). For him, it is important to show how much the human body is connected with the ocean that constitutes most of our Earth, and so we have to take care of it. "[O]ceania is five parts lands to a thousand parts water," writes Perez (*from unincorporated territory [Saina]* 129), emphasizing the connectedness between water and land, but also showing how small and vulnerable island communities are. He calls attention to the rising water level around these defenseless islands; "i didn't know 'sea level' / would remind me of 'shelter'" (ibid. 106). Once the sea level reaches a certain point, there will be more and more climate refugees from the Pacific, he warns.

Perez, a father, is concerned about his daughter's future. His child was born in Hawai'i and she met with water at an early age. She was rinsed in the sink, bathed in the tub, and while still a baby, in the ocean. These intimate moments of the infant meeting the purest element are set side by side with the environmental problems caused by militarism and foreign developments. Perez paints a sinister picture of the environment while he and his wife are bathing the baby in the ocean: "pilot whales, deafened / by sonar, are bloated and stranded / ashore," "schools of recently spawned fish, lifeless, / spoil the tidelands," and the parents and the daughter "shiver like generations of coral reef / bleaching" (*from unincorporated territory [lukao]* 13). Although the setting of the poem seems peaceful, there are problems hidden "under water." He utilizes water as an object to talk about serious issues and uses poetry to call the reader's attention to them.

Water (the ocean) can connect the author to a community, as well as the past, present, and future generations on and away from Guam. The opening poem of *from unincorporated territory [saina]*, titled "from sourcing," starts with "water": "'[hanom] [hanom] [hanom]' / ~ / what echoes across waters: / taotaomo'na— (ancestors)" (13). Perez, living in diaspora in Hawai'i, still connects with his homeland through water. He can still "hear" the calling of his ancestors. He recalls a happier period of his people "before / contact before / colonialism before / history" and draws strength from the ancestors who remain with him in "histories" and "in our bodies." The poem ends on a positive note: "[we] / will continue after in / all afters" (13). This idea echoes the Native American writer, Gerald Vizenor's idea of survivance. As long as the ocean connects Chamorros and other indigenes, as long as they remember history, traditions, and their ancestors, and as long as they resist foreign domination, they will survive and they will succeed even in colonial circumstances.

An important, traditional object of the Chamorros that was connected to everyday life and carries traditional knowledge, the *sakman* (canoe), is another recurring topic in Perez's poems. In the past, Chamorros used canoes to discover the islands around them, to connect with other Indigenous communities, to fight in wars, to obtain food from the ocean, and so on. Below is the explanation and history of the *sakman* after colonization by Perez:

> the sakman—an outrigger canoe—once numerous in the waters of the mariana islands ... sometimes exceeded forty feet in length and were known as the fastest sailing vessels in the world—following the chamorro-spanish wars [1671–1698] the spanish colonists began destroying the sakman and forbade chamorros to sail the ocean ... the sakman was later burned. By the mid 19th century the knowledge of how to build and sail them was lost. [...] In 2007 members of tasi [traditions about seafaring island] ... built a 33-foot sakman ... they named [it] "saina": "parents elders spirits ancestors"—on 9/20/08 the sakman was blessed and entered the waters—it was the first time in centuries a sakman could be seen in the waters around guam.
>
> (*from unincorporated territory [Saina]* 14–15)

Hence, the title of Perez's second book of the series includes the word "saina" and the cover page of the poetry collection juxtaposes two different types of boats: an old black-and-white drawing of a sakman on the top of the page and a color photograph of five seafarer US Navy ships at the bottom. The sakman, once an everyday object of the Chamorros, has returned to the ocean and it symbolizes resistance and activism. As long as sakmans sail the seas, Chamorros and their culture will survive. In the poem titled "from aerial roots," Perez explores the process of the "building and launching of the sakman with [his] own memory of canoe paddling as a student at Chief Gadao Academy" (Hsu 301). The paddling experience as a young boy had left a deep impact on Perez. After moving away from Guam for more than a decade, "[he] can still feel the burn of movement in [his] body from pulling the currents—still the movement rooted in—[his] body still overseas areal" (Perez, *from unincorporated territory [Saina]* 129). Through him and his memories and representations, traditions of sailing will live on.

The third book of the series, *from unincorporated territory [guma']*, focuses on an object, the latte, which is symbolic of the foundation of Chamorro culture because it used to give the basic infrastructure to buildings in Guam in the pre-contact times. Perez describes it in his book:

> Latte, or latde, are stone structures composed of two parts: a haligi (vertical pillar) and a tasa (bowl-shaped capstone) the fallen latte is the sign. The haligi—carved from limestones, basalt, or sandstone—ranges in height from three to nine feet and is wide at the base bullets ricochet and narrow towards the top. The tasa, made from inverted coral head or carved from limestone, sits atop the haligi this raised house to sing. Completed latte structures give us their message were arranged in parallel rows of at least four pairs evenly spaced. They formed the foundation of homes, schools, canoe shelters, food sheds, and communal spaces momongmong.
>
> (18)

Archival images of latte structures are shown on the cover page of the book and placed side by side with a photograph of a US military airplane, a tank, and a large selection of bombs. The juxtaposition of the two images is clear: while the Chamorro culture is supported by natural stone pillars, the American values are built on war and violent occupation.

Because of the earlier mentioned military buildup at Pågat, the archeological remains of the latte village are in danger of disappearing forever. Moreover, besides the latte remnants, there are other valuable elements on the land that need to be taken into consideration:

> The Department of the Navy prepared the Draft Environmental Impact Statement (DEIS) to access the military buildup *this cage*. [...] According to the DEIS, the military planned to build their live firing range complex in an area along the northeastern coast of Guåhan *[we] have* known as Pågat, an ancestral latte village *bullets fragment and*. Many people *ricochet* travel to Pågat to fish, hike, and collect medicinal herbs; to learn about Chamorro culture and history *cues to navigate*; and to seek guidance from the ancestral spirits that dwell there to *sing future*. Pågat is also home to Mariana eight-spot butterfly, an endangered native species that *is born and fed and grows and*
>
> (*from unincorporated territory [guma']* 60; emphasis original)

If the military firing range is built, traditional customs, local animals, and plants will be lost, and the ancestral spirits, important components of the old religion, will be disturbed. Perez, to emphasize the importance of the issue, visually juxtaposes other texts by italicizing and inserting them into the main text. The italicized texts, since visually distinctive, catch the readers' attention. The placement and the content of these inserted texts are both important. "The fallen latte is the sign" of the ancient spirits "giv[ing] their message" to the living, explains Perez on another page in the same book (*from unincorporated territory [guma']* 14). Latte used to be the base of "homes, schools, canoe shelters, food sheds, and communal spaces" and they were the heartbeat (momongmong), the vital force, of the community. The firing range would symbolize quite the opposite. Soldiers would train there day by day and practice how to take life. By adding the sound of the heartbeat to the text in Chamorro, the poet accentuates the message that there will be no heartbeat (instead, there will be death) if the firing range was built.

Moreover, it would resemble a "cage," a prison, and the ancestral village would be soon covered with "bullets fragment and ricochet." Chamorros hold great respect for their ancestors and Indigenous culture and they have historically relied on their guidance. If the space of these practices is taken from them, there won't be much left to "navigate" them towards the future. At last, the endangered creatures of Pågat could not reproduce and would go extinct if the ecological conditions are changed.

In another poem titled "ginen tidelands" Perez compares the human skeleton to the latte architecture: "[our] bones: / acho' latte / removed from— / to museums" (ibid. 16). If latte is removed from Guam and placed in museums, where only dead objects are preserved, the culture will die the same way humans could not live without their skeletons. Therefore, by emphasizing the importance of such an object in these poems and throughout the book, Perez's text can be interpreted as an activist statement against the military buildup on Pågat.

Man-made objects, the maps of Guam, and the Pacific are other recurrent subjects in Perez's poetry. There are actual maps, maps that are made up of texts and poems about his experience with maps in his series. In an interview with Lantern Review, he explained the function of maps in his work:

> The "actual maps" in my first book are ... both visual poems and illustrations of the rest of the work. [...] [T]hey function in two ways: first, they center "Guam," a locating signifier often omitted from many maps. Secondly, the maps are meant to provide a counterpoint to the actual stories that are told throughout the book. While maps can locate, chart, and represent ... they never show us the human voices of a place. I place this abstract, aerial view of "Guam" alongside the more embodied and rooted portraits of place and people.
>
> (Iris n.p.)

In his first poetry book *from unincorporated territory [hacha]*, Perez incorporates four actual maps. The first map (28) shows the historical "Spanish Galleon trade route between Acapulco and Manila" on which Guam was a crucial stop (Perez, "Transterritorial Currents" n.p.). The second one is a Second World War Pacific Map that shows the Japanese control over Guam (Perez, *from unincorporated territory [hacha]* 29). It is significant because most history books make no mention of the history of Guam under the Second World War, even though it was attacked just like Pearl Harbor and occupied by Japan for 3 years—the only US territory taken over during the war (Perez, "Transterritorial Currents" n.p.). The third map shows the importance of Guam as an air travel transit center between the United States, Asia and other islands of the Pacific (Perez, *from unincorporated territory [hacha]* 30). The last, fourth, map reveals the US military bases on Guam which occupies one-third of the island (ibid. 85). These four maps show not only the great significance of Guam in the Pacific but also the succession of the (ongoing) colonization. First, the Spanish exploited the island's favorable location. Later the Japanese controlled it, and last, American militarism and tourism took it over. The visual map poems can disclose and (visibly) connect politics, history, and culture more precisely than written ones (Lai 16). Although Guam always has been and still is an important place in the Pacific and beyond, it is not often mentioned in history books and media. "We are invisible," says Perez ("Transterritorial Currents" n.p.). In the preface of *from unincorporated territory [hacha]*, he explains what he means by "invisible":

> On maps, Guam doesn't exist: I point to an empty space in the Pacific and say, "I'm from here." On some maps, Guam is a small, unnamed island; I say, "I'm from this unnamed place." On some maps, Guam is named "Guam, U.S.A." I say, "I'm from a territory of the United States." On some maps, Guam is named, simply, "Guam"; I say, "I am from Guam."
>
> (7)

Before European travels, Chamorros relied on different kinds of navigation tools such as song maps. After journeys were completed, a song would be created that would weave geographic, biological, and sensory elements together to form a map. These songs would take on features such as the stars, the color of the water, the features of shorelines, changes in clouds, the songs of birds. So long as these songs were remembered and passed on, a return journey was always possible (Bevacqua 84). After the arrival of the European explorers, who treated the Pacific Ocean as an empty space, cartographic representations of it were developed, where the area typically separated Asia and the American continent (Iris n.p.). Since then, Chamorros, as well as other Pacific communities, have been forced to look at the world in another way. Instead of song maps and remembrance, they had to learn to "read" and understand visual maps which were created by and for Western navigators (Lai 15). In the same way, Perez cannot help but search for his homeland on the vast Western world map and try to find it through the different names that foreign powers attached to it.

In his fourth book, *from unincorporated territory [lukao]*, Perez returns to map poems again and includes four of them. The first one is the "Telegeography cable network" that connects countries in and on the two sides of the Pacific Ocean. Here again, Guam plays a central role in distributing the cables among communities. In a note below the picture, Perez states that "more cables have landed on Guam than in either Hawai'i or California" (9). The second map is an illustration and combination of three other maps and shows the "Key US Bases in Pacific Pivot Buildup" (25). By combining three maps ("Mariana Island Training Area EIS," "NOAA IOOS: Pacific Ocean States, territories, etc." and "DITC: Acoustic Effects on Marine Mammals"), Perez shows the overlapping effects the military buildup causes in the area. The third map is of Guam titled "Toxic Chemicals of Guam," and it reveals the locations of the more than a hundred dumpsites of the island (41). The fourth map is the plan of the Fire Training Airforce field and the text below describes how the buildup will negatively affect wildlife (57). While the first book and its four map poems took us through historical points and showed the importance of Guam in the region as well as opposed it to its invisibility, the last book and its maps reflect on the negative consequences of colonization. They show the present but also predict a pessimistic future for Guam.

Perez, like other Chamorros, locally and abroad, tries to make sense of and find his identity in the colonial context. As Lai argues, maps are important approaches to determine one's roots of origin and also to establish how one will be perceived by others (15). The fact that Perez cannot find his homeland on the map because it is absent or it is there, but constantly named differently by various powers and for diverse political reasons, is of course symbolic. His experience is shared by many Chamorros who try to hold on to maps and names, hoping they will provide answers regarding their origin. Instead of looking for Guam on the world map, Perez provides us with his collection of maps. This time, he chooses what to show us—the different definitions of Guam: as a center of trade and later of air travel, occupied nation throughout post-contact history, militarized island, and the effects of militarization on people and environment. This definition is not only one or the other or nothing at all as presented by foreign powers but a mixture of various definitions—the truth told by a man who is both a Native Chamorro and an American and whose dual identity is tied to more than one land. In this sense, maps are representations of guidance for one's spiritual journey. We can look at these maps as important objects that display activist messages. Through them, the reader can see the problems Indigenes in Guam encounter: social and environmental issues brought by modernization and militarization. Perez places these maps strategically and sometimes adds a few notes or explanations. However, he does not comment on them; instead, he lets the pictures and numbers speak for themselves. This way these map poems can act as activist texts that signal resistance without stating it directly.

The stone is the final (natural) object with mission discussed in this chapter. The stone carries more than its literal meaning and demonstrates the importance of connection to the land. The significance of the stone derives from an old Chamorro myth, "How the Women Saved Guåhan from a Giant Fish," that emerges again and again in Perez's poetry. It tells the story of a large fish that attacks Guam every night and slowly eats away the island, stone by stone. The men try to thwart the fish by chasing it on canoes, but all their efforts are unsuccessful. Finally, the women use their hair to weave a large net and manage to capture the fish and save Guam from the giant fish. However, Perez's "version" is not the first modern emergence of the old story. In the past years, Chamorro activists reached back to such "traditional wonder histories," as Bevacqua and Bowman call them because they incorporate the old values and teachings of the ancestors which can be applied and used to inspire Indigenous movements and activism (70). The giant fish, of course, symbolizes the American army that takes away the land little by little. The well-known story helps to pass on the vision of activist groups, such as Nasion CHamoru (Chamorro Nation) and others, and speaks against colonialism and militarism. At the same time, it encourages environmental sovereignty and political and cultural independence of the Chamorros (Bevacqua and Bowman 72). This tale became essential in activist rhetoric because it shows the possible destruction of the land due to military developments and the feasibility to speak up against it and confront it (ibid. 79).

Interestingly, Perez includes two different versions of the myth in *from unincorporated territory [saina]*. The first one is told by the poet's grandmother:

> Once / in days of / our / before time / ancestors / in days / when chaifi (god of the underworld) / virgin mary / not yet come … / a huge fish / lived underground / tunnel between / pago and agana bays / each night ate / stone until / hole / [we] afraid / be no earth / after many generations passed / to days of spanish / mary came / she / knew how to help [us] / she / takes a long silken hair / from / her head makes a loop / she throws it over the fish's head / captive / she / ties the fish / of reach / of earth / so today / if you stand / over tunnel / listen / you can hear / angry beating / tail against / walls / forever / trying to escape from / her hair.
> 
> (26–28)

This version clearly shows the Christian influences on the ancient tale. Many Chamorro tales, that once had great cultural relevance, have been replaced by stories that served the building of a powerful empire of the Westerners. Even though Chamorro stories did survive the colonization of the tales, they were changed and contorted to accommodate the Eurocentric, Christian colonial ideology (Bevacqua and Bowman 73). Undoubtedly, this happened to this myth, too. Virgin Mary came to Guam to save the Chamorros from their unchristian lifestyle. Although the beast is captured and locked under the earth, perhaps to hell, it is still trying to come back to corrupt the people of Guam, and they are only safe as long as their belief in Virgin Mary is strong.

The second "version of the story of i guihan dångkolo (big fish) [as told before]" appears in a later part of the book:

> once / the center / of [our] island / eaten away both sides / land between agaña bay and pago bay / becoming more narrow / "if this keeps on [guam] will be cut into two / we must do something to stop it / as [we] talked s messenger brought word / a giant fish had been seen in pago bay / nibbling nibling / deeper / deeper.
> 
> (*from unincorporated territory [Saina]* 55).

Later the men go "looking / for the giant fish / [we] didn't find it / for it [is] hiding" (ibid. 71). At last, the women of Guam "cut / off some of their long / beautiful / hair / and wove / it into a net / spread out in every direction / then they / began to sing / the fish heard the sound / it swam in to the / underland waters / to hear more clearly" (ibid. 97). After it swam close enough, lured by the women's singing, "[we] dived into the water / spreading net / great fish became tangled / … / save [our] island / with the magic / of [your] hair / singing" (ibid. 122). The original version is not infiltrated with

Western culture yet and it shows how a community working together can maintain the security of the land and continuation of the culture. By setting the stories next to each other, Perez shows that it is not only the military that endangers Chamorros; foreign ideas, values, lifestyle, and religion can be just as devastating. The island that disappears stone by stone refers not only to the land but also to Chamorro culture. The texts are therefore a call for resistance.

   The literal meaning of losing the land is shown in another poem as parts of the official documents of the Organic Act are contrasted with the myth. A short passage of the story ("'each night ate / stone until / hole / [we] afraid / be no earth'" (ibid. 33) is inserted into a three pages long text from the Organic Act that includes the lengthy list of the areas that were seized by the US government (ibid. 31–33). Perez also shows the magnitude of the portion of the land that was taken through the signing of the act by inserting such a limited passage of the traditional story. One can sense how little the Chamorro voices had been taken into account when dividing the land simply by looking at this poem. While the text of the Organic Act is italicized, the lines from the myth are normal and stand out clearly from the official document. The poet plays with visuals to show the small, remaining voice of his people. Despite colonization, they are still present and their voices can still be heard.

## Conclusion

Indigenous peoples in Guam and elsewhere in the Pacific struggle for sovereignty and decolonization. Local activists often express resistance by displaying cultural identity, such as connecting to their history, traditions, local customs, and everyday objects from their culture, and stories. Besides giving the joy of reading, literature can also be a medium to pass on activist messages. As Perez said in an interview, poetry is empowering and it has always been a powerful tool in political movements and the other way around; authors were always inspired to create by these movements (Perez, "Poet to Poet Interview" n.p.). In his work, he addresses cultural, historical, ecological problems that his people have to endure every day due to the centuries-long colonization and militarization of Guam. Often, he does not state his opinion directly but instead uses different techniques to deliver his messages. He gives clues to his readers; plays with numbers and visuals, pictures, and maps; and arranges texts in an impactful manner. He translates Chamorro words only pages later to force his readers to reread previous passages and search for meaning throughout the books very consciously. Sometimes he sends his readers to websites where one can get more information and understand the activist message more precisely. His clues often include everyday objects that convey deep meaning in Chamorro culture. Some of them, such as traditionally made objects and food from Guam, the sakman (canoe), latte building structures, different kinds of maps, and slowly disappearing stones, are employed as metaphors of the land. By mentioning these ordinary objects and placing them strategically in his poems, Perez reveals the consequences of colonialism and militarism on Guam. The survival of the traditional objects and activities that surround them symbolizes the survival of Chamorro culture and it depends on the Indigenous community. Perez assists the continuation by including these objects and acts in his poetry, emphasizing their importance, and addressing the urgent issue of their (objects and culture) approaching possible disappearance. "Our native voices are political expressions," says Perez, and as long as Indigenous activists "express the politics of survival, resistance, and resurgence," for example, "through poems of protest, critique, and witness," (n.p.), the culture and the people of Guam will live on and thrive in the future.

## Works Cited

Bevacqua, Michael Lujan. "The Song Maps of Craig Santos Perez." *Transmotion*, vol. 1, no. 1, 2015, pp. 84–88.

Bevacqua, Michael Lujan, and Isa Kelley Bowman. "Histories of Wonder, Futures of Wonder: Chamorro Activist Identity, Community, and Leadership in 'The Legend of Gadao' and 'The Women Who Saved Guåhan from a Giant Fish.'" *Marvels & Tales*, vol. 30, no. 1, 2016, pp. 70–89.

Cabral, Amilcar. "National Liberation and Culture." *Colonial Discourse and Postcolonial Theory: A Reader*, edited by Patrick Williams and Laura Chrisman, Harvester Wheatsheaf, 1993, pp. 53–65.

DeLisle, Christine Taitano. "Destination Chamorro Culture: Notes on Realignment, Rebranding, and Post-9/11 Militourism in Guam." *American Quarterly*, vol. 68, no. 3, 2016, pp. 563–72.

DeLoughrey, Elizabeth M. "Toward a Critical Ocean Studies for the Anthropocene." *English Language Notes*, vol. 57, no. 1, 2019, pp. 21–36.

Diaz, Vicente M, and J. Kēhaulani Kauanui. "Native Pacific Cultural Studies on the Edge." *The Contemporary Pacific*, vol. 13, no. 2, 2001, pp. 315–42.

Hauʻofa, Epeli. "The Ocean in Us." *Culture and Sustainable Development in the Pacific*, edited by A. Hooper, ANU P, 2005, pp. 32–43.

Heim, Otto. "How (Not) to Globalize Oceania: Ecology and Politics in Contemporary Pacific Island Performance Arts." *Commonwealth Essays and Studies*, vol. 41, no. 1, 2018, pp. 131–45.

Hsu, Hsuan L. "Guåhan (Guam), Literary Emergence, and the American Pacific in Homebase and from Unincorporated Territory." *American Literary History*, vol. 24, no. 2, 2012, pp. 281–307.

Iris. "The Page Transformed: A Conversation with Craig Santos Perez." *Lantern Review Blog*, Mar. 12, 2010, http://www.lanternreview.com/blog/2010/03/12/the-page-transformed-a-conversation-with-craig-santos-perez/. Accessed Feb. 10, 2022.

Keown, Michelle. *Pacific Islands Writing: The Postcolonial Literatures of Aotearoa/New Zealand and Oceania*. Oxford UP, 2007.

Lai, Paul. "Discontiguous States of America: The Paradox of Unincorporation in Craig Santos Perez's Poetics of Chamorro Guam." *Journal of Transnational American Studies*, vol. 3, no. 2, 2011, pp. 1–28.

Merriam-Webster Dictionary, www.merriam-webster.com/dictionary/object.

Naʻputi, Tiara R. and Michael Lujan Bevacqua. "Militarization and Resistance from Guåhan: Protecting and Defending Pågat." *American Quarterly*, vol. 67, no. 3, 2015, pp. 837–58.

Peek, Michelle. "Kinship Flows in Brandy Nālani McDougall's *The Salt-Wind: Ka Makani Pa'akai*." *Feminist Review*, vol. 103, 2013, pp. 80–98.

Perez, Craig Santos. *from unincorporated territory [hacha]*. Tin Fish P, 2008.

———. *from unincorporated territory [saina]*. Omnidawn Publishing, 2010.

———. *from unincorporated territory [guma']*. Omnidawn Publishing, 2014.

———. *from unincorporated territory [lukao]*. Omnidawn Publishing, 2017.

———. "Poet to Poet Interview: Rajiv Mohabir and Craig Santos Perez." *Kenyon Review*, Feb. 20, 2019, https://www.kenyonreview.org/2019/02/poet-to-poet-interview-rajiv-mohabir-and-craig-santos-perez/. Accessed Feb. 10, 2022.

———. "The Poetics of Mapping Diaspora, Navigating Culture, and Being from (Part 1)." *Doveglion Press*, 2011, http://www.doveglion.com/2011/04/craig-santos-perez-the-poetics-of-mapping-diasporanavigating-culture-and-being-from-part-1/. Accessed Apr. 3, 2018.

———. "Transterritorial Currents and the Imperial Terripelago." *American Quarterly*, vol. 67, no. 3, 2015, pp. 619–24.

Rowe, John Carlos. "Transpacific Studies and the Cultures of US Imperialism." *American Studies as Transnational Practice: Turning toward the Transpacific*, edited by Y. Shu and D. E. Pease, Dartmouth College P, 2015, pp. 259–75.

South, Todd. "Marine Corps Plan to Relocate from Okinawa to Guam Needs a Review, Commandant Says." *Marine Corps Times*, May 4, 2019, https://www.marinecorpstimes.com/news/your-marine-corps/2019/05/03/marine-corps-relocation-from-okinawa-to-guam-worthy-of-review-commandant-says/. Accessed Feb. 10, 2022.

Steiner, Candice Elanna. "A Sea of Warriors: Performing an Identity of Resilience and Empowerment in the Face of Climate Change in the Pacific." *The Contemporary Pacific*, vol. 27, no. 1, 2015, pp. 147–80.

Vizenor, Gerald. *Survivance: Narratives of Native Presence*. U of Nebraska P, 2008.

Woodward, Valerie Solar. "'I Guess They Didn't Want Us Asking Too Many Questions:' Reading American Empire in Guam." *The Contemporary Pacific*, vol. 25, no. 1, 2013, pp. 67–91.

# 6

# Remapping Mānoa Valley in Hawaiian Literature

Chia-hua Lin

As a result of the deeply problematic Western mapping practices and ideology, the landscape of Hawai'i as well as the lifeways and food ways of Kānaka Maoli (Native Hawaiians) have been drastically changed since the arrival of the white settlers. Despite the exploitative settler-colonial cartography, Kānaka Maoli continue to survive and strive. Native Hawaiians unceasingly remap their (is)land through bringing back the *moʻolelo* (hi/story, myth, and legend) and their traditional practices, thereby constituting their everyday resurgence. In this chapter, I will first discuss the problem of Western mapping practice as well as the anthropocentric and capitalist ideologies that lie behind capitalist colonial cartography. This chapter then investigates how Kānaka Maoli confront the Western mapping with their worldview and ways of knowing. I will draw examples from literary maps—poems by Albert Wendt and Brandy Nālani McDougall—as well as the revitalization project at Ka Papa Loʻi O Kānewai, a restored *loʻi kalo* (water taro fields) near the University of Hawai'i at Mānoa (UHM), which I considered to be a physical/embodied mapping. Through these examples I argue that Kānaka Maoli claim their presence and resist Western ideologies through their own way of remapping the *'āina* (land) and *wai* (water).[1,2]

The first problem of Western mapping practices I would like to name is the viewing of land as an object or even commodity without life, its own rights, feelings, and agency. Western maps are exploitative in their nature since they are a means for the exploitation of both natural resources and the colonized people. As T. V. Reeds argues, "Mapping was one of the key objectifying strategies that enable colonist expropriation" (32). Western maps, which view the land as void of life, are employed as a tool to assist the exploitation of the land. Maps, in other words, become the weapon of colonialism in complicity with capitalism to drain the life out of the land and degrade it to an exploitable commodity. As Candace Fujikane contends, "[c]apital expands its domain

---

[1] In the first part of this chapter where I discuss the problem of Western mapping practices, I will use certain English words instead of 'Ōlelo Hawai'i (Hawaiian language) partly because in that context I am still discussing Western conception. It is also my rhetorical resistance since I do not want to discuss the degrading ideology in Hawaiian words that have deep and significant cultural meaning.

[2] Here I want to briefly point out that water is so important in Hawaiian culture that wealth in 'ōlelo Hawai'i (Hawaiian language) is *waiwai*. This discussion, however, is not the focus of this chapter.

through the evisceration of the living earth into the inanimacies of nonlife, depicting abundant lands as wastelands to condemn them and make way for the penetration of black snake oil pipelines under rivers, the seeding of unexploded ordnance in militarized zones, and the dumping of toxic wastes on sacred lands" (3). Along with the objectification and commodification, Western mapping ignores the feelings, emotions, and tempers of the land and water, let alone their agencies.

The objectification and commodification of the environment, I would like to further point out, is the result of Western mapping practice's failure to capture the depth of a certain place. As Ryden, Kent C. suggests, "[Western map] compresses the landscape's ambiguities into an arbitrary and simplified flatness—it is all surface, lacking depth" (21). In addition to how Western cartography cannot convey the depth of a place, it is also important to note that the degrading of the natural environment to nothing more than a few lines and figures on the Western map also deprives lands and waters of spiritual and cultural significance. I argue that Western mapping practice which simply "take[s] a fandom lump of geography and flatten it out, reduce it to graphic symbols, draw grids and coordinates on it" (Ryden 53) also drains the life out of the land. As I argue and elaborate on throughout this chapter, while the land is merely some curved lines or other symbols on a map for the white settler in Hawaiʻi, Kānaka Maoli learn to view the land as "alive with mythic and scared meaning" (ibid. 44) through the stories. Kānaka Maoli learn about their spiritual relationship through the moʻolelo, and they restore this relationship by tending to the land and water.

The lines on the Western map mentioned above also symbolize boundaries. Western mapping practices, in other words, tend to separate rather than connect places. Seashore, for example, is viewed as the division between land and ocean. As Edward Cashman Jr. states, "A lot of people think that the ocean stops at the beach" (qtd. in Schuler n.p.). This ideology fails to recognize how streams and rivers are connected to the ocean, which explains white settlers' failure to manage the streams properly. In Kānaka Maoli worldview, however, land/water divisions are not understood as separations but as relations. According to Fujikane, land divisions "are defined by their relationality with that which lies on their edges, borders that are not boundaries of separation but seams of relationality" (19). Waters, by the same token, are also connected. In-land freshwater and the ocean are not two separated, but joined, ecosystems. This kind of understanding allows Kānaka Maoli to manage the streams in a way that will sustain both inland water and marine ecosystems.

The anthropocentric and capitalist ideology underlying Western cartography also results in the separation of humans from more-than-human beings. This brings me to another reason why I consider Western cartography shallow and problematic: it fails to address the relationship and connectedness between Indigenous peoples and their environment and thus serves to alienate people from a place. In Western settler ideology, moreover, humans are often considered as superior to, and thus have dominance over, the land and all other-than-human beings, which justifies and neutralizes the exploitation of nature. The exploitative Western ideology, in a sense, results in the belief that neither destroying the taro fields nor altering the streams will have devastating consequences because it fails to recognize the relationship between Native Hawaiians and taro as well as the connectedness of waters. Through

Kānaka Maoli worldview, I endeavor to explore a nonhierarchical and kincentric way to relate to the environment.

The land, streams, and taro fields in Hawai'i have been ravaged by the Euro-American settlers. This chapter focuses not so much on how the landscape of Mānoa Valley has changed since the arrival of the white settlers; instead, I discuss how Kānaka Maoli map this place through their stories and embody their worldview through their practice of everyday resurgence to restore the *lo'i kalo*. Elspeth P. Sterling and Catherine C. Summers document in *Sites of Oahu* that Mānoa Valley was once covered by potato and taro patches (282). However, due to urbanization, most of the invaluable traditional crops are gone. The valley is now "covered by streets and houses" (Ibid.). To be more exact, potatoes can no longer be found in the valley, and only a few taro patches as well as the traditional irrigation systems are preserved with great effort now. In addition, most in-land freshwater (streams) are either damaged or in some way altered. As Timothy A. Schuler quotes from the state's Commission on Water Resource Management that "roughly 20 percent of Hawaii's streams are lined, straightened or otherwise channelized. On Oahu, where most of the state's population lives, the figure is closer to 100 percent" (n.p.). In addition, UHM unfortunately also became an accomplice in the destroying of taro fields "when the university evicted [the kalo farmers] to make way for new dormitories" that were never built (Gregory n.p.). With the above examples, I want to put forth that settlers' ignoring of Kānaka Maoli worldview can have a devastating effect on Native Hawaiian culture as well as the natural environment of Hawai'i.

Against all odds, however, Kānaka Maoli and Hawaiian culture continue to survive and thrive! After examining the downgrading and threatening Western ideologies and mapping practices, I will now move on to discuss how, in the face of the devastations, challenges, and "an ever-changing environment over which [Native Hawaiians] have limited control" (Lane-Kamahele 128), Kānaka Maoli show their resilience by upholding *kalo* (taro) culture, Hawaiian values, and wisdom of their *kūpuna* (elders/ancestors), which manifest in their land and water management. In order to push back against the degrading Western mapping, I would like to draw examples from literary maps (by Albert Wendt and Brandy Nālani McDougall) as well as everyday practices (at Ka Papa Lo'i O Kānewai) that are grounded on Native Hawaiian culture, values, and worldview.

One distinction between Kānaka Maoli and Western mapping of Mānoa Valley I want to point out is that while Western cartography, as mentioned earlier, only represents *superficial* features of the land with lines or other symbols, Kānaka Maoli map the 'āina through their mo'olelo, which captures the depth of a place. As Joni Adamson eloquently suggests:

> The outsider follows a map's pattern of contours, symbols, and colors over geographical surface, but the insider annotates the map, tracing the invisible landscape through mythic tales, labeling the land with the worlds and *stories* of their songs, sketching imaginative contours and dramatic peaks through repeating their *traditional narrative*.
>
> (7; emphasis added)

**Figure 6.1** Mānoa Valley by Albert Wendt (photographed by the author).

One of the literary maps I would like to refer to is the poem about Mānoa valley, on a painting, by Albert Wendt, a well-known Samoan poet, writer, and scholar (Figure 6.1). This piece is currently displayed in one of the rooms of the English Department at UHM. Although Wendt is a Samoan, the Oceanian connections have brought him to Hawaiʻi where he has taught at UHM for years. Moreover, his literary map is also rooted in Kānaka Maoli worldview. In his mapping, Wendt points out how the land has an agency and power in that it watched the people move in; "The Koʻolau watched the first people settle in the valley" (n.p.).[3] Furthermore, knowing Kānaka Maoli's

---

[3] In ancient time, Koʻolau Range is a sacred site for Native Hawaiians. It is also at this range that King Kamehameha I waged the late battle after which he had all the Hawaiian islands under his reign.

moʻolelo (which will be given later in the chapter) and worldview, and placing them at the center, Wendt rightly refers to kalo as their ancestor in the poem; "The Kānaka Maoli planted their ancestor the Kalo" (n.p.). Wendt maps out the deep genealogical relationship of Native Hawaiians with the Kalo as well as with the ʻāina. Wendt further points out how, in Mānoa Valley, the kūpuna of Kānaka Maoli (both human and the kalo) have "flourished for generations" (n.p.). In his literary map of the valley, Wendt also calls the stream as well as the loʻi kalo the *kūpuna* have constructed "the valley's black blood" (n.p.) in order to designate their significance.

In Wendt's poem, he doesn't see the land simply as an exploitable natural resource and taro as simply a plant or staple food. Instead, Wendt depicts the kinship between Kānaka Maoli and the ʻāina and kalo. This kind of relationship teaches Kānaka Maoli to fulfill their *kuleana* (right and responsibility) to their relatives. In other words, Wendt's literary map depicts the depth of a kinship that cannot be captured by Western capitalist mapping. I will elaborate on the idea of kuleana later in this chapter.

As a reciprocate for Wendt's poem and alliance, McDougall, a Kanaka Maoli poet and scholar, also writes a poem about Wendt and his connection to this place. The poem is titled "He Mele Aloha no Albert Wendt a me Reina Whaitiri," and it is included in *The Salt-Wind: Ka Makani Paʻakai* (2008). In the poem, McDougall writes that "the makana of kalo, / niu, ʻuala, ʻula, maiʻa and iʻa / this ʻāina has fed you [Wendt], too" (85).[4] Here we are reminded again that, in Hawaiian worldview, ʻāina means "that which feeds." ʻĀina is not merely a commodity but that which feeds the people. Kalo, too, is the older sibling that feeds. The poet goes on to write, "and the ʻili ʻili birthing themselves / in the naʻau of Papa / bathed by the rain of Wākea– / they've shown you / how they make themselves / mountains" (85). McDougall invokes the *moʻolelo* of Papa (earth mother), *Wākea* (sky father), and *Hāloanaka* (who turned into the first kalo) in this poem. By doing so, she maps out the genealogical link of Kānaka Maoli with not only kalo but all beings. This is what Fujikane defines as "Kānaka Maoli cartographies" which "map familial relationality among humans, lands, and elemental forms, plant and animal ʻohana (family)" (18).

The moʻolelo of Hāloanaka will be given later in this chapter, but I'd like to bring forth here that according to the *Kumulipo*, the Hawaiian creation chant, all beings are birthed, and thus genealogically related. Both Hawaiian islands and Native Hawaiians are born of Papa and Wākea, and so Native Hawaiians and the islands are, again, genealogically connected. In "Embracing the Sacred: An Indigenous Framework for Tomorrow's Sustainability Science," Kekuhi Kealiikanakaoleohaililani and Christia Giardin also put forth the Hawaiian idea of *kinolau* to discuss how in the Hawaiian worldview all (natural) elements are the manifestation of *nā akua* (deities), to whom Kānaka Maoli have a genealogical link (63–64). This spiritual and familial relationship of Kānaka Maoli with all more-than-human beings, in turn, lay the foundation of the Hawaiian concept of *aloha ʻāina* (love the land) and *mālama ʻāina* (care for the land) (63). These ideas will be further elaborated later in this chapter, but I want to point out

---

4   *Niu* is coconut in Hawaiian. *ʻUala* means sweet potato. *ʻUlu* is breadfruit. *Maiʻa* is banana. *Iʻa* is fish.

here that through her poem, McDougall is able to map this deep relationship which is ignored, disregarded, and discredited by Western colonial cartography.

In another poem titled "Papatuanuku" McDougall further maps out the kinship between Kānaka Maoli and kalo and refute Western cartography. In the first line of the poem, She writes: "E hoʻolohe ʻoukou e nā mamo o Hāloa—" (62). In English it is translated to "Listen, you descendants of Hāloa." Through the moʻolelo of kalo, we learn that Hāloa can refer to both the firstborn of Papa and Wākea and the first kalo as well as his brother, the first *kanaka* (man). Descendants here refer to Kānaka Maoli. McDougall more explicitly portrays the genealogical connection between kalo and Kānaka Maoli by writing, "It is my [Hāloa's] blood coursing/ through you, and lush fruit of my body/ feeding you" (62). To be more exact, the poets specify the connectivity by blood between kalo and Native Hawaiian in this poem. Moreover, in this poem, McDougall writes, "Nation rise and fall / with the tides, and your boundaries / of pepa might as well be written / in dust" (62). In a sense, the poet repudiates the borders/boundaries of nation-states on *pepa* (paper)—map. This literary map of McDougall's reveals the deep connections instead of separation.

In the following paragraphs, I will draw examples from Ka Papa Loʻi O Kānewai, a restored loʻi kalo and traditional irrigation system, to discuss how Kānaka Maoli embody their worldview and physically counter the problematic Western cartography and ideologies mentioned above. That is, whereas Western mapping only captures the superficial features of a place, Kānaka Maoli's moʻolelo maps the deep meaning of a place. Moreover, while the capitalist ideology views the land as an exploitable commodity, Kānaka Maoli consider ʻāina as a living being—elemental forms of *nā akua*, to be more exact—to whom we should pay our love and respect. Also, unlike the anthropocentric ideologies that divide humans and other-than-human beings, Kānaka Maoli learn from their moʻolelo that kalo is their kūpuna and older siblings. Native Hawaiians also understand how streams and the ocean are connected. This worldview is celebrated in the restoration of loʻi kalo and the traditional irrigation system at Ka Papa Loʻi O Kānewai, and thus I argue that it can be seen as the demonstration of the resilience of Kānaka Maoli as well as the hope for the continuance of Hawaiian culture and for a sustainable future.

In order to preserve the kalo culture of Hawaiʻi, a group of UHM students—with the help of Uncle Harry Mitchell from Maui and other traditional farmers—established Ka Papa Loʻi O Kānewai near the Kamakakūokalani Center for Hawaiian Studies of UHM. Its establishment, however, didn't go without challenge. On the contrary, it raised some controversies. For example, a part of Ka Papa Loʻi O Kanewai and its surrounding area were displaced by the building of the Center for Hawaiian Studies building, which leads Penn to ask, "[S]hould a cultural use area be sacrificed to a facility for academic cultural scholarship?" (134).[5] In the website, *The EcoTipping Points Project*, Gregory

---

[5] There is a controversy over the relationship between Kapapa Loʻi O Kanewai and UHM. However, this controversy will not be further examined or discussed since it is beyond the scope of this chapter.

also documents that "[i]n the late 1980s a conflict arose because, somewhat ironically, construction of the new Center for Hawaiian Studies destroyed some of the loʻi as well as the spring. Most egregious, according to [Lolana] Fenstemacher, was the destruction of some rare cultivars" (n.p.). Despite all the difficulties, Ka Papa Loʻi O Kānewai, "the last remnant of extensive Waikīkī taro pondfield systems" (Penn 134), continues to be very well maintained and even starts to bring people from the community to work together. This is a great example of how the Indigenous knowledge and traditions of Kānaka Maoli can, and will, carry into the future.

To counter the Western colonial mapping of Mānoa Valley, there are a number of important things Kānaka Maoli learn and teach at Ka Papa Loʻi O Kānewai, for instance, the moʻolelo of the valley and of Kānewai and the moʻolelo of kalo in Hawaiian culture. These moʻolelo are examples of Kānaka Maoli cartography, which captures the deep cultural significance that is missing in Western maps. Via these moʻolelo, Kānaka Maoli are taught the cultural importance of the place, Kānewai, as well as kalo. Native Hawaiians, moreover, are connected to the ʻāina and wai at a deeper level, which is what I meant by depth earlier. Furthermore, through taking care of kalo, Kānaka Maoli learn about and put into practice the traditional values in their culture—*malama ʻāina, laulima*, and *puʻu honua*. Finally, two other important Hawaiian values—*aloha ʻāina* and *kuleana*—are also learned and embodied at Ka Papa Loʻi O Kānewai. All these Hawaiian terms will be explained later.

Every day, students and faculties work at the *loʻi* to *mālana* (take care of) the kalo. There is also a workday at the loʻi on the first Saturday of every month during which people from the community come to work together at the loʻi. Through their moʻolelo and mālana the ʻāina, Kānaka Maoli learn and maintain their deep connections to the ʻāina as well as kalo. For instance, "Kānewai" means so much more to Kānaka Maoli and their settler allies than to white settlers because they know that the name came from a deity, Kāne. As Gregory points out, "[t]he little area of Honolulu called Kānewai gets its name from a spring created there by the god Kāne when he first came to Oʻahu" (n.p).[6] This is the first moʻolelo given to the participants of the workday at Ka Papa Loʻi O Kānewai, and it is also documented in *Sites of Oahu*: two brother deities—Kāne and Kanaloa—came to Oʻahu one day, and they decided to rest in Mānoa Valley. Kanaloa got thirsty so he asked Kāne for freshwater. Kāne smiled at Kanaloa's request because he could hear the water running underground. Then Kāne struck the ground with his ʻōʻō (staff) and water came forth in abundance from the place where Kāne struck (283–84). Through the moʻolelo, Kānaka Maoli are taught to see Kānewai as the "healing waters of Kāne" (Sterling et al 281). This is a great example of how Kānaka Maoli cartography depicts the depth of a place instead of superficial geographical features.

Kānaka Maoli are also taught to respect the ʻāina as a living being with power and agency via the moʻolelo. To illustrate this point, I would like to draw an example from my own personal experience at Ka Papa Loʻi O Kānewai. It was my first time working

---

[6] It is worth pointing out that Kāne and Kanaloa created numerous springs besides the one we tell of at Kānewai. These other springs, however, are not the focus of this chapter and thus will not be discussed here.

at the loʻi, and our group leader asked us to first introduce our names. After we have all given our names, the leader explained that we were not just introducing ourselves to each other but also to the ʻāina so it can recognize us. In other words, along with the group I worked with, I learned that the recognition between me and the ʻāina is not, and should not be, unilateral. The ʻāina has its own feeling, and thus I should show it the proper respect it deserves by introducing myself to it before I start working on it. In this kind of worldview, the land is no longer viewed as an object or commodity, and humans can no longer claim dominance over the land.

In their worldview, Kānaka Maoli also recognize kalo as their ancestor instead of simply a commodity or staple food as white settlers do. In other words, kalo is a significant crop in Hawaiʻi not only because it is the primary food source but also because of its familial tie to Kānaka Maoli. It is through this relationship that Native Hawaiians remap Mānoa valley. Here I would like to recount the moʻolelo through which Kānaka Maoli are taught the genealogical connection of kalo and Native Hawaiians: In the ancient time, there were two deities—Papa and Wākea. After their sexual union, Papa first gave birth to the Hawaiian islands. Later, they produced a child named Hāloanaka. He was stillborn and was buried. Then, from where Hāloanaka's body was buried grew the first kalo plant. The next child, named Hāloa after the first child, became the first kanaka (human) to live on the islands. The second Hālona was the ancestor of all Kānaka Maoli. Understanding the relationship between Native Hawaiians and kalo through this moʻolelo leads people to believe that "the kalo plant, arising from the prior-born child, is superior to and more sacred than man" (Cho et al. 2).[7]

The moʻolelo that reminds Kānaka Maoli of their relationship to the kalo is also retold in many different forms such as the mural on the pillar under a bridge and the carving at Kapapa Loʻi O Kānewai (Figures 6.2 and 6.3). These different ways of telling the moʻolelo all reveal Kānaka Maoli worldview that neither separates humans from other-than-human beings nor views kalo and ʻāina as objects or commodities. The retelling of the moʻolelo and the restoring and maintaining of the loʻi kalo, I would add, also demonstrate Kānaka Maoli resilience. Despite the invasion of (neo)colonialism and capitalism, Native Hawaiian culture continues to flourish from this deep familial relationship. Kalo, in other words, acquires cultural and spiritual significance through the moʻolelo. At Ka Papa Loʻi O Kānewai, Mānoa valley is also remapped through the moʻolelo of Kāne and Hāloa. Because of this mapping, Kānaka Maoli learns to see kalo as their ancestor, and they show respect to their kūpuna and

---

[7] Hawaiian moʻolelo are incredibly rich and they are passed down orally for generations. Therefore, it is inevitable that there are different versions of the moʻolelo. I am recounting the version I heard at Kapapa Loʻi O Kanewai and as written in the article of John J. Cho et al. It is pointless to argue for the orthodoxy of a particular version of the moʻolelo. The existence of multiple versions of a moʻolelo should serve to remind us the importance of being open-minded and to the ʻŌlelo Noʻeau (proverbs or wise sayings): "ʻAʻohe pau ka ʻike i ka hālau hoʻokahi" (Knowledge is not exhausted/learned in one school).

Figure 6.2 Mural on the Pillars (photographed by the author).

demonstrate their resilience by taking care of the ʻāina, wai, and kalo. Now that we know the moʻolelo, we also realize that the destruction of kalo loʻi as well as the spring have severe consequences in both cultural and ecological terms.

On the workday at Ka Papa Loʻi O Kānewai, after retelling the moʻolelo of Kānewai and the kalo, the group leader said to the participants: "Now that you know the moʻolelo, you have a kuleana to this place." Regarding Kuleana, Melia Lane-Kamahele defines it as "the uniquely Hawaiian concept of a reciprocal relationship between a person who is responsible and the thing that he or she is responsible for" (128). We can see from this definition that in Native Hawaiian understanding, rights and responsibilities are inseparable. Moreover, I would like to point out that through the moʻolelo Kānaka Maoli, as well as non-Hawaiians, learn about not only their reciprocal relationship with, but also their kuleana to, the ʻāina. Taking care of the ʻāina and kalo at Ka Papa Loʻi O Kānewai and ensuring the continuance of Kānaka Maoli worldview are an example of how Kānaka fulfill their kuleana. It is an honor for me, a non-Hawaiian, to be able to share the moʻolelo and thus kuleana. Participating in the workday and writing the experience down to voice with Kānaka Maoli and the ʻāina are my endeavors to carry out my kuleana.

In contrast with the exploitative Western cartography that leads to global environmental challenges, Kealiikanakaoleohaililani and Giardina suggest how Indigenous peoples' ecological views can contribute to the study and practice of

Figure 6.3 Wood carving at Ka Papa Lo'i O Kānewai (photographed by the author).

sustainability; "with a sacredness ethic [in Indigenous cultures], taking of resources is viewed as an exchange and privilege that comes with stewardship and responsibilities" (59). In this time of global environmental crisis, Kānaka Maoli mapping can provide us with a different way of thinking that can establish a harmonious, non hierarchical, and reciprocal relationship with the environment that opens the possibility to a sustainable future.

One thing I would like to point out here is that among the participants at the workday, there are people from different cultural backgrounds as well as generations. At the workday, we were also asked to tell the group where we are from. After our introduction, the leader explained to us that by asking us to introduce ourselves through our home countries, or the land we are from, she recognizes that we all bring into the group something from our own cultural background, and thus we all have something to contribute. People of different ages and ethnicities, in a sense, are brought together and connected at Ka Papa Loʻi O Kānewai through storytelling, and now we all learn about our kuleana to the ʻāina and start to contribute from our own viewpoints and cultural backgrounds.

Earlier I mentioned how Western mapping conceives of the ocean as stopping at the shore, at Ka Papa Loʻi O Kānewai we also observe how this ideology is challenged through Kānaka Maoli cartography. Kānaka Maoli, through experiences of working closely with the ʻāina and the kai (sea or area near the sea) for generations, know that land, inland freshwater, and the ocean are actually connected. Together they constitute an interwoven ecosystem. Moreover, Native Hawaiians understand this connectedness as not simply that in-land freshwater flows into the ocean but also that fish and other animals travel upstream as well through various underground water systems. For example, "Hawaiian freshwater gobies that are found only in the 50th state and its surrounding waters spend a portion of their lives in the ocean but swim upstream to spawn, just like salmon" (Schuler n.p.). William Puleloa also mentions that "[u]nique species of fishes, shrimps, and shellfishes moved upstream into the plains and mountains to become the ʻoʻopu, ʻōpae, and hīhīwai" (n.p.).

With the knowledge of how waters are connected, Kānaka Maoli developed ʻauwai (traditional Hawaiian irrigation ditch system) and a way of managing loʻi kalo to ensure that the water flows constantly so ecosystems are kept healthy (Figure 6.4). One special thing about the Hawaiian irrigation system is that, instead of building a dam or blocking/diverting the water completely, water is only slowed down enough to move part of the water into the ʻauwai (irrigation ditch). After the water flows through the loʻi kalo, it is directed back to the main stream again. The place where the irrigation water goes back to the stream is called *hoʻi wai*. The *ʻauwai* system demonstrates Kānaka Maoli's belief that people well as all other-than-human beings living downstream have equal rights to water. Native Hawaiians respect water rights and will not deprive others of their access to water. This is why, in the Hawaiian worldview, water should always flow. Unfortunately, it is also the reason why the alteration of the waterways after the arrival of the white settlers has a severe effect on Native Hawaiian cultures and lifeways.

This practice is important to the ecosystem also because it turns loʻi kalo into a natural filter. As Schuler points out, "[i]f managed properly, [the kalo patches] would also filter runoff, reducing the amount of pollutants entering Honolulu's waterways and, ultimately, the ocean" (n.p.). In addition to being a natural filter, loʻi kalo is also a significant in that the watering running through the loʻi kalo will bring nutrients to the fishponds downstream to nurture the fish. This had been how the kūpuna of Kānaka Maoli had managed the water and loʻi for thousands of years. From this delicate and

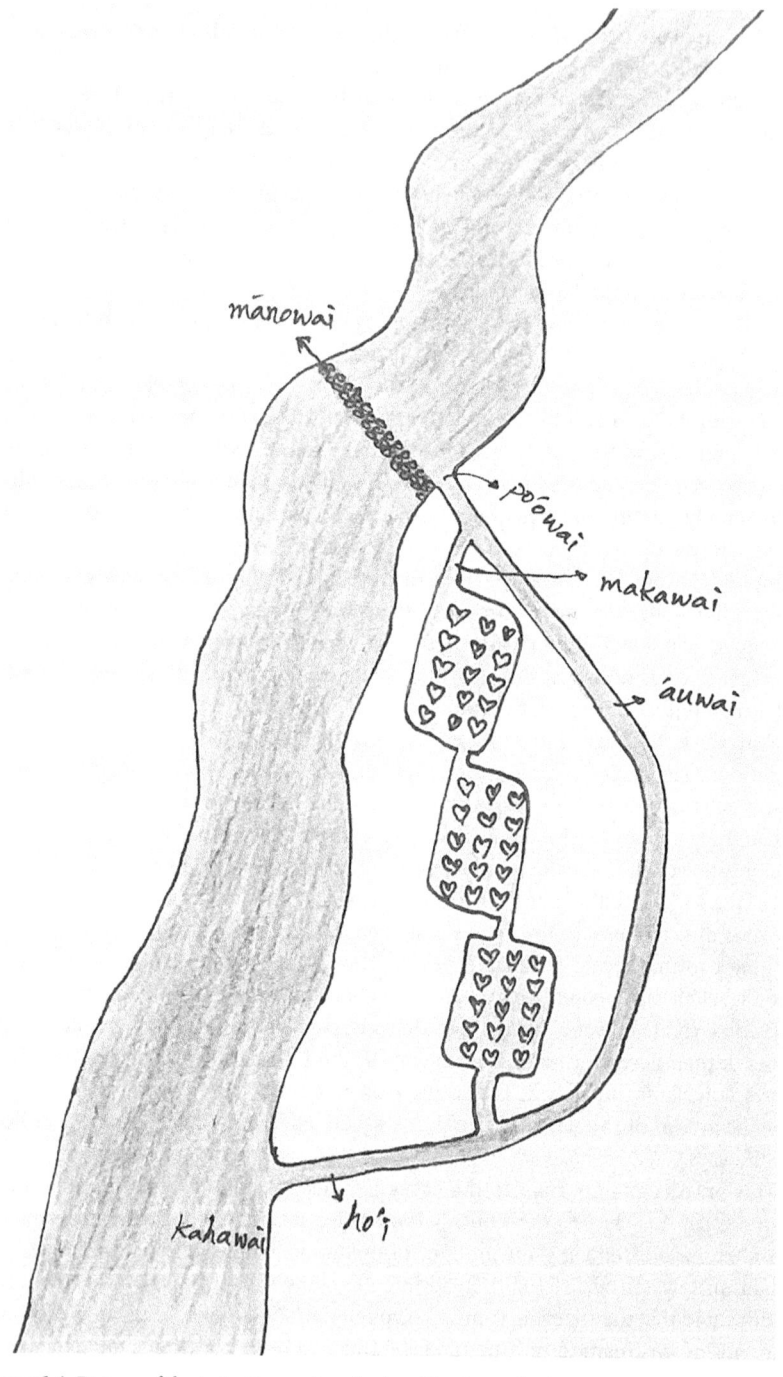

**Figure 6.4** Picture of the irrigation system (painted by the author).

complicated system we can really see the wisdom of Kānaka Maoli's ancestors, and the restoration of this system shows Kānaka Maoli's capability not only to carry this wisdom into the future but also to adapt to a constantly and rapidly changing environment. The restoration of the water, in addition, "is a vital opportunity to improve the health of the island's freshwater and saltwater resources, while also potentially protecting communities from flooding and sea level rise" (Schuler n.p.). This again shows that Kānaka Maoli worldview and traditional knowledge are crucial in a time of global environmental crisis.

Another educational objective and benefit of Ka Papa Loʻi O Kānewai is the cultivation, through growing kalo and reconnecting to ʻāina, of three important Hawaiian values in Kānaka Maoli: first, Malama ʻāina, which means to "take care of the ʻāina." It is important to keep in mind that the ʻāina "feed[s] and nurture[s] you to make you healthy so you can help others" (qtd. in DeSilva n.p.). Second, laulima, which means "many hands working together." At the workday, the leader explained to us that laulima in this context means more specifically to work together to care for the ʻāina as well as each other, so we have to take care of other group members as well. Finally, Puʻuhonua, which means "a safe place where people can learn and practice Hawaiian culture" (ibid.). The leader at the workday, also, told the participants that the goal is to build a safe place for both human and other-than-human beings to exist together (Figure 6.5). We can thus infer how important the restoration of loʻi kalo is to upholding Hawaiian values.

**Figure 6.5** People working in the loʻi kalo (photographed by the author).

Another important Hawaiian values I would like to put forth is *aloha ʻāina*. Through working on the ʻāina and taking care of the kalo, Kānaka Maoli deepen their relationship with, and love for, the land, which is aloha ʻāina. One of my tasks when I participated in the workday at Ka Papa Loʻi O Kānewai was to walk in the loʻi to even out the field so that the water can flow through the whole loʻi. It was an easy enough task, but because there were so many little stones and pebbles in the field, every step was extremely painful to my feet which have never walked bare on the land and were unaccustomed to this kind of labor. After the workday, moreover, my lower back and legs hurt for three days. One thought that came to me while experiencing the pain was "Those who are willing to suffer and sweat everyday to work on the ʻāina must be really in love with it!" But I chose to go back again next month because I now share the love for the ʻāina. I think the physical pain ties me more tightly to the ʻāina. Also the dirt that stuck in my fingernails and toenails gave me a sense of intimacy with the ʻāina.

My experience of working on the ʻāina with my body didn't just connect me to the ʻāina; it reveals to me how the phrase aloha ʻāina is overused or even abused. Intense as it is, the workday was just a 4-hour activity after all. Some Kānaka Maoli, however, have to work longer hours every day in the field. Witnessing how Native Hawaiians are actually loving, caring, and fighting for the ʻāina, I realize that aloha ʻāina is not, and should never be, merely a slogan but an everyday practice. It is the everyday resurgence of Native Hawaiians. Thinkers of everyday resurgence challenge us to move beyond the state-centered recognition of Indigenous rights and look at how everyday acts of resurgence "create spaces in which Indigeneity is centered" (Elliott 70). Through their everyday act of resurgence, Michael Elliot also argues, Indigenous peoples "[reconnect] with land, culture, and community" (67). At Ka Papa Loʻi O Kānewai, Native Hawaiians create a space where Kānaka Maoli values are centered and they are reconnected to the ʻāina. For Kānaka Maoli, aloha ʻāina is a way of life, and I argue that we should stop appropriating the term in a way that is draining the profound and deep meaning and feeling out of the phrase.

In conclusion, whereas the anthropocentric and capitalist Western mapping commodifies land as well as alienate human from the land, the moʻolelo of Kānaka Maoli function to strengthen the relationship between Native Hawaiians and the ʻāina as well as human and other-than-human beings. In other words, moʻolelo, to borrow the language of Adamson, "eloquently reveal[s] the depth of a [Kānaka Maoli's] sense of place in which they live" (7). Moreover, the Hawaiian values and worldview mentioned above have been passed down for hundreds of years by the kūpuna of Kānaka Maoli, and it continues to thrive. At Ka Papa Loʻi O Kānewai, the Hawaiian worldview and values are still being passed down to the next generation. This is an example not only of how Kānaka Maoli map and honor their deep relationship with the ʻānia but also of Native Hawaiian resilience. This is why Craig DeSilva considers Ka Papa Loʻi O Kānewai "a piko (center) for Hawaiian teaching and learning" (n.p.).

The landscape of Mānoa Valley has changed dramatically since the arrival of white settlers, and the streams and kalo were, and still are, gravely threatened. This is because, to borrow Fujikane's words, "Capital produces a human alienation from land and from the elemental forms that constitutes a foundational loss" (5). However, Kānaka Maoli shows their resilience by reviving the kalo culture at Ka Papa Loʻi O Kānewai.

Furthermore, as Lane-Kamahele contends, through moʻolelo we can cultivate "engagements across time and generations between communities, place, and people that we are able to personalize relationships" and "by *talking story* and hearing the *stories* we keep the connections alive, connections that become timeless" (133; emphasis added). In other words, moʻolelo tie different generations of Kānaka Maoli and non-Hawaiians together so that we can "[continue] to work together and embracing change" (Lane-Kamahele 128) and to push back against the exploitative Western cartography.

## Works Cited

Adamson, Joni. *American Indian Literature, Environmental Justice, and Ecocriticism: The Middle Place*. U of Arizona P, 2001.

Cho, John J., Roy A. Yamakawa, and James Hollyer. "Hawaiian Kalo, Past and Future." *Sustainable Agriculture*, U of Hawaiʻi, 2007, pp. 1–8.

DeSilva, Craig. "Caring for Kalo Teaches Hawaiian Values." *Island Scene*, May 30, 2018, https://islandscene.com/caring-for-kalo-teaches-hawaiian-values?utm_source=wellbeingHI. Accessed Mar. 29, 2019.

Elliott, Michael. "Resurgence: The Drive for Renewed Engagement and Reciprocity in the Turn Away from the State." *Canadian Journal of Political Science*, vol. 51, no. 1, 2018, pp. 61–81.

Fujikane, Candace. *Mapping Abundance for a Planetary Future: Kanaka Maoli and Critical Settler Cartographies in Hawaiʻi*. Duke UP, 2021.

Gregory, Regina. "USA-Hawaii-Restoring the Life of the Land: Taro Patches in Hawaiʻi." *The EcoTipping Points Project*, Aug. 2014, http://ecotippingpoints.org/our-stories/indepth/usa-hawaii-taro-agriculture.html. Accessed Mar. 23, 2019.

Kealiikanakaoleohaililani, Kekuhi and Giardina P. Christian. "Embracing the Sacred: An Indigenous Framework for Tomorrow's Sustainability Science." *Sustain Sci*, vol. 11, 2016, pp. 57–67.

Lane-Kamahele, Melia. "Further Considerations of Community, Culture, and Change." *The George Wright Forum*, vol. 34, no. 2, 2017, pp. 128–33.

McDougall, Brandy Nālani. *The Salt-Wind: Ka Makani Paʻakai*. Kuleana Oiwi, 2008.

Penn, David C. "Water Needs for Sustainable Taro Culture in Hawaiʻi." *Sustainable Taro Culture for the Pacific Conference*, edited by L. Ferentinos, Sept. 24–25, 1992, Honolulu, pp. 132–34.

Puleloa, William. "Native Hawaiians and Streams." *State of Hawaiʻi: Division of Aquatic Resources*, http://dlnr.hawaii.gov/dar/habitat/streams/cultural-importance/. Accessed Mar. 29, 2019.

Reed, T. V. "Toxic Colonialism, Environmental Justice, and Native Resistance in Silko's *Almanac of the Dead*." *MELUS*, vol. 34, no. 2, 2009, pp. 25–42.

Ryden, Kent C. *Mapping the Invisible Landscape: Folklore, Writing, and the Sense of Place*. U of Iowa P, 1993.

Schuler, Timothy A. "Uncovering the Potential of Honolulu's Hidden Streams." *Next City*, Aug. 22, 2016, https://nextcity.org/features/view/honolulu-sustainable-development-auwai-howard-hughes. Accessed Mar. 12, 2019.

Sterling, Elspeth P. and Catherine C. Summers. *Sites of Oahu*. Bernice P. Bishop Museum, 1978.

# 7

# Planetary Boundaries, Planetary Imaginary: Homing Pacific Eco-poetry

Hsinya Huang

Deriving from the Greek *oikos*, the term "eco" means house, home, household, family, and dwelling place. This chapter examines Indigenous Pacific eco-poetry of "homing in" to represent the unique Indigenous experience of islands as ecosystems that are dynamic and interconnected. Drawing on poetry by Kathy Jetñil-Kijiner of Marshall Islands, I investigate Indigenous homing experiences in conjunction with the violent history of nuclear militarism in the Pacific. Addressing the "slow violence" of nuclear radiations and enforced dislocation, a "delayed destruction that is dispersed across time and space" (Nixon 2), Jetñil-Kijiner's poetry testifies the drastic changes of Indigenous Pacific in lands and waters. The advancement of a violent colonial agenda could only be made possible at the expense of the Indigenous people's expulsion from their home(is)lands. The idea of "home" propels us to critique the imbrication of imperial power and environmental disruption by contemplating on the loss of home for Pacific islanders, who live or die at the forefront of global crisis. I contest Johan Rockström's idea of planetary boundaries (PB), which defines the environmental limits within which human beings can safely operate, with the concept of planetary imaginary as evidenced in Jetñil-Kijiner's eco-poetry to examine Indigenous voices of "homing in." I argue that while colonialism has inflicted pervasive and oppressive influence on the ecosystems as home, planetary thinking in Jetñil-Kijiner's eco-poetry anchors the islanding creativity that enacts a recognition of Indigenous peoples and their home(is)lands as entities deserving to thrive with dignity and reciprocity. This chapter centers on Indigenous experiences of militarization and nuclearization in Marshall Islands to lay bare the colonial trajectory in Oceania and the islanding resistance through Indigenous contestation and voice. Ultimately, it showcases the epidemic violence integral to the Anglo-European cleaving of the world and concludes with planetary kinship, through which the Indigenous contacts and combats the colonial, and PB crossed over to become planetary imaginary.

## From Planetary Boundaries to Planetary Imaginary

Never in human history as now in the twenty-first century has our species' ability to cope with planetary change been so urgent. The geochemist Paul Crutzen and ecologist Eugene Stoermer nominate the concept of the Anthropocene to suggest the massive human impact on the Earth system (Crutzen and Stoermer 2000; Castree 2014). This is complemented by the PB hypothesis of Rockström et al., who identified nine earth system processes to create "a safe operating space for humanity."[1] "A safe operating space for humanity" indicates the planetary life support systems essential for human survival; wherever and whenever these boundaries are crossed, there would be abrupt and irreversible changes to the Earth. To observe these limits becomes the precondition for sustainable development (472–73).

This hypothesis of PB in examining the current impact of the Anthropocene, however, has its oversight. While it emphasizes the significance of human action in relation to the capacity of the Earth to sustain it, the biophysical constraints or thresholds cannot address the extreme impact of radioactive militarism since the first atomic bomb blast in 1945, immeasurable due to the possibility of a total annihilation of human civilization. Boundaries no longer hold, and the world then seems to have no other horizon than an apocalyptic one, which, for Jacques Derrida, also encompasses the possible obliteration of every archive; it was against that horizon of "remainderless destruction" (30). Deprived of any real referent, the nuclear regime, as Derrida mobilizes it, can simply be set up "through that fabulous textuality": "a myth, an image, a fiction, a utopia, a rhetorical figure, a fantasy, a phantasm" (23).

Pivoting on Derrida's idea of "textuality," part of my work postulates how, in the face of the nuclear devastating effects, literatures or imaginaries become essential to arouse awareness and forge a model of shared agency to make possible a collective urgent response to the nuclear catastrophe. Opposing Derrida's theoretical abstraction, however, I hold that radioactive toxicity should not be rendered as apocalyptic fantasy; it is rather, as Elizabeth DeLoughrey puts it, "a historical, global, and ongoing presence" ("Radiation Ecologies and the Wars of Light" 476). The toxicity is especially pervasive across the Pacific region, which does not merely destroy human life but remains in the oceanic body and in the risk of continued ecological degradation. For those who suffer, survive, or die in the midst, it results in extreme traumatic experiences, and for the ocean planet we call home, it marks the start of a new unit of geological time, the Anthropocene epoch, and usher in slow and pervasive environmental violence. Jan Zalasiewicz et al. propose that the Anthropocene commences with the first A-bomb test in 1943 of the Manhattan Project and the stratigraphic presence of radioactive elements from that blast and the much larger nuclear ones that took place over the following decade (Zalasiewicz et al. 2011, 2018; Monastersky 2015; Jacobs 2015;

---

[1] The nine processes include ocean acidity, chemical balances, atmospheric aerosols, biodiversity, land use types, freshwater, nitrogen and phosphorous cycles, and stratospheric ozone density. See Rockström et al. 472–75.

Pugh 2021). The radionuclides, such as long-lived plutonium-239, continue to wreak havoc, which we have no reason not to "equate with the annihilation of humanity as a whole" (Derrida 28).

Specifically relevant to this current study is the US detonation of sixty-seven nuclear bombs between 1946 and 1958, which vaporized the Marshall Islands and caused the islanders exiling from their home. These islands were chosen precisely because of the colonial/imperial myth of islands as isolated and remote sites, apt for any scientific (nuclear) or laboratory experiments (Hau'ofa 2008; DeLoughrey 2013; Keown 2020).[2] While the Marshall Islands were exploited as segregated testing grounds, the islanders exposed to nuclear fallout became human subjects for radiative experiments. The catastrophe occurs with each individual death and as it accumulates, the loss may involve the entire Oceania islands' society, culture, tradition, and memory. Despite his abstraction, Derrida is accurate in saying that the nuclear war "can only come about in the name of that which is worth more than life, that which, giving its value to life, has greater value than life" (30). Life destroyed is not to be limited to human species; it also entails a whole universe of the islands and the environment of the Pacific. The entire archive of island culture, values, knowledge, and tradition about the ocean, which constitutes 70 percent of our planet and which the world relies on for survival, could have been gone. What is at stake is the entire cultural and social memory, which is a large part of human civilization on the expansive waters and (is)lands.

Derrida's conceptualization of an "archive," as applied to the context of the nuclear Pacific, unveils a violent history of colonial brutality and Indigenous suffering. By the time the testing ended, Bikini Atoll was pronounced to be uninhabitable for at least 24,000 years, the half-life of the plutonium-239 (DeLougrey 2013; Keown 2020). Not until the US belatedly completed a partial decontamination in the late 1970s and 1980s, did the islanders of the Bikini and Enewetak Atoll return to find their entire lagoon still severely contaminated (Rust 2019; Keown 2020). The US deposited the most lethal debris and soil into Runit Dome on Enewetak Atoll. To date, the Dome still holds more than 3.1 million cubic feet of US-produced radioactive debris, including lethal amounts of plutonium (Rust 2019).

The Dome, reminiscent of the A-bomb Dome in Hiroshima and known as "the Tomb" to ri-Enewetak, becomes the visible manifestation of the nuclear legacy, a symbol of the sufferings which the Marshallese experienced for the US security. The whole island remains heavily contaminated, and alarms arise about the fact that rising sea levels and expanding cracks within the concrete are speeding up radioactive isotopes leaking from the Dome into the lagoon (Keown n.p.). The Runit Dome represents a "concrete archive" of the nuclear and colonial legacies in the Pacific, as Michelle Keown puts it brilliantly (n.p.). To further illustrate, the word "concrete" may literally convey two other senses: first, it represents the military "concrete" infrastructure which is the storage

---

[2] That the Euro-American construct of small islands as enclosure to provide a ready-made laboratory for studying science has been vital to theories of ecology in ways that inform much of modernity in complicity with colonialism and imperialism. See DeLougrey (2013, p. 14, n. 10).

of radioactive debris—the "concrete shell"; second, the Dome is precisely "concrete" evidence of the legacies of US nuclear violence across the Pacific. While Keown's idea of "concrete archive" addresses the forces of radiative colonialism on the Indigenous past, my reading of Jetñil-Kijiner poetry explicates what is lived and experienced as the "lifeworld" of shared islanders' experiences. The site of nuclear detonation is, in the words of humanist geographers such as Anna Buttimer and Charles Travis, the "lifeworld" (*lebenswelt*) of the Marshallese islanders (Buttimer 1976; Travis 2017). The islanders' sense of belonging to the Pacific stems from the fact that they live together for thousands of years across this oceanic world. Viewed as an "ongoing historical process," the nuclear militarism results in devastating human suffering and brutality, which disrupts the "lifeworld" of the Pacific islanders—"lifeworld" as constituted by the islanders' spatial, temporal, and cultural experiences from which all things in their environment emerge as meaningful as home.

It is against this backdrop of the "lifeworld" of Indigenous Pacific that nuclear colonialism needs to be investigated. Islands are "lifeworld" rather than void isolates as the imperial discourse of modernity and science has construed. The nuclear regime is not to be understood in abstract terms but rather it must be grounded in the "concrete" (material, cultural, and historical) experiences of Indigenous Pacific, that is, in the "lifeworld" of the islanders who experience nuclearism first-hand. Buttimer observes that human consciousness embraces "a world of values, a world of goods, a practical world. It is anchored in a past and directed towards a future; it is a shared horizon, though everyone may construe it in a uniquely personal way" (281). She translates "lifeworld" as the "culturally defined spatiotemporal setting or horizons of everyday life" (277). As the Anthropocene posits human agency as a geological force and PB define the thresholds within which human agency can operate safely, the concept of "lifeworld" facilitates alternative geographical perspectives by retrieving the islanders' sense of their waters and dwelling, of place and environment, which they embrace as "home."

By examining culturally defined horizons of everyday life, this chapter provides a dynamic version of the islanders' place and time attuned to the entire human survival and thriving in the face of planetary catastrophe. Whereas the many sites of life and culture in the nuclear Pacific become vulnerable or dismantled, how can a responsible nuclear criticism be aligned with anticolonial practice of the Pacific Indigenous people? How does such a criticism shed light on our common planetary future on which the survival and thriving of human life depends? Given the many dimensions and enormous scales of the crisis, how can we collectively constitute ourselves and think and act "planetarily"?

In considering the notion of home, we turn toward ecology. Judith Plant stresses the importance of "the practice of coming to terms with our ecological home" (ix). Environmental action is based on a revaluing and redefining of the (ocean) planet as home (ibid. 21). The planet as home becomes the locus of liberation from a culture of violent divides. It is at home where people have a measure of command over the creation of common goods and values. It is through everyday encounters at home in their "lifeworld" that we perceive Indigenous Pacific as the contested site of ecological crisis and opportunities. For these encounters nurture stories, meanings, and imaginaries we tell and utilize. The planetary imaginaries, which Pacific islanders' poetry powerfully construe—the imaginaries of "a species of alterity," a way Gayatri Chakravorty Spivak names as the planet—carry us away from the epistemologically patronizing and analytically confusing proximity of "global," "globalization," and the like. By focusing on "the planetary," we call for humility, care, sharing, and other ways of feeling and sensing the otherness that makes relationality possible in the first place. The ensuing crisis of the nuclear militarism is not understandable if we situate the harm elsewhere in a remote sea. Not until we make sense of the consequences by thinking, feeling, and acting with the Indigenous people of Oceania, do we envision an opportunity for the ultimate threat to the survival of the entire human race.

## Contesting Nuclear Pacific as (Non)Home

More than any other site, the Marshall Islands are victims of the nuclear Pacific, associated with the "contained space of a laboratory" (DeLoughrey, "The Myth of Isolates" 167–84). Jetñil-Kijiner's poetry emerges from her "island home" to bear witness to radiation ecologies in the Pacific (*Iep Jāltok* 20). By invoking eco-poetry from "island home" as a form of resistance against nuclear militarism, her poetics explores the legacy of nuclear and atomic age as common and contemporary experiences of the islanders on the (is) lands and waters they call "home," or rather, "without a home" (*Iep Jāltok* 24).

Jetñil-Kijiner charts the trajectory of the Indigenous subject that refuses to be subordinated to nuclear powers of Euro-American imperialism. The devastating US hydrogen bomb test at Bikini Atoll on March 1, 1954, was a thousand times more powerful than the atomic bomb dropped on Hiroshima. It exposed thousands of islands in the surrounding area to radioactive fallout. The exiled islanders said they are too fearful to ever go back because of nuclear contamination (Rust n.p.). The US nuclear experiments in the Marshall Islands ended in 1958 but the effects were long-lasting, including irreversible environmental contamination and indefinite displacement of the islanders with "only a passport to call home," to use Jetñil-Kijiner's words in her poem "Dear Matafele Peinam," which she read in the 2014 United Nations Climate Summit (*Iep Jāltok* 70).

As "Dear Matafele Peinam" addresses the impact of climate change on Indigenous islands, it nevertheless involves "more than climate change," which Donna Haraway insightfully pinpoints: It is also "extraordinary burdens" of toxicity, "vast genocides of people and other critters, etc., etc., in systemically linked patterns that threaten major system collapse after major system collapse after major system collapse" ("Anthropocene, Capitalocene, Plantationocene, Chthulucene" 159). The nuclear militarism in the Pacific results from "systemically linked patterns." A systemic violence has been sustained and reproduced by pervasive forms of imperialism, colonialism, and modernity in complicity with one another. This legacy continues to impact the island space and its inhabitants, transforming the islanders' lifeworld into imperial laboratory and nuclear testing ground. What is more, the damages have cumulated toward a situation where we call "ecological collapse," i.e., a drastic reduction of the ecosystem in carrying capacity for all organisms to the extent that often results in mass extinction. Jetñil-Kijiner was saddened at the age of fifteen when she conducted a "history project" and "read firsthand accounts of what we call / jelly babies / tiny beings with no bones / skin—red tomatoes" (*Iep Jāltok* 20). It was not just the case of birth defects, but it also invoked the vast genocides and radical extermination of the Pacific islanders alongside the sea creatures they feed on in a planetary scale as the ocean disseminates the nuclear toxicity over generations.

While the exilic climate refugees have "only a passport to call home," hair in Jetñil-Kijiner's nuclear poem "Fishbone Hair" is said to be "rootless," "without home" (*Iep Jāltok* 24). The poem is dedicated to her niece Bianca, who suffered from leukemia and passed away in 2011. Jetñil-Kijiner seeks to make sense of Bianca's death and disclose the sophisticated nature of the US nuclear legacies in the Marshall Islands. The harmed Indigenous body comes to merge with the planetary body in nuclear disasters. Jetñil-Kijiner uncovers the consequence of nuclear militarism by alluding to heliotrope as traces of modernity and nuclearization. Representing the nuclear testing on Bikini Atoll in a solar metaphor, she renders the explosion as a disruptive event to the islanders' everyday life: "over 50 years ago / when they were out at sea just miles away from Bikini / the day the sun exploded / split open / and rained ash on the fishermen's clothes" (29). As much as the islanders savor the sun in their oceanic lifeworld, the nuclear weapons came to them in the form of solar/cosmic explosion on one of the common days, as it took place in Hiroshima and Nagasaki, disrupting the labor of the fishermen without their knowing where these weapons came from. It was enormous in scale for the explosion is likened to that of our solar/comic center. The enlightenment of the Western nuclear science ironically led to the immediate darkness and disorientation of the ocean planet.[3]

Jetñil-Kijiner performed the poem in a video clip that was released in time for Nuclear Remembrance Day when Marshallese commemorated the detonation of the Bravo bomb. The poem starts inside Bianca's bedroom, where Jetñil-Kijiner found "two ziplocks / stuffed / with rolls and rolls of hair": "Maybe it was my sister / who stashed away Bianca's locks in ziplock bags / locked it away so no one could see / trying to save that / rootless hair / that hair without a home" (*Iep Jāltok* 24). Reading hair as a part object, which retrieves the repressed traumatic memory, she does not merely mourn the passing of a young life but muses on the common death of many islanders and loss

---

[3] Elizabeth DeLoughrey's seminal essay on radiation ecologies "Heliotropes: Solar Ecologies and Pacific Radiations" explores the complex relationship between ecology as a discipline and the radiative legacy of the militarized Pacific, through which she delves into the imperial intention to normalize nuclear energy to that of the sun. Rehistoricizing nuclear explosions within the context of atomic discourse, she discloses a heliocentric global modernity in complicity of imperial militarism and colonialism. See also Rebecca Hogue on nuclear normalization and Robert Jocobs's article on the impact of the nuclearization of the Pacific on the global ecosystem.

of their island home. She reaches a point of convergence where physical fallout of hair conflates with radioactive fallout of the bomb. The fallout of hair as "rootless" signifies the effacement of any possible trace of home and root, and culture and memory. Bianca's tiny body maps the nuclear Pacific: "There had been a war / raging inside Bianca's six-year-old bones / white cells had staked their flag / they conquered the territory of her tiny body / they saw it as their destiny / they said it was manifested / It / all / fell / out" (25). The individual body is "conquered" as "the territory," reminiscent of the waters and islands that are colonized. The bombs which killed numerous civilians in the Pacific left even more sickened by the fallouts. The toxic body merges with the toxic planetary body. As the islanders feed on the contaminated fishes, the nuclear war turns the 6-year-old girl's body into a battlefield. Bianca contracts leukemia, doubtfully resulting from having polluted fish, which is the islanders' daily diet: Bianca loved / to eat fish / she ate it raw ate it fried ate it whole / she ate it with its head / slurping on the eyeball jelly / leaving only / tiny / neat / bones" (27).

The poem ends with a fragmentary stanza, projecting the disastrous and long-lasting impact of not only the bomb (explosive event) but the fallout (prolonged progress of slow violence):

Thin
    rootless
        fishbone hair
   black
      night
  sky
net
       catch
  ash
    catch
   moon  catch
star

for you Bianca
for you.

As this visual image reminisces about the brokenness of the Indigenous body and dwelling place, it also fosters a model of shared agency from which it can become possible to respond to the catastrophe collectively and urgently. By retrieving nuclear toxicity as an everyday reality and process in "lifeworld," Jetñil-Kijiner does not merely tell a story of a singular person but forges shared agency in her planetary imaginaries which involve the sky, stars, ocean, and the (is)lands in totality. Pivoting on the relationship between the I and the second person addressed here and now, the poem evokes an uncanny sense of living amidst accumulated disruption, rendering the nuclear catastrophe an ongoing ecological process.

## Testifying from Island Home/Dome/Tomb

In her Dome poem, Jetñil-Kijiner testifies this present nuclear process from the farthest atolls in the Marshalls, where she witnesses the disastrous confluence of the cracked Runit Dome, sea-level rising, and leaking nuclear waste into the lagoons, turning "island home" into "a concrete shell that houses death" ("Dome Poem Part III: 'Anointed'"). The Runit Dome was once just Runit, one of the islets that made up Enewetak atoll. As the US nine nuclear explosions burned down the atoll, in its place was a crater into which a huge amount of highly radioactive plutonium-239 was later collected, dumped, and concreted. The islanders were forced to depart and do not return until this day. With her distinct lyricism, Jetñil-Kijiner composed the Dome poem and performed it from the Dome itself. This act of performing what may have been buried underwater constitutes a ritual for the poet to mourn the death of numerous lives, both human and more-than-human. Jetñil-Kijiner asks what would happen if she used "this monstrosity to create art" ("New Year, New Monsters, New Poems")?

The Dome poem consists of three parts. "Part I: The Voyage" features the voyage Jetñil-Kijiner takes to Enewetak, and by way of Bikini Atoll, returns to where she starts, Majuro. Her journey over four to five days and nights passes with "swapping life stories, staring at the horizon, watching the crew steer and change sails, spotting baby whales, dolphins, and flying fish, watching the line for a tugging mahimahi (dolphin fish), tracing stars, wave patterns, singing ukuleles." Her voyaging experience is oceanic in totality. She encounters an ocean of multispecies connectivity, in which sea creatures such as flying fish and its predator mahimahi migrate along a path created by the Pacific currents and form the vibrant matter of the wide and vast waters. She observes the sky as well as the ocean, tracing what is above in the galaxies and underneath the patterns of waves, and in this way, discloses a cosmic order of time and space pertaining to the islanders. In her narrative, the vertical dimension of the planet intertwines with the flow and liquidity of the ocean. It features a collective journey in the sense that there are also her fellow Fijian crew alongside more-than-human beings. It is furthermore a ceremonial return to the nuclear ground zero. She becomes the one to witness and recover the hidden stories of her island home in its oceanic totality.

"Part II: Of Islands and Elders," as Jetñil-Kijiner renders it, appears "counterintuitive" in the sense that the Dome poem reverses the physical journey by starting from the last stop at Bikini. Thereby, it denotes multiple layers of significance to formulate a poem from the end which yet meets the beginning writ large. For Bikini evokes memories and visions of the nuclear testing as "just one—albeit a most pernicious one—of the many colonial phenomena and processes that affect the Pacific region" (Teaiwa, "bikinis and other s/pacific n/oceans" 87). The A-bombs in Hiroshima and Nagasaki did not end the world wars, but quite the contrary, the nuclear legacies continue until this day, which Teresia Teaiwa details and critiques in her lengthy volume (2001). Bikini epitomizes all these legacies of nuclear violence.

Part II of the Dome poem commences with a photo of what ostensibly looks like a regular lagoon but is in effect the crater created by the Bravo bomb. The tiny speck of the canoe only appears to contrast the spacious blue that was once the site of the largest nuclear blast ever detonated in the world. Framed in an initial narrative among panoramic visuals of the poet's island home, which has now been turned into a site of toxicity, Part II explores how the bomb inflicts extreme violence and the ongoing Indigenous erasure, physically and ideologically. The journey is, nonetheless, a reluctant detour. For Jetñil-Kijiner has never prepared herself enough to "reflect on what it would mean to visit this site that was the source of so much pain and legacies of trauma" ("Dome Poem Part II: Of Islands and Elders"). How to accommodate or commemorate a wound that is too deep to bear?

Part II delivers a contemplative process before the story can be told and lyricism formed to confront a history buried and an island home incinerated. After taking a wrong turn as if the arrival were to be deferred, in front of the poet is a burned-out bunker, and to the side "an islet that look[s] as if it [were] missing a limb." The visuality of dismemberment retrieves the apocalyptic moment when the island was partially vaporized by the blast. She then realizes that what was physically gone is no longer a part of their cultural and mnemonic scape, either. For no one, not even an elder, is able to remember its name. The only clue is the neighboring island called Nam, which is still alive. The name "Nam" refers to the once "pantry" of a ri-Bikini Irooj or chief and was one of the islands reserved for food for the ancient community when the rainfall made these islands abundant with food. Whenever supplies ran low on the main island that housed most population of the Bikinian community, the islanders would sail to these farther islands for provisions. The islands also nurtured massive breadfruit trees that supplied most of the materials to build their "walaps," large canoes that ri-Bikini and ri-Enewetak were known for. Approaching the dismembered island, she reimagines and maps the islands' ancient abundance through a powerful narrative of her islanding and seafaring ancestry. It is in this remapping of her island home that she contrasts and confronts the traumatic impacts of the nuclear legacies at home as an irreversible rupture. Jetñil-Kijiner comes to testify that the bomb blast incinerates a once thriving island home that would have provided materials for nurturing plentiful and lavish island community and for making their voyaging canoes. An island does not merely provide materials for physical well-being but is key to their lived experience and heritage. Its elimination means the disappearance of the material base on which the islanders rely to keep their oceanic tradition intact. The removal of the islanders' lifeworld as well as the entire voyaging knowledge is a condition near to cultural and etho-genocide.

It is then not surprising that upon return to Majuro, Jetñil-Kijiner learns about the passing of Elder Limeyo Abon, who, at the age of 14, lived on Rongelap Atoll the day when the Bravo bomb exploded in Bikini, and radioactive ash rained down on her island of Rongelap. While Abon spent the rest of her life traveling worldwide to tell her stories, her passing symbolizes the crisis of a significant part of Indigenous testimony on nuclear militarism. It denotes the passing of "a walking encyclopedia of nuclear legacy knowledge," as the poet returns to face the death of still another elder, Bill Graham, former Peace Corp volunteer and RMI Nuclear Advocate, whom she has recently consulted for her poetry. This passing of the generation of islanders' elders who experienced the nuclear Pacific first-hand alerts the poet to the urgency of telling the story and passing it on. The story is precisely about "a place to call home, a place to live freely," as Abon said to *Japan Times* ("Dome Poem Part II: Of Islands and Elders"). For not only is the geographical space of an island gone due to nuclear detonations, but the removal and displacement of the islanders threatens to eradicate and exterminate their culture, tradition, and heritage, all embodied in "island home."

Part II is trigged by the passing of the elders. "Should there be a ceremony? A prayer perhaps? A poem"? Jetñil-Kijiner realizes that a poem is a ceremony, mourning, and prayer. Conflating images she spots earlier over her journey shape and reshape the constellations of meaning and enlighten her to fabricate a pome of interconnectivity and entanglement. She desegregates in disaggregation of all these entangled images: "the Bravo blast, the canoe in an empty lagoon, the obliterated island, the stunted island, the burnt trees that once fed her ancestors and built canoes, and the deaths of two legacies of nuclear activism." For her, writing is a way of generating meaning and understanding in the aftermath of enormous loss:

> What happens when islands
> that nourished us with the wisdom of their bodies
> become barren
> amputated—
> do they mourn the unfurling greenery
> of canoes never birthed?
> massacred
> murdered
> and no one remembers
> And how do we mourn elders
> who were islands
> lush with knowledge and story?

It is precisely the crisis of memory in "no one remembers" that puts her embarking on the journey for understanding the nuclear atrocity. The journey brings her to mourn for island home, now "barren" and "amputated," and for her relations and fellow islanders, "massacred" and "murdered." At the end of a series of questionings for "how" and in a subordinate clause, she converges the bodies of the elders with "islands lush with knowledge and story." In the elders' bodies resides repressed Indigenous memory of the nuclear impact, a racial memory that exists beyond conscious remembering. The tortured bodies of the islanders conflate with the altered body of the incinerated island. Both bodies bear the colonial/nuclear inscription and constitute a material base for remembering the displaced past and population. Jetñil-Kijiner recounts the elders' stories which are trans-generated from the communal body of the elders and islands. To be precise, the elders and islands are not segregated bodies; they merge into a communal body. This communal body becomes the very site from which words, stories, knowledge, and testimonies of nuclear violence originate. It provides "the index of a *history* yet to be made," to borrow from Michel de Certeau (227).

Jetñil-Kijiner poetic endeavor commences with her history project in her teens and matures as she writes to become a historian, awakened to the unspoken and unspeakable past of her "island home." She recognizes that the elders are "islands lush with knowledge and story." "Knowledge and story" refer to truth in the bodying forth of the islands' nuclear legacies and Indigenous resistance against them. They represent the character of a people and of its lifeworld as an integrated whole to fight against historical amnesia. The elders and islands merge as an evocative synonym for culture and heritage of resistance under the hegemonic dominance and nuclear abusive powers. Cultural coding returns in the elders' testimonies and stories, which she is eager to catch up and pass on.

The ending of Part II goes beyond "sorrow" and "fury" into a transitional conjunction of "but" to transcend victimhood: "*But look– / right there / There exists / still/ some / green / Even after / a nuclear blast / life / continues to unfurl / its leaves*" (emphasis original). The islands' ecological flourishing brings forth a lifeworld amidst and despite "a nuclear blast." Jetñil-Kijiner transforms and re-historicizes Marshallese experiences by recovering "knowledge and story" as a "regenerative healing practice" (Hogue 2). Part II ends in a beacon of hope in ecological futurity, in which she foreshadows "the narratives of creation" (ibid. 13) in the final part of the Dome Poem, "Anointed."

Indeed, as Rebecca H. Hogue pinpoints, the poem frames the Island's two existences, one being that of life, ecology, and regeneration and the other, of nuclear waste, concrete shell, and death (14). Dome Poem Part III "Anointed" inextricably converges these two existences in recognizing "Runit's past as place of life, productivity, and generativity against what the ri-Enewetak now call Runit 'the tomb'" (ibid. 14–15). Unlike A-bomb Dome of Hiroshima, which has been memorized as an icon of the atomic ruins, Runit Dome is an imperial infrastructure to cover up precisely those ruins by burying them underneath into a "concrete shell," a "tomb." Both domes, nonetheless, bespeak the historical process of the nuclear Pacific and ongoing suffering of those afflicted. The nuclear explosions and subsequent interment of radioactive waste on the island transform the originally bountiful home of Enewetak's Indigenous peoples into a wasteful land, and in this way, efface the history and presence of the islanders (Keown n.p.).

In "Anointed," by addressing her home island as a second-person "you," Jetñil-Kijiner reinscribes Marshallese presence by exploring the cultural memories and legends. She enlivens the intimate stories relating to Runit Island to contest and combat the hegemonic powers of nuclearization. The opening line "I am coming to meet / see you" indicates Indigenous presence in the island-scape. Thereby, her affective encounter with the island discloses a landscape of past bounty. She maps its original abundance, replete with "breadfruit trees heavy with green globes of fruit whispering promises of massive canoes," "crabs dusted with white sand scuttled through pandanus roots," "looming coconut trees," "beds of ripe watermelon, swollen with juice," etc. And yet all these are no longer visible as she frames them within the past temporality of "you were a whole island, once." She repeats "green globes of fruit, pandanus roots, and whispers of canoes" only to punctuate the line with a question mark. It is this sense of loss that triggers her quest. She comes to uncover and remember the stories and (is)landscapes that have been usurped: "What stories will I find?"; "Will I find an island or a tomb?"; "Who knows the stories of the life you led before?"; "How shall we remember you"?

In effect, Jetñil-Kijiner epitomizes the generations of Marshall Islanders who have suffered the consequences of US nuclear testing and journeyed to experience and explore the island first-hand. The poem juxtaposes the former natural fecundity with the nuclear destruction archived in the "solidified history" of "incinerated trees, a cracked dome, a rising sea, a leaking nuclear waste with no fence" ("Dome Poem Part III: 'Anointed'"). The refrain of "you were a whole island, once" evokes a current fragmented image of her island home:

> Then you became testing ground. Nine nuclear weapons consumed you, one by one by one, engulfed in an inferno of blazing heat. You became crater, an empty belly. Plutonium ground into a concrete slurry filled your hollow cavern. You became tomb. You became concrete shell that houses death.
>
> (ibid.)

The verb "house" does not delineate shelter but rather problematize any connections to life and home. It ironically bespeaks the ways in which the island is haunted by a state of "unhousedness." The islanders do not simply face the loss of a material house but experience a sense of psychological homelessness. The passage constitutes remnants of nuclear detonations and evokes the collective trauma suffered by the islanders. The young mind searches for "more stories" by posing more questions:

> Who remembers you beyond your death? Who would have us forget that you were once green globes of fruit, pandanus roots, and whispers of canoes? Who knows the stories of the life you led before? ... I am looking for more stories. I look and I look.
>
> (ibid.)

The stories Jetñil-Kijiner summons pivot on "the shell," and taking it as a point of departure, she looks beyond the nuclear infrastructure to probe into an empowering legend of the island's first civilization. The legend has it that the turtle goddess gifted one of her sons, Letao, a piece of her shell, "anointed with power." The word "anoint" comes from the ancient Latin word *unguere*, which means "to smear." It denotes a sacred ritual of blessing by smearing a person with any perfumed oil to introduce a divine presence. The shell gave Letao the power to transform into anything, into trees and houses, and even to kindle the first fire. He gave this fire to a small boy, who almost burned his entire village to the ground. The poem thereby contrasts the elemental energy of Letao's first fire with the blast of the nuclear detonations that "consumed" Runit (Keown n.p.). Elizabeth DeLoughrey has noted that as a smoke screen to the nuclear denotations, the US invokes tropes of "a new dawn, a rising sun, and the birth of a new world," giving the bomb "a new kind of divinity" invented through technological innovation ("Heliotropes" 246). "Anointed" powerfully questions "this human usurpation of power over elemental forces," as Michell Keown suggests (n.p.). Jetñil-Kijiner ends the poem by questioning the legitimacy of the unnatural fire of the nuclear testing: "Who anointed them with the power to burn"?

William Bevis conceptualizes Indigenous experiences of "homing in," which highlights return to the state that includes a community, a place, and a past (585). Returning to one of her home islands, which has gone through immense nuclear catastrophe, operates to shape the poet's connection with the past and place. Unlike the examples of gain and reunion cited by Bevis, however, Jetñil-Kijiner maps her trajectory toward a collective loss. Homing in does not bring joy of reunion but painful recognition of a bountiful past and a lush island now destroyed. And yet it is through this homing voyage that the poet conveys value and meaning of returning to her home, past, and people. Jetñil-Kijiner uncovers the rich repository of Marshallese oral history and legend attached to Runit Island and its people. Performing the poem at the wounded site of her island nation, she resists hegemonic colonial and neocolonial powers through affirming the right to her historical and cultural heritage engrained and embedded in the island. The stories represent conditions necessary for a decolonial dignified life and finally for rejecting displacement and remaining in their communities of origin.

As she utters the final words of the poem, Jetñil-Kijiner stands firmly on the "shell concrete" and positions herself at the center of the Runit Dome. Her physical presence resists colonial erasure of her island, tradition, and heritage and reasserts the endurance of the Marshallese people. This island, as Michelle Keown states, should not have been a site of nuclear testing and waste dump; instead, it is "an integral part of a vast Marshallese 'sea of islands'" (n.p.). The island is the history, conveyed to the world through the poet's affective narrative, lyricism, and performance. The poem thus fashions a model of Indigenous articulation, in which home becomes an action of homing, and by "homing in," she renounces displacement and erasure and reclaims her "island home."

## Coda: Making Kin

In the same blog post she publicized her Dome poem, Jetñil-Kijiner reflects on another poem, "Monster," also linked to nuclear legacy ("New Year, New Monsters, New Poems"). "Monster" was performed in front of the A-bomb Dome in Hiroshima. The poet immediately recognized emotional and powerful connections as she encountered a *hibakusha*, A-bomb survivor, at Hiroshima Peace Museum. Such an encounter brings forth "many intersections," as she puts it, "with the nuclear legacy of the Marshalls." She testifies to how permeative the nuclear militarism is across the Pacific and yet how Indigenous survival should be taken seriously through mutual care, relational resilience, and interdependence, and by imagining a widening circle of associations pertaining to nuclear survivors.

Donna Haraway's idea of "making kin" formulates new associations in the contemporary world of planetary damage: "make-with—become-with, compose-with" ("Anthropocene, Capitalocene, Plantationocene, Chthulucene" 161). "Making 'kin'" means something other/more than entities tied by ancestry or genealogy (Haraway 2015, 2016; van Dooren and Chrulew 2022). Refracting on kinship beyond genetics, Haraway imagines a transformative and more just future, based on "kindness" beyond "ties by birth": "The kindest were not necessarily kin as family; making kin and making kind (as category, care, relatives without ties by birth, lateral relatives, lots of other echoes) stretch the imagination and can change the story" (161).

Jetñil-Kijiner demonstrates precisely such a category of care and relations by stretching her imagination and telling a story big and inclusive enough to accommodate kinship beyond blood ties. Her poetry performance with Aka Niviâna from Greenland, a collective poem titled "Rise," is still another distinct example. She traveled to Greenland's capital city Nuuk, where she met Inuk Artic poet Niviâna. Together, they embarked on a spiritual, planetary, and poetic journey to a crevasse-scarred melting glacier. As Greenland's glaciers melt and flow into the sea, Pacific islanders suffer from rising sea levels. They lay bare the climate impact on their respective island home as a shared process of environmental catastrophe. Thereby, they demonstrate an imagination of co-belonging and co-agency within cultures of Indigenous collective dissent.

The complex terrain of the imagination remains a way of understanding and exploring the manifestations of anthropogenic catastrophes. It is a way of seeing, sensing, thinking, and interpreting based on Indigenous sensibilities to their home places in connection with others. Facing planetary disasters, Haraway explains, "requires sympoiesis, or making-with, rather than auto-poiesis, or self-making" ("Anthropocene, Capitalocene, Plantationocene, Chthulucene" 162). For Jetñil-Kijiner, the survivors come together as she summons the islands and lands that suffer. Indigenous species, human or more-than-human, who suffer the impact of planetary catastrophes provide "the stories (and theories) that are just big enough to gather up the complexities and keep the edges open and greedy for surprising new and old connections," to put in the words of Haraway: "It matters what stories tell stories, it matters what thoughts think thoughts, it matters what worlds world worlds" (162).

In "Rise," Jetñil-Kijiner addresses her fellow islander of the Northern country: "I'm coming to you / from the land my ancestors chose. / Aelon Kein Ad, / Marshall Islands, / a country more sea than land. / ... / I bring with me these shells / that I picked from the shores / of Bikini atoll and Runit Dome." "Shells" from the islands of nuclear testing evoke "nuclear uncanny," using Jessica Hurley's words (95). Jetñil-Kijiner spreads and retells the story in front of the melting glaciers, home to many Inuit/Inuik people. The Freudian "uncanny," in its German original "das unheimliche" or in Homi Bhabha's translation "unhomely," refers to something familiar and rooted in the everyday life experience of "home" and yet becomes alienated, "unhomely." Jetñil-Kijiner's encounter with another Indigenous subject designates a jarring moment of disjunction that projects other island (home) time and space as a radical site to mourn for her lost community, place, and past, evolving around the very idea of "home," at once "ours and other" (Bhabha 165):

> I offer you this shell
> and the story of the two sisters
> as testament
> as declaration
> that despite everything
> we will not leave.
> …
> that our lives matter more than their power
> that life in all forms demands
> the same respect we all give to money
> that these issues affect each and everyone of us
> None of us is immune
> And that each and everyone of us has to decide
> if we
> will
> rise

By offering, a symbolic gesture of "making kind," she assembles a world of survivors, who "will not leave" home, and testifies by converging her stories with other stories. As the ice recedes and melts, Niviâna similarly experiences the vanishing of her traditional way of life evolving around the vibrant matter of the ice. And yet their joint reflections and lyricism as actions revive and reshape the islands by affirming the resistance of the Indigenous inhibiters who refuse to leave or vanish. The powerful end note of "rise" features Indigenous resurgence, ushering in a precious moment of trans-Indigenous connectivity. The performative power of their lyricism constitutes one of the "dissident acts," which, as Mary Louise Pratt's title shows, stems from "planetary longings" for symbiotic sustainability and flourishing (2022).

This chapter shows how abstract versions of nuclear criticism should be replaced with (is)landed Indigenous voices, practices, and actions, which connect multiple sites of Indigenous "island home" under siege. Reflecting on the word "Indigenous," Philip Deloria notes that "Indigenous peoples have been emigrants who left their homes for elsewhere. They have been migrants, travelers, and movers across the continents. […] And they have been refugees, people in flight, making their way with only the clothes on their backs" (2). It is precisely the Indigenous people on the (forced) move that eventually produce survivance relations, which will end the time of "hypersubjects," as Timothy Morton and Dominic Boyer construe. Out of planetary chaos, as they put it, we witness the emergence of "hyposubjects" instead, plural in its becoming-with and subscendent (moving toward relations) rather than transcendent (14). The first time in history, humans must deal with a problem and a responsibility of this magnitude and the young Indigenous poets-activists shoulder them fearlessly, shouting out their "testament" and "declaration" in decolonial solidarity. Telling stories of their home islands, which need to be shared and spoken, give them the space to connect, understand, testify, and declare that the Indigenous (hypo)subjects resist to vanish and they "deserve more than just to survive." They deserve to thrive.

## Works Cited

Bevis, William. "Native American Novels: Homing In." *Recovering the Word*, edited by Brian Swann and Arnold Krupat, U of California P, 1987, pp. 580–620.
Bhabha, Homi. *The Location of Culture*. Routledge, 1994.
Buttimer, Anne. "Grasping the Dynamism of Lifeworld." *Annals of the American Association of Geographers*, vol. 66, no. 2, 1976, pp. 277–92.
Castree, Noel. "The Anthropocene and Geography I: The Back Story." *Geography Compass*, vol. 8, no. 7, 2014, pp. 436–49.
Crutzen, Paul J. and Eugene F. Stoermer. "The Anthropocene." *Global Change*, Newsletter, vol. 41, 2000, pp. 17–18.
de Certeau, Michel. "Politics of Silence: The Long March of the Indians." *Heterologies: Discourse on the Other*. U of Minnesota P, 1986, pp. 225–33.
DeLoughrey, Elizabeth. "Heliotropes: Solar Ecologies and Pacific Radiations." *Postcolonial Ecologies: Literatures of the Environment*, edited by Elizabeth DeLoughrey and George B. Handley, Oxford UP, 2011, pp. 235–53.
———. "The Myth of Isolates: Ecosystem Ecologies in the Nuclear Pacific." *Cultural Geographies*, vol. 20, 2013, pp. 167–84.
———. "Radiation Ecologies and the Wars of Light." *MFS Modern Fiction Studies*, vol. 55, no. 3, 2009, pp. 468–98.
Deloria, Philip J. "Immigration and Indigeneity." *The American Historian*, 2021, pp. 1–2.
Derrida, Jacques. "No Apocalypse, Not Now (Full Speed Ahead, Seven Missiles, Seven Missives)." *Diacritics*, vol. 14, no. 2, 1984, pp. 20–31.
Hauʻofa, Epeli. *We Are the Ocean: Selected Works*. U of Hawaiʻi P, 2008.
Haraway, Donna. "Anthropocene, Capitalocene, Plantationocene, Chthulucene: Making Kin." *Environmental Humanities*, vol. 6, 2015, pp. 159–65.
———. *Staying with the Trouble: Making Kin in the Chthulucene*. Duke UP, 2016.
———. *When Species Meet*. U of Minnesota P, 2008.
Hogue, Rebecca H. "Nuclear Normalizing and Kathy Jetñil-Kijiner's 'Dome Poem.'" *Amerasia Journal*, vol. 47, no. 2, 2021, pp. 208–29.
Hurley, Jessica. "The Nuclear Uncanny in Oceania." *Commonwealth Essays and Studies*, 41, no. 1 (Autumn 2018), pp. 95–105.
Jacobs, Robert. "The Bravo Test and the Death and Life of the Global Ecosystem in the Early Anthropocene." *The Asia-Pacific Journal*, vol. 13, no. 29.1 (Jul. 20, 2015), pp. 1–17.
Jetñil-Kijiner, Kathy. "Dome Poem Part I: The Voyage." https://www.kathyjetnilkijiner.com/dome-poem-part-i-the-voyage/. Accessed Nov. 10, 2021.

Jetñil-Kijiner, Kathy. "Dome Poem Part II: Of Islands and Elders." https://www.kathyjetnilkijiner.com/dome-poem-part-ii-of-islands-and-elders/. Accessed Nov. 10, 2021.

———. "Dome Poem Part III: 'Anointed' Final Poem and Video." https://www.kathyjetnilkijiner.com/dome-poem-iii-anointed-final-poem-and-video/. Accessed Nov. 10, 2021.

———. "Fishbone Hair." Poetry Performance. https://www.kathyjetnilkijiner.com/videos-featuring-kathy/. Accessed Aug. 19, 2021.

———. *Iep Jāltok: Poems from a Marshallese Daughter*. The U of Arizona P, 2017.

———. "New Year, New Monsters, New Poems." Jan. 25, 2018. https://www.kathyjetnilkijiner.com/new-year-new-monsters-and-new-poems/. Accessed Nov. 10, 2021.

———. UN Climate Summit Poem "Dear Matafele Peinem." https://www.kathyjetnilkijiner.com/videos-featuring-kathy/. Accessed Sept. 28, 2021.

———. Videos. https://www.kathyjetnilkijiner.com/videos-featuring-kathy/. Accessed Nov. 10, 2021.

Jetñil-Kijiner, Kathy, and Aka Niviâna. "Rise: From One Island to Another." Poetry Performance, https://www.kathyjetnilkijiner.com/videos-featuring-kathy/. Accessed Oct. 7, 2021.

Keown, Michelle. "'A Story of a People on Fire': Nuclear Archives and Marshallese Cultural Memory in Kathy Jetñil-Kijiner's 'Anointed.'" *Art and Australia* Online, 2020, https://www.artandaustralia.com/online/image-not-nothing-concrete-archives/%E2%80%98-story-people-fire%E2%80%99-nuclear-archives-and-marshallese. Accessed Oct. 7, 2021.

Monastersky, Richard. "First Atomic Blast Proposed as Start of Anthropocene." *Nature: International Weekly Journal of Science*, Jan. 16, 2015, http://www.nature.com/news/first-atomic-blast-proposed-as-start-of-anthropocene-1.16739/. Accessed May 11, 2022.

Morton, Timothy and Dominic Boyer. *Hyposubjects: On Becoming Human*. Open UP, 2022.

Nixon, Rob. *Slow Violence and the Environmentalism of the Poor*. Harvard UP, 2011.

Plant, Judith. "Growing Home." *Home! A Bioregional Reader*, edited by Van Andruss et al., New Society Publishers, 1990, pp. ix–xi.

Pratt, Mary Louise. *Planetary Longings (Dissident Acts)*. Duke UP, 2022.

Pugh, Jonathan and David Chandler. *Anthropocene Islands: Entangled Worlds*. U of Westminster P, 2021.

Rockström, Johan et al. "A Safe Operating Space for Humanity." *Nature*, vol. 461, 2009, pp. 472–75.

Rust, Susanne. "How the U.S. Betrayed the Marshall Islands, Kindling the Next Nuclear Disaster." *Los Angeles Times*, Nov. 10, 2019, https://www.latimes.com/projects/marshall-islands-nuclear-testing-sea-level-rise/. Accessed Mar. 2, 2022.

Spivak, Gayatri Chakravorty. *Death of a Discipline*. Columbus UP, 2003.

Teaiwa, Teresia K. "bikinis and other s/pacific n/oceans." *The Contemporary Pacific*, vol. 6, 1994, pp. 87–109.

———. *Militarism, Tourism and the Native: Articulations in Oceania*. 2001. University of California, PhD dissertation.

Travis, Charles. "GeoHumanities, GIScience and Smart City *Lifeworld* Approaches to Geography and the New Human Condition." *Global and Planetary Change*, vol. 156, 2017, pp. 147–54.

van Dooren, Thom, and Matthew Chrulew. eds. *Kin: Thinking with Deborah Bird Rose*. Duke UP, 2022.

Zalasiewicz, Jan et al. "The Anthropocene." *Geology Today*, vol. 34, no. 5, 2018, pp. 177–81.

Zalasiewicz, Jan et al. "The Anthropocene: A New Epoch of Geological Time?" *Philosophical Transactions of the Royal Society*, 2011, pp. 835–41.

# 8

# The Ecological Vision of the Ainu Reflected in Their Oral Tradition

Hitoshi Oshima

The Ainu are culturally one of those "northern peoples" who reside in the regions around the North Pole. They used to be numerous, living in Hokkaido, the northern islands of the Japanese Archipelago, but actually, they have become very few and their traditional culture is almost dead because of Japanese colonization that took place at the end of the nineteenth century.

Japanese colonization over the Ainu was so terrible that it would not be unjust to use the term "cultural genocide." The colonizing government forced the Ainu to abandon their land, language, and way of living based on hunting; they had no other choice than going to Japanese schools, becoming farmers or factory workers only to lose their tradition. Today, very few of them speak Ainu and know little of their culture.

The Ainu have also suffered racial discrimination from the Japanese. In fact, many of them have hidden their ethnic identity for a long time just to avoid being discriminated against. Today, they are officially admitted as a distinct ethnic group in the Archipelago,[1] but few of them can feel freed from discrimination.[2]

The tragedy they have suffered can be seen in the discourse of Yukie Chiri (1903–1922), the first Ainu who translated their oral tradition into Japanese. In the preface of her book *Ainu Shin-yo-shu, the Anthology of Ainu Divine Songs* (1923), we find the following words:

> Long ago, this broad land of Hokkaido was a world in which our ancestors lived lives of freedom. Like children of unspoiled innocence, they lived their carefree lives in the embrace of Mother Nature, whose beloveds they were—what happy people they must have been! Oh, what a wonderful way of life their life must have been! That tranquil state of mind is already a thing of the past, a dream torn apart by the passing decades, for this earth is changing quickly, with hills and meadows becoming villages and villages becoming cities one after another.

---

[1] The Ainu Law was established in 1997 to protect Ainu culture and ethnicity, to promote respect for them, and to prevail knowledge of them.

[2] According to Ainu Association of Hokkaido, more than 30 percent of the Ainu have experienced racial discrimination. See their website: https://www.ainu-assn.or.jp/english/

Somehow, almost unnoticed, the form that Nature had worn in ancient times began to fade, and of the people who once dwelt so happily in field and mountain, most are no longer to be found. The few of us who remain of our race do nothing but stare in astonishment at the way the world has gone. Yet what we see from these eyes is that the radiance of the beautiful spirits of our forebears, whose every gesture was ruled by a sense of the spiritual, has been burdened with unease, consumed with discontent, weakened, dizzied, become helpless, gone beyond the reach of outside help, a miserable sight, something doomed to annihilation … Such is the name we have now–what a sad name it is that we now bear ….

But … the language that we use each day to share our feelings with our beloved ancestors has become worn with use. Even the beautiful words that have been handed down to us are mostly timid things, things which will surely be extinguished along with their weak, doomed users. Oh, what a heartbreaking thing—and almost already only a memory.

(Peterson 159-81)[3]

Her discourse is so powerful and beautiful that we cannot but applaud the brilliant skill of language she possessed. Yet the words are full of pain so much so that a normal Japanese reader could not but feel ashamed of their ancestors' barbarous deeds against them. He or she could feel all the more shame because Chiri apparently expresses no resentment to the Japanese.

The preface of Chiri's anthology quoted above surely indicates the barbarity of Modern Japan, but it reveals some ecological principles of the Ainu as well. The phrase "their carefree lives in the embrace of Mother Nature" shows their sense of harmony with the natural environment; the phrase "our forebears, whose every gesture was ruled by a sense of the spiritual" indicates their everyday life impregnated with the sense of the sacred. To the Ainu, Nature was definitely divine and sacred. Their ecology was based on that religious vision.

\* \* \*

To see their ecological worldview more in detail, let us look into *Kamui yukar*, especially the above-mentioned songs Chiri chose and translated into Japanese. *Kamui yukar* means "divine songs" believed by the Ainu to be "songs sung by a god or a goddess." Usually, they take the form of an autobiographical story narrated by a god or a goddess.

Among many of those songs, I choose a song titled "the Song the Owl God Sang," the first song in Chiri's anthology. I choose it because it reflects the Ainu ecological vision in quite a typical way.

The song begins with these beautiful phrases:

"Silver drops fall all around, golden drops fall all around," Thus I sang as I glided
    above a stream and over a village,
And as I passed I gazed down—

---

[3] Hereafter, translations of Chiri's text are by Benjamin Peterson. See *The Song the Owl God Sang: The Collected Ainu Legends of Chiri Yukie*, BJS Books, 2013, Kindle.

> Those who had been poor had become rich,
> Those who had been rich were now poor, it seemed.
> On the beach, human children were playing
> With toy arrows and toy bows.
> "Silver drops fall all around, Golden drops fall all around,"
> I sang as I flew over the children.
>
> (Peterson 192)

As you see, it tells a story about humans seen from above by the Owl God flying in the sky. From the phrase "Those who had been poor had become rich, Those who had been rich were now poor," we can see the Ainu conception of human society in which a poor human can be reborn as a rich one in the future and vice versa.

The next quotation presents a scene where the rich children tried to shoot an arrow to kill the Owl God in vain.

> The children of those who had been poor
> And were now rich
> Putting gold arrows to their gold bows
> Shot at me in turn with their gold arrows
> Which I caused to pass below me and above me.
>
> (Peterson 201)

The most interesting point of the quotation above is doubtlessly the last phrase: "Which I caused to pass below me and above me." To the Ainu, it is not the hunter but the prey that could choose the result of hunting. If the hunter is successful, it is thanks to the prey's benevolence; if not, it is due to the prey's resistance.

This does not mean that the Ainu disliked hunting. They were a hunting people as I said earlier; they lived on it. But their notion of hunting was different from ours. If they killed animals, they thought it is because the prey did a favor to them. As the following quotation shows, the Owl God chose a poor boy bullied by rich children and allowed him to kill Him.

> The boy, taking up an archer's stance,
> Biting his lower lip, took aim,
> And loosed the arrow.
> The little arrow flew well,
> It reached me, and with my hand
> I reached out and received that little arrow.
> I spiraled downward, the air rushing past me;
> I plummeted to the ground.
>
> (Peterson 214)

The reason for the Owl God's choice of the poor boy is that He knew the boy's ancestors were rich and noble. This judgment resembles our tendency to judge the poor people with nobility better than the nouveau riche who are mean, but it is not exactly the same.

The Ainu believed those who suddenly became rich knew little of how to treat the dead and that those who used to be rich would treat the dead body more respectfully so that the soul could get free from the body without difficulty. To the Ainu, knowing how to liberate the soul from the dead body was of utmost importance.

The Owl God's choice can also be attributed to a sense of social justice the Ainu possessed. He must have found it more judicial to be killed by a poor boy bullied by rich children than the contrary. In general, an Ainu divine song has a moral teaching. In the case of this song, it shows that the poor bullied by the rich should have more benefit than the others.

As I said above, the Owl God chose to be killed by the poor boy whose ancestors were rich, hoping the boy's family would treat His body decently. The following passage of the song shows that His hope was realized. The boy's family treated His body duly in accordance to the Ainu ritual tradition.

> He put me in at the east window, and then
> With well-chosen words, fluently told his tale.
> From inside the house, an old couple
> Came along, raising their hands up over their eyes.
> To look at them they were obviously terribly poor
> Yet they had a gentlemanly and a ladylike quality.
> They were startled to see me and bowed deeply;
> Respectfully adjusting their sashes
> They petitioned me thus:
> "Great owl god,
> You favor us by appearing at the inadequate hut
> Of mere peasants; accept our thanks.
> Once we were counted among the wealthy and great,
> And although now we are reduced to these straits,
> Mere paupers, in times past the local gods
> Often graced our home with their presence;
> Therefore, as today's sun
> Has already gone down, tonight allow us
> To shelter you, Great God …."

(Peterson 229–37)

What is remarkable about the quotation is that the Owl God whose body was dead could see everything happening to Him. He saw the boy and the boy's family sanctifying Him by a series of prayers and rites. You may wonder who it is that could see all that was happening. The answer is in the following quotation:

> Then, everyone lay down, and soon
> With resounding snores they all fell asleep.
> I sat there between the ears of my earthly body
> But before long, when midnight came,
> I arose.

"Silver drops fall all around,
Golden drops fall all around,"
I sang quietly,
As from the left side of the house to the right,
With beautiful sounds, I flew.

(Peterson 245)

It is this "I" sitting "between the ears" of the Owl's body that saw all. The speaker, "I," is of course the Owl God's soul. After having seen it, He arose, sang, and flew to Heaven, from where He gave thanks and a lot of presents to the boy's family who treated Him so well.

From a literary point of view, this "I" in the Ainu divine songs is quite interesting. The songs are similar in structure to our modern autobiographical novels, but "I" in an Ainu divine song is entirely the soul without the body whereas a modern autobiographical "I" is just a person in flesh and blood. If some writers such as Marcel Proust insist that their "I" is not a person in flesh and blood but a soul, they may have a literary vision similar to the Ainu's.

Let us see the end of the song of the Owl God who returned home in Heaven, satisfied with what He received from the poor family. He saw from above that the family became rich and happy because of the gifts He gave them; He also saw that they invited all the village people to their house to share their happiness instead of having an arrogant attitude toward them. Thanks to their generosity, even those who used to be unkind to them became kind now. The story has thus a happy ending, teaching us a lesson that we should always be generous and tolerant to others.

As for the soul that becomes independent from the body, I would like to add that the belief in the soul that the story allows us to see is a common trait among the Northern peoples living around the North Pole (Obayashi 15–20). The Inuit in Alaska and Canada, the Sami in Finland and Sweden, the Nivkh in Siberia, share more or less the same vision of the soul. You can see the practice of it, for example, in a Russian film titled *Kukushka*.[4]

According to Kyosuke Kindaichi (1882–1971), a Japanese pioneer of the Ainu studies, the Ainu conceived human beings and other beings as visible forms of the same invisible spirit residing in Heaven. Each being on earth or in the sky was considered by them as a visible form of the invisible spirit (Kindaichi 78–81). No wonder the Ainu worshiped all of them as gods or goddesses.

As for artifacts, they worshiped them in the same way because they thought each artifact was made from a divine natural being, by divine human's hands. A house, for example, was considered divine because it was made from a "divine" tree and by "divine" human hands. However, this does not mean that they never killed beings or destroyed anything on earth. As a hunting people, they admitted to men's killing of other creatures, of course. The important thing to the Ainu was not the killing itself, but how and for what purpose the killing was done. They placed great emphasis on the hunters' attitude

---

[4] The English title is *The Cuckoo*. The film is directed by Aleksandr Roghozhkin and distributed to many countries in 2002.

when they killed. The Ainu knew quite well that humans had to kill animals to survive, but they believed people should kill the animals with respect or awe for them. They never thought of killing the animals for pleasure or economical benefit.

Their respect and awe toward the prey are seen in the ritual they practiced for the animals they killed. As the above-quoted song shows, they purified the body of the prey by a series of rites and prayers so that the victim's soul could leave the body to return to Heaven.

Some may say that such beliefs and rituals are no more than childish justifications for their hunting and that they did not really treat animals as kindly as it appears. This thought is wrong because the Ainu never killed animals for pleasure or economical purposes. They had a religious vision of the relation between humans and their prey, which is inexistent in any of the so-called modern peoples.

Let me remind you of a fact. The Ainu killed the deer with bows and arrows just for living while the modern Japanese have been killing them with guns in order to sell the meat for wealth. After taking the Ainu's land, the Japanese built canneries for deer meat in different places in Hokkaido toward the end of the nineteenth century (Miyajima 145).

\* \* \*

Let us take a look at another divine song of the Ainu that shows another aspect of their ecological vision. It is not in the above-mentioned anthology compiled and edited by Yukie Chiri, but in another anthology compiled by Itsuhiko Kubodera (1902–71). The title of the song is *The Song Sung by the Goddess of the Old Boat*. It narrates an autobiographical story of a divine boat, beginning with Her birth and ending with Her death and rebirth.

The song consists of six parts. The first part narrates the birth of the Goddess of the Boat coming out of a tree; She is the narrator of the whole story. The second part narrates Her wonderful navigation over the ocean with Oki-kurumi, Her creator. The third part is about Her fatigue and distress on shore after the long navigation and the sudden disappearance of Oki-kurumi whom She loves. The fourth part shows Her joy in meeting a young god called Pon Okikurumi, the son of Oki-kurumi. This young god invites Her on a new journey across the sea, which She accepts willingly. The next part narrates the misfortune of the goddess. Her navigation proves to be fatal because of a storm. She finds herself onshore, torn into pieces. She is in deep sorrow.

But Ainu songs never end unhappily. The last part of the song tells that thanks to the ritual performed by Pon Okikurumi, She recovers Her soul and is freed from the body. She can now go back to Her home in Heaven. Thus the whole story makes a complete circle from life to death, and then from death to life, representing a happy and harmonious world.

At the beginning of the song, the soul of the Goddess of the Boat narrates how she was made into a boat:

> I was born and raised alone
> Just on the top of the Fall

Of the Sorachi River.
I was doing nothing special
Passing day by day.
One day,
I heard somebody talking
Down by the River.
Then appeared Samai-un-kur, a female human
Coming with six axes toward me.
Samai-un-kur said to me:
"You who are pretty
You are just a useless tree!
I will make a boat out of you so that you can be useful
And then take you for trading
And then make you a goddess;
I will dress you finely with liquor,
With good traded liquor
And some rice as well."

(Kubodera 176)[5]

As the quotation tells, a human goddess called Samai-un-kur comes to see the divine tree and tells her that She is going to do Her a favor by making a boat out of her. The goddess is far from gentle, so the divine tree gives a negative attitude to her:

I revealed to her
The hardest part of my skin
Hiding the softest part
She tried to chop me down in vain
The edge of her six axes chipped
Because of me.

(Kubodera 177)

By showing the "hardest part" of the skin, she refuses to be cut down by Samai-un-kur.
    The same tree, however, shows a totally different attitude to Oki-kurumi, Samai-un-kur's brother. Seeing his sister being refused, Oki-kurumi comes up to propose to the divine tree the same thing as his sister did, but much more gently and respectfully. This time, unhesitatingly, the divine tree accepts his proposal:

I hid from him
The hardest part of my skin
To expose the softest part
Soon came his axes

---

[5] All the translations of Kubodera's version are mine.

Big ones and small ones
To chop me down.

(Kubodera 177)

The ecological lesson we can learn from this is simple and clear: humans should be polite, gentle, and respectful to Nature if they want to make use of her. The Ainu as well as other peoples surely needed to kill some part of Nature to live on, but they were taught from generation to generation to be respectful to Nature, never to be abusive.

Now, the part of the song in which Oki-kurumi, the human god who made a boat out of the tree, left her alone on shore after the first navigation is interesting from a literary point of view. The divine boat confesses to having felt lonely and sad just like a human female who has lost her beloved one. She laments, "I was abandoned alone on the shore," "seeing nothing but sands and dusts," and feeling "tired and gloomy" (Kubodera 220–31). Seeing those expressions, we cannot but accept that the song is realistic in its own way.

Her sadness does not last long because the young human god Pon Okikurumi, the son of Oki-kurumi, comes up to see her. She expresses the joy of meeting him in the following way:

One day
From the hill behind
I heard a sound of sand
Someone walking on it, coming near me little by little
I turned around and saw
A god, a small Okikurumi
A young lad
Who has just become a lad
His beard has not grown fully yet
Yes, a young lad has come!

(Kubodera 236–53)

Here again, the emotion of the Goddess of the Boat is described like that of a human. Her joy is the same as that of a lonesome woman who finally encounters a handsome young man.

Seeing all this, some may think that the Ainu projected human emotion onto Nature, but that is a wrong interpretation. We should rather see that the Ainu felt they were part of Nature and that all beings and things were from one and the same source to them. In other words, they perceived Nature as human in the same way that they perceived themselves as part of Nature. They naturalized humans and humanized Nature at the same time.

This double vision of Nature is the very key to understand the particularity of the Ainu ecological vision. It consists in the sympathy-antipathy relationship among humans and animals, plants, and even artifacts. The relation between the human-like goddess Samai-un-kur and the divine tree in the song quoted above, for example, indicates the antipathetic relation between them, whereas the one between the human-like young god Pon Okikurumi and the Goddess of the Boat indicates a sympathetic relation. It is this alternate vision of the Nature-human relation in terms of sympathy and antipathy that forms an essential part of the Ainu ecology.

We said above that the Ainu conceived all the beings and things as born out of one and the same invisible spirit. This spirit was considered eternal and invariable, and only its incarnations in visible forms were thought to be ephemeral and variable. The Owl God in the first song could see everything happening to Him after death because His soul survived His body. The Goddess of the Boat in the second song could do the same because Her soul, eternal and invariable, could see everything that happened to Her. What the soul needed in both cases is freedom from the body to go home to Heaven, and it is only the humans' special rites and prayers that enabled the soul to return.

You may wonder what kind of ritual they practiced to liberate the soul from the body they killed. The main Ainu ritual for sending the soul to Heaven was the offering of *inau*, a kind of ritual wood stick. When the Owl God was killed by the poor boy whose ancestors were rich, His soul was revitalized by the offering of many *inau* on the part of the boy's family. In the case of the Goddess of the Boat, Her soul could be freed from the body because the young god Pon Okikurumi ornamented Her with a lot of *inau*. He offered Her some additional liquor and tobacco so that She could bring souvenirs to Her divine colleagues in Heaven. His words of prayer dedicated to Her were as follows:

Come on, come on
Oh, Madame the Boat!
Please listen carefully
To the words of my prayer
That recovers your life.

His prayer worked so well that She could return home safely. Once in homeland, She joyfully greeted the gods and goddesses living there and gave them the liquor and tobacco.

You may have remarked through those divine songs of the Ainu that they had a vision of life and death as a cycle. It begins with birth, passes through death, recovers the soul free from the body, brings it back to Heaven, and turns back to be reborn on Earth by taking a new visible form. The ritual with *inau* is a necessary means to realize the transition from death to life. The *inau* works here as a lubricant.

As we have seen, the Ainu worldview and their religious practice reflect an ecological view quite different from ours. As their divine songs confirm, it is based on the notion of sympathy-antipathy between humans and other beings or things in the world. This explains why they did not think of environmental protection in the same way as our ecologists. Seen from the Ainu point of view, our idea of protecting Nature must have been too much anthropocentric. To them, it was obvious that Nature acts on humans no less than humans on Nature and that the whole world is a place of emotional interactions among all the existing beings and things. This interactive and alternate emotional vision is totally lacking in our ecological thought.

## Works Cited

Kindaichi, Kyosuke. *Ainu no Kenkyu*. Naigai Shobo, 1925.
Kubodera, Itsuhiko. *Ainu no Sjhin-yo*. Sofu-kan, 2004.
Miyajima, Toshimitsu. *Ainu-minzoku to Nihon no Rekishi*. San-ichi Shobo, 1996.
Obayashi, Taryo. "Hoppo Minzoku no Sekai-kan." *Northern Peoples*. Hokkaido Museum of Northern Peoples, 1995.
Peterson, Benjamin. *The Song the Owl God Sang, the Collected Ainu Legends of Chiri Yukie*. BJS Books, 2013. Kindle.

# Part Three

# Ocean and Ecology

# 9

# Becoming Oceania: Toward a Planetary Ecopoetics or Reframing the Pacific Rim

Rob Wilson

*Walking on water wasn't built in a day.*

—Jack Kerouac

Vexed by animosities of post–Cold War history and emerging forms of global antagonism and military crisis, the South China Sea has become "Asia's Roiling Sea," as a *New York Times* editorial puts it in August 2012: "The sea is not only an important trade route but is also rich in oil, natural gas, fishing and mineral resources. Nations are fighting over islands and even specks of rocks to stake their claims."[1] Pacific Rim sites, islands, and their modern nation-coded coasts and borders—from China, Taiwan, Korea, and Japan to Malaysia, Vietnam, and the Philippines—are getting caught up in those "heavy waters" of military surveillance, resource extraction, and industrial waste, as Elizabeth DeLoughrey shrewdly calls them (705). Such everyday conflicts can challenge the very telos of trans-oceanic globalization that (since the late 1970s) presumes "a [Pacific] Rim that is an imagining of transnational capital, [as] a co-prosperity sphere" (Connery, "Pacific Rim Discourse" 36).[2] But this bio-kinetic and turbulent Pacific Ocean, which "zones the world's whole bulk around it [and] makes all coasts one bay to it" (to use Melville's co-presencing trope from *Moby-Dick*, Chapter CXI, "The Pacific"), remains un-amenable to such territorial demarcations of national, contractual, or marine sovereignty. From the Bikini Atoll atomic testing during the Cold War era down to the latest nuclear disaster in Fukushima, Japan, in 2011, citizens of late-capitalist modernity threaten not just the water, ground, and air of local dwelling but the interconnected Pacific as a planetary bioregion. This latest tsunami traumatically reminds Pacific Ocean dwellers from Sendai in coastal Eastern Japan to Santa Cruz along the Northern California coast that the Pacific Rim is not just discourse or trope; it is also a geologically interactive bioregion.

---

[1] *New York Times* editorial, "Asia's Roiling Sea," Aug. 18, 2012.

[2] Connery has gone on to reiterate his claim that "[i]n both China and the United States, the oceanic imaginary has lost much of its force since 1989. In the United States, *Pacific Rim* is now mostly confined to fusion restaurants and universities" ("Ideologies of Land and Sea: Alfred Thayer Mahan, Carl Schmitt, and the Shaping of Global Myth Elements" 196).

In effect, we need another bigger and better way of framing this shared oceanic horizon; that is to say, another way of converting the Pacific Rim into a shared if wary figure of geo-poetic and ecological interest, as I will go on to evoke through a conjuration of experimental poets and writers whose works enact forces of "becoming oceanic" and formally as well as in content, suggests a different mode of belonging to region and globe than the post-Hegelian will to dominion. For, in an environmental sense as well, we can all but forget the ocean while dwelling in an urban life world (in huge, consumption-rich cities like Shanghai, Honolulu, Kaohsiung, and San Francisco, or Berlin and London in the Northern Atlantic for that matter) that depends for its very modern well-being *on, from, and across the ocean*. This *ocean commons* so-called, if figured as a vital biospheric element necessary to sustaining life and planetary health, could help build up tactics and affects of ecological solidarity and modes of co-dwelling. To do so, the ocean would have to be framed in terms that can inspire an imagination of co-belonging, mutual interest, and care. The Pacific Ocean could come to signify a bioregional site of coalitional *promise* as much as a geopolitical danger zone of *peril*, and, as I will aim to show in this essay, the forging of an ocean-based ecopoetics can help in this regard.

Hawai'i, at least since the 1840s when the United States manifested its interest in securing Pearl Harbor as a strategic coaling station on route to markets of Asia, until its annexation in 1898, has long been entangled in US struggles to secure Pacific maritime space as some kind of extra-continental territory and element of modern dynamism. As Charles Olson evoked Melville's wildly American drive for space as "oceanic deliverance" in *Call Me Ishmael* (1947), "Now in the Pacific. THE CARRIER. Trajectory. We [Americans] must go over space, or we wither" (114).[3] Pro-imperial diplomat Whitelaw Reid summarized US policy during its war with Spain in 1898: "To extend now the authority of the United States over the great Philippine Archipela go is to fence in the China Sea and secure an almost equally commanding position on the other side of the Pacific. [...] Rightly used, it enables the United States to convert the Pacific Ocean almost into an American lake."[4]

As if activating its own version of a Monroe Doctrine in the region, China has a long historical claim to these sea-access routes to the Western Pacific and the Indian Ocean via the Malacca Strait, as Robert D. Kaplan argues in *Asia's Cauldron: The South China Sea and the End of a Stable Pacific*. He calls it a space geo-strategically akin to the US Caribbean, a kind of "blue national soil" to the PRC navy (13, 41).[5] Recalling

---

[3] Christopher Connery tracks this movement "as a journey that begins and ends in terrestriality to a pure trajectory, a pure oceanic deliverance" ("The Oceanic Feeling and the Regional Imaginary" 303).

[4] Reid is quoted in Bruce Cumings, *Dominion from Sea to Sea: Pacific Ascendancy and American Power* (140–1). For the long duration of this "American Pacific" as a chain of military bases secured via coaling stations and harbor ports, particularly Pearl Harbor in the interior Pacific and Juan de Fuca on the Rim, see John Eperjesi's "Basing the Pacific: Exceptional Spaces of the Wilkes Exploring Expedition, 1838–1842."

[5] Arif Dirlik has urged that we drop the Europe-originated use of "South China Sea" and "East China Sea," instead of using "SE Asia Sea" and "East Asia Sea" which were historically used by "dynastic regimes" in the region (email to Rob Wilson, May 27, 2014). See also John J. Mearsheimer's "The Gethering Storm: China's Challenge to US Power in Asia" (2010) on the Chinese challenge to contemporary US hegemony as to some extent a mimicry of some of its tactics and doctrines.

world war history and the invocation of the Monroe Doctrine as a "great space" (*grofsraum*) principle of foreign exclusion and imperial expansion, we might well be wary of its belated use in Asia and on the Pacific Rim.⁶ Still, the larger geo-territorial context for this struggle presumes what is called "the competition for dominance in the Asia-Pacific region."⁷ Here, the United States has maintained uneasy hegemony at least since the defeat of Japan and Germany in the Second World War, despite Nixon and Mao's world-altering 1972 Shanghai communiqué that affirmed, "Neither [side] should seek hegemony in the Asia-Pacific region and each is opposed to efforts by any other country or group of countries to establish such hegemony."⁸

"The Pacific is big enough for all of us," declared then US Secretary of State Hillary Clinton—like some American Adam—at the 2012 Pacific Forum in Fiji. This did not satisfy China Rising not to mention interior Pacific countries grown wary of neoliberal "Rimspeak" since the end of the Cold War.⁹ President Obama's "Pacific Pivot" in 2011 toward increased US military presence has only aggravated the problem of definition, interest, and strategy, generating blowback and populist resistance in naval-base sites like Jeju Island in South Korea and Okinawa in Japan, as well as across the oceanic commons of so-called *Moana Nui* from Hawai'i to Taiwan.¹⁰ Along with twenty-one other nations and despite maritime tensions in the Pacific, China is for the first time participating in the US-led Rim of the Pacific (RIMPAC) naval and security exercises held in Hawai'i.¹¹ In short, caught between re-nativizing visions of "Moana Nui" or a re-securitizing RIMPAC, the Pacific remains riddled with antagonisms of political, territorial, and commercial conflict any version of "Pacific Rim" needs to conjure.

"Earth is a misnomer. The planet should be called Ocean," Ed DeLong has urged, registering his marine biologists' sensibility for the ocean as regenerative life fluid that comprises some 90 percent of our biosphere.¹² We need to see ourselves as oceanic citizens as much as earth-dwellers, ocean-beholden peoples enmeshed in a tenuous, Gaia-like system. Here authors of oceanic eco-poetics from Gary Snyder in the Pacific Northwest and Epeli Hau'ofa in Tonga to Craig Santos Perez and Brandy Nālani

---

[6] See Carl Schmitt, "The Monroe Doctrine as a Precedent for a *Grofsraum* Principle."

[7] On the US struggle to maintain hegemony in the Pacific region during the Obama regime see, for example, "U.S., China Clash on Key Issues," *New York Times*, Sept. 5, 2012, and "Too Small an Ocean," *The Economist*, Sept. 8, 2012. See also *New York Times* editorial, "Asia's Roiling Sea," Aug. 18, 2012.

[8] See Henry Kissinger on this world-altering Shanghai accord in his memoir, *On China*, 270.

[9] See, for example, "U.S., China Clash on Key Issues," *New York Times*, Sept. 5, 2012. As U.S. Secretary of State Hillary Clinton optimistically avowed at the 2012 Pacific Forum before she headed to tenser meetings with China in Beijing, "the Pacific is big enough for all of us": see "Too Small an Ocean," *The Economist*, Sept. 8, 2012.

[10] See Koohan Paik and Jerry Meander, "Blowback in the Pacific," *The Nation*, Dec. 31, 2012, accessed online on Asia-Pacific resistance to securing the Pacific Ocean as a "massive 'US commons,'" as in the struggle to turn Jeju island into a joint South-Korean US naval base and to resist this buildup via an anti-military coalition called *Moana Nui*.

[11] See Jim Stevenson, "China Makes Debut in RIMPAC Naval Drills," *Voice of America* online, Jul. 4, 2014.

[12] Quoted in Stefan Helmreich, *Alien Ocean: Anthropological Voyages in Microbial Seas* (3).

McDougall in Guam and Hawaiʻi and Juliana Spahr of California can help disturb the environmental unconsciousness that often reigns. The ocean can help to figure a vision of planetary belonging.

As Rob Nixon has warned about mounting imbalances of power, wealth, resource, risk, and vulnerability taking place across world oceans during neoliberalist regimes in this, our "geomorphic" Anthropocene:

> Neoliberalism loves watery metaphors: the trickle-down effect, global flows, how a rising tide lifts all boats. But talk of a rising tide raises other specters: the coastal poor, who will never get storm-surge barriers; Pacific Islanders in the front lines of inundation; Arctic peoples, whose livelihoods are melting away—all of them exposed to the fallout from Anthropocene histories of carbon extraction and consumption in which they played virtually no part.

Threatened with techno-human endangerment and systemic distortion, the ocean calls for broader reckoning as species origin, resource, and horizon. Whales, dolphins, coral reefs, and marine microbes—from the era of Melville and Darwin down to Walt Disney and postcolonial works like *Life of Pi* and *Cloud Atlas*—appeal for a sense of co-dwelling that would connect beings across various scales of lung/brain/blood/water/air linkage. "This connection of everyone with lungs" is how American poet Juliana Spahr puts this imperiled wholeness in a collection by that name, tracing forms and forces of biopolitical relationality across militarized waters and polluted airs that extend from the United States Pacific Command at Pearl Harbor to Manhattan Island, post-9/11 and post-Kyoto (*this connection of everyone with lungs*).[13]

Juliana Spahr's timely book *Well Then There Now* (2012) offers another work of experimental ecopoetics, deeply oceanic in the way it situates Hawaiʻi and the United States not just in relation to Native Hawaiian struggles and multiculturalist movements in altered English, but also in relation to global forces like arctic melting, species extinction, and resource extraction. While Spahr challenges the first-personal plural "we" of Robert Frost's manifest-destiny poem, "The Gift Outright," showing how such US claims like "this land was ours before we were the land's" fall apart in an occupied native space like Hawaiʻi, she offers a more broadly oceanic vision of planetary and insular interconnection, indicting her own and "our" consumptive and polluting patterns from Ohio, to Oʻahu, to Manhattan:

> They often lived on an island in the Pacific and they often lived on an island in the Atlantic. *Lake Chubsucker*. They thought of these two residences of theirs as opposites although both were place of great economic privilege and resources, places that themselves consumed large amounts of resources and consumed more and more resources all the time. *Lake Sturgeon*.
>
> (84; emphasis original)

---

[13] Spahr is working on a new poem called "Transitory, Momentary" that tries to measure ecological damages and reach of the "oil wars" and oils spills via the palpably feeble device of using iambic pentameter as a medium of human control and response.

The "unnamed dragonfly species" and myriad fish she lists, in broken catalogues, are invoked as endangered species, endangered by us-and-them binaries large and small, local and global ties, near and far spaces that are overlain as interconnected relations: "Things of each possible relation hashing against one another," as she names this systemic process in another poem (67). Land and ocean frames clash, overlay, and split apart yet (as Spahr puts it) *hash together* in discrepant perspectives endangering the planet, thus calling out for a multi-relational vision of commonality and care this work of experimental ecopoetics would enact.

These oceanic ties and flows in the interior Pacific, pulling back from the past and across into the future, also mark contemporary re-Indigenizing Hawaiian poetry, as represented across English-Hawaiian languages by Brandy Nālani McDougall in her poetry collection *The Salt Wind: Ka Makani Paʻakai* (2008), whose "protagonist" binding family and self to history and place is not so much the human presence as it is the ocean wind full of salt resonances and Hawaiian remembrances recalling modes of place-based and oceanic belonging. In her opening poem "Pō," she invokes a mode of primordial oceanic belonging via an updated, reframed translation of the Hawaiian epic poem *Kumulipo*, recalling a land-ocean space deeper than and prior to modern plantations, Pearl Harbor, and tourist history in Hawaiʻi:

Before the land was tamed by history,
the oceanside resorts and pineapple plantations,
before the cane knife's rust, the dark time of sickness,
the coming of cannons, the bitter waters drunk,
before the metallic salt of blood, the rain emptied
into rivers, the winds carved valleys and mountains,
before the earth spurted fire, birthed islands.

Re-worlding Hawaiʻi back into salt winds and geo-energies of ancestral memory and postcolonial futurity, she opens readers to oceanic modes of ecological co-belonging to sea and place. As Wai Chee Dimock remarks in *Through Other Continents*, "Literature is the home of non-standard space and time" (4), and such poems help bring these other "nonstandard" spaces and times of a *Pacific-becoming-Oceania* into uncanny figuration.

Book-length poems by Perez also enact a related feat of repossessing Oceania and the Marianas, projecting a mode of world-belonging in which Guåhan/Guam can no longer be named (or forgotten as) just another "unincorporated territory" of the post-1898 imperial American Pacific. Resisting Guåhan's being called the "Pacific hub to Asia" (30) in *from unincorporated territory [hacha]* (2008), and *from unincorporated territory [saina]* (2010), or being referred to as "USS Guam" (11), poet-scholar Santos Perez would resist the centuries-long Spanish and US "reduction" process of "subduing, converting, and gathering natives through the establishment of missions and the stationing of soldiers to protect those missions" (11). His poems (tied to transpacific tidelands as much as to the experimental writings of *Tinfish* in Honolulu and Bay Area open-field poetics) proliferate counter-namings and trace alternative routes and roots in a counter-geography of archipelagic belonging: not to an American Pacific (where Guåhan is as a militarized security site) but to Oceania, challenging the call "to prove the ocean/ was once a flag" (47).

In *Be Always Converting, Be Always Converted*, decentering "American poetics" as such via long-standing transnational Pacific ties, I focused on *the* crucial postcolonial figure of Pacific-world reframing, the Tongan writer and social scientist Epeli Hauʻofa (1939–2009), who turns away from the telos of capitalist hyper-development that has gotten the modern ocean into the trouble it is in as "Great Pacific Garbage Patch" ecoscape (87–142). "Oceania" stands for Hauʻofa's New Pacific ecumene of counter-conversion, a strategic mode of refiguring this Pauline universality of address for Pacific Islanders for whom globalization discourse would hail them into market dependency, subaltern labor, and secular difference. Oceania, vast, watery, evocative, at core mysterious (like the earlier PNG pidgin-vernacular term "wansolwara" for the Pacific as "one salt water" meaning "one ocean, one people") becomes a way of reframing and forming a new regional and global identity. "South Seas," "Australasia," "South Pacific" (introduced via James Michener, Rodgers, and Hammerstein et al. during the postwar American hegemony in the cold war ethnoscape of "militourism"), "Pacific Basin," and "Pacific Islands" all give way to "Oceania" as the self-identified signifier of interior Pacific choice.[14]

Hauʻofa's paradigm-shattering figure for coalition-building is called "Oceania" and its poetic vagary of definition becomes a re-signifying form of watery unity by which Polynesian, Micronesian, and Melanesian and all such colonial-imposed definitions of race or nationhood could be sloughed off as boundary lines, false confinements into smallness, irrelevance, and global dependency. "Oceania" was originally a French geographical term ("l 'Océanie") coined in 1831 by the French explorer Dumont d'Urville; it was also a still-used Roman Catholic signifier for the Pacific (starting from appointing a Bishop of Oceania to New Zealand in the 1840s). And it has now become the name for one of eight planetary eco-zones on the Earth. Following Albert Wendt's call for a poetics and ecology of a "New Oceania," Hauʻofa framed his rebirth-turn toward this re-signified and refigured postcolonial Oceania along a trans-oceanic road leading from Damascus via Suva to Kona and Volcano on the Big Island.[15] Oceania stands for a hope-generating turn away from insular models of smallness, lack, disconnection, or belatedness installed by colonial discourse.

All but dematerialized into cyberspace *netizens* of urban space, we dwell on the verge of "forgetting the [material] sea" as a site of co-belonging, resistance, and co-history, as filmmaker Allan Sekula documents in works like *Fish Story* (1995) and *The*

---

[14] Meditating on the semiotics and politics of "Oceania," Hauʻofa admits having "Wansolwara" in mind, as the name for a newspaper produced by Pacific Islander journalism students at the University of South Pacific in Fiji, when he founded the Oceania Centre for Arts and Culture in 1997 where the "Red Wave Collective" emerges ("The Ocean in Us" 114–17).

[15] See director Shirley Horrock's documentary portrait of Albert Wendt's oceanic trajectory from Samoa and New Zealand into the world of postcolonial literature, *The New Oceania* (Point of View Productions, 2005).

*Forgotten Space* (2011).¹⁶ The ocean, in many sites, remains the *unthought* as such. We can forget this material-semiotic ocean even on a Pacific Rim that houses thirteen of the twenty largest container ports in the world from Hong Kong to Long Beach (Cumings 386). Living on landed edges, we trope the sea as *alien other*, as a quasi-Biblical antagonist as site of the void, waste, or oblivion: some kind of blue-black abyss creating monsters from inhuman depths linking Job's Leviathan or Melville's *Moby-Dick* to *Aliens of the Deep* (2005).¹⁷ The Pacific houses the deformed byproduct of our chemical transpacific waste in the South Korean movie (linking Seoul's Han River to the American Pacific), *The Host* (2006) not to mention Guillermo del Toro's film *Pacific Rim* (2013) with its bio-phobic vision of sea monsters (*Kaiju*, the Japanese word for Godzilla-like creatures) about to devour San Francisco, Tokyo, and humanity itself. *Pacific Rim*, the movie, is the latest strike on "Pacific Rim discourse": less ecological subject or political allegory than a projected market for circulating genre phantasies, despite a PLA officer's rather prescient cultural studies like claim that "[t]he decisive battle against the monsters was deliberately set in the South China Sea adjacent to Hong Kong" to provoke China and maintain US hegemony in the region.¹⁸

*Pacific Rim* recalls the mounting ecological catastrophe of disappearing coral reefs and native islands being submerged, oceanic acidification, thermal shifts, amid the mounting North Pacific garbage gyres of transnational detritus between Japan and the United States. What is coming to be called a *blue poetics* of "oceanic becoming" needs to deal with such matters to register the submarine forms, coastal cities, and oceanic sites impacted by the hyper-capitalist world.¹⁹ International search-and-rescue teams scouring vast reaches of the Indian Ocean off the west coast of Australia for missing signs of Malaysia Airlines Flight 370, as Barbara Demick observed, "discovered what oceanographers have been warning—that even the most far-flung stretches of ocean are full of garbage." The flotsam and jetsam of the far-flung ocean digests the everyday life of global capitalism. Here, an oceanic feedback system of "blue" and "green"— suggesting planetary equilibrium and renewal—now radiates a more dangerously "prismatic ecology" of violet-black, red, brown, and grey warning signs.²⁰

---

[16] See Sukhdev Sandhu, "Allan Sekula: Filming the Forgotten Resistance at Sea."

[17] See Christopher Leigh Connery, "There Was No More Sea: The Supercession of the Ocean from the Bible to Cyberspace" and "Sea Power."

[18] Ben Child notes a Chinese military officer's phobic allegorization of *Pacific Rim* as a military fable of oceanic domination: "The decisive battle against the monsters was deliberately set in the South China Sea adjacent to Hong Kong," [PLA officer] Zhang wrote. "The intention was to demonstrate the US commitment to maintaining stability in the Asia-Pacific area and saving mankind." The Chinese military is currently concerned over US plans to transfer 60 percent of American naval assets to the Pacific by the end of the decade. Zhang added: "Soldiers should sharpen their eyes and enforce a 'firewall' to avoid ideological erosion when watching American movies. More importantly, they should strengthen their combat capability to safeguard national security and interests" (Child, "*Pacific Rim* designed to advance US cultural domination of China").

[19] See Steve Mentz, *At the Bottom of Shakespeare's Ocean*, 97–9; and John R. Giles, "The Blue Humanities."

[20] "[B]athal, abyssal, and hadal zones [as] empty, void, null—an abyss of [deeper oceanic] concern," as Stacy Alaimo puts this for her entry on deep-ocean ecopoetics called "Violet Black" (233).

The poet Bill Knott warned in a rebuke to Jack Kerouac and the Beats's overdependence on fossil-fuel consumption to power their cross-country roads and God-quests across the planet in: "On the Road (Kerouac)" (2014). Such prophecy of "ecocide" often goes unheeded as everyday news. As Peter Sloterdijk warns in *Neither Sun nor Death*, "[p]eople born today do not develop any oceanic consciousness— neither in the phobic nor the philobatic [self-avoiding of dangerous objects] sense," leading into disaster zones of global ("spherical") forgetting we face as shared planetary horizon (239). While a biogenetic object of planetary magnitude and interconnection, the ocean remains one of those "sublime imaginary constructs of wholeness" we cannot fully conjure into the spherical globe given terrestrial predispositions that often still hold (Sloterdijk, *In the World Interior of Capital* 5). Jasper Bernes has portrayed this dystopian sense of spatial captivity inside late-capitalist Los Angeles, excavating the ocean in a bleak theory-haiku from *Starsdown* (2007):

> Under the parking lot, the beach.
> Under the beach, the parking lot.
>
> (82)

We try to map the ocean with treaties and legal conventions rooted in straight lines, contracts, and bounded spaces, in an uneasy dialectic of *mare liberum* and *mare clausum*. These projections of Exclusive Economic Zones (EEZs) regulated by the 1982 United Nations Convention on the Law of the Sea (UNCLOS) fail to take lasting dominion, as in the recent dispute over uninhabited islands known as the Diaoyu in China and the Senkakus in Japan.[21] "China thinks of the South China Sea much as the U.S. thinks of the Caribbean [if not the entire Pacific as such]: as a blue-water extension of its mainland," to invoke Kaplan again, recalling the primacy of geography to international conflicts of land and sea amid collapsing distances and border-crossing euphoria along the global market ("Geography Strikes Back").[22] Admiral Alfred Thayer Mahan's "wide commons" of global commerce and military power defended as the US-secured high seas has shrunk in the wake of such territorial extensions of exclusive economic zones and resource scarcity.[23]

---

[21] "Once defined by the range of a cannon shot from the shore, sovereignty over coastal waters has since 1982 been guided by the United Nations Convention on the Law of the Sea (UNCLOS). Signatories can claim a 'territorial sea' up to 12 nautical miles (22km) from their shoreline, inside which they can set laws but not meddle with international shipping. Beyond the territorial sea there is a 200-mile 'exclusive economic zone' (EEZ), where coastal countries have the sole rights to resources. When two EEZs collide, UNCLOS calls for an equidistant line between the coasts, splitting the shared gulf or strait down the middle. The theory sounds simple, but the practice is complicated: islands, rocks, historic sovereignty and natural resources can bend the line." For an analysis of these current conflicts in the Northern Pacific, see "Make Law Not War: How to Solve Spats over Sea Borders," *The Economist*, 25 Aug. 2012.

[22] See also Bill Hayton, *The South China Sea: The Struggle for Power in Asia* on the genealogy of the South China Sea as "both fulcrum of world trade and a crucible of conflict" (n.p.).

[23] On the "neo-Mahanian" importance of "maritime geography" in contexts of a shrinking global commons and contemporary struggles over resource scarcity, see James C. Hsiung, "Sea Power, Law of the Sea, and China-Japan East China Sea 'Resource War.'"

In his ethno-scientific study of microbial oceanography, *Alien Ocean* (2009), Stefan Helmreich elaborates a "dual [romantic-scientific] imaginary" bespeaking ambivalence toward planetary waters: the ocean has become both *trouble to us* (as with tsunamis or climate turbulence) and *in trouble from us* (as in our Pacific garbage patch or overfishing). The ocean figures as elemental sublimity: an immensity at once threatening us and yet a healing "source of its own curative powers" (114–15), as in these little heroic deep-sea microbes that eat up the potent greenhouse gas, methane, we overproduce globally (31). Perhaps *the* Pacific sign of oceanic endangerment remains our contemporary global installation, so to speak, in the "ocean commons" created by overproductive waste and ecological unconsciousness on both sides of the Northern Pacific. The *Great Pacific Garbage Patch* is a gyre of plasticene detritus twice the size of Texas, weighing some 100 million tons, that lies just below ocean surface between California, Hawai'i, and Japan. This slimy image of late-capitalist sublimity is formed from throwaway bottles, chemical sludge, and polymers harmful to marine wildlife.[24]

Such "ecopoetic" images of oceanic endangerment could be multiplied: Tuvalu island disappearing due to global warming and rising tides, the US military buildup from Guåhan and Cheju Island to the Persian Gulf and Australia, the melting arctic, mounting typhoons of Taiwan, the nuclear waste waters of tsunami-stricken Japan. At the same time, John Luther Adams (whose music often integrates sonic effects from his coastal environment in the Northern Pacific) has composed a symphony called "Become Ocean" which won the Pulitzer Prize in 2014, as "a haunting orchestral work that suggests a relentless tidal surge, evoking thoughts of melting polar ice and rising sea levels."[25] "Life on this earth first emerged from the sea. And as the polar ice melts and sea level rises, we humans find ourselves facing the prospect that, once again, we may quite literally become ocean": this is how Adams explained the environmental context that led him to compose "Become Ocean," a work full of sonic echoes from oceanic waves and whales and patterns drawn from planetary slow time.

Aesthetic figurations of oceanic-becoming might help move urban citizens, early and late, into a more trans-oceanic vision of solidarity, co-dwelling, and shared peril. The Pacific might become that "last world ocean" where the post-Greco Roman civilizational imperative—*translatio imperii maris*—falls apart into modes of rhizomatic becoming, multiplicity, and trans-species belonging. Building outward from this shared commons spreading across Oceania, such a decentered imaginary of the Rim might move us toward "the promise" of the Ocean as space of altered belonging, ecological confederation, and planetary solidarity. The United States, fronting this nexus to Asia-Pacific on many fronts, needs to overcome what has been

---

[24] This paragraph draws on information from the following sources accessed online: Jane Palmer, "Junk Accumulating on Monterey Bay Ocean Floors: Scientists Find Increasing Levels of Debris in the Deep Sea," *Santa Cruz Sentinel* (Feb. 2, 2010); and Maggie Shiels, "Boat Made of Trash [the Plastiki] Prepares to Set Sail," *BBC News* (Mar. 3, 2010).

[25] See "John Luther Adams's 'Become Ocean' Wins Pulitzer Prize for Music," *WQXR blog*, Apr. 14, 2014. With thanks to Paul Bové for this reference.

called, in Singapore, its "self-identification [as] a missionary superpower" across this region of China Rising.[26]

Becoming ocean still figures as a threshold experience in some double sense—miraculous and catastrophic, liberating and threatening, amazing yet horrifying, overwhelming any land-centric categories and affects of homeliness and bounded belonging, shuttling between utopic and dystopian affects, narratives, and images that would comprise a "blue" ecopoetics. In a brilliantly conjunctive hip-hop song by Mos Def (Yasiin Bey) called "New World Water," the polluting effects of worldwide industrial capitalism and waste-production of bottled water create a "lopsided" ecology of contamination that cannot be dispelled from drinking "New World Water":

> New World Water make the tide rise high …
> The sun is settin in the treetops burnin the woods
> And as the flames from the blaze get higher and higher
> They say, "Don't drink the water we need it for the fire!"
> New York is drinkin it (New World Water)
> Now all of California is drinkin it (New World Water)
> Way up north and down south is drinkin it (New World Water)
> Used to have minerals and zinc in it (New World Water)
> Now they say it has lead and stink in it (New World Water)
> Flourocarbons and monoxide
> Push the water table lopside
> Used to be free now it costs you a fee
> Cause oil tankers spill they load as they roam cross the sea.[27]

In Mos Def's eco-jeremaic 1999 chant, "New World Water" becomes a toxic, far-flung betrayal of whatever the "New World" stood for as redemptive promise in the Americas, across world oceans, from the Atlantic to the Pacific. Dystopia now rules the water. But, if the ocean has been figured in traumatic terms of war, disaster, shipwreck, monsoon, hurricane, and accident, the ocean abides as a fundamental planetary origin, full of poetry, enchantment, and the magic blue waters of the humanities, as a turn to the writings of Jack Kerouac can still help us to see even in this contemporary moment of what is coming to be called the Anthropocene.

---

[26] See George Yeo, "For the Rest of Asia, America Might Be a Friend, But China Cannot Be an Enemy," *Huffington Post online*, Aug. 20, 2014 who argues this stark contrast: "The U.S. is, by self-identification, a missionary superpower. It judges others by its own standards and tries to shape them in the U.S.' own image—by hard and soft power. If China is also a missionary power, like the Soviet Union, perhaps a titanic struggle will again be inevitable. However, China is, by self-proclamation, not a missionary power. For China, a cardinal principle of statecraft, not just the PRC but also its earlier incarnations, is non-interference in the internal affairs of others unless those affairs affect China's core interests."

[27] Lyrics and recording of this song from the album *Black on Both Sides* can be accessed at: http://rapgenius.com/Yasiin-bey-new-world-water-lyrics

The first *road* Kerouac ever dreamed of as a path across the world and as an awakening call to his vocation as a writer was not a highway but ocean. As he worked on a draft of his first novel in 1942 at the age of 20, he wrote, "Into this book, 'The Sea is My Brother' I shall weave all the passion and glory of living, its restlessness and peace, its fever and ennui, its mornings, noons and nights of desire, frustration, fear, triumph, and death" (*The Sea Is My Brother: The Lost Novel* 11). The sea-as-road Kerouac dreamed of—while still a student at Columbia University in New York City where he had begun to meet those life-hungry writers like Allen Ginsberg and William Burroughs who would form the subterranean homesick Beats—was huge, world-encompassing, sweeping across the North Atlantic and the Mediterranean down to the Caribbean and around to the Pacific: "the old ports of Spain and Belfast, Glasgow, Manchester, Sidney, New Zealand; and Rio and Trinidad and Barbados and the Cape; and Panama and Honolulu and the far-flung Polynesians." *The Sea Is My Brother*, "the lost novel" published posthumously in 2011, survives as a rough sketch of those ever-early energies, drives, dualities, dreams, flights, hints at the more wildly oceanic style and scope that would give the world the amazing body of work in prose, poetry, and prose poetry that Kerouac wrought.

Kerouac was writing this vow to his soulmate Sebastian Sampas in 1942, this "mad poet brother" from Lowell and fellow writer in a group they termed the Young Prometheans who were haunted by communism, war, brotherhood, love, restlessness, and literary ambition. Sampas would lose his life in the battle against Axis forces at Anzio in 1944, but Kerouac would remain faithful to these high writerly ambitions he first outlined in letters to Sebastian, and he would marry his sister Stella Sampas in 1966 as if to keep these ties to Lowell intact after the fame and abandonment hit. "Port debaucheries then back to sea" (38) went the rhythm of Ti Jean's lifelong de-territorializing flights from Lowell to New York to San Francisco to Mexico City to Tangier to Paris to Florida and back to Lowell. "I hit the road [away from family and married life], bummed all over the U.S.A., finally took to shipping out," says Wes, a thinly disguised, hard-drinking, and quest-driven Kerouac. This lost novel shows Kerouac breaking not just from the academic life at Columbia, but from what Jack Spicer called "the English Department of the soul," a kind of living death masquerading as middle-class success.

The Atlantic Ocean Kerouac would soon cross and briefly labor upon as merchant marine on the *SS Dorchester* (a transport ship later sunk by a German submarine in 1943) would provide this world-influential writer with his first huge metaphor for world brotherhood and incarnational longing in sentences that began to encompass the energy of body and soul fusing in Whitmanic rhythms of some libidinal-political en masse. Written in a spontaneous drug-induced 3-week burst in 1951 and not published until 1957, *On the Road* would more fully bring this poetic vision of crazed unity into world-circulating recognition in the Beat idiom, through bebop prose and the questing God-hungry figures of Sal Paradise and Dean Moriarty, energized by the postwar dream of a restless America opening up with "all that raw land that rolls in one unbelievable huge bulge over to the West Coast, and all that road going, all the people dreaming in the immensity of it."

The ocean, in spatial effect, proved to be Kerouac's first interstate highway system, as it were, and it led not across the continent to the wilder US leftcoast freedoms of California, but across global waterways to the world as horizon, pushing history beyond war and murderous rivalry into something more blessed and worthy of the human quest. *The Sea Is My Brother*, now published with an array of other uncollected writings from those juvenilia years of self-formation that have also been gathered by Kerouac's hard-working literary estate in *Atop an Underwood* (1999), admittedly remains what Allen Ginsberg called "just a lot of reverie prose." But Kerouac was a writer driven by such youthful dreams across the forties and fifties and on until his death in 1969 at the age of 47. As Sam Sacks has noted of Kerouac, "He did not, ultimately, want to flee from his youth; he wanted to enlarge it and live in it perpetually." "The ocean wild like an organ played" for Kerouac, who was tired of that weary tune of war and death, as was Bob Dylan in his post-Beat wake.

The sea was crossed as an ocean of war, risk, commerce, and death, but it also stood for oceanic consciousness and connection, the dream of cosmic unities and "shipping out" across imaginative frontiers—"as if California had stretched around the world back to New England" (Kerouac, *The Sea Is My Brother* 35). Here were spaces of wonder, bliss, and terror Melville, Thomas Wolfe, Coleridge, Poe, and Whitman had opened up that still called to Kerouac—"for the future world of never-war" (Kerouac 27) as a character rants in *The Sea Is My Brother*. Like Dylan, Kerouac is always early, always getting started, always writing a drunken experiment that is utterly sober in range, reach, uncanny eruption. As Gilles Deleuze has brilliantly noted of Kerouac's quest for transformation through writing and life as filled with oceanic flux,

> Writing carries out the conjunction, the transmutation of fluxes, through which life escapes from the resentment of persons, societies, and reigns. Kerouac's phrases are as sober as a Japanese drawing, a pure line traced by an unsupported hand, which passes across ages and reigns. It would take a true alcoholic to attain that degree of sobriety.
>
> (51)

The trope-laden afterlife of this restless road to world-becoming keeps going, as Kerouac has become "posthumously prolific" as David Barnett puts it in the *Independent*,

> The novella follows two characters, old-hand seaman Wesley Martin and Columbia professor Bill Everhart, who hook up and ship out for Greenland carrying war cargo—a journey that Kerouac himself undertook on the SS Dorchester. The plot is minimal, and in both style and construction the novel betrays Kerouac's immaturity as a writer.

If the execution leaves much to be desired, as reviewers have noted, the novel does show the foundations Kerouac was laying for his future work: "There are wonderful bursts of

Kerouackian jazz-prose which break through the strictures of the conventional novel, and even then his ear for dialogue was sharp and naturalistic." As Sam Sacks measured and dismissed such Beat work for his *Wall Street Journal* readers,

> Instead [of the will to finished novelistic form] there was Mexico, Burroughs and Benzedrine; "On the Road" banged out in 20 days on a 120-foot scroll (dictated by the Holy Ghost, the writer told [Robert] Giroux, who rejected it); the veneration of spontaneous prose and the whole baggy, unending, self-aggrandizing iconography of the Beats.

But, in *The Sea Is My Brother* and later more Pacific-based and global works like *Big Sur* (novel) and *Lonesome Traveler* (travel book), the sea loomed as a horizon of world infinitude and experimental movement, not just as the history-drenched space of torpedo-ridden danger, militarism, lacklove, wanhope, and death: "To make the sea your own, to watch over it, to brood your very soul into it, to accept it and love it as though only it mattered and existed!" (47). The world-pitching, world-heaving sea called to Kerouac as it had to Melville and Dana if not Whitman and Gary Snyder: "[N]ext to the smell of salt water," says this early model of Kerouac, "I'll take the smell of the highway ... Whitman's song of the open road, modern version" (58).

The oceanic quest is at core not just material but figurative, driven by writer models—"life at sea—[becoming] a Thoreau before the mast" (76). As Martin's more learned sidekick Everhart hymns it about such drives to explore land and sea in *The Sea Is My Brother*, "the pioneer is free because he moves on and forgets to leave a trace. God!" (63). Kerouac's first novel over-signals its romantic quest with portmanteau character names like "Everhart" and "Earthington," as point of view shifts with unstable abandon, unsure of who is hero. Still, an ordinary seaman is figured forth as if reborn into an oceanic communism shorn of class consciousness, for these fictive sailors of a war-torn planet had "entered into the Brotherhood of the Sea—these men considered the sea a great leveler, a united force, a master comrade brooding over their common loyalties" (113). The masculinist metaphors that circulate in *The Sea Is My Brother* must by now stand in stark, anachronistic contrast to Rachel Carson's ecological mandate to planetary co-dwelling in *The Sea Around Us* (1951) as maternal, caring, interconnected, trans-human: "The sea is mother to all life on the planet."

The more macho Kerouac knew well the murky reach and depths of the military-industrial sea, his ear was marked and marred by it as was his modernizing era, but he also invoked more joyous transformations of the ocean as world-transforming force that pointed toward another history and way of being—global space as calling out for the Buddhist-compassion way of the "dharma bum." In his amazing Pacific-based experimental poem "Sea" (appended as ending to his ocean-haunted novel *Big Sur*), Kerouac invoked the myriad, multilingual, globally crisscrossed voices (French, Chinese, Alaskan, Pomo, Spanish, English, Hawaiian, Japanese, Russian, and more) that go on deeply lurking inside the ever-lapping Pacific waves of this huge ocean from Big Sur and Nagasaki to China and even back to his Brittany origins in France:

> O the cities here below!
> The men with a thousand
> arms! the stanchions of
> their upward gaze! the
> coral of their poetry! the
> sea dragons tenderized, meat
> for fleshy fish—
> Navark, navark, the fishes
> of the Sea speak Breton—
> wash as soft as people's
> dreams—We got peoples
> in & out the shore, they call
> it shore, sea call it
> pish rip plosh—The
> 5 billion years since
> earth we saw substantial
> chan—Chinese are
> the waves—the woods
> are dreaming.[28]

Along these lines of oceanic interconnection and awakening urban readers to world consciousness via the subterranean and trans-oceanic quest for something different, Kerouac once advised fellow Beat poet Bob Kaufman—as they looked out upon a New York City that was becoming the *Pax Americana* Rome of global finance, world culture, and military empire—to stay hopeful, vigilant, vision-hungry, upbeat, "Walking on water wasn't built in a day."[29] *Walking on water* here means, as I trope upon Kerouac as a "becoming Oceania" mentor of planetary compassion and cosmic belonging across space and time, to learn "oceanic consciousness" even in urban sites: to learn how to flow and mix; to learn how to coexist with the elements and other species; to learn a mode of being linking together of waters and lands; to learn how to form figures and affects of conjunctive beatitude and modes of co-belonging; to learn how to detoxify *new world waters* on this planet, before it is too late.

---

[28] This experimental-world-language poem activating the oceanic environment (composed and signed "21 August 1960 Pacific Ocean at Big Sur California") can be found online here: http://www.beatsupernovarasa.com/ARCHIVE/SEA.htm. Kerouac's *Big Sur* novel contains a long excerpt as its Appendix. Allen Ginsberg later wrote in a blurb for Penguin's 1991 reprinting of Kerouac's alcohol-drenched novel, "[H]ere at the peak of his suffering humorous genius, he wrote through his genius to end with 'Sea,' a brilliant poem appended, on the hallucinatory Sounds of the Pacific at Big Sur."

[29] Kerouac's remark is quoted in David Henderson, Introduction to *Cranial Guitar: Selected Poems by Bob Kaufman*, 15.

# Works Cited

Alaimo, Stacy. "Violet-Black." *Prismatic Ecology: Ecotheory beyond Green*, edited by Jeffrey Jerome Cohen, U of Minnesota P, 2013, pp. 233.
"Asia's Roiling Sea." *New York Times*, Aug. 18, 2012.
Bernes, Jasper. *Starsdown*. Small Press Distribution, 2007.
Child, Ben. "*Pacific Rim* Designed to Advance U.S. Cultural Domination of China." *British Guardian*, Aug. 28, 2013.
Cohen, Jeffrey Jerome, ed. *Prismatic Ecology: Ecotheory beyond Green*. Minnesota UP, 2013.
Connery, Christopher Leigh. "Ideologies of Land and Sea: Alfred Thayer Mahan, Carl Schmitt, and the Shaping of Global Myth Elements." *Boundary 2*, vol. 28, 2001, pp. 173–201.
———. "Pacific Rim Discourse." *Asia/Pacific as Space of Cultural Production*, edited by Rob Wilson and Arif Dirlik, Duke UP, 1995, pp. 30–56.
———. "Sea Power." *PMLA*, vol. 125, 2010, pp. 685–92.
———. "The Oceanic Feeling and the Regional Imaginary." *Global/Local: Cultural Production and the Transnational Imaginary*, edited by Rob Wilson and Wimal Dissanayake, Duke UP, 1996, pp. 284–311.
———. "There Was No More Sea: The Supercession of the Ocean from the Bible to Cyberspace." *Journal of World Geography*, vol. 32, 2006, pp. 495–511.
Cumings, Bruce. *Dominion from Sea to Sea: Pacific Ascendancy and American Power*. Yale UP, 2009.
Def, Mos. *Black on Both Sides*. Rawkus Records and Priority Records, 1999.
Deleuze, Gilles and Claire Parnet. *Dialogues*, translated by Hugh Tomlinson and Barbara Habberjam. Columbia UP, 1987.
DeLoughrey, Elizabeth. "Heavy Waters: Waste and Atlantic Modernity." *PMLA*, vol. 125, 2010, pp. 703–12.
Demick, Barbara. "Malaysia Plane: Confronting Searchers Is an Ocean Full of Garbage." *Los Angeles Times*. Mar. 30, 2014.
Dimock, Wai Chee. *Through Other Continents: American Literature across Deep Time*. Princeton UP, 2006.
Eperjesi, John. "Basing the Pacific: Exceptional Spaces of the Wilkes Exploring Expedition, 1838–1842." *Amerasia Journal*, vol. 37, 2011, pp. 1–17.
Giles, John R. "The Blue Humanities." *NEH*, vol. 34, 2013, n.p.
Hau'ofa, Epeli. "The Ocean in Us." *We Are the Ocean: Selected Works*. U of Hawai'i P, 2008, pp. 41–59.
Hayton, Bill. *The South China Sea: The Struggle for Power in Asia*. Yale UP, 2014.
Helmreich, Stefan. *Alien Ocean: Anthropological Voyages in Microbial Seas*. U of California P, 2009.
Henderson, David. *Introduction to Cranial Guitar: Selected Poems by Bob Kaufman*. Minneapolis, 1995.
Horrocks, Shirley, dir. *The New Oceania*. Point of View Productions, 2005.
Hsiung, James C. "Sea Power, Law of the Sea, and China-Japan East China Sea 'Resource War.'" Forum on China and the Sea. Macao, China. Oct. 9–11, 2005.
"John Luther Adams's 'Become Ocean' Wins Pulitzer Prize for Music." *WQXR Blog*. Apr. 14, 2014.

Kaplan, Robert D. *Asia's Cauldron: The South China Sea and the End of a Stable Pacific*. Random House, 2014.
———. "Geography Strikes Back." *The Wall Street Journal*. Sept. 7, 2012.
Kerouac, Jack. *Atop an Underwood*. Penguin, 1999.
———. *Big Sur*. Bantam Books, 1962.
———. *Lonesome Traveler*. Grove Press, 1977.
———. *The Sea Is My Brother: The Lost Novel*, edited by Dawn Ward, Penguin, 2011.
Knott, Bill. *The Unsubscriber: Poems*. Farrar, Straus and Giroux, 2004.
Kissinger, Henry. *On China*. Penguin, 2011.
"Make Law Not War: How to Solve Spats over Sea Borders." *The Economist*. Aug. 25, 2012.
McDougall, Brandy Nālani. *The Salt-wind: Ka Makani Pa'akai*. Kuleana 'Ōiwi P, 2008.
Mearsheimer, John J. "The Gathering Storm: China's Challenge to US Power in Asia." *The Chinese Journal of International Politics*, vol. 3, 2010, pp. 381–96.
Mentz, Steve. *At the Bottom of Shakespeare's Ocean*. Continuum, 2009.
Nixon, Rob. "The Great Acceleration and the Great Divergence: Vulnerability during the Anthropocene." *Profession*. 2014.
Olson, Charles. *Call Me Ishmael*. Johns Hopkins UP, 1997.
Paik, Koohan and Jerry Meander. "Blowback in the Pacific." *The Nation*, Dec. 31, 2012.
Palmer, Jane. "Junk Accumulating on Monterey Bay Ocean Floors: Scientists Find Increasing Levels of Debris in the Deep Sea." *Santa Cruz Sentinel*, Feb. 2, 2010.
Perez, Craig Santos. *from unincorporated territory: [hacha]*. TinFish Press, 2008.
———. *from unincorporated territory: [saina]*. Omnidawn, 2010.
Sandhu, Sukhdev. "Allan Sekula: Filming the Forgotten Resistance at Sea." *The Guardian*, Apr. 20, 2012.
Schmitt, Carl. "The Monroe Doctrine as a Precedent for a *Grofsraum* Principle." *Writings on War*, translated and edited by Timothy Nunan, Polity, 2011, pp. 83–90.
Shiels, Maggie. "Boat Made of Trash [the Plastiki] Prepares to Set Sail." *BBC News*, Mar. 3, 2010.
Sloterdijk, Peter. *In the World Interior of Capital: Towards a Philosophical Theory of Globalization*, translated by Wieland Hoban. Polity, 2013.
———. *Neither Sun nor Death*, translated by Steve Corcoran. Semiotext(e), 2011.
Spahr, Juliana. *This Connection of Everyone with Lungs*. U of California P, 2005.
———. *Well Then There Now*. David R. Godine, 2012.
Stevenson, Jim. "China Makes Debut in RIMPAC Naval Drills." *Voice of America*, July 4, 2014.
"Too Small an Ocean." *The Economist*, Sept. 8, 2012.
"U.S., China Clash on Key Issues." *New York Times*, Sept. 5, 2012.
Wilson, Rob. *Be Always Converting, Be Always Converted: An American Poetics*. Harvard UP, 2009.
Yeo, George. "For the Rest of Asia, America Might Be a Friend, but China Cannot Be an Enemy." *Huffington Post Online*. Aug. 20, 2014.

# 10

# Island Imaginations, Bioregionalism, and the Environmental Humanities

Kathryn Yalan Chang

The Eighth Naphtha Cracker Project was proposed in 2006, the site for it was selected in 2008, and it was halted in 2011.[1] The project was supported and invested in by Kuokuang Petrochemical Technology Corporation, the state-owned oil refinery Chinese Petroleum Corporation (CPC) of Taiwan, and several other Taiwanese petrochemical companies and major firms. The temporary termination of the Eighth Naphtha Cracker Project, a project that would have damaged land, air, and water as well as threatened the endangered pink dolphin, was a major achievement for the environmental movement in Taiwan. Based on their support for the anti-Kuokuang campaign and anxiety about Taiwan's future, two Taiwanese poets and environmental writers, Sheng Wu (Sheng-Xiong Wu) and Mingyi Wu, co-edited *Wetlands, Petrochemicals, and Imagining an Island* (2011), a collection of essays and interviews giving voice to an alternative imagination of Taiwan's future during the anti-Kuokuang campaign.

*Wetlands, Petrochemicals, and Imagining an Island* represents the voices of regional residents, environmental protection activists, artists, cultural critics, and university teachers and students from around the country. It offers an insight into grassroots bioregionalism through its mixture of local voices, place-related poetry, songs, essays, analyses of the Sixth Naphtha Cracker Plant (1991) in Yunlin County, discussions of the environmental impact assessment of petrochemical technologies in Changhua County, records of community events, and details of environmental activism. Wu and Wu and the other authors represented in the collection share the same concerns about how the petrochemical industry has greatly impacted the environment and public health.

---

This chapter is the partial results of a research project funded by the Ministry of Science and Technology Projects in Taiwan (MOST 109-2410-H-143-004).

[1] The term "cracker" derives from "cracking," which refers to "the process of breaking down chemical compounds by heat." The term applies in particular to the process of the "cracking of hydrocarbons in the kerosine fraction obtained from petroleum refining to give smaller hydrocarbon molecules and alkenes" (*Oxford Dictionary of Chemistry*).

Sheng Wu is a local poet whose poems and essays are inspired by his life experiences. His works, which are best known for expressing a vivid Taiwanese identity, convey a deep affection for the land without superficial nostalgia. For example, *Guarding River of Mother: Notes on the Jhuoshuei River* (2002) reflects a deep understanding of ecological issues and concerns about the Jhuoshuei River, the longest river in Taiwan. Mingyi Wu has also written extensively on environmental issues and social movements in Taiwan. He has attracted global attention with his novel, *The Man with the Compound Eyes* (2011) and the latest novel *The Stolen Bicycle* (2017). As he comments in the preface of *Wetlands, Petrochemicals, and Imagining an Island*, each sentence of the book contains imaginings of the island (5).

In this chapter, I first discuss how environmental activists have adopted an island/environmental imagination and bioregional practices as these specifically refer to the Da-chen wetlands and issues of community health in Changhua County. This imagination and these practices strengthen effective/affective work as it reflects environmentalists' efforts to protect the Jhuoshuei River and its watershed by interrogating and challenging state power and economic modernization. I then argue that Wu and Wu's book exemplifies work in the "environmental humanities," a synthesis of knowledge produced out of the humanities, scientific data, and public opinion and policies, and it uses that knowledge and evidence to analyze how the communities and organizations that formed the anti-Kuokuang campaign successfully halted Changhua County's Eighth Naphtha Cracker Project.

## The Bioregional Imagination: A Life Place versus a Toxic Island

*The place where we're living is actually just a small island. I sometimes feel that in a way the size of the island is not for us to decide ... I often think that if you stroll from town to town, from village to village, the island would get really big.*
—Mingyi Wu, *The Man with the Compound Eyes*

*With the environmental crisis comes a crisis of the imagination, a need to find new ways to understand nature and humanity's relation to it.*
— Lawrence Buell, *The Environmental Imagination*

The term "bioregionalism," coined by Peter Berg and Raymond Dasmann in 1974, refers to "both geographical terrain and a terrain of consciousness—to a place and the ideas that have developed about how to live in that place" (Aberley 19, 36). It connotes place or landscape but also how one conceptualizes place and alters landscape through one's imagination. As Kirkpatrick Sale explains the term "bioregionalism":

> There is nothing so mysterious about the elements of the word, after all—*bio* is from the Greek word for all forms of life, as in *biology* and *biography*, and *region* is from the Latin *regere*, a territory to be ruled—and there is nothing, after a moment's thought, so terribly difficult in what they convey together: a life-territory,

a place defined by its life forms, its topography and its biota, rather than by human dictates; a region governed by nature, not legislature.

(43)

Sale's definition of "bioregionalism" reveals that to consider bioregionalism is to take fauna and flora into account as well as political and administrative boundaries.[2]

John Elder proposes eight categories for defining a local region: the "geological processes producing the main landforms of [the] watershed"; "its characteristic climate, seasons, and weather"; "the lifecycles and habitats of notable local plants and animals, and the communities to which they belong"; "the fluctuations of forest history in our region"; "indigenous human cultures and some of their own stories about the area"; "immigration and settlement from other countries"; "nearby farms and their products"; and "ways people in the watershed presently make their living" (14–15). These are useful for discussing the bioregionalism issues that relate to the proposed petrochemical plant in Changhua County and the Da-chen wetlands and watershed. In addition, ecocritic Lawrence Buell's distinction between regionalism and bioregionalism is useful to include here. As he states, instead of traditional regionalism, "[m]odern bioregionalism" increases one's sense that "regions remain permeable to shock waves potentially extending worldwide" (*The Future of Environmental Criticism* 81).

Taiwan has multiple bioregions, stretching from the north to the south and from coastal areas to inland and mountainous regions. As the diversity of Taiwanese cultural groups and landscapes make each region unique, each area requires different governmental responses, and nuanced environmental checks and balances. "Ilha Formosa!" was the first word shouted by the Portuguese when they saw Taiwan on their voyage for the first time. The ancestors of Taiwanese people called Taiwan by the names "dolphin," "taro," and "sweet potato." Taiwan, as an island nation, is surrounded by the ocean and its marine and coastal environments reveal the complexity of water-related issues in relation to terrestrial environmental problems. As Yi-chun Yeh observes, each

---

[2] Robert L. Thayer prefers the term "life place" to "bioregion" (3). The former refers to "a unique region definable by natural (rather than political) boundaries with a geographic, climatic, hydrological, and ecological character capable of supporting unique human and nonhuman living communities" (3). Thayer also uses the term "ecoregion," one that underscores that territories are "nested" and one that pays attention to the significant roles of "abiotic influences, such as climate and landform" (16). Tom Lynch draws attention to the term "nested bioregionalism," accentuating bioregional "overlapping and permeable borders" and the notion that bioregions "are nested and interwoven at various scales, from the most local to the planetary" (29). Pointing to the need to soften borders, Lynch challenges older distinctions between the local and the global: every local place is part of a broader and larger (global) place. As Thayer points out, "[e]ach of us lives somewhere within a watershed or hydrological region (although we are only now coming to that realization), and these watersheds are relatively distinct and do not always correspond with city, county, state, or national boundaries" (19). As a consequence, to focus on the bioregion in one's research is to place a high value on shared commons such as river systems, ecozones, oceans and waterways, or mountain ranges. This valorization is "the basis for understanding the place of human history within a clearly delineated environmental context" (Spence 429), and it should be sustained for future generations.

island has a unique and irreplaceable value. Without adequate protection, the island's fecund biodiversity is overused or exploited. It is possible that the island will no longer be an island in the future but an irretrievable space (Yeh 20). Yeh's imagination of the island's future relates to the anti-Kuokuang campaign's opposition to any industry and construction, such as incinerators, dumps, and petrochemical plants. The campaign recognizes the importance of wetlands in terms of human and environmental health and pictures an alternative future for Taiwan.

The role of the environmental imagination, as described by Buell, is significant for promoting bioregional practices. Wu and Wu offer an alternative vision to that of proponents of the Eighth Naphtha Cracker Project. They envision a fruitful island (Formosa) instead of a toxic island. As the blurb for Buell's *The Environmental Imagination: Thoreau, Nature Writing, and the Formation of American Culture* states, environmental protection starts with the environmental imagination. The following question thus is asked: What counts as the Taiwan environmental imagination in the event of the anti-Kuokuang campaign? The environmental imagination in Wu and Wu's book is not an exclusively anthropocentric one; rather, it takes into consideration the threats to nonhuman species and the habitats of these species.

The alternative future that anti-Kuokuang campaign creates and imagines points to a debate in 2010 between Chia-yang Tsai, the director of the Changhua Coast Conservation Action and the chairman of the Changhua Environmental Protection Union, and Bao-lang Chen, the former chairman of Chinese *Petroleum Corp* (CPC) of Taiwan and Kuokuang Petrochemical Technology Corporation, on one of the TV programs in Taiwan Public Television Service (PTS). Tsai and Chen present diametrically opposite views about Taiwan's future. Having great expectations for the petrochemical industry, Chen argued that due to the high value of the products of petrochemical manufacture in industrial countries, people in those countries are not only wealthy but also have higher life expectancies. In Chen's view, Taiwan has limited resources and heavily relies on raw materials imported for the manufacturing of export goods, so developing petrochemical industries is the way to boost Taiwan's economic development ("Chia-yang"). Against Chen, with regard to the construction of the Eighth Naphtha Cracker Project, Tsai argued that the Da-chen wetlands should be at the very least categorized as a national wetlands area ("Chia-yang"; Wu and Wu 80).[3] For petrochemical companies, the wetlands are an infertile and valueless place, but for supporters of the anti-Kuokuang campaign, the wetlands are "the kidneys" of the earth, comparable to forests, "the lungs of the earth" ("Devoted in [sic] Preserving Wetlands?").[4]

---

[3] Tsai also pointed out that although the government is unwilling to list Da-chen as a wetland due to political and commercial pressures, it was suggested in both 2007 and 2010 that Da-chen wetland be listed as national and even international wetland.

[4] According to the World Wildlife Fund (WWF), wetlands are "one of the most undervalued ecosystems but provide a range of vital services. They provide food, they filter water and offer a unique habitat for many different species" ("The Value of Wetlands"). They purify and break down toxic substances in water, prevent seawater invasion, protect coasts against erosion, recharge groundwater, and reduce the temperature, or the so-called heat island effect. They play a vital role in the ecology of any region. They are a tightly protective network guarding a region. Without them, natural ecological cycles become unbalanced.

The bioregion of the Da-chen wetlands, an area of 4,000 hectares, was proposed to be the site of Taiwan's eighth petrochemical park, the Eighth Naphtha Cracker Project. The wetlands are part of the Changhua coastal intertidal zone, which spans four kilometers along the intertidal zone and is the largest estuary. According to Chia-yang Tsai,

> There are 15 kilometers of mudflats stretching from the estuary of the Jhuoshuei River to the mouth of Erlin Creek in Fangyuan. This is the last stretch of natural coastline in Taiwan, serving not just as a foraging habitat for the humpback dolphin, but also as a fishery and aquaculture region of Changhua County as well as feeding grounds for the Eurasian curlew and Saunders' gull, both protected migratory birds.
>
> (qtd. in Nelson, n.p.)

Sheng Wu's poem "Write You a Poem," as well as Tsai's description of the Da-chen wetlands, evokes Una Chaudhuri's term "theater of species." Dedicated to the anti-Kuokuang campaign and published in Wu and Wu's collection, the poem articulates principles and practices of bioregionalism. Da-chen wetlands is home to fiddler crabs, mudskippers, far eastern curlews, long-legged chickens, and egrets, and a "life territory" or bioregion where Taiwan pink dolphins migrate regularly. The poem also reminds readers that farmers and fishermen have lived here for centuries (Wu and Wu 34). As the Da-chen wetlands are the last remaining intertidal mudflats in the mouth of the Jhuoshuei River, the Eighth Naphtha Cracker Project *would* cause irreparable havoc to the region.[5] The mouth of the Jhuoshuei River, known as "the mother river of Taiwan," not only supports many seabird species but also is a region that people have long depended upon for agriculture, took root in the land, lived on the land contentedly, and passed on their knowledge from generation to generation (Wu and Wu 218).

However, the Da-chen wetland's case exemplifies how the Kuokuang project reflects socio-political and economic forces uniformed by fundamental environmental principles of sustainability. For instance, there have been conversations on whether or not the Da-chen wetlands should be listed as wetlands of national-level importance. Bao-lang Chen himself said that if Da-chen had been officially designated as wetlands, he would not have "shot himself in the foot" by negotiating with local government and environmental groups ("Chia-yang"). As Sheng Wu and Mingyi Wu argue, because

---

[5] Tsai also points out that the intertidal zone along the country's west coast is a critical part of Taiwan's aquaculture, agriculture, history, and culture (169). It is internationally recognized as a wetlands area. More specifically, Da-chen wetland, located in the southwest corner of Changhua County, is the southernmost alluvial fan of Jhuoshuei River. It is located next to the Taiwan Strait, across from Yunlin County. As Tsai indicates, the southern coast of Changhua, which includes the wetlands of Hanbao, Fangyuan, to Da-chen, may be the last intertidal mudflats in Taiwan. They have a high biological productivity, are rich in species diversity, attract hundreds of water birds in winter, are a site of oyster aquaculture, and act as a natural coastal defense (Tsai 79).

the government refused to attach even a local or "national-level" importance to the wetlands, they have been "erased" from the possibility of being given "international" importance (9).

The televised debate between Chen and Tsai also reflects the interests of the petrochemical industry to continue to expand its operations. It is important to understand the history of economic and industrial development in Taiwan and the role that the petrochemical industry has played in this history. According to Mingyi Wu, American investment as well as public and private capital in Taiwan gave birth to two giant monsters, Taiwan CPC and Formosa Plastics, which subsequently devoured the island's future ("Preface" 3). As the petrochemical industry expanded, the Taiwanese government's slogan—"Energy Efficiency and Carbon Reduction"—has become for many Taiwanese people a joke, for they consume more energy than they produce. When Bao-lang Chen argued that the Eighth Naphtha Cracker Project would differ from Formosa Plastics' Sixth Naphtha Cracker Plant because low-carbon green energy goals would be met, Chia-yang Tsai retorted that this would not reduce the pollution from the plant ("Chia-yang"). Tsai and other individuals involved in the anti-Kuokuang campaign were especially concerned about the impact of the petrochemical industry on the coastal fisheries in Taichung, Changhua, and Yunlin. They were worried about the impact of the industry on the air and water as well as the large-scale land reclamation of the Da-chen. Since the CPC first built a plant in Kaohsiung in 1968, the petrochemical industry has continued to develop in Taiwan; over the past 42 years, the industry has polluted and contaminated hundreds of hectares of land. The contaminated land can never be recovered, regardless of the amount of money that is spent on recovery programs (Wu and Wu 193).

Chen's promise to meet low-carbon green energy goals sounds like lies to the people who are familiar with the debate that took place in 1987 between Yung-ching Wang, the founder of Formosa Plastics, and Ding-nan Chen, Chief of Yilan County. It was about whether or not the construction of Formosa Plastics' Sixth Naphtha Cracker Plant should be in Yilan County. Chen expressed concern from a bioregional perspective. He was reluctant to welcome polluting industries such as naphtha cracker parks. He and others were more interested in establishing so-called chimney-free industries in order to maintain the region's local and unique bioregional value (Wu and Wu 63). Due to Chen's environmental imagination, Yilan County continues to have clean water, air, and land today,[6] and it contrasts markedly with Yunlin County, where Formosa Plastics' Sixth Naphtha Cracker Plant is located (Wu and Wu 52).

After the founding of the Formosa Petrochemical Mailiao Plant in 1994, Yunlin became a deeply compromised bioregion. It and the nearby townships of Mailiao, Taisi, Dongshih, Lunbei, and Sihhu were threatened by high concentrations of dioxin pollution. Dioxin is a substance that can disrupt endocrine and other hormonal

---

[6] Yilan County is the site of Taiwan's first locally produced whisky. One of the reasons that King Car Corporation chose Yilan to be "the center of production" for its whisky products was because of "the excellent waters from the Central and Xueshan ranges, the mountain breezes, and the damp Pacific air," all of which "impart a wonderful character to the whisky" (Chang, Chiung-fang).

processes in the human body including "sex changes in men and increased risk of breast cancer in women" ("Open Letter").⁷ Yunlin County's high cancer rates evoke Stacy Alaimo's statement that "the recognition that human health is undeniably affected by the health of the environment impels global environmental justice movements" (92). Petrochemicals and their byproducts cause an array of health problems (Wu and Wu 116). Cancer and other diseases that are caused or exacerbated by environmental pollution are "political not because either subject—bodies or environment—is inherently political, but rather because of the silence and secrecy surrounding the overlapping intersections of these subjects" (Knopf-Newman 134). Moreover, the town and region of Taisi, once known for its oyster farming, now suffers from coastal erosion as well as declining fish populations, which is due to acidification of the oceans. The adjacent town of Mailiao was once filled with fish farms and now is comprised of an industrial park, concentration camp like dormitories for Thai and Filipino laborers, the KTV *chamuro* (a tea house, karaoke bar, and a place where prostitution may clandestinely occur), and betel-nut stalls (Wu and Wu 66). Financial compensation was given to Mailiao in return for the building of Sixth Naphtha Cracker Plant. Although Taisi does not receive any compensation (Wu and Wu 70), cancer does not bypass Taisi and adjoining towns. Research indicates that local residents in Mailiao and Taisi are exposed to high levels of pollution from the Sixth Naphtha Cracker Plant (Wu and Wu 49–50).

Poems in Wu and Wu's book contain strong appeals to principles of environmental justice and equality. In a poem titled "Protest at the North," Ken-cheng Lee alludes to the fact that cancer cases in Yunlin County are typically blamed only on individuals' consumption of tobacco and alcohol. He writes, "Head for a place that decides our destiny/that place is called Taipei … Illness, cancer, they said: smoke cigarettes and drink alcohol, it is our bad habit, / no proof of industrial pollution. / Head of county, village mayor, local representatives / sell our health, soul, dignity for their local development" (38). As Alaimo states: "the material world becomes the very substance of self" and is entangled with "volatile scientific and political struggles" (3). The "unpredictable and always interconnected actions of environmental systems, toxic substances, and biological bodies" (3) have made it relatively easy in the past for industrial developers in Taiwan to deny accountability. The anti-Kuokuang campaign has made it more difficult for them, but environmentalists in Taiwan still face an uphill battle in their fight to halt the continued expansion of Taiwan's petrochemical industry.

Sheng Wu's poems narrate the history of Formosa Plastics' Sixth Naphtha Cracker Plant. Wu uses the metaphor "chimney kingdom" to describe a toxic Taiwan:

Chimney kingdom in the name of petrochemical industry, / determines location without explanation / in Lin-yuan / Giant chimneys tower above the town,

---

[7] In the "Open Letter from Taiwan Civil Society to the Formosa Plastics Group," the authors report that in June 2009 Public Health Professor Chang-chuan Chan (National Taiwan University) found significant correlations between the Sixth Naphtha Cracker Plant in Yunlin County and cancer rates among residents in the nearby townships of Mailiao, Taisi, Dongshih, Lunbei, and Sihhu.

reaching the sky, / small chimneys stand in great numbers, just like / the guards in front of a magnificent empire, rich and powerful families / raging flames burn down the whole day.

(Wu and Wu 47)

Formosa Plastics Corporation and other industrial developers have transformed Taiwan into a chimney kingdom of naphtha cracker plants: the Fourth Naphtha Cracker Plant in Lin-yuan (1984), the Fifth Naphtha Cracker Plant (1994) in Houching, and the Sixth Naphtha Cracker Plant (1999) in Mailao.

Min Yung Lee's short poem, "Pollution," resonates with Wu and Wu's commentary:

In order to maintain the giant chimney
Riot-control *police* blockade the whole village
Spray smog makes the green fields turn black
Blocks the sky
That is the net weaved by power
In order to subdue the thoughtful brain
In order to make touching heart submissive
Grand reasons for development
Development is to chop off the hope of forestation
Dead land
Stinking dead birds' bodies exposed to the sun.

(Wu and Wu 191)

The petrochemical industry in Mailiao in Yunlin County uses excessive amounts of water. The bioregions of Changhua and Yunlin Counties are complex marine and estuarine ecosystems and both are experiencing shrinking water supplies. Both share the same ocean currents, wind systems, and greater weather systems. These current and systems define bioregions (Thomashow 130). If the Kuokuang project is implemented, it will result in land subsidence problems and groundwater overdrafts. It also will endanger Taiwan's high-speed transportation (Wu and Wu 197). Rejecting the metaphor of "chimney kingdom," Wu and Wu point out that Taiwan is facing a raft of environmental, social, economic, and cultural problems that are being ignored by policy-makers. Catriona Mortimer-Sandilands's idea of "preventing metaphoric closure and opening the need for ongoing conversation" (181) is worth noticing in this context. The people of Taiwan are searching for a new metaphor to describe an alternative future for Taiwan, a future where the environment, society, and economy can flourish.

When the government of Taiwan planned for the future of Taiwan several decades ago, it focused exclusively on industrially stimulating the economy. It has been promoting that kind of economic growth and development since the 1970s, making it appear as if industrial growth is the only factor to consider with regard to the country's future. In the name of progress and economic revitalization, state-led industrialization walks hand in hand with private corporations. Together, they compete for the world's largest petrochemical plants. The industrial development policy of Taiwan is one of the factors in the loss of Taiwan's coastal wetlands, the subsiding of land from industrial water withdrawal and sand mining, and the increase of toxic air emissions, contaminated water, and toxic buildup of metals in soils (Wu and Wu 171–2). This "macroeconomy" policy ruins bioregions. Robert L. Thayer points to this as follows: "Matter and energy flow from the natural capital of ... natural regions into the macroeconomy, and the macroeconomy delivers products, waste matter, and waste heat back to the biosphere via its specific bioregions" (113). Advocates of industrial high energy consumption and industrial high water usage disregard the associated problems of economic vulnerability, growth volatility, the compromised health of people, and social inequity (Wu and Wu 221). As Vandana Shiva describes common understandings of progress and development, these refer to the introduction of "scientific agriculture," "scientific animal husbandry," "scientific water management," and so forth, and they are reductive, universalizing, and inherently violent and destructive (14). The two main political parties in Taiwan, the Kuomintang political party (KMT) and the Democratic Progressive Party political party (DPP), both seem intent upon industrializing Taiwan's bioregions (Wu and Wu 186). They are promoting mass production, and mass waste and pollution. Both have changed older "definitions of proper land use and appropriate national development" (Spence 430). As various globalizing economic, technological, and political powers influence and affect contemporary bioregions, these regions lose their heterogeneity. Reduction and universalization bring about the homogeneity and standardization of cultures, societies, ideologies, and ways of life.

The government along with large corporations has "change[d] our island into a toxic distribution center" (Wu and Wu 188). Taiwan must stop relying on the petrochemical industry, which has already destroyed much of Taiwan's fragile island environments. In the past, the petrochemical industry helped to boost local and national trade and economic growth. However, Taiwan now needs to transit to an environment-based economy instead of the industry that is the cause of high levels of pollution and high environmental risks. Proponents of the Kuokuang project argue that without the Eighth Naphtha Cracker Project, 600,000 job opportunities will be lost ("Petrochemical Project"). They imply that "if the industry's environmental impact [can] be reduced, causing less damage to human health and to ecosystems," the project will be a viable option ("Petrochemical Project Highlights Economy, Environment Conflict"). In reality, this is very difficult and costly to accomplish. Moreover, real estate prices fall dramatically in regions where there are high concentrations of petrochemical plants. The anti-Kuokuang campaign, which successfully halted the Eighth Naphtha Cracker Project, calls for people's awareness of Taiwan's bioregions (Wu and Wu 160).

## The Future We Want: The Environmental Humanities and Ecological Engagement

*I'm afraid the main issue right now is the necessity of the project, not the technical challenge. It's about what kind of island you want.*
　　　　　　　　—Mingyi Wu, *The Man with the Compound Eyes*

"The Future We Want" is an outcome document of the United Nations (UN) Conference on Sustainable Development, signed by all UN member states. It takes into consideration "a high quality of life" that is "equitably shared and sustainable" for all species around the globe (Adamson, "Roots" 125). Although Taiwan is not a member of the UN, the anti-Kuokuang campaign undertakes advocacy work based on this document. Wu and Wu's book is an example of how literary expression affirms environmental justice principles including "the interdependence of all species" and "responsible uses of lands and renewable resources in the interest of a sustainable planet for humans and other living things"; moreover, the book also calls for "universal protection" from toxic wastes that threaten and intimidate "the fundamental right to clean air, land, water, and food" ("The Principles of Environmental Justice" 1, 3, 4).

As Taiwanese culture continues to be influenced by liberalization, modernization, and westernization, social movements and political reforms are not taking, and need not take, the form of a radical political revolution or violent acts against the government. Anti-Kuokuang campaign actions include spiritual blessings and ceremonies, music videos, and social media petitions against Kuokuang Petrochemical Corporation Factory. Wu and Wu's *Wetlands, Petrochemicals, and Imagining an Island* is also particularly significant, for it provides a historical and political environmental analysis of the Kuokuang.[8] Even if a reader has no idea about the Kuokuang project, he/she can learn about the project through the more creative material in the book such as poems and other creative writings.

Wu and Wu's book is part of the growing body of literature on environmental justice. This literature includes, in addition to "poetry and fictional prose," as Adamson notes, "movement manifestos, EPA documents, and international trade agreements" (*American Indian Literature* 129). The environmental humanities as a whole also is contributing to environmental justice literature in the areas of "history, philosophy, aesthetics, religious studies, literature, theater, film and media studies" (Adamson, "Humanities" 135). These areas are "informed by the most recent research in the sciences of nature and sustainability" (Adamson, "Humanities" 135). Connecting with disciplines outside of the humanities—with disciplines in the areas of technology, science, and politics—the environmental humanities is breaking the "bureaucratic inertia" and altering "the tendency of governments, academia, and other groups to work in isolation" (Adamson, "Humanities" 138).

Environmentalists' use of a diverse range of artistic expression to oppose the establishment of the Kuokuang project reflects the importance of the arts in effecting change. Wu and Wu's book includes, for example, "poetry and short essays that give voice to individuals from the arts as well as academic circles and the medical profession" (Chen, n.p.). Chung-ming Liu, a global climate-change expert and Chairman of the Environmental Quality Protection Foundation, makes the argument that Taiwan needs to pursue an economic path that will effectively reduce carbon dioxide emissions and efficiently promote economic growth (Wu and Wu 114–15). As part of his argument,

---

[8] For a historical review of Taiwan's petrochemical industry since the 1960s, see Shieh and Ho.

Liu advises that Taiwan ought to implement policies which encourage more investment in art and culture industry, as he believes that creating a prosperous economy based on industrial production is not as applicable to Taiwan today as it was in the past (Wu and Wu 114–15).

Understanding local stories helps people to comprehend how complex issues of environmental justice influence people's lives on a daily basis. The role of literature and art is significant because "dramatised narrative, poetic invocation, aesthetic experiment, and stylistic innovation" are able to deconstruct "an array of powerful connotations such as 'home,' 'locality,' 'ground' and 'belonging' and attendant powerful notions of identity" (Harris 110). The protagonists in the stories speak for themselves (Cole and Foster 1). Wu and Wu's book includes some stories which lay stress on the spirit of engagement as well as personal narratives and testimonies. Jin-lang Lin and Bao-feng Zheng's story tells how their lives have been destroyed by the Six Naphtha Cracker Plant. Since 1990, the Lin family has made their living through oyster farming in Taisi. After the construction of the Six Naphtha Cracker Plant, their lives changed: "Due to the sand pumping, the seascape was altered, and the ecology of the intertidal oyster reef was damaged. Oyster seeds were covered in sand and oyster harvests declined sharply. The old men living in the country had no idea how the Six Naphtha Cracker Plant would impact oyster farming" (Wu and Wu 71). The government broke the promise that the plant would not have any impact on oyster farming. However, the burden of providing the proof requested by the Environmental Protection Administration lay on the oyster farmers themselves. Moreover, the "no compensation" rule was based on the government's position that "industry comes first" and "the land of the emerging industrial park" does not belong only "to oyster farmers" (Wu and Wu 71).

Bao-feng Zheng's story is a particularly powerful testimony in terms of ecofeminist engagements. Women in Taiwan's fishing villages play a vastly under-recognized role. They wear traditional bamboo hats, nondescript clothes, aprons, rain shoes, face masks with small floral prints, and sleevelets, and their two eyes and two hands are always busy opening the oysters. They work in oyster farms with their husbands during the early morning at low tide and with other women during high tide. When they open, clean, process, and cook the oysters, they perform the same tasks as local men, reducing the pressure on men, and they are equally exposed to pollution. Yet, due to sexism in fishing villages, as Zheng testifies, women often endure insults when they stand up for the rights of illiterate fishermen and protest sand pumping and sea reclamation. Zheng has since passed away, but her husband Lin carries on her passion, keeping an eye on every development plan along the seashore of Yunlin and asking the Six Naphtha Cracker Plant for more details regarding the depleting fish populations. As Wu and Wu also note, "either local factions or gangsters control Yunlin" (Wu and Wu 73). The Six Naphtha Cracker Plant and the offshore industrial island at Mailiao village are intertwined with political interests and huge profits (Wu and Wu 72). Lin claims, "Without knowing, we [he and his late wife] are on the same boat. Fighting persists. It is responsibility that drives our common mission" (Wu and Wu 73). This is how local people such as Lin and Zheng engage with the complicated personal and political forces in the area. If the Eighth Naphtha Cracker Plant is built in Da-chen, on the other side of Jhuoshuei River, Yunlin will still experience air and other forms of pollution as it is in the same bioregion.

Transformation means reimagining more "equitable, cooperative relations among ourselves and everything else on the planet" (Hofrichter 87). For Lin and Zheng, achieving that reimagination is necessary for survival and requires what Hofrichter calls "a politics that challenges principles of growth, consumerism, and corporate power that ... permit the burden of ecological devastation to be born" (87). Their work critically contributes to and forms the environmental humanities. As Adamson notes, this area of study in the humanities, which brings together a wide range of disciplines (philosophy, ethics, history, literature, etc.), "has long worked as an imaginative force" toward the "transformations of the world and its inhabitants" ("Humanities" 139). "Transformation," as Luke W. Cole and Sheila R. Foster define it, works at the individual, group, and community level, and it influences "institutions, government, and social structure" (14). Many individuals feel vulnerable (and understandably so) in the face of unequal distributions of resources, social benefits, and pollution caused by big industries. Some will (be able to) choose to fight to change these conditions. Such individuals are "transformed through the process of struggle" (Cole and Foster 14). As "residents in marginal communities," they acquire power through "networking with other groups" and they can shape environmental policy, "both locally and nationally," as well as to create "more opportunities for community input into the spectrum of policy making that affects their material conditions" (Cole and Foster 15).

Many people who have experienced the magnificence of the wetlands are willing to devote themselves to the anti-Kuokuang campaign even though they do not reside in areas directly affected by the Kuokuang project. One proponent of the Kuokuang project, a local representative, asks outsiders to mind their own business because they know nothing about the needs of people who live near the project. Indeed, as Linda Martin Alcoff also argues, "outsiders" can sometimes cause problems in environmental justice movements because a speaker's location "has an epistemically significant impact on that speaker's claims and can serve either to authorize or de-authorize her speech" (98). Furthermore,

> not only is location epistemically salient but certain privileged locations are discursively dangerous. In particular, the practice of privileged persons speaking for or on behalf of less privileged persons has actually resulted (in many cases) in increasing or reinforcing the oppression of the group spoke for.
>
> (98)

However, as Mingyi Wu argues, this is an era of no bystanders (Preface 6). Every piece of land in Taiwan ought to be treasured by every citizen regardless of where he/she lives. Local residents must form alliances with so-called outsiders including legal, academic, medical, religious, and environmental groups.⁹ Take Wu and Wu's book as an example. Sheng Wu, a Changhua-native local farmer as well as poet, is an "insider," while Mingyi Wu, who also admits he can hardly be called an environmental activist, is an "outsider." Yet his voice and contribution represent the collaborative power that the movement requires. Moreover, in the case of the anti-Kuokuang campaign, their fight for preserving the Changhua wetlands reflects a strong commitment to community engagement. Working with others enables local residents to feel empowered and interconnected. As Mary L. Stokrocki and Michael Delahunt define "empowerment," this is the act of "transferring power" and "giving confidence" to, and "building self-esteem" among, locals (1). As Karla Armbruster also argues, such "small steps in the direction of sustainability" are multiple and have significant positive outcomes (240).

The Matsu Fish Conservation Union of Taiwan creates alliances with other non-governmental organizations (NGO) to buy land from the government as part of a strategy to save Taiwan's endangered pink dolphins.¹⁰ As Adamson points out about the contemporary discourse of the rights of species other than human species:

> In a globalizing and corporatizing world, some communities are pushing the notion of "rights" and "citizenship" beyond the confines of legalistic and political structures based only on "the human," since these terms often problematically promote notions of identification, symmetry, totality, and unity employed to justify hegemonic and totalitarian actions, by both state and corporations, in the name of community.
>
> ("Environmental" 181)

If humans are unable to survive without relying on other species, the narrow sense of anthropocentric domination over other species needs some reconsideration. As Zhao-lun Chen argues, voicing the arguments of many opponents of the Kuokuang project, "[o]nly when a healthy ocean exists, will healthy white dolphins survive; only when healthy white dolphins live, will the well-beings of humans continue" (Wu and Wu 92).

Stories about the Taiwan pink dolphins play an important role in the anti-Kuokuang campaign. Those narratives, as with the stories found elsewhere in the world, contribute

---

⁹ On August 8, 2010, various civil groups including religion groups based in central Taiwan—the Roman Catholic Diocese of Taichung, Buddhist groups, Taiwan Ecology Academic, the Bicycle Group, Changhua Environmental Protection Union, Wang Gong Oyster Art Culture Association, and Providence University Woodpecker Environmental Working Team—collectively urged for protection of the Changhua wetlands and protested against the Kuokuang group's proposal to develop land close to the estuary of the Jhuoshuei River.

¹⁰ The Matsu Fish Conservation Union, Taiwan, was established in 2007 by six environmental groups: Taiwan Academy of Ecology (台灣生態學會), Taiwan Sustainable Union (台灣永續聯盟), Taiwan Environmental Protection Union (台灣環境保護聯盟), Wild at Heart Legal Defense Association (台灣蠻野心足生態協會), Wild Bird Society of Yunlin (雲林縣野鳥學會), and Changhua Environmental Protection Union (彰化環境保護聯盟). Taiwan Society for Wilderness (荒野保護協會) joined in 2011, and Oceanus Honors Gaia (台灣海龍王愛地球協會), and Taiwan Coast Network (台灣西海岸保育聯盟) participated in 2012 and 2013, respectively.

to "the languages spoken, the dances and rituals of culture" (McGinnis 1). They include folklore, fairy tales, games, poetry, art, ritual, literature, myth, dancing, singing, music and religious imagery. According to Michael Vincent McGinnis, "[a]nimals play key roles, perhaps as a totem or emblem of a family or clan, in linking humanity to place" (2). The Matsu Fish Conservation Union of Taiwan combined images of the Taiwanese goddess Matsu, protector of fishermen, with images of the Taiwan pink dolphin in order to bring more public attention to the anti-Kuokuang campaign. As argued by Peter S. Ross, Chairman of the Eastern Taiwan Strait Sousa Technical Advisory Working Group (ETSSTAWG), protecting dolphins and their habitat helps to protect and improve the health and productivity of coastal fisheries: the more dolphins there are, the stronger the food chain is, and the more abundant fishery resources there are (Huang).

Other narratives also play a vital role in educating people about the Kuokuang project. In "Write You a Poem," Sheng Wu expresses:

How much I hope my lines and poetry / are able to cast bullets,/to penetrate avaricious and insatiable brains, / or, to smelt metal and swords / to stab the breast full of insatiable desire. / But I can't. What I can do is to endure over and over again. / Write a sad and vain poem, / swallow excessive grief and indignation. / My lines and poetry are neither bullets nor swords. / They neither intimidate somebody / nor know before whom to kneel down. / Only is every line full of tears of sorrow. / Recite over and over again. / Cry out loud over and over again.

(Wu and Wu 36–37)

The passage expresses Wu's affection for Changhua and condemnation of the government. Likewise, Yong-lai Liao's ironic poem "Let's Make a Turn!" counters an argument that one often hears among people when they are asked to join in the struggle to save Taiwan's pink dolphins: "Humans have no food to eat, / so why care about these dolphins?!" (Wu and Wu 41). Liao responds by way of irony: "[To those] whose hair color is like that of our skin, / a super big governor announced: / Tell them [dolphins] to make a turn! / ... / Give 'Home' to humans!" (Wu and Wu 41).[11]

---

[11] CWDs cannot make a turn or take a route that avoids the area (Wu and Wu 125). This is why supporters of the anti-Kuokuang campaign were disappointed when National Taiwan University professor Chiu-long Chou, known as the "mother of the dolphins," reported that the coastal areas from Miaoli to Yunlin are "a certain important passage" for white dolphins' in their daily activities of swimming, finding food, socializing, and so forth. In stressing "passage" instead of "habitat," Chou and her research group unintentionally offered the Kuokuang project group the chance to argue that passage of the dolphins could be easily altered; that the dolphins could be trained using food baits and sound seduction to alter their course; and that the government could construct artificial arc-shaped seawalls to make the dolphins change their course. The government now is even promising that when the Kuokuang project is completed, when white dolphins approach it, the Kuokuang plants will be immediately shut down and the operators will wait for the dolphins to pass. Such promises mean little to ecologists and others who have observed for a long time how other similar projects have failed, including the development of other artificial corridors for wild CWDs (Wu and Wu 91, 92, 175).

The anti-Kuokuang campaign resists top-down regulatory controls and solutions by working at the grassroots level to draw public attention to issues. For example, the campaign invites pop singers and local lyric writers to reach out to different ethnic groups and generations.[12] Taiwanese singer Bobby Chen wrote the song "My Grandmother is a Matsu Fish" (Chang, Tie-zhi) to raise awareness about the impact of the petrochemical plants on the endangered dolphins. It refers to Matsu, the sea goddess widely worshipped by people in Taiwan and southeastern China as the protector of fishermen and sailors, as well as to the Chinese white dolphin (CWD), an animal species that also is known as a friend of shipwrecked sailors. The lyrics include these lines: "Rank and riches decreed by heaven, / Safety is property, / rich deposits, / how it would be spent in one's whole life, / Fate has marked the next generation, / petrochemical plants frighten us to death."[13] In "After the Eighth Naphtha Cracker Industrial Park," nature/ecological writer Ka-hsiang Liu writes of dolphins that are "now on the verge of death, / [and] could be the most deplorable [beings] on earth" (464). Liu does not romanticize pink dolphins; rather, he laments the fate of the CWD if Kuokuang Petrochemical Technology is successful in its bid to "build a naphtha cracker plant on 4,000 hectares of unpolluted wetlands in central coastal Taiwan" (463). Hopefully, the beauty of the CWD and Liu's verse will trigger people's empathy and ensure that environmental considerations are prioritized. The campaign will not be successful without the public's empathy and broad-based environmental awareness.

Wu and Wu's book ends with an appeal to people to buy wetlands in an attempt to save Taiwan's dolphins. They can do this through a trust fund set up by the Changhua Environmental Protection Union and other environmental groups (Wu and Wu 233). Chia-yang Tsai and others set up this national trust fund, the first of its kind in Taiwan, when they became aware that if regional plans were approved by the government, 2,000 hectares of tidal mudflats could be sold to Kuokuang Petrochemical at the low rate of NT$100 per square meter (Nelson). The operators of the trust competing with Kuokuang project stakeholders offer to purchase land from the government for NT$119 a share. If enough people buy a share, the land can be saved from industrial development (Nelson). As Rui-bin Chen says, "[o]ne share or 100 shares, anyone can be a landowner!" (qtd. in Nelson). The national trust fund represents the power of the general public, and it stresses spontaneity and participation in maintaining the commons (ecological environments and cultural and historical sites). People are the biggest "corporation" with the highest potential in Taiwan. In order to develop

---

[12] A-Da is a singer in The Village Armed Youth band, founded in Taichung in 2007. The band gives attention to Taiwan's farmers, and its members insist on the correlation between rock music and social praxis. A-Da's song about Jhuoshuei River is collected in Wu and Wu's book (26). Another song about the Jhuoshuei River included in Wu and Wu's book is written by Ming-chang Chen (Wu and Wu 28). Chen is a folk song musician who devotes himself to Taiwanese lyrics and songs. Another Taiwanese musician represented in Wu and Wu's book, Kou Chou Ching (a member of a hip-hop Taiwanese band), writes "what we have is seafood culture, no oceanic culture at all" in one of the band's songs entitled "Gray Coastlines" (Wu and Wu 30–31).

[13] My own English translation of Chen's lyrics. The Chinese lyric can be reached through the following link: https://www.mymusic.net.tw/ux/w/song/show/p000001-a0091241-s000257-t008-c0

a sustainable future for Taiwan, environmentalists are reaching out to the people to protect Taiwan's environment (Wu and Wu 233). In the preface of Wu and Wu's book, Mingyi Wu indicates that E. F. Schumacher's notion of "free goods" is akin to the idea of "the commons" or to the idea of communal lands (Wu 5). This land is often the most vulnerable to being exploited and manipulated in the name of development and economic management. Hence, environmental groups can purchase the "commons" of Taiwan's wetlands to prevent them from being turned into naphtha cracker plants.

When the Executive Yuan of Taiwan first supported the Eighth Naphtha Cracker Project, recognizing it as a major national investment plan, social groups, college professors, senior high students, local residents, and cultural activists protested against the endorsement. Fighting against the project, they sought to protect Taiwan's wetlands and the human populations that depend upon them. They reflect what Cole and Foster characterize as groups that "help to transform marginal communities from passive victims to significant actors in environmental decision-making processes" (14). They are fighting for their children, their communities, their quality of life, and their health. Wu and Wu's book portrays the strong grassroots opposition to the Kuokuang project and the call for a total ban on its construction. As a result of that opposition, in 2011, President Ying-jeou Ma announced that the government would not support the Kuokuang Petrochemical Plant Project in Da-chen, Changhua. The environmental movement was revitalized by the anti-Kuokuang campaign ("Petrochemical Project Highlights Economy, Environment Conflict"). It was a milestone in Taiwan's environmental movement and mobilized people nationally, kick-started an environmental movement that had been silent for a long time, and caused the government to reverse its policy. Through it, many people are more optimistic about influencing government policy through citizen action ("Petrochemical Project Highlights Economy, Environment Conflict").

The campaign's successful halting of Taiwan's Eight Naphtha Cracker proves that the people of Changhua refuse to be victims or to allow to take place what took place in Yunlin County. Most importantly, it demonstrated "community cohesion" (Cole and Foster 17). Changhua County residents and many other Taiwanese successfully halted a project that, like similar projects elsewhere in the world, threatens businesses, homes, and schools (Cole and Foster 17). The public has "begun to consider whether [Taiwan needs] more heavy industry," says Chen-yi Kan, secretary of the Matsu Fish Conservation Union of Taiwan, a group that represented the anti-Kuokuang campaign (qtd. in Jennings). Nonetheless, the battle still rages.[14]

## Conclusion

A nation can grow stronger economically in 10 years but also suffer irretrievable damage in this same amount of time. Where is Taiwan heading in the Anthropocene?

---

[14] In 2020, the controversy over solar panel installations can be observed in Changhua and other wetlands throughout the island.

Will the people of Taiwan choose again to believe the "lies" of the stakeholders of petroleum companies or will they recognize that a clean environment is irreplaceable (Wu and Wu 64)? As an island, it is difficult for Taiwan's natural environments to deal with high polluting industries. An alternative future for Taiwan ought to include low pollution-producing, non-petrochemical industries. This future would reflect the development of environmentally sustainable industries (Wu and Wu 212). Because of Ding-nan Chen's environmental imagination, Yilan County has retained its local uniqueness, and it has prospered. It has a Dongshan River Water Park (which hosts the Yilan International Children's Folklore & Folkgame Festival), a Luodong Sports Park, a Yilan Sports Park, a National Center for Traditional Arts, and the Lanyang Museum. All of these have enabled Yilan to grow and flourish in a sustainable way.

The anti-Kuokuang campaign represents not only the opposition to short-sighted, "blind" forms of economic development but also people's desire to transform Taiwan into a place where natural environments and local cultures are respected and where people take care of vulnerable and marginal groups. Such a future would make Taiwan a real "Ilha Formosa!" (Wu and Wu 208–09) and would reflect that the imagination of Taiwanese people matches the health of the land (Wu and Wu 237).

The petrochemical industry has existed in Taiwan for 40 years. Since the industrial gas explosion in Kaohsiung in August 2014, people have been wary of the government's calls for more industrialization. An expansion plan for the Sixth Naphtha Cracker Plant in Mailiao now has been turned down by locals and environmental activists because of the accident in Kaohsiung. Petrochemical companies are bleeding dry Taiwan's rivers and ruining much of the island's remaining wetlands. As Mingyi Wu claims, the petrochemical industry overlooks generation justice, environmental justice, and class justice (qtd. in Lu). Eva Horn and Hannes Bergthaller indicate in their book, *The Anthropocene* (2020), that "[t]he 'thing' of the Anthropocene are too close to be objectified, too big to be pictured, too complex to be fully accounted for" (102). Fatal industrial accidents ought to act as a warning: it is time for us to prioritize health and life over monetary profits in the precarious times of the Anthropocene. Many literary works and advocacies that this chapter has discussed reveal that we are so entangled with nonhumans on the same land in Taiwan that we need to uphold ethical obligations to imagine the future of a symbiotic island.

## Works Cited

Aberley, Doug. "Interpreting Bioregionalism: A Story from Many Voices." *Bioregionalism*, edited by Michael Vincent McGinnis, Routledge, 1999, pp. 13–42.

Adamson, Joni. *American Indian Literature, Environmental Justice, and Ecocriticism: The Middle Place*. U of Arizona P, 2001.

———. "Humanities." *Keywords in the Study of Environment and Culture*, edited by Joni Adamson, W. Gleason, and D. N. Pellow, New York UP, 2015, pp. 135–39.

———. "Roots and Trajectories of the Environmental Humanities: From Environmental Justice to Intergenerational Justice." *English Language Notes*, vol. 55, nos. 1–2, 2017, 121–34.

Alaimo, Stacy. *Bodily Natures: Science, Environment, and the Material Self.* Indiana UP, 2012.
Alcoff, Linda Martin. "The Problem of Speaking for Others." *Who Can Speak? Authority and Critical Identity*, edited by J. Roof and R. Wiegman, U of Illinois P, 1995, pp. 98–99.
Buell, Lawrence. *The Environmental Imagination: Thoreau, Nature Writing, and the Formation of American Culture.* Harvard UP, 1995.
———. *The Future of Environmental Criticism: Environmental Crisis and Literary Imagination.* Blackwell, 2005.
Chang, Chiung-fang. "King Car Whisky: Distilling the Kavalan Spirit." *Taiwan Panorama*, translated by Scott Williams, Mar. 3, 2014. Accessed Oct. 27, 2021.
Chang, Tie-zhi. "Rock and Roll as a Power of Resistance." *Environmental Information Center*, Jul. 10, 2011. Accessed Nov. 3, 2021.
Chaudhuri, Una. "'There Must Be a Lot of Fish in That Lake': Toward an Ecological Theater." *Theater*, vol. 25, no. 1, 1994, pp. 23–31.
Chen, Jyun-jyun. "藝文行動在反國光石化運動中的現象分析 (Analysis of Art and Culture Act in Anti-Guoguang Petrochemical Campaign)." Mar. 3, 2014. Accessed Oct. 27, 2021.
"Chia-yang Tsai and Bao-lang Chen Debate on the Construction of the Kuokuang Park." *PTS News Networking, Taiwan.*, Oct. 21, 2010. Accessed Mar. 3, 2014.
Cole, Luke W. and Sheila R. Foster. *From the Ground Up: Environmental Racism and the Rise of the Environmental Justice Movement.* New York UP, 2001.
"Devoted in [sic] Preserving Wetlands?" CTS (Chinese Television System), Mar. 3, 2014. Accessed Oct. 27, 2021.
Elder, John. *Stories in the Land: A Place-based Environmental Education Anthology.* The Orion Society, 1998.
"Future We Want—Outcome Document." Jan. 15, 2015. Accessed Oct. 27, 2021.
Harris, Stephen. "Book Review of *The Bioregional Imagination: Literature, Ecology, Place*. Edited by Tom Lynch, Cheryll Glotfelty, and Karla Armbruster." *AJE (Australasian Journal of Ecocriticism and Cultural Ecology)*, vol. 2, 2012/2013, pp. 109–11.
Hofrichter, Richard. "Cultural Activism and Environmental Justice." *Toxic Struggles: The Theory and Practice of Environmental Justice*, edited by Richard Hofrichter, New Society Publishers, 1993, pp. 85–117.
Horn, Eva and Hannes Bergthaller. *The Anthropocene: Key Issues for the Humanities.* Routledge, 2020.
Huang, Vicky. "Where White Dolphins and Industry Collide." *Taiwan Info.* Jan. 2, 2011. Accessed Oct. 27, 2021.
Jennings, Ralph. "Oil Refinery Snub Marks Arrival of Taiwan's Environmental Movement." *The Christian Science Monitor.* Apr. 26, 2011. Accessed Oct. 27, 2021.
Knopf-Newman, Marcy Jane. *Beyond Slash, Burn, and Poison: Transforming Breast Cancer Stories into Action.* Rutgers UP, 2004.
Liu, Ka-hsiang. "After the Eighth Naphtha Cracker Industrial Park." Trans. Chia-ju Chang. *ISLE*, vol. 18, no. 2, 2011, pp. 463–64.
Lu, Yi-rong. "Records for Anti-Kuokuang, Poet Agitated by Tears." *Li Pao Daily.* Jan. 10, 2011. Accessed Oct. 27, 2021.
Lynch, Tom. *Xerophilia: Ecocritical Explorations in Southwestern Literature.* Texas Tech UP, 2008.
McGinnis, Michael Vincent. "A Rehearsal to Bioregionalism." *Bioregionalism* edited by Michael Vincent McGinnis, Routledge, 1998, pp. 1–9.

Mortimer-Sandilands, Catriona and Bruce Erickson, eds. *Queer Ecologies: Sex, Nature, Biopolitics and Desire*. Indiana UP, 2010.
Nelson, Chris. "Anyone Can Be a Landowner! Buy Land to Save Dolphins—The First National Trust." *China Times*, translated by Coral Lee. Mar. 5, 2014. Accessed Oct. 27, 2021.
"Open Letter from Taiwan Civil Society to the Formosa Plastics Group." Wild at Heart Legal Defense Association, Taiwan. May 19, 2010. Accessed Nov. 3, 2021.
*Oxford Dictionary of Chemistry*. Mar. 3, 2014.
"Petrochemical Project Highlights Economy, Environment Conflict." *Taiwan Insights: Keeping You Up-to-Date on Taiwan*, June 16, 2014. Accessed Oct. 27, 2021.
"The Principles of Environmental Justice (EJ)." *NRDC* (Natural Resources Defense Council). June 6, 2018. Accessed Oct. 27, 2021.
Sale, Kirkpatrick. *Dwellers in the Land: The Bioregional Vision* (1985). Sierra Club Books, 1991.
Shieh, Jyh-Cherng and Ming-sho Ho. *The Naphtha Cracker That Travels around Taiwan: The Story of Kuokuang Petrochemical Project* (八輕遊台灣: 國光石化的故事). Rive Gauche Publishing House (左岸文化), 2011.
Shiva, Vandana. *Staying Alive: Women, Ecology and Development*. Zed, 1989.
Spence, Mark. "Bioregions and Nation-States: Lessons from Lewis and Clark in the Oregon Country." *Oregon Historical Quarterly*, vol. 103, no. 4, 2002, pp. 428–38.
Stokrocki, Mary L. and Michael Delahunt. "Empowering Elementary Students' Ecological Thinking through Discussing the Animé Nausicaa and Constructing Super Bugs." *Journal for Learning through the Arts*, vol. 4, no. 1, 2008, 3–30.
Thayer, Robert L. *Life Place: Bioregional Thought and Practice*. U of California P, 2003.
Thomashow, Mitchell. "Toward a Cosmopolitan Bioregionalism." *Bioregionalism*, edited by Michael Vincent McGinnis, Routledge, 1998, pp. 121–32.
Tsai, Chia-yang. "Love and Death in Changhua Coastal Wetlands." *Wetlands, Petrochemicals, and Imagining an Island*, edited by Sheng Wu and Mingyi Wu, You Lu Wenhua (有鹿文化), 2011, pp. 78–81.
"The Value of Wetlands." *WWF Global*. Jan. 5, 2015. Accessed Oct. 27, 2021.
Wu, Mingyi. "Preface: The Era of No Bystanders." *Wetlands, Petrochemicals, and Imagining an Island* (濕地、石化、島嶼想像), You Lu Wenhua (有鹿文化), 2011, pp. 2–6.
———. *The Man with the Compound Eyes*. Harvill Secker, 2013.
Wu, Sheng. *Guarding River of Mother: Notes on the Jhuoshuei River* (筆記濁水溪), Unitas A Literary Monthly Magazines (聯合文學), 2002.
Wu, Sheng and Mingyi Wu. *Wetlands, Petrochemicals, and Imagining an Island* (濕地、石化、島嶼想像). You Lu Wenhua (有鹿文化出版社), 2011.
Yeh, Yi-chun. "Among Islands." *Our Islands*. Taiwan Interminds (玉山社), 2006.

# 11

# Decolonizing Oceanic Realms: Voices from Australia Pacific

Iris Ralph

The term, the Oceanic imaginary, traces to a 2001 essay of the same name by the Fijian writer Subramani. A key critical source for Pacific literature, Indigenous studies, and postcolonialism and postcolonial ecocriticism scholars, Subramani's work is a call to recognize and support literature about the Pacific by writers from the Pacific and to critically interrogate literature about the Pacific that is produced by "western travelers" and other outsiders. The deployment of the Oceanic imaginary thus brings attention to how "the West's often stereotypical perception of the Pacific" dominated understandings of the Pacific up through the end of the twentieth century, and the imaginary speaks today, as it did 20 years ago, for strengthening the "regional consciousness" in the Pacific, achieving "collective self-determination" for Pacific Islanders, and reclaiming "what several centuries of western colonialism" in the Pacific "diminished or destroyed" (Huggan and Tiffin 53–54). This chapter is inspired by that imaginary, and by a closely related concept, decolonization. This chapter postulates decolonization of oceanic realms through a reading of two works of literature from Australia, an island-continent that geographically and geopolitically overlaps with Oceania and has borders in the Pacific Ocean.

The two works of Australian literature that form the basis of this chapter are Ray Lawlor's play, *Summer of the Seventeenth Doll*, first performed in 1954, and Tim Winton's novel, *Shallows*, published in 1984. Lawlor's play is haunted by the nefarious practice of blackbirding by the sugarcane industry in the South Pacific in the nineteenth and twentieth centuries. Today, much more is known about that practice because of Australia's South Sea Islanders (SSI) community and its vital spearheading of and contribution to the work of decolonization. Winton's novel reflects and engages with decolonization insofar as it is a critique of colonial and postcolonial whale slaughter

---

The origins of this chapter trace to the 4th Cross-Strait Ecological Conference (National Sun Yat-sen University, Kaohsiung, Sept. 19, 2014) and "Environmental Humanities on the Ground" conference (Shanghai Normal University, Shanghai, Nov. 6–8, 2015). I thank the organizers, foremost among them Professor Hsinya Huang (National Sun Yat-sen University) and Professor Lily Hong Chen (Shanghai Normal University), for inviting me to present early drafts of this chapter.

in the Indian Ocean off the west coast of Australia in the nineteenth and twentieth centuries. Set in an oceanic realm that lies to the distant west and south of Oceania, the novel nonetheless supports and complements the work of decolonizing Oceania and its oceanic neighbors, bringing attention to regions of the world dominated by colonial and postcolonial foundation myths of prosperity.

Coined by the German economist Moritz Julius Bonn in the 1930s, decolonization refers in broad terms to the self-governance of countries after the collapse, defeat, or withdrawal of colonial powers (qtd. in O'Dowd and Heckenberg, n.p.). Decolonization also is about taking responsibility for the acts of one's colonial forbears, learning about and remembering the "violated bodies" of the people and the environments that were colonized by one's forebears, recognizing and endeavoring to dismantle the postcolonial and neocolonial outcomes of the past, and listening to and supporting First Nations people in their struggle to be heard in the present (DeLoughrey and Handley 6). Decolonization has "no illusion that ancestry proves an unambiguous and exclusive claim to land as territory" (6), and it does not seek "to reify a pristine past" (Haebich 77). Rather, decolonization functions to "bring the past into the present" (ibid.) and "sacralize ... what can never be recovered" (DeLoughrey and Handley 6). Decolonization involves, further, the "return of stolen lands," "reparations for the descendants" of colonized people, and "question[ing] the bounds and the legitimacy of the nation-state structure" (Davis and Todd 774). For those who first embarked on the boats of decolonization, decolonization also begins with asking where one's people came from; how one got to the place where one now is; whose land one now leases, rents, or owns; and what was done to the people and the land before one got there (Sanchez, n.p.).

## *Summer of the Seventeenth Doll* and Sugarcane

*Summer of the Seventeenth Doll* takes place in the year 1953, in the southeastern Australian city of Melbourne, in the state of Victoria. Two seasonal sugarcane workers, Roo and Barney, have come south from the far north, from the state of Queensland, the center of Australia's sugarcane industry. They are visiting Olive, Roo's longtime girlfriend; Emma, Olive's mother, who runs a boarding house, where Roo and Barney stay; and Bubba, a young woman who has known Roo and Barney since she was a child, when they first brought her a doll. For the past sixteen summers, Roo and Barney have made the trip south during the layoff season of sugarcane cultivation. The men are seasoned workers but also older, and Roo now can no longer brag that he's a top cutter. He has suffered a back injury and been replaced by a younger man in his gang, and now he is looking for a factory job in the city. He may not return to the cane fields up north. He proposes to Olive, but she has never wanted to marry and settle down, or at least not with Roo. Olive's rejection of him is a harbinger of the end of the summers that she and Roo, Emma, Barney, and Bubba have found happiness in for more than 16 years.

Scholars today and in the past note that *Summer of the Seventeenth Doll* speaks for an emerging national consciousness in Australia in the post–Second World War period, and for "national self-expression as a means of self-assertion" (Rees qtd. in Valentine, n.p.). Specifically, Lawler's use of the "Australian vernacular" (as well as "frank approach to sexuality") was "bold and unprecedented" for the time (Jose 683). This language—a "strident, distinctive Australian accent that became part of the play's hallmark" (Damousi qtd. in Valentine, n.p.)—was that of Australia's working and lower-middle classes. Roo and Barney are seasonal cane workers; Emma runs a boarding house in Carlton, a tough, inner-city, working-class suburb of Melbourne in the 1950s; and Olive's friend Pearl is a single mother (widow) who has been "driven back to earning a living by the one job she knows well, that of a barmaid, though she would infinitely prefer something more classy—head saleswoman in a frock salon, for instance" (Lawler 683). Olive introduces Pearl to Barney in the hopes that they will take a liking to one other, for Nancy, whom the men had met in past years, has now married and moved on.

The lives of Australia's working classes and lower-middle classes in the 1950s and 1960s were marked by long working hours, low incomes, and little or no social security. These classes comprised the descendants of Anglo-European colonial-settler people who migrated to Australia in increasing numbers after 1788. These classes also included Australia's oldest human populations—Aboriginal and Torres Strait Island people (First Nations Australians)—as well as recent arrivals from Europe. In addition, these classes comprised Pacific Islanders. Many in the last group worked in the sugarcane fields of Queensland and New South Wales alongside such figures as Roo and Barney and were brought to one of those two states under the nefarious practice of blackbirding.

Stephen Gapps, a senior curator of Voyaging and Early Colonial Maritime History of the Australian National Maritime Museum, writes about blackbirding in a recent article published on the museum's website. The practice dates as far back as the 1860s, when demand for labor in the "burgeoning sugar cane industry" in Queensland "saw trading ships turn into … 'recruitment' vessels across the Pacific" (Gapps, n.p.). Many Pacific Islands people were "indentured" (ibid.). "Unscrupulous traders" also resorted to "kidnapping" Pacific Islanders, practices that were tantamount to, or indeed were, slavery practices (ibid.). The Pacific Islanders who worked in Queensland came from eighty Pacific islands. These included the Solomon Islands, modern-day Vanuatu, Papua New Guinea, Fiji, Tuvalu, and Kiribati. In 1901, blackbirding ended. Ironically, the ending of the practice was the outcome of the Immigration Restriction Act of 1901, a law that underpinned Australia's White Australia policy. The Immigration Restriction Act of 1901, and the Pacific Island Labourer Act of 1901, then paved the way for the deportation of approximately 10,000 Pacific Islanders from Queensland and northern New South Wales between 1906 and 1908.

Gapps's summary of the practice of blackbirding is similar to another recent account, written by Ben Doherty for *The Guardian*. Both of these accounts represent the effort to portray Australian colonial and postcolonial histories more fairly and accurately or to decolonize those foundation narratives. In "'Full Truth': Descendants of Australia's 'Blackbirded' Islanders Want Pioneer Statues Amended," Doherty focuses on these histories in the context of two major cities in north Queensland, Mackay, and Townsville, which were named after two men who became wealthy from blackbirding practices. Sixty thousand South Sea Islanders (another term for Pacific Islands people) were brought to sugarcane plantations near these towns. Many were "kidnapped," "tricked," or "coerced" into leaving their own islands (Doherty, n.p.). Fifteen thousand died prior to the outlawing of the practice. When blackbirding was banned, thousands more were forcibly deported—"press-ganged on to ships and taken back to the Pacific" (ibid.). Many of these people were returned to islands other than their own. In 1994, the Commonwealth (federal government) recognized those who had remained behind and their descendants for being a distinct cultural group. In 2000 and 2013, respectively, the state governments of Queensland and New South Wales—the states where the sugarcane industry was first established or expanded to, and the states where the industry continues to flourish today—belatedly followed suit, formally recognizing Australia's South Sea Islanders (SSI) community.

Today, the "unalloyed veneration" of the owners of the sugarcane industry is "insulting" to the SSI community (Doherty, n.p.). It and other Australian communities inclusive of First Nations communities are engaging in a "broader discussion" of the industry and so drawing attention to the environmental degradation as well as horrific human rights abuses of cash crop industries such as sugarcane (ibid.). The sugarcane industry is still a major industry in Australia: sugarcane production is the largest export crop after wheat ("Industry Information," n.p.). Vast areas of Queensland are used up by the industry. Marine environments in the Pacific Ocean also have been terrifically impacted. For years, one of the most popular yet uncared for of those environments, the Great Barrier Reef, has suffered from large quantities of "effluents, pesticides, and sediment from sugar farms" ("Sugar Produces Bitter Results for the Environment," n.p.).[1] Industrial sugarcane cultivation also deleteriously impacts wetlands, "an integral part of" marine environments (ibid.). Not far from the shores of Australia, in Papua New Guinea, the sugarcane industry has caused similar degradation. Soil fertility there has declined by approximately 40 percent because of the industry (ibid.). Elsewhere on the planet, industrial sugarcane cultivation pollutes major rivers: the Niger in West Africa, the Zambezi in Southern Africa, the Indus River in Pakistan, and the Mekong River in Southeast Asia. Colonial and postcolonial industrial sugarcane cultivation has as dark a history in the Caribbean as it has in the region of the Pacific (Paravisini-Gebert 73; Niblett 271). Industrial crop plantation took and continues to take an incalculable toll on the environment, and it betrays the continuation of colonialist ideologies.

*Summer of the Seventeenth Doll*, set against the backdrop of the sugarcane industry in the northeast of Australia and a novel that can be situated in a body of literature that scholars call "canefield fictions" (Zeller 217), barely if at all alludes

---

[1] See also an article posted by the World Wildlife Fund (WWF), "Sugarcane Farming's Toll on the Environment."

to the colonial and postcolonial contours of the sugarcane industry in its portrait of two cane cutters who migrate south every summer from the far north during the off season. Yet, in its notice of the lives of workers employed by the industry, the play provokes notice of those contours and so brings readers to the practice of blackbirding in the South Pacific. Australia's SSI communities are at the forefront of bringing attention to that practice, and their work illustrates, reflects, and supports the decolonial imaginary and so closely identifies with critical studies that engage with the decolonial imaginary in the specific context of colonial and postcolonial histories of sugarcane cultivation.

## *Shallows* and Cetacean Slaughter

Another Australian colonial and postcolonial history that is being decolonized, is that of whaling, a euphemism for whale slaughter. It is the explicit subject of Timothy Winton's novel. Published in 1984, almost 30 years after Lawler's play, *Shallows* captured a moment in time, 1978, when industrial and other commercial whaling ground to a halt off the coast of Western Australia. The reason for that cessation arguably may be due less to the mounting public protest against the industry at the time and more to do with the fact that industrial whaling had exhausted the oceans of whales by then— "[a]n ocean without whales is like a wilderness without trees" is how one character in the novel describes what is happening in the Indian Ocean in the 1970s (Winton 137). However, public protest did play a role in that terminal route. *Shallows* alludes to that protest. It included the blockade of the Cheynes Beach Whaling Company, at Frenchman Bay, in Albany, in the winter of 1977. The group that led the blockade, the Whale and Dolphin Coalition, an offshoot of Greenpeace, was formed in 1974, in Sydney, New South Wales, by Jonny Lewis, an Australian, and Jean-Paul Fortom-Gouin, a Frenchman ("Workers and Protestors Meet at Cheynes Beach Whaling Station"). They "drew world attention to whaling activities in Australian waters" and, at the end of 1978, the station closed down its operations (ibid.).

Most of the events of *Shallows* take place in the momentous year of 1978. Interspersed between those events are events that take place much earlier, in the nineteenth century. In 1831, Nathaniel Coupar, an American whaler (and "American deserter"), abandons the whaling ship, *The Family of Man*, at Angelus, a port in Western Australia at the southern tip of the state (Winton 39). The town of Angelus, which Nathaniel remembers being "dubbed ... the Bay of Whales" by a fellow American whaler (ibid. 16), is more or less a naked allusion to the historic whaling town of Albany, one of Western Australia's three major whaling towns. American whalers dominated whale killing in the Indian Ocean up through the end of the nineteenth century. They pulled out at the end of the nineteenth century as a direct result of following the common industrial practice of "exhausting limited resources for quick profits," but, in the early twentieth century, other whalers, Norwegian whalers, took up where their American peers had left off ("Whaling" n.p.). During the Second World War, whaling again slowed, and then when the war ended it accelerated again when there was a "world shortage of fats" and the price of whale oil "rose to six times the prewar price" (ibid.). In 1955, 60 percent of all whales killed in Australia were killed in Western Australia at Albany, Point Cloates, and Carnarvon (ibid.). By 1963, the state had prohibited whaling except for the operations at Albany (at Cheynes Beach, Frenchman Bay). In 1978, due to the "dwindling numbers" of whales, this whaling station also finally closed (ibid.).

In Winton's novel, in 1978, a century and a half after Nathaniel Coupar jumps ship at Angelus, Nathaniel's grandson, Daniel Coupar, gives a journal that had belonged to Nathaniel Coupar to Cleveland (Cleve) Cookson, an outsider to Angelus and the newly married husband of Daniel's granddaughter, Queenie. As Cleve reads through the pages of the journal (one man's personal record of whaling in the nineteenth century), Queenie, who works as a tour guide, becomes caught up in an anti-whaling demonstration in Angelus and joins forces with the leaders: Georges Fleurier, a Frenchman; Marks, a US-American; and Brent, a Canadian. The leaders call themselves Cachalot & Company, a reference to cachalot whales (also known as sperm whales), animals valued primarily for their fat and the waxy perfumed substance of ambergris (found in their stomachs). The main aim of Cachalot & Company is "to close down" Paris Bay, the whaling company that became an Australian-owned company in 1918 and has operated in Angelus since 1910 (Winton 31, 40). Cleve at first objects to Queenie's involvement with Cachalot & Company, and the couple separate. In the final pages of the novel, there are signs that Cleve and Queenie will reconcile, but this positive turn in events contrasts with the much smaller gains of the anti-whaling protesters. Although they have succeeded in bringing more attention to cetacean slaughter, the demonstrators continue to face hostility and opposition, and considerable apathy as well. On a cold winter day, on July 4—a date that carries a reference to Queenie's North American ancestor, Nathaniel Coupar, and his bid for freedom (albeit a different kind of freedom from either that which the date of July 4 symbolizes in the United States or that which the anti-whaling protest at Angelus represents)—Cleve and Queenie drive out to a remote area of the beach. They wake up the next morning to "the cries" of a large group of stranded whales (ibid. 260). Their "huge, stricken bodies" have been caught "in the shallows" (ibid.). Many are already dead; many others are dying. In the light of the torch (flashlight) that Cleve and Queenie carry, they helplessly move among the whales, now reduced to "[m]asses of flesh" and "heaving monuments" (ibid.).

Queenie and the Coupar family as a whole stand against the interests of another old Angelus family, the Pustlings. The commercial Pustling faction is openly hostile to the animal rights activists who come to Angelus to protest the slaughter of whales (humpback, southern right, sperm, and other cetacean species). The pro-whaling faction is led by Des Pustling, a real estate developer and property manager and the descendent of "Benjamin Pustling of Surrey [England]," the reputed founder of Angelus (Winton 9). The Pustlings have steered the course of the town since 1938. The tides are turning against them, as Queenie (Coupar) Cookson and the Cachalot & Company anti-whaling group threaten to thwart Pustling's plans to further exploit Angelus, but the Pustling faction continues to be a formidable force, insensitive and openly antagonistic toward calls to live more modestly, that is to say, environmentally, in the world at the bottom (of many of the oldest maps) of the world.

The southern oceanic realm continues to be hammered by the dreams of politically conservative local and state governments colluding with big industry. One of the most recent of these dreams refers to the ambitions of Equinor (a Norwegian oil company) to drill in the Great Australian Bight. Since at least 2016, oil companies have been trying to gain access to drill for oil in the Bight, one of the last remaining areas of an ocean not crippled by human enterprises ("Great Australian Bight"). Equinor's bid follows on the heels of those of British Petroleum (BP), Chevron, and Karoon Energy (ibid.). In 2020, the company finally abandoned its plans, but until today many local and state government officials are bent on working with energy companies to transform the Bight into a vast aqueous industrial pit, detonate the deep-sea floor of the ocean, eradicate the marine ecologies in it, and leave behind a dead zone. That intent was apparent in the government's response to the pullout of Equinor in 2020. The government said the withdrawal was "disappointing" (ibid.).

Queenie's empathy for cetaceans traces back to her childhood when she used to converse with dolphins and whales. She no longer does, for she is no longer a child, and in the conventional thinking of the time, communication with and sentimental feelings for whales is something one must let go of when one reaches adulthood. Philip Armstrong, an early leading figure in critical animal studies—an area of critical inquiry that shares common grounds of interest with postcolonial ecocriticism and Indigenous studies—comments on the general tendency to "underestimate" the historical role of states of affect or "emotion" in the context of twentieth-century historical as well as fictional records of human-cetacean communication ("Cetaceans and Sentiment" 169). Armstrong summarizes one of those accounts, the story of Opo, a 2-year-old bottle-nosed dolphin who in the 1950s regularly visited a beach at Opononi—"a small settlement on New Zealand's Hokianga Harbour"—and played with other beachgoers (human beachcombers) (ibid. 170). In 1960, a cultural historian "produced a book-length treatment" of the story of Opo (ibid. 171). More productions followed. These included two novels, a series of paintings by a well-known artist, a children's story, a documentary film, and a "hit song" by the Kiwi singer-songwriter, Don McGlashan (ibid.). In all but one of the productions, the focus was on the aspects of the selfhood and subjectivity of Opo and the moral and emotional bonds between Opo and his human companions. Some of the productions also documented or otherwise recorded the death of Opo on March 9, 1956, the day after legislation to protect dolphins was enacted (ibid. 174). The exception to these kinds of productions of the Opo story was Maurice Shadbolt's novel, *This Summer's Dolphin*, published in 1969 (ibid. 176).

Shadbolt's novel divested the story of Opo of all of its sentimental content, content which in fact was largely accurate in the context of the actual history of Opo at Opononi (Armstrong, "Cetaceans and Sentiment" 176). Shadbolt instead produced a narrative of "bold, savage, modernist authenticity," depicting Opo as being an animal that was "rough and dangerous in play," a "sublime rather than sentimental presence," and a figure that "provides a kind of exhilaration bordering on terror and annihilation" (ibid. 177). Nonetheless, Shadbolt would never claim that his novel "represented a more accurate version" of the Opi story, and he later wrote "a non-fiction account of the actual events," which supported "the sentimental content and tone of all other manifestations of the Opo story" (ibid.). Shadbolt's nonfiction account, which appears in *Love and Legend*, published in 1976, was based on a summer that he had spent in Opononi, between 1955 and 1956; in this account he described those few months as being "the only-fairy tale" he was ever likely to have lived in his life (Shadbolt qtd. in Armstrong, "Cetaceans and Sentiment" 177).

Armstrong explains the divergence of Shadbolt's novel from "all other manifestations of the Opo story" (inclusive of Shadbolt's second Opi story) in terms of the decline in the taste, beginning in the early twentieth century and extending past the middle of that century, for sentimental narratives, a body of literature that associates with nineteenth-century Anglo-American literature ("Cetaceans and Sentiment" 177). Armstrong relates the "disdain for sentiment" to Shadbolt's novel, which was published in 1969 (ibid. 175). That "contempt," both "cultural and intellectual" in its manifestations (ibid. 176), stamps accounts and representations of nonhuman animal behavior in the sciences as much as in the arts (ibid.). "[C]ompassionate feelings for nonhuman animals … were perceived as obstacles, either to progress or profit" up through "at least the 1970s," and key stakeholders in "commerce," "industry," and the "sciences" were "more or less invincible to challenges based on human sympathy for the suffering of animals" (ibid.). "During much of this same period," for those who were "charged with the task of considering animals at a professional level" (biologists, agribusiness professionals, literary and cultural studies scholars, and so forth), "the dominion of science, industrial capitalism, and modernism made sentimentalism something between a crime and a sickness" (ibid.).

Pushing against the "anti-sentimentalist hegemony" that extends up through "at least … the 1970s" (Amstrong, "Cetaceans and Sentiment" 176), in both the arts and the sciences, are records and stories of the affective bonds and the moral ties between humans and other animals. The vast majority of the versions of the Opo story represent such records and narratives. Winton's novel, a very different kind of narrative, also draws attention to the affective bonds between humans and other animals in the figures of Queenie and Queenie's grandmother, Maureen Bolt.

*Shallows*, a work of literary realism, includes several descriptions of Queenie that speak for the affective bonds between humans and other animals. Queenie empathizes with the whales who are being commercially caught and killed at Angelus, and when she was a child she bonded with cetaceans and other marine animals in a way that the adults around her did not understand. At school, she told "stories … about conversations with dolphins and hearing God in seashells" (Winton 7). She also is described as being cetacean- or fish-like herself. Queenie is "broadbacked," supports a "big body," and "ought not to have been born a land mammal" (ibid. 4). Her lungs are unusually strong, "fantastic," and she is "lithe and quick in the water" (ibid. 4). When Cleve first meets her, he comes across her "lying in a rock-pool," completely at home in the water (ibid. 15). In high school, she quickly advances to lead the school's swimming team (ibid. 121). Queenie's grandmother, Maureen Bolt similarly is a water creature.

When Daniel Coupar first meets his future wife, she appears like a breaching cetacean exhaling air from her spiracle. Daniel, in a boat on the Hacker River, distinguishes

> a shape in the coppery water moving towards him. Platypus? Crocodile? Neither belonged in the Hacker. He slipped an oar from its rowlock and waited with it raised. When the surface broke just near the gunwhale ... a human, a woman [emerged] ... Tossing her hair back she blew a jet of air and smiled.
>
> (ibid. 85)

Further, Winton's descriptions of Queenie as a child bring to mind the 13-year-old girl, Jill Baker, a "lonely girl, and only child," who played with Opo at Opononi in New Zealand (Shadbolt qtd. in Armstrong, "Cetaceans and Sentiment" 177). The figure of Jill Baker is a "key element" of the Opo story (Armstrong, "Cetaceans and Sentiment" 171). In Winton's novel, Queenie is somewhat like this figure; she is a lonely child, although she is lucky that her grandfather, Daniel Coupar, has raised and dotes on her. No one knows who Queenie's father is, and Queenie's mother, Eileen, abandoned Queenie when she was a child.

Since 1984, other novels that draw attention to cetacean exploitation, cetacean loss, and cetacean suffering, and the questionable rationales for that exploitation, loss, and suffering, have joined ranks with Winton's *Shallows*. Such novels include Maori writer Witi Ihimaera's *The Whale Rider,* first published in 1987 and subsequently made into a film; Indian writer Amitav Ghosh's *The Hungry Tide*, published in 2004; South African writer Zakes Mda's *The Whale Caller*, published in 2005; and Chickasaw writer Linda Hogan's *People of the Whale*, published in 2008.[2] The authors of these novels focus on content that includes the laws and practices defining humans' relationships with whales or other cetacean species in precolonial times. Those ancient governances reflected respect for and knowledge of cetaceans, and they included recognition of the affective bonds between cetaceans and humans, and so the inclusion of considering these animals in hardly superficial moral terms. In Australian contexts, the oldest set of laws that give human rights to whales are those of the country's oldest human populations. First Nations Australian people continue to be at the forefront of the effort to restore those old laws, which have little to do with where one most likely is to encounter a cetacean in Australia today, in an aquatic entertainment park or dolphinarium such as Sea World Marine Park in Queensland. That effort is one of decolonization and exemplifies the decolonial imaginary. It includes a recent art project led by a group of women from the South Australia town of Ceduna and the Aboriginal community of Yalata, situated a couple of 100 kilometers west of Ceduna. The women craft whale art from nets that the fishing industry dumps or loses and from other marine debris that

---

[2] For an analysis of these four texts, see Jonathan Steinwand's "What the Whales Would Tell Us." Another key text for literary and cultural studies scholars who study cetacean representation is Herman Melville's *Moby-Dick*. For more on this iconic text, see Iris Ralph's "Tall-Fins and Tale-Ends in Taiwan: Cetacean Exploitation, Oil Refineries, and *Moby-Dick*"; and Philip Armstrong's "Rendering the Whale."

strews the beaches of South Australia where it meets the Great Australian Bight in the Indian Ocean (Hamilton and Pedlar). One such piece of art, named Jidirah, is a right whale sculpture showcasing the seven sisters dreaming story of the Mirning people. In 2021, at the time of the penultimate drafts of this chapter, Jidirah was "migrating through art galleries in Europe," and two similar "ghost net art pieces"—a harlequin fish and an orca whale sculpture—were in line for an overseas trip and possible permanent home (ibid.).

When *Shallows* was published in 1984, Australia's post-1788 environmental movement was barely a decade old, as was the Aboriginal (First Nations Australian) land rights movement (Heiss and Minter 4–6), a movement symbolized by the hoisting of the Australian Aboriginal Flag in Victoria Square, in the South Australia capital city of Adelaide, on July 9, 1971. Most Australians in the 1970s and 1980s were only just beginning to pay attention to the ecocide of cetaceans as well as countless other animal or plant species in the oceans and seas of Australia (and to the genocidal policies relating to the treatment of Australia's oldest people). *Shallows* is about that notice in the context of protests against whaling in the 1970s. The novel reflects Winton's long involvement in environmental causes that refer in particular to fights to save Australia's oceanic environments. Four-time winner of Australia's highest literary award, the Miles Franklin Literary Award, and the only writer in addition to Thea Astley who has won the award four times, Winton donated the Miles Franklin award money that he received for the novel, *Dirt Music*, to a successful campaign to save the Ningaloo Reef in the Indian Ocean (Edemariam).[3] For years, he has been closely involved with the Australian Marine Conservation Society, a society that began in central Queensland in 1965 and was formed for the purpose of protecting marine environments, which include the Ningaloo Reef in the Indian Ocean. That involvement is an important aspect of the decolonial imaginary; it reflects the belief that environments and people are related by powerful moral and affective bonds. Those have been terrifically damaged by colonial and postcolonial powers, but these powers have been unable, so far, to entirely eradicate them.

The foregoing reading of Tim Winton's novel *Shallows* and Ray Lawler's play *Summer of the Seventeenth Doll* seeks to contribute to the arts and humanities from perspectives generated and shaped by scholars situated in the areas of critical inquiry of Pacific literature, postcolonial ecocriticism, Indigenous studies, and critical animal studies. Two key concepts identified in this chapter are the Oceanic imaginary and decolonization. The first concept was proposed by Subramani and is widely discussed in the scholarships on Pacific literature. Decolonization is associated with the commitments of First Nations writers and thinkers of postcolonial ecocriticism. Decolonization is germane to the study of Australian literature, for it is a body of literature that is steeped in colonial and postcolonial ideologies that roughly date back to 1788, the year that British Empire sought to colonize the island-continent now known as Australia.

---

[3] Winton's two other Miles Franklin Award winners are *Breath* (2009) and *Cloudstreet* (1992).

This chapter reads how Winton's novel voices out against colonial and postcolonial industries of cetacean slaughter in the nineteenth and twentieth centuries in waters claimed by the Australian government. Lawler's play, haunted by the practice of blackbirding in the South Pacific, likewise propels us to reconsider colonial hegemony in Australia Pacific. In reading Australian literature in the context of broader colonization in the Pacific, this chapter elucidates the ways Australian literature contributes to (re-) worlding the Pacific by laying bare the connections between ongoing colonial practices and waters.

## Works Cited

Armstrong, Philip. "Cetaceans and Sentiment." *Considering Animals: Contemporary Studies in Human–Animal Relations*, edited by Carol Freeman, Elizabeth Leane, and Yvette Watt, Ashgate, 2011, pp. 169–82.

———. "Rendering the Whale." *What Animals Mean in the Fiction of Modernity*. Routledge, 2008, pp. 99–133.

Damousi, Joy. *Colonial Voices*, Cambridge UP, 2010.

Davis, Heather and Zoe Todd. "On the Importance of a Date, or Decolonizing the Anthropocene." *ACME: An International Journal for Critical Geographies*, vol. 16, no. 4, 2017, pp. 761–80.

DeLoughrey, Elizabeth and George B. Handley. "Introduction: Toward and Aesthetics of The Earth." *Postcolonial Ecologies*, edited by DeLoughrey and Handley, Oxford UP, 2011, pp. 3–39.

Doherty, Ben. "'Full Truth': Descendants of Australia's 'Blackbirded' Islanders Want Pioneer Statues Amended." *The Guardian*, Aug. 24, 2017, https://www.theguardian.com/australia-news/2017/aug/24/full-truth-needs-to-be-told-descendants-of-blackbirded-south-sea-islanders-want-memorials-amended. Accessed Dec. 6, 2021.

Edemariam, Aida. "Waiting for the New Wave." *Guardian News*, June 28, 2016, http://www.theguardian.com/books/2008/jun/28/saturdayreviewsfeatres.guardianreview9. Accessed Dec. 6, 2021.

Gapps, Stephen. "Blackbirding: Australia's Slave Trade?" *Australian National Maritime Museum*, Aug. 23, 2019, www.sea.museum/2017/08/25/australias-slave-trade. Accessed Dec. 6, 2021.

"Great Australian Bight: Equinor Abandons Controversial Oil Drilling Plans." *BBC News*, Feb. 25, 2020, https://www.bbc.com/news/world-australia-51623764. Accessed Dec. 6, 2021.

Haebich, Ann. "Biological Colonization in the Land of Flowers." *Ecocritical Concerns and the Australian Continent*, edited by Neumeier and Tiffin, Lexington, 2020, pp. 75–90.

Hamilton, Jodie and Emma Pedlar. "Migrating Whale Sculpture Makes Waves for Indigenous Art Overseas." *ABC News*, Aug. 5, 2021, https://www.abc.net.au/news/2021-08-05/jidirah-ghost-net-whale-sculpture-migrating-overseas/100236764. Accessed Dec. 6, 2021.

Heiss, Anita and Peter Minter. "Aboriginal Literature." *Macquarie Pen Anthology of Aboriginal Literature*, edited by Heiss and Miner, Allen & Unwin, 2008, pp. 1–8.

Huggan, Graham and Helen Tiffin. *Postcolonial Ecocriticism: Literature, Animals, Environment*, Routledge, 2010.

"Industry Information." Sugar Australia Company Ltd 2018. http://www.sugaraustralia.com.au/sugar-australia/about/industry-information/. Accessed Dec. 6, 2021.

Jose, Nicholas. "Ray Lawler." *Macquarie Pen Anthology of Australian Literature*, edited by Nicholas Jose, Allen & Unwin, 2009, pp. 682–83.

Lawler, Ray. "Act 1, Scene 1." *Summer of the Seventeenth Doll* (1954). Excerpted in *Macquarie Pen Anthology of Australian Literature*, Allen & Unwin, 2009, pp. 683–90.

Niblett, Michael. "Oil on Sugar: Commodity Frontiers and Peripheral Aesthetics." *Global Ecologies and the Environmental Humanities*, edited by Elizabeth DeLoughrey, Jill Didur and Anthony Carrigan, Routledge, 2015, pp. 269–85.

O'Dowd, Mary Frances and Robyn Heckenberg. "Explainer: What Is Decolonisation?" *The Conversation*, June 22, 2022, https://theconversation.com/explainer-what-is-decolonisation-131455. Accessed July 1, 2022.

Paravisini-Gebert, Lizabeth. "Bagasse: Caribbean Art and the Debris of the Sugar Plantation." *Global Ecologies and the Environmental Humanities*, edited by Elizabeth DeLoughrey, Jill Didur and Anthony Carrigan, Routledge, 2015, pp. 73–94.

Ralph, Iris. "Tall-Fins and Tale-Ends in Taiwan: Cetacean Exploitation, Oil Refineries, and *Moby-Dick*." *JoE: Journal of Ecocriticism*, vol. 6, no. 1, 2014, pp. 1–12, ojs.unbc.ca/index.php/joe/article/view/553/482. Accessed Jan. 28, 2022.

Rees, Leslie. *The Making of Australian Drama*. Angus and Robertson, 1973.

Sanchez, Nikki. "Decolonization Is for Everyone." *TEDxSFU*, Mar. 12, 2019, www.youtube.com/watch?v=QP9x1NnCWNY. Accessed May 18, 2022.

Shadbolt, Maurice. *Love and Legend: Some Twentieth-Century New Zealanders*. Hodder and Stoughton, 1976.

———. *This Summer's Dolphin*. Cassell, 1969.

Steinwand, Jonathan. "What the Whales Would Tell Us: Cetacean Communication in Novels by Witi Ihimaera, Linda Hogan, Zakes Mdea, and Amitav Ghosh." *Postcolonial Ecologies*, edited by Elizabeth DeLoughrey and George B. Handley, Oxford UP, 2011, pp. 182–99.

Subramani. "The Oceanic Imaginary." *The Contemporary Pacific*, vol. 13, no. 1, 2001, pp. 149–62.

"Sugar Produces Bitter Results for the Environment." *ThoughtCo*. https://www.thoughtco.com/effect-of-sugar-on-the-environment-1204100. Accessed Dec. 6, 2021.

"Sugarcane Farming's Toll on the Environment." *World Wildlife Fund (WWF)*. https://www.worldwildlife.org/magazine/issues/summer-2015/articles/sugarcane-farming-s-toll-on-the-environment. Accessed Dec. 6, 2021.

Valentine, Alana. "Cue the Chorus: An Ever-Changing Idiom." *Australian Plays Transform*, Currency Press Digital, 2014. https://apt.org.au/script/CPD-7. Accessed Dec. 6, 2021.

"Whaling." *Western Perspectives on a Nation*. LISWA: Library and Information Service of Western Australia. https://slwa.wa.gov.au/wepon/sea/html/whaling.htm. Accessed Dec. 6, 2021.

Winton, Tim. *Shallows*. Penguin Books, 1984.

"Workers and Protestors Meet at Cheynes Beach Whaling Station." Australian National Maritime Museum 2018. Collections.anmm.gov.au/objects/192722. Accessed Dec. 6, 2021.

Zeller, Robert. "Tales of the Austral Tropics: North Queensland in Australian Literature." *The Littoral Zone: Australian Contexts and Their Writers*, edited by C. A. Cranston and Robert Zeller, Amsterdam, Rodopi Press, 2010, pp. 199–218.

# 12

# Whale as Cosmos: Multispecies Ethnography and Contemporary Indigenous Cosmopolitics

Joni Adamson

*He would watch [the whale], its great shining side, the eye with its old intelligence, the gentleness of it in the body covered with barnacle life and sea creatures. It was loved by his people. It was a planet.*

—Linda Hogan

Both Niki Caro's 2002 film, *Whale Rider*, and Linda Hogan's 2008 novel, *People of the Whale*, feature children chosen by their whaling communities to carry the traditions of their peoples into the future. Both children are linked to canoes associated with the whales considered by many Indigenous whaling peoples to be not only companion species but ancestors. In a pivotal scene in Caro's film, 12-year-old Paikea Apirana recites the same family genealogy that is carved into the hull of an unfinished canoe that sits behind her house. "I come from a long line of chiefs stretching all the way back to the original whale rider, also named 'Paikea,'" she declares. According to Maori oral tradition, Paikea rode on the back of a whale from Hawaki (Hawai'i) to Aotearoa (New Zealand) (Cawthorn 1–2). There, he established the Ngati Porou, a subgroup of the Maori who still live in Whangara, a small village on the northeast side of New Zealand's North Island. This is the village where Caro sets the film.

In an authoritative reading of Whiti Ihimaera acclaimed 1987 *The Whale Rider*, the novel Caro adapts for her screenplay, Chadwick Allen writes that for the Maori, "whakapapa," or genealogy, is the preeminent form of Maori scholarship and covers the descent of all living things from the gods to the present time (Allen 131). The "relationships encoded in whakapapa serve as a primary terminology—a system of names and a set of coordinates—for the analysis of one's rightful place in the universe" (Allen 131). In each Maori subgroup, "certain members will be selected when they are children to be trained as experts in the genealogy" of the tribe, the cosmos, the gods, the primal genealogies of humankind, and the *waka* (canoes) that carried the ancestors

---

This article is a reprint of "Whale as Cosmos: Multispecies Ethnography and Contemporary Indigenous Cosmopolitics." Special Issue: "Ecocriticism in English Studies." *Revista Canaria de Estudios Ingleses* 64 (2012): 13–46.

to Aotearoa (Allen 131). Thus, standing on the stage of her village meeting house, "Pai's" recitation of her whakapapa shows her to be the expert who will carry Ngati Porou knowledge of Maori "spiritual relationships with the earth and cosmo" into the future (Allen 209).

In *People of the Whale*, Chickasaw writer Linda Hogan also puts a child expert at the center of her story of a North American coastal whaling people she calls the "A'atsika." Hogan's novel fictionalizes the controversy set off when the Makah of Washington State hunted and killed a gray whale in 1999. A small tribe of only 2000 people, the Makah were thrust into the harsh glare of the global spotlight when they approached the International Whaling Commission (IWC) for permission to resume hunting whales. During the media frenzy surrounding the hunt, arguments both pro and con pitted members of the Makah tribe, and other coastal whaling peoples around the world, dualistically against environmentalists and reporters who accused them of being "Ecological Indians." This term, coined in anthropologist Shepherd Krech's *The Ecological Indian* in 1999, has come to be associated with the notion that neither contemporary Indigenous groups and nations nor their ancestors were as ecologically sensitive as stereotypes about "people close to nature" have implied.

Major twenty-first-century field studies of ecocriticism problematize the notion that premodern cultures lived in perpetual harmony with nature (Garrard 120–21, 133; Buell 23). To question this notion, both Garrard and Buell reference Krech's work which was groundbreaking and controversial for examining evidence that not all North American Indian tribes hunted animals such as the buffalo "sustainably," as that term has come to be used in modern contexts. Krech concludes that the dominant image of the Indian in nature is based on assumptions that take for granted that each Indigenous person "understands the systemic consequences of his actions, feels deep sympathy with all living forms, and takes steps to conserve so that the earth's harmonies are never imbalanced and resources never in doubt" (Krech 21). He then analyzes evidence that both supports and confronts the image of the "Ecological Indian" thriving in "public culture" today (213). Krech's conclusions about the mixed and contradictory anthropological record have been used by some scholars to imply that species extinctions have not entirely been the fault of Europeans and therefore Indigenous peoples should not be held up as models of ecological awareness. However, Krech himself concludes that while not all Indigenous groups could be said to be "conservationist," many "clearly possessed vast knowledge of their environment" and "understood relationships among living things in the environment" (Krech 103, 212).

Greg Garrard's use of Krech's research is notable for picking up on the finer points of the argument. In *Ecocriticism*, he argues that the relationship between Europeans and Americans was based "on destruction and consumption of forests and wildlife so astonishingly voracious that, in places, it amounted to an 'ecocidal' campaign to exhaust and refashion whole habitats" (123). Garrard emphasizes Krech's most salient point which is that Indigenous resistance movements (from the occupation of Alcatraz Island in the 1970s forward) employ tropes of ecological Indigeneity as they organize to resist land appropriation and ecological degradation (Krech 20). This argument is essential for ecocritics to understand, Garrard concludes, since contemporary

Indigenous writers continue to employ images of the Ecological Indian in strategic ways that provide "some Indians with a source of pride and aspiration for themselves and their societies" (125).

Hogan's novel challenges simplistic arguments about the Ecological Indian by setting her story in a modern context and placing a young Indigenous man, Marco, in the lead canoe paddling out to the ocean in search of a whale. The grandson of the A'atsika people's most famous whaler, Marco is born with webbed feet and is able to dive in the ocean for long periods of time, suggesting that he is the "incarnation of an ancestor" (Hogan 38). In the context of the oral traditions of many North American Indigenous cultures, Hogan's description of Marco implies that he is a transformational being about to take the shape of human or whale. As I explain in an earlier article, transformational characters depicted in Indigenous oral traditions, whether human or animal in form or name, are considered to be supernatural but *not* impersonal, universal beings. Instead, they are thought of as supernatural personal beings who are able to transform themselves into other forms for the purpose of interacting with humans (Adamson, "Why" 41, n. 11). Recognizing Marco as one of these special beings, A'atsika elders teach him traditional whaling practices and place emphasis on how to paddle a traditional cedar canoe. Hogan also writes that before the whale hunt, few A'atsika men know how to paddle a canoe, so it falls to Marco to teach them proper techniques (87).

In Caro's film, Paikea, or "Pai," is also linked to a traditional fishing and whaling vessel, or "waka" that sits, unfinished, behind her house.[1] The novel on which the film is based, Witi Ihimaera's *The Whale Rider*, does not focus on a waka. However, when Ihimaera, who acted as executive producer for the film, came together with Caro to collaborate on *Whale Rider*, the canoe became central (see *Te Waka* and *Behind the Scenes*). The choice to feature a waka so prominently can be explained, as I will discuss at more length below, by the fact that "paddling," or the rowing of traditional canoes, is an activity increasingly associated with a loosely networked global Indigenous rights movement that is seeking legal and political protections not only for humans but for ecosystems and the interrelated species upon which they depend for survival.

Focus on the waka also allows Caro to transform Ihimaera's novel into a 100-minute film that concisely conveys a concept, linked to Maori activism, which Allen describes as "building the ancestor." Contemporary Maori, explains Allen, continue to carve elaborate meeting houses in their villages which are considered the "body of the ancestor" (134). This is the reason why the meeting house where Pai gives her genealogical recitation has a wooden carving of the first Paikea sitting over its entrance. Inside these elaborately carved meeting houses, figures of the gods of the Maori cosmos can be read as if they were an ethnography of the Maori cosmos (Allen 125, 134). The "events" that take place in Maori meeting houses—school plays, traveling art exhibits, or protest marches—are often dramatically "staged" in ways that allow Maori groups to draw connections between local land claims and struggles for

---

[1] For more on how a waka is built for the film, see *Te Waka: Building the Canoe*, a special feature documentary included with the *Whale Rider* DVD.

environmental justice and "a burgeoning international indigenous rights movement" (Allen 7). This movement, as I argue in *American Indian Literature*, began centuries ago with the first Indigenous uprising and slave revolts (Adamson 29, 47). More recently, this movement has created what Allen describes as the collective notion of "Indigenous people" without privileging any particular Indigenous group. The documents and international meetings emerging out of the movement, Allen observes, might be described as "autoethnographic," meaning that they often "negotiate a single narrative out of the worldviews, memories, and aspirations of disparate Indigenous cultures while also constructing a dialogue between Indigenous and non-Indigenous understanding of Indigenous experience" (Allen 209). These forms and forums participate in "a number of distinct meaning systems simultaneously—those of North American First Nations and American Indians, the Maori, the Sami, the Aboriginal peoples, *and* Western culture" (Allen 208).

As I will argue below, the collaborative construction of a waka by Maori wood carvers and Hollywood production crew members, and the launching of the finished canoe at the end of Caro's film, can be seen as an "event" that offers insight into the "autoethnographic" activities of Indigenous and ethnic minority groups organizing a movement that is lately being described as "indigenous cosmopolitics."[2] Hogan also associates her novel with this movement by featuring Indigenous Northwest American "paddlers" and "paddling Nations" that represent the ways in which whaling cultures are revisioning their relationship to the whale and to the planet (Hogan 303, 267). This chapter will examine how notions of "cosmos" are represented in Caro's film and Hogan's novel by transformational characters and explore the relevance for ecocriticism of a cosmopolitical movement that is being articulated in "autoethnographic" legal instruments and documents such as the 2007 United Nations Declaration on the Rights of Indigenous Peoples (UNDRIP) and the 2010 Universal Declaration on the Rights of Mother Earth (UDRME). UDRME, for example, claims for Indigenous peoples "a cosmic spirituality linked to nature thousands of years in the making" (see Preamble). This will allow me to explore how Caro and Hogan defy simplistic conclusions about the trope of "the Ecological Indian" and offer, instead, interesting characters and scenarios that can be used to illustrate a new mode of research being referred to as "multispecies ethnography."

## From Animals That Are "Good to Think" to Species That Are "Good to Live With"

In a recent essay, Jonathan Steinwand examines what he terms the "cetacean turn" in environmentalist iconography as it is exemplified by Indigenous-authored novels about human relationships to whales (182). Reading Ihimaera's novel, *The Whale Rider*,

---

[2] I focus on Caro's film rather than Ihimaera's novel because of its focus on the waka and its association with Maori activist events that represent the "building of the ancestor."

and Hogan's novel, *People of the Whale*, Steinwand observes that both whales and Indigenous peoples are depicted as compelling figures because of their "liminality and ambiguity." While whales constantly negotiate the boundaries between the worlds of air and water, modern Indigenous and marginalized ethnic groups of people are "liminal figures negotiating the boundaries of the dominant 'civilization' and wild nature, of traditional premodern and postmodern late capitalist lifestyles" (184). Steinwand's argument builds on Lawrence Buell's analysis in *Writing for an Endangered World* of the relationship between whales and Indigenous peoples in contemporary environmentalist iconography. From the publication of Herman Melville's *Moby-Dick* in 1850 to the present, creative writers have been expanding modern imagination around whales as charismatic megafauna while environmentalists hope concern for these animals will move people to care not only for whales, but for ecosystems and other species threatened by pollution, overfishing, and a warming ocean (Buell 201–02).

But more intriguing for the purposes of this chapter, *Moby-Dick* points toward a mode of research that Buell terms "comparative ethnology." As an illustration, Buell analyzes Ishmael as a literate "outsider" traveling on the Pequod, the notorious industrial whaling ship pursuing the famous White Whale. Ishmael fashions a mental space in which whaling reduces the humanity of people and "whale-beholding" ennobles whales and impels humans to imagine "people and whales as semi-interchangeable" (Buell 212). The "species boundary is perpetually being blurred, and the reader pulled back and forth across it" with dozens of playful personifications, including whales with brows, whales who carry on like "colleagians," whales who care for their young and for each other, etc. (Buell 207–08). Ishmael, then, is "a lens through which humans and sea creatures become coordinated into an informal comparative ethnology" (Buell 212).

"Comparative ethnology" might also be an apt phrase for describing the work that transformational characters perform in Caro's film and Hogan's novel. As anthropologist Claude Lévi-Strauss articulated it, the oral traditions of various Indigenous cultures include animals capable of transforming into other shapes not because they are "good to eat" or "good to prohibit" but because they are "good to think" (qtd. in Adamson, "Why" 35–36). When included in contemporary Indigenous literature, stories about transformational animals—bears, snakes, and frogs—with their quasi-human qualities (their intelligence, their ability to shed skin or walk upright, or to move easily through air and water) teach lessons about the relationship between humans and animals because they reveal the animality of humans and the humanity of animals. As I argue in *American Indian Literature*, novels by Native North American writers as diverse as N. Scott Momaday, Louise Erdrich, and Leslie Marmon Silko illustrate that characters with transformational qualities are often employed to address social and environmental injustices by suggesting that "boundaries are permeable" (106). Thus, these novels encourage readers to think about how they might alter "the power relations at the root of social and ecological problems" (Adamson, *American Indian Literature* 112).

Early ecocritical work, then, including Buell's analysis of Ishmael's "comparative ethnology" and my analysis of transformational characters in Indigenous literatures, points to an emerging field whose sensibilities have been gathered by Donna Haraway, Bruno Latour, Isabelle Stengers, Marisol De la Cadena, and other scholars who study a host of organisms that are not just "good to think" but "good to live with" (Haraway's formulation). Called "multispecies ethnography," theorists and practitioners in this field, write S. Eben Kirksey and Stefan Helmreich, have moved well beyond anthropological studies that account for animals and other-than-human species only within the confines of "food," "taboo," or "symbol." They consider humans within a context of their entanglements with other kinds of living selves (546). In her "ethnographically inspired" study of Latin American "Indigenous cosmopolitics," anthropologist De la Cadena examines the interactions between humans and "earth-beings," defined as sacred mountains known to demand respect from humans and "other-than-humans" including animals, plants, and "lesser beings" recognized as lakes, forests, or smaller mountains. De la Cadena draws from Isabelle Stengers's work to explicate how earth beings are taking the stage in a political arena coming to be known as "Indigenous cosmopolitics."

Stengers extracts from the word "cosmopolitan" its two constituents: cosmos and politics. "Cosmos" refers to the unknown constituted by multiple, divergent worlds and "politics" to the articulation of which "they would eventually be capable" (Stengers 995). In the Andean ethnographic record, "earth beings" with "individual physiognomies more or less known by individuals involved in interactions with them" are enlisted when their material existence and that of the worlds to which they belong is threatened by the siting of a mine, clear-cutting, pollution, erosion, overfishing, overhunting, etc. (De la Cadena 341–42). While these beings might be categorized as "things" or "natural resources" within Western politics or science, Indigenous activists confront the monopoly of discourses that provincialize "the universe" as a world inhabited by humans who are distanced from "Nature" (De la Cadena 345). For Indigenous peoples, "earth-beings" have never been separated from "nature" and have always interacted with humans. Their increasing presence on regional, national, and international political and public stages, writes De la Cadena, is extraordinary only because of its recent "public visibility" (348).

Caro's film provides a wonderful illustration of how a geological formation might be recognized as an "earth-being" that could be represented ethnographically through a story or film "staged" to remind humans that "other" species are not just good to think but are entities and agents that are good "to live with" (as Haraway maintains). According to Maori legend, when Paikea arrived on the East Coast of New Zealand one thousand years ago, he had been instructed by his elders never to let the whale on which he rode touch land. But when he arrived in Aotearoa, he was too tired to swim to land, so he coaxed the whale to shore, where it died. In Ihimaera's first iteration of Paikea's story, when the whale touches the sand, it becomes "an island. You can still see it, near Whangara" (qtd. in Allen 134). In Caro's film, this rock formation, seen just offshore from Whangara, provides a visual reminder of the Maori's connection to and responsibility for the whale. The formation becomes, literally, a mnemonic for the entanglement of humans with whales and thus a kind of shorthanded "comparative ethnography."

Caro observes that she welcomed the opportunity to "work collaboratively" with Executive Producer Ihimaera and "collectively" with the villagers of Whangara who played every role in the film except those of the lead actors to portray this complex entanglement (*Behind the Scenes*). Every time the island is featured in the background of a scene, the intimate, 1,000-year-old relation of the Maori to the whale is reiterated. The Nagati Porou have no pre-European history of maritime whaling since their canoes were more suited to fishing than whaling. However, both before and after the arrival of Europeans, they relied on incidental captures and strandings which were considered a gift from the sea, to be used for meat, fat, oil, and bone. Strandings, mnemonically represented by the island, were and still are an "occasion for awe, for sorrow (at the death of a distant relative), and ultimately a cause for elation at the bounty provided" (Cawthorne 3). The mass stranding of whales that occurs in the film, and the sorrow expressed by the villagers who play themselves, is powerfully portrayed because they are not simply acting; they are "there to protect the story" (*Behind the Scenes*). The island itself is also "protecting the story" because it suggests that "living with" a particular species can take many forms, from companion species to food to ancestor, and is a responsibility to be taken seriously. In this way, the film becomes an "activist event," as Allen defines that term, that draws attention to a the political and artistic ways that the Maori are drawing connections between local issues and an international movement working not only for human rights but for the protection of "Mother Earth" as an entire "cosmos" of relations (UDRME, Preamble).

## The Ecological Indian and the Emergence of Indigenous Cosmopolitics

Recently, Annette Kolodny has shown that Indigenous peoples were actively constructing images of the "Ecological Indian" for their own ends much earlier than the 1970s date that Krech avers as the historical moment in which American Indians embraced and strategically began marshaling images of themselves in support of the environmental movement (Krech 20). Kolodny analyzes Penobscot writer Joseph Nicolar's 1897 text, *The Life and Traditions of the Red Man*, to show that the Penobscots of Maine in North America understood "the political usefulness of publicly declaring themselves protectors, conservators, even kin to the worlds they hoped to save as early as the late 1700s" (Kolodny, "Rethinking" 18). For the Penobscots, the world was everywhere alive with the spiritual powers of "kin beings" (often depicted as transformational characters). These beings taught that the "plants and animals were their helpers and companions, just as the people, in their turn, were to act as kin and companions to the living world around them" (Kolodny, "Rethinking" 12). Nicolar's ethnography is not an expression of desire for a premodern past, but a manifesto declaring the Penobscot to be in active resistance to the illegal appropriations of their land and the decimation of the beings who live there. In 1823, they presented the first of many petitions to the governor of Maine documenting that "in years past the beasts of the forest, Moose and Deer, were very plenty […], [but] in consequence of the white people killing them off merely for the sake of their skins, they have now become nearly extinct" (Kolodny "Rethinking" 5). After Nicolar died, his book became the basis of a successful 1972 land claims lawsuit brought by the Penobscots against the US government which resulted in the recovery of 300,000 acres of land for the tribe. Also, from the 1940s to the 1960s, the Penobscots staged Nicolar's book as a pageant for tourists visiting Maine (Kolodny, "Saving" 95–96).

The Penobscots were not the only Indigenous group to begin staging activist events focused on transformational animals, ancestral migrations, or relationship to "earth-beings" before the 1970s. From the 1950s to the 1970s, many North American tribal groups waged successful land claims suits which resulted in returned territories (Adamson, *American Indian Literature*, 175–76). These lawsuits were energized by the even earlier efforts of other Indigenous groups around the world to organize nationally and internationally. In 1923, Haudenosaunee (Iroquois) Chief Deskaheh traveled to Geneva to speak to the League of Nations about incidences of genocide and injustice in North America. In 1925, Maori religious leader T. W. Ratana similarly sought to protest the breaking of the Treaty of Waitangi in New Zealand, which had given the Maori ownership of their lands in 1840. Both leaders were turned away by the League of Nations, but Indigenous groups did not cease their attempts to petition what would later become the United Nations ("About UNPFII"). Their activities led, by 1982, to the organization of the United Nations Working Group on Indigenous Populations (WGIP), and in May 2002, to the first meeting of the UN Permanent Forum on Indigenous Issues ("About UNPFII"). This organization worked concertedly toward the adoption in 2007 by the United Nations of the Declaration on the Rights of Indigenous Peoples (UNDRIP). This international legal instrument has drawn attention to the decades-long transnational activities of coalitions of Indigenous and non-Indigenous nongovernmental organizations (NGOs) and civil society groups that have been campaigning for global recognition of Indigenous cultural, legal, and environmental rights ("About UNPFII"). In 2010, drawing their authority from UNDRIP, Indigenous peoples from around the globe gathered for the World People's Conference on the Rights of Mother Earth in Cochabamba, Bolivia. In the Declaration that emerged from this gathering, "Mother Earth" is recognized as an "earth-being" that is not female-gendered but, rather, the "Source of Life" (De la Cadena 335, 350). As defined by UDRME, "Source of Life" or "Mother Earth" is understood as "ecosystems, natural communities, species and all other natural entities" (UDRME, Art. 4.1).

In the nearly two centuries leading up to the UNDRIP and UDRME, many "autoethnographic" documents, summits, and conferences have emerged out of the Indigenous rights movement. These forms and forums, though highly syncretic, are being recognized not only by Indigenous peoples themselves but by a "concert of nations" whose attention Indigenous and ethnic minority groups have sought to "direct and whose judgment they [endeavor] to persuade" (Allen 197). However, establishing an "authentic Indigenous identity" has not been the goal of this activism. Rather, since the 1980s, regional, national, and international coalitions of Indigenous peoples have consistently rejected clichéd stereotypes of "ethnic purity" or "proximity to nature" as they organize to oppose economic development models that are causing large-scale environmental degradation and displacement among the Indigenous and the poor

(Adamson, *American* 31–50, 128–79). Indigenous politicians and their allies have recognized that a politics based only on ethnic identity will ultimately fail, since the trade liberalization schemes linked to extractive industries, large-scale development projects, and corporate capitalism and agribusiness can be a problem not just for Indigenous peoples but for ethnic minorities, the poor, and for the non-Indigenous. Thus, Indigenous cosmopolitical organizers have moved away from debates about "identity" and toward renewed attention to achieving civil, human, and environmental rights through alliance-making and capacity-building among diverse Indigenous and non-Indigenous groups who are working together to achieve adoption of international legal instruments or passage of national or regional legislation protecting civil and human rights and the rights of "Mother Earth."

## Rebuilding the Ancestor as Activist Event

Ihimaera recalls that he wrote his first story about the whale rider for his own 12-year-old daughter to encourage the idea that new generations of Maori people do indeed possess the ability to interpret or reinterpret Maori tradition in contemporary times (*Behind the Scenes*). While living in New York, he looked out his high-rise window and saw, to his amazement, a whale swimming up the Hudson River. This inspired him to write the story of Paikea, but with a twist that is dramatically portrayed in Caro's film. After the death of his wife and baby son, the main character Porourangi goes against tradition and names his surviving twin daughter, "Paikea," after the boy whale rider who links the Ngati Porou to the whales that taught them to navigate the Pacific and became the inspiration for the canoes that allowed them to engage in coastal fishing and an occasional whale hunt (Cawthorn 2). Porourangi is hurt by his father's insistence that he marry immediately after his wife's death so that he can produce a male heir. He decides to move to Germany where he can grieve in peace and exhibit his celebrated wood carvings in European art galleries. He leaves Paikea, also known as Pai, in Whangara to be raised by her grandmother, Nanny Flowers, and her grandfather, Koro Apirana.

Koro believes that tradition dictates that the leader of the Ngate Porou must be a male. He is alarmed that so many young men in the village are engaged in drug and gang activity. He hopes to stem these trends by gathering them in the meeting house and teaching them more about their traditions as he tries to identify who among them should be the next leader. He excludes Pai from his school because she is a girl. However, she takes her future into her own hands by enlisting the aid of her uncle, who secretly teaches her to fight like a warrior, just as Koro is teaching these lessons to the young men. When her grandfather finds out about this breach in tradition, he is enraged. He loses himself in despair when none of the boys prove worthy of the title "koro" or leader. Later, when a pod of whales strands themselves on the beach, Koro believes it is because the people/ancestors/whales have no leader. He admonishes Pai against touching the distressed and dying creatures. But when Koro walks away, Pai lovingly strokes the largest whale's barnacled body and climbs onto its back. Coaxing it to lift itself, she leads the surviving members of the pod back to the ocean and remains on the whale's back as it dives beneath the ocean.

By filming Pai descending under the water, Caro and Executive Producer Ihimaera accomplish two things. Because Pai is a girl, they open stereotypical notions of the "Ecological Indian" and Indigenous "tradition" to question. From what time period must legitimate tradition come? Can leadership traditions that no longer make sense in modern contexts change be adapted or even improved? By showing Pai descending under the water, Caro and Ihimaera also imply that Pai may be a transformational being who illustrates that "boundaries are permeable" and power relations at the root of social and ecological problems can be altered (Adamson *American Indian Literature* 106, 112). This scene also blurs the boundaries between human and animal and engages in a kind of multispecies ethnography, to use the language of Kirksey and Helmreich, that does not seek to "give voice, agency or subjectivity to the nonhuman—to recognize them as other, visible in their difference" but to advocate a radical rethinking of categories of analysis "as they pertain to all beings" (Kirksey and Helmreich 562-3). Caro and Ihimaera are calling upon the audience not only to rethink Indigenous traditions but Linnaean classifications of genus, family, order, class, phylum, kingdom, and domain as these supposedly "natural" categories delineate the differences between male and female and human and "other-than-human." Pai's possible transformational qualities question the hidden ontology which makes "the human" the central reference in any study of "multiple species" and calls upon the audience to rethink all categories in the cosmos including the "natural" ones.

When Pai survives and returns, Koro realizes she is a leader for new times. The film ends as he joins her for a celebratory voyage in Porourangi's beautifully finished and feathered waka which "builds the ancestor" as it literally represents a multispecies ethnography. The voyage is an "activist event" that illustrates a powerful "grandparent-grandchild bond" that has become emblematic in Maori cultural productions of a Maori political renaissance in Aotearoa. As Allen explains, representations of this bond have been "mobilized as a symbol of unity and political power" that has worked to restore Maori pride in their artistry and cultural heritage and assert their legal and political claims to illegally appropriated Maori lands and natural resources (128–30). This bond is strongly represented as Porourangi and a full complement of traditionally dressed Maori paddlers launch the waka with Paikea and her grandfather sitting in the position where the original whale rider would have sat on the back of a whale. The waka itself is built by a team of traditional Moari woodcarvers and Hollywood production crew members (*Te Waka*). Together they articulate the multispecies genealogy of the Maori cosmos on the hull. Father Sky and Mother Earth are carved on either side and a carving of Paikea sits on the bow. The vessel itself represents the body of the whale. The generations of men and women, in all their modern diversity, are carved along the length of both sides of the canoe. As the waka cuts through the water, humans and figures of Maori gods and ancestors are literally and symbolically interacting with multiple species living in the ocean.

On the beach, a group of multiracial, international people, including Porourangi's pregnant German wife, can be seen cheering and chanting. This group could be seen to represent over 200 years of activism and collaboration among multiracial groups working for regional, national, and international civil, legal, and policy protections not only for threatened groups of people, but for multiple species functioning together in a complex cosmos of relations. Porourangi's children, one unborn and one in the waka, "rebuild the ancestor" as they reclaim community's "significant past" as well as "its significant present and possible future" (Allen 147). The waka, in the context of this last scene, reinterprets and resignifies Indigenous genealogies and traditions in the context of complex contemporary realities among Indigenous, ethnic minority, civil society groups, and artistic/cultural producers who are working in coalition to claim the "cosmos" as a dynamic space that includes humans and the whole community of beings that exists in the world. Porourangi's German wife illustrates how people from around the world, not just Indigenous people, are coming together to imagine a politics built not on clichéd notions of the Ecological Indian but upon regional, national, and international laws and policies seeking the "recovery, revalidation, and strengthening of Indigenous cosmovisions" (UDRME, Preamble).

## Transformational Animals and Sentient Earth Beings

Multispecies ethnography calls upon humans to radically rethink categories of analysis as they pertain to life at multiple scales. Linda Hogan, a passionate whale activist who was invited by seven Makah women elders to join them in a collaboration that would "revision" Makah's relationship to the whale, wrote *People of the Whale*, as a part of that project.[3] She creates Marco, a human/whale being, to represent the relationship between humans and other-than-humans as she calls upon readers to become more aware of evolutionary worlds that exist outside the "measured time" of a single human life (Hogan 17). Hogan represents evolutionary time with the "old intelligence" of a whale's eye set in a "body covered with barnacle life and sea creatures" that is conceptualized as a "planet in its universe" (267). The whale's eye calls upon readers to engage in a comparative ethnography that reveals the ways in which multiple species conduct their interrelational lives. The novel shows that for many Indigenous peoples, these worlds have never ceased to exist. The whale's "old intelligence" also helps to explain why the Cochabamba delegates call upon the world to grant all species the "right" to the "time and space" necessary for the regeneration of "biocapacity" and "vital cycles" (UDRME, Preamble).

---

[3] Hogan and her friend, naturalist and writer Brenda Peterson, along with oceanographer, Jean Michel Cousteau, visited the Makah village in the years before the now infamous whale hunt. In turn, the Makah women were invited to go with Hogan, Peterson, and Cousteau on a National Geographic mission to trace the migration routes of gray whales from Baja, Mexico, to the Artic. These collaborations are documented in Peterson and Hogan's *Sightings*.

In order to illustrate the concepts of evolutionary time and imperceptible threats to the earth's "vital cycles," Hogan creates a multispecies ethnography in which two human characters, Thomas and Ruth, act in relation to their child, Marco, who is represented as a transformational being. Thomas is a Vietnam War veteran and the grandson of the A'atsika people's most famed traditional whaler, Whiti. Thomas's story illustrates how modern Indigenous communities must deal with complicated social and economic issues that challenge their relationship to environmentalism. Before he is born, the forests are clear cut and the whales have been overhunted. The resulting high unemployment at Dark River and lack of economic opportunity compels Thomas, newly married to his childhood sweetheart Ruth, to follow his best friend Dwight to the US army recruitment office and sign up to serve in the Vietnam War. In the jungles of Vietnam, and later, Cambodia, Thomas is ordered to burn the rice paddies of the local Indigenous peoples, the Muong. When the fields will not ignite in the dense humidity, Thomas and his unit are ordered to contaminate the fields with chemicals. Hogan writes, "In his world, his old world, these things were not done, but now he knew worlds overlapped, many of them, as if they were transparent pages in a book" (166). Thomas's cultural world, which is shaped by A'atsika values and reverence for living organisms, overlaps with a modern political world in which crimes take place at both the micro- and macro-scopic scales.

Here, Hogan employs toxins, which operate at levels invisible to the human eye to suggest comparative multispecies ethnographies operating at multiple scales. The deliberate contamination of rice paddies indicates that Hogan is concerned about how the world's Indigenous, minority, ethnic, and poor communities are affected by toxins, released in wars or in agricultural practices, which transgress the boundaries of human and other-than-human bodies at microscopic, imperceptible levels that nevertheless have implications for the continued survival of all life on earth. Although he has no formal education, Thomas's A'atsika upbringing has made him aware that his participation, voluntary or involuntary, in the release of toxins has ethical and moral implications for the socionatural worlds crucial to the survival of both humans and other-than-humans living side by side in a state of interdependence.

Ashamed of his wartime crimes, and after many years away from Dark River, Thomas cannot bring himself to return to Ruth or Marco, the son born shortly after he left for Vietnam.[4] Instead, he takes up residence in San Francisco. When he finally returns home, it is to join Dwight on the whale hunt. Dwight, also a Vietnam veteran, has become a powerful man and successfully persuades the A'atsika tribal council that the village should reclaim their "tradition" by reestablishing the practice of "cultural whaling." Dwight argues that the hunt will renew the tribe culturally and economically after years of disastrously high rates of unemployment, poverty, alcoholism, domestic violence, and drug abuse exacerbated by the economic pressures caused when the tribe voluntarily agreed to stop hunting whales in 1946. However, Dwight fails to base

---

[4] In the novel, Thomas deserts the US army and spends many years living with a Muong wife and daughter in Cambodia. Because of space, this chapter will not address those years.

his petition on a complete cultural history of the A'atsika. As feminist ecocritic Greta Gaard explains, in pre-1800s Makah society, only elite, wealthy males, who inherited their status, were allowed to be whale hunters (5). Dwight's petition purposely equates A'atsika cultural identity with only the most famous practice of the tribe's elite, upper-class male ancestors. Thus, Hogan uses the character of Dwight to acknowledge "indigenous complicity in environmental destruction" and avoid "any suggestion that the local people necessarily have exclusive access to nature" (Steinwand 187).

Thomas's estranged wife, Ruth, and a group of women elders oppose the whale hunt. They insist that the A'atsika no longer need whale meat to survive and gray whales are not numerous enough to be hunted regularly (Hogan 70). They have also discovered that Dwight is motivated by potential business deals with industrial whaling nations, including Japan and Norway, which are advancing him under-the-table bribes he is using to pay for a new addition to his house (Hogan 68–69).[5] On the day Marco paddles the lead canoe out to the ocean in search of a whale, they stand on the beach to demonstrate their opposition to the notion of a "cultural hunt."

Ruth's son, Marco, has been charged by the elders to follow A'atsika traditions in determining whether or not any given whale should be hunted. When a young, inquisitive gray whale playfully swims up to the side of the canoe and greets the men, Marco commands the whalers not to kill the juvenile but his orders are ignored. The already drunken crew fire shots from high-power rifles and in the chaos that follows, Marco disappears under the bloody water along with the dying whale. Because his body is never found, Hogan implies that he may be an earth-being, capable of living on. Later Thomas, Marco's father, who fired the first shot, acknowledges the part he played in the disappearance of his son and the death of the young whale. He thinks about all the whales he has seen over the course of his lifetime. They are covered with barnacles and other sea life. This suggests that whales are not single creatures but a cosmos of life. In killing a whale or a person, Thomas concludes, humans kill "a planet in its universe" (Hogan 267).

After the disastrous hunt, Thomas is so sorrowful and ashamed that he moves across the bay to live with the elders. He spends hours in the ocean, learning to swim and regulate his breath, just as a whale regulates its oxygen when it dives beneath the sea and just as Marco did while Thomas was away in Vietnam. This suggests that Thomas is consciously thinking about his relationship to the whale as planet/cosmos. According to De la Cadena, when contemporary Indigenous people or politicians put earth beings at the center of their actions, they see these creatures not as proposals for what "is" or "what ought to be." Rather, earth beings provoke thought, or to use Isabelle Stengers's terms, they "slow down reasoning" and create an opportunity to arouse a slightly different awareness of the problems and situations under analysis (qtd. in De la Cadena 360–61). Thomas's long dives invite readers to "slow down reasoning" and

---

[5] Traditional Makah elders who opposed the 1999 hunt discovered that whaling nations like Japan, Norway, and Russia were supporting and encouraging Makah whalers to set a precedent for "cultural whaling," since this new International Whaling Commission category would then open the way for those countries to file similar petitions (Gaard 23, n. 3; Peterson and Hogan 107–08, 143).

to see the world not as "universe" (singular) but as a cosmos of worlds teeming with life spanning multiple scales from the molecules of oxygen Thomas must control to stay under the water to the pulmonary system he must expand to stay alive. Like the body of a whale or any living creature, Thomas's body is also a "planet in its universe" (Hogan 267).

While thinking and breathing like a whale, Thomas slows down reasoning and comes to understand how his blind faith in traditions that he had not really understood when he left for Vietnam—nationalism, patriotism, patriarchy—"had led him to crimes" (Hogan 95). Yet there are crimes taking place at a much larger scale—war, deforestation, extractive industries that are destroying socionatural relationships between humans and other beings. Thomas's experiences set human multispecies relationship not in the context of a single "universe" described by Western science as the separation of the "Human" from "Nature" but in a context that contemporary Indigenous activists and multispecies ethnographers are describing as a "pluriverse" that does not separate human or "other-than-human beings and the worlds in which they [exist]" (De la Cadena 345). Hogan illustrates the possibility for rethinking human relationships to the pluriverse by showing Thomas's moving away from a position supportive of Dwight. Near the end of the novel, Ruth sees Thomas visibly "transformed" from lifeless war veteran to caring member of the whale clan (Hogan 238). This suggests that Hogan holds out hope, to use the words of the UDRME, that humans might rediscover and move to protect not individual charismatic megafauna but an entire cosmos imagined as a "living being with whom [humans] have an indivisible and interdependent relationship" (UDRME, Art. 2).

## A Cosmopolitical Pluriverse

Caro and Ihimaera and Hogan create human/whale children that provoke a kind of thinking that might enable humans to undo, or more accurately, unlearn, classificatory social and scientific systems that have separated male from female and human from nature. These children suggest that contemporary people may indeed have something to learn from stories about transformational characters who suggest worlds of multispecies relationships. Ruth prays to earth beings, but she is also a single woman who must provide for herself through her salmon fishing operation. Her need to sustain herself financially illustrates that allowing earth beings to count in politics does not remove all proposals for economic growth and development from the negotiating table. People—Indigenous or not—can still side with a mine or dam, operate a fishing or agricultural business, and chose jobs or money, depending on local needs.

However, Ruth has observed for herself that there are fewer salmon in the ocean (Hogan 70). She sees that her people will need to imagine new ways to support themselves economically in the future. As she and her fellow A'atsika elders "slow down reasoning," they imagine how they might advocate, as did the Makah women activists upon which their characters are based, the development of a whale-watching enterprise that will provide jobs that flow "from the same past of whale hunting" but which are adapting premodern traditions to a "new and environmentally fragile world" (Peterson and Hogan 165). After the 1999 whale hunt, the Makah women elders entered into coalition with their Quileute neighbors to the north and began meeting together with the goal of taking both human economic and whale ecological health into account. *New York Times* writer William Yardley has reported that in North America, one of the forms this revisioned relationship to the whale has taken is the revival of "paddling" or rowing traditional cedar canoes. Since 1998, tribes scattered across coastal regions of Washington State and British Columbia have paddled traditionally designed cedar canoes "as many as 40 miles a day, some times more, over two or three weeks, camping at a series of reservations until they converge at the home of a host tribe" (Yardley). There, a host tribe welcomes several thousand people for a week of traditional dancing, singing, and celebration staged to "recapture cultural, linguistic and intertribal connections" nearly lost after European settlers and more recently substance abuse and suicide have threatened their survival and continuance as distinct tribal groups (Yarkley). Funded by several new tribal enterprises, including casinos, and a small but growing industry that feeds tourists fresh fish and locally made beers and wines, this re-commenced traditional practice began after an elder studied traditional "seagoing canoes in museum exhibits and even those on display in a Seattle restaurant, because none were left in their village" (Yardley).

The tradition of paddling has also been revived among Austronesian-speaking people throughout the Pacific, including the Maori. Just as elders in the American Northwest had to find and study canoes archived in museums because they no longer had any of their own, the Ngati Porou of Whangara did not possess a waka because they are very expensive to build (*Te Waka*). For this reason, the waka in Caro's film, a fully functioning ceremonial canoe, is given to the people of Whangara after the film wraps as a gift that will allow them to "rebuild the ancestor." In the last scene of the film, Pai and Koro sit in a vessel that represents a true collaboration between the villagers of Whangara and a Hollywood film crew. This is an "event" that brings an Indigenous group into coalition with non-Indigenous people and suggests something that goes far beyond the "tactical essentialism" described by Krech. Ihimaera, Caro, and Hogan are employing film and literature to urge audiences and readers to revision the planet as a cosmos of multispecies communities existing in intimate, entangled relations.

## Works Cited

"About UNPFII and a Brief History of Indigenous Peoples and the International System." *The United Nations Permanent Forum on Indigenous Issues*. 2006. Aug. 17, 2009.

Adamson, Joni. "Why Bears Are Good to Think and Theory Doesn't Have to Be Another Form of Murder: Transformation and Oral Tradition in Louise Erdrich's *Tracks*." *Studies in American Indian Literatures*, vol. 4, no. 1, 1992, pp. 28–48.

———. *American Indian Literature, Environmental Justice, and Ecocriticism: The Middle Place*. U of Arizona P, 2001.

Allen, Chadwick. *Blood Narrative: Indigenous Identity in American Indian and Maori Literary and Activist Texts*. Duke UP, 2002.
*Behind the Scenes of* Whale Rider. Dir. Jonathan Brough. Special Feature. *Whale Rider*. New Market Films, 2002.
Buell, Lawrence. *Writing for an Endangered World: Literature, Culture, and Environment in the U.S. and Beyond*. Harvard UP, 2001.
———. *The Future of Environmental Criticism: Environmental Crisis and Literary Imagination*. Blackwell, 2005.
Cawthorn, M.W. "Maori, Whales and 'Whaling': An Ongoing Relationship." *Conservation Advisory Science Notes*. No. 308. Wellington: Department of Conservation, Head Office, New Zealand, 2000, pp. 1–15. May 28, 2009.
De la Cadena, Marisol. "Indigenous Cosmopolitics in the Andes: Conceptual Reflections beyond 'Politics.'" *Cultural Anthropology*, vol. 25, no. 2, 2010, pp. 334–70.
Gaard, Greta. "Tools for a Cross-cultural Feminist Ethics: Exploring Ethnical Contexts and Contents in the Makah Whale Hunt." *Hypatia*, vol. 16, no. 1, 2001, pp. 1–26.
Garrard, Greg. *Ecocriticism*. Routledge, 2004.
Haraway, Donna. *When Species Meet*. U of Minneapolis P, 2008.
Hogan, Linda. *People of the Whale*. W. W. Norton, 2008.
Kirksey, S. Eben, and Stefen Helmreich. "The Emergence of Multispecies Ethnography." *Cultural Anthropology*, vol. 25, no. 4, 2010, pp. 545–76.
Kolodny, Annette. "Rethinking the 'Ecological Indian': A Penobscot Precursor." *ISLE: Interdisciplinary Studies in Literature and Environment*, vol. 14, no. 1, 2007, pp. 1–23.
———. "Saving Maine for the Indian: The Legacy of Joseph Nicolar's *The Life and Traditions of the Red Man*." *MELUS*, vol. 34, no. 2, 2009, pp. 81–101.
Krech, Shepherd III. *The Ecological Indian: Myth and History*. Norton, 1999.
Steinwand, Jonathan. "What the Whales Would Tell Us: Cetacean Communication in Novels by Witi Ihimaera, Linda Hogan, Zakes Mda, and Amitav Ghosh." *Postcolonial Ecologies: Literatures of the Environment*, edited by Elizabeth Deloughrey and George Handley, Oxford UP, 2011, pp. 128–99.
Peterson, Brenda and Linda Hogan. *Sightings: The Gray Whale's Mysterious Journey*. National Geographic, 2002.
Stengers, Isabelle. "The Cosmopolitical Proposal." *Making Things Public: Atmospheres of Democracy*, edited by Bruno Latour and Peter Weibel, MIT, 2005, pp. 994–1004.
*Te Waka: Building the Canoe*. Dir. Jonathan Brough. Special Feature. *Whale Rider*. New Market Films, 2002.
"United Nations Declaration on the Rights of Indigenous Peoples." The United Nations Permanent Forum on Indigenous Issues. Adopted by the United Nations General Assembly in 2007. Aug. 11, 2009.
"Universal Declaration on the Rights of Mother Earth." World People's Conference on Climate Change and the Rights of Mother Earth. Sept. 17, 2010.
*Whale Rider*. Dir. Niki Caro. Perf. Keisha Castle-Hughes, Rawira Paratene, Vicky Haughton, Cliff Curtis. New Market Films, 2002.
Yardley, Willam. "A Northwest Journey by Canoe to Reconnect with the Old Ways." *The New York Times*, Jul. 25, 2011, A9. Nov. 22, 2011.

# Notes on Contributors

**Joni Adamson** is Professor of Environmental Humanities in the Department of English and Senior Sustainability Scholar at the Julie Ann Wrigley Global Institute of Sustainability at Arizona State University. In 2012, she served as President for the Association for the Study Literature and Environment (ASLE) and, for over 10 years, led the American Studies Association's Environment and Culture Caucus. She is co-editor of five collections and special issues, including *Keywords for Environmental Studies* (New York University Press 2015), *American Studies, Ecocriticism and Citizenship: Thinking and Acting in the Local and Global Commons* (Routledge 2013), and *The Environmental Justice Reader* (U of Arizona P 2002). She is author of *American Indian Literature, Environmental Justice and Ecocriticism* (U of Arizona P 2001) and has written over forty articles and reviews focusing on the environmental humanities, Indigenous perspectives on sustainability, material ecocriticism, environmental literature and film, environmental justice, contested notions of "the commons," food sovereignty, and critical plant studies.

**Kathryn Yalan Chang** is Professor in the English Department at National Taitung University in Taiwan. Her current research interests include nature therapy, material ecocriticism, medical and environmental humanities, environmental justice and activism, food and animal studies, and ecofeminism. Chang's recent project was entitled "Resilient Healing: Eco-Narratology, Neuroplasticity, and Matters of Care in Environmental Literary Texts." Her latest publications include "'Slowness' in the Anthropocene: Ecological Medicine in *Refuge* and *God's Hotel*," *Neohelicon* (2017), and "'Seeing Connections:' An Ecofeminist Peace Study of Mingyi Wu's *The Stolen Bicycle*" (Routledge, 2021).

**John R. Eperjesi** is Professor in the Department of English Linguistics and Literature at Kyung Hee University in Seoul. He received his PhD in the Literary and Cultural Theory program at Carnegie Mellon University and is the author of *The Imperialist Imaginary: Visions of Asia and the Pacific in American Culture* (University Press of New England, 2005). His work has appeared in *Amerasia*, *Asian Studies Review*, *boundary 2*, *The Contemporary Pacific*, *Inter-Asia Cultural Studies*, *Interdisciplinary Studies of Literature and the Environment* (ISLE), *Journal of American Studies*, *Minnesota Review*, and *Pacific Historical Review*. His current research and teaching is in the field of postcolonial ecocriticism.

**Hsinya Huang** is Distinguished Professor of American and Comparative Literature, National Sun Yat-Sen University (NSYSU), Taiwan. She is former Dean of Arts and

Humanities and Provost of Academic Affairs and Faculty Advancement, NSYSU, and served as Director General of International Cooperation and Science Education, Ministry of Science and Technology, Taiwan, 2018–19. She is the author or editor of books and articles on transnational and transpacific studies, Native American and Pacific Islander literatures, and humanities for the environment, including *(De)Colonizing the Body: Disease, Empire, and (Alter)Native Medicine in Contemporary Native American Women's Writings* (2004) and *Native North American Literatures: Reflections on Multiculturalism* (2009), *Aspects of Transnational and Indigenous Cultures* (2014), *Ecological Literature: Ecology, Subjectivity, and Technology* (2015), *Chinese Railroad Workers: Recovery and Representation* (2017), *Diaspora, Memory and Resurgence: Trans-Pacific Indigenous Writing and Practice* (2021), and *After Hiroshima: Radiation Ecologies in Trans-Pacific Indigenous Literature* (forthcoming). She serves on the advisory board of *The Journal of Transnational American Studies* and *Routledge Series on Transnational Indigenous Perspectives* and on the editorial board of *Transmotion: A Journal of Vizenorian Indigenous Studies*. Her current research project investigates the Anthropocene in the transpacific writing.

**Chia-li Kao** is Associate Professor at the Graduate Institute of Taiwan Literature and Transnational Cultural Studies at National Chung Hsing University. Kao received a PhD in Comparative Literature from Indiana University at Bloomington. Her research areas include comparative literature, pre–Second World War Japanese and Taiwanese literature, and Caribbean literature. Her recent research focuses on nature writing in Taiwan under the Japanese rule. She published *Writing Tropical Islands: Empires, Travel and Imagination* (2016) and co-edited *Crossing Southeast Asia* (forthcoming).

**Chia-hua Lin** is a PhD candidate in the English Department of the University of Hawaiʻi at Mānoa. She is the recipient of 2018 Fulbright Graduate Study Grant as well as the 2020 Government Scholarship to Study Abroad (GSSA) from the Taiwanese Ministry of Education. Her research interests include trans-Indigenous studies, ecopoetics, Hawaiian literature, and Pacific literature. She currently works as the secretary for the Asia Pacific Observatory of Humanities for the Environment. She is the co-editor of *Chinese Railroad Workers in North America: Recovery and Representation* (2017).

**Paul Lyons** was Professor of English at the University of Hawaiʻi at Mānoa, where he taught courses in US and postcolonial literatures, literary theory and criticism, and Pacific regional poetics. His work includes projects on collaborative relations and friendship among Kānaka Maoli and settlers, and on influences and affinities between African American and Pacific literatures. His publications include a monograph, *American Pacificism: Oceania in the U.S. Imagination* (Routledge 2006), and articles and reviews in journals such as *American Literature, American Literary History, Studies in American Fiction, Arizona Quarterly, Journal of Commonwealth and Postcolonial Studies, Boundary 2, Philosophy East & West, Anglistica*, and the *Contemporary Pacific*. He was the co-editor of "Pacific Currents," a special issue of *American Quarterly* (2015).

**Hitoshi Oshima** is Professor of Comparative Literature at Fukuoka University, Japan, and interested in understanding both Japanese literature in a global context and general literature in terms of cognitive and neurosciences. He used to be a member of the Executive Council of International Comparative Literature Association (ICLA) and President of Japanese Comparative Literature Association (JCLA). Among his publications in Western languages, "Le Développement d'une pensée mythique pour comprendre la pensée japonaise," "El Pensamiento Japonés," "Science, Literature and Art, An introduction to Modern Criticism Through Kobayashi Hideo," "The World according to Nishida Kitaro," etc.

**Craig Santos Perez** is an Indigenous CHamoru from Guåhan (Guam). He is the co-editor of six anthologies and the author of five books of poetry and the monograph, *Navigating Chamoru Poetry: Indigeneity, Aesthetics, and Decolonization*. He is a professor in the English Department and an affiliate faculty with the Center for Pacific Islands Studies and the Indigenous Politics Program at the University of Hawai'i at Mānoa.

**Iris Ralph** teaches English language and literature courses at Tamkang University. Her areas of teaching and research include Australian literature, British literature, American literature, animal studies, posthumanism, and ecocriticism. She is a member of ASLE, ASLE-Taiwan, and ASLEC-ANZ (where she has served in the past in the role of treasurer and where she now serves in the role of bibliographer). Her most recent publications include "The Systemic Approach, Biosemiotic Theory, and Ecocide in Australia" (*CLCWeb: Comparative Literature and Culture*, December 2014); "Posthumanist Readings" (*Ted Hughes*, ed. Terry Gifford, Palgrave Macmillan, Houndmills, UK, December 2014); book review of *Ecocriticism and Shakespeare: Reading Ecophobia* by Simon C. Estok (*Tamkang Review*, June 2014); "Pedagogical Literary Environmental Activism and 'The Dream of the Rood'" (*Forum for World Literature Studies*, June 2014); and "Tall-Fins and Tale-Ends in Taiwan: Cetacean Exploitation, Oil Refineries, and *Moby-Dick*" (*Journal of Ecocriticism*, Spring 2014).

**Syaman Rapongan** is a prominent Tao aboriginal writer. He received his BA in French, MA in Anthropology, and PhD candidacy in Taiwan literature from National Cheng Kung University. He spent his school years in Taiwan until the 1980s when he returned to take part in the civil protest against nuclear waste deposit on his home island, *Pongso no Tao* (Orchid Island). In 1992, he published *The Myths of Ba Dai Bay* 八代灣的神話, a bilingual collection of traditional tales and myths of the Tao. Other titles, forming a part of the tradition of Indigenous literature of Taiwan and the Pacific, include *Cold Sea, Deep Passion* 冷海情深 (1997), *Black Wings* 黑色的翅膀 (1999), *The Memories of the Waves* 海浪的記憶 (2002), *The Sailor's Face* 航海家的臉 (2007), *The Old Seaman* 老海人 (2009), *Eyes of the Sky* 天空的眼睛 (2012), *Drifting Dreams of the Ocean* 大海浮夢 (2014), *The Death of Ngalumirem* 安洛米恩之死 (2015), *The Eyes of the Ocean* 大海之眼 (2018), *I Wish to Be a Fish Scale of* *the Ocean* 我願是那片海洋的魚鱗 (2021), *A Man without Mailbox* 沒有信箱的男人 (2022), etc. His work has been translated into English, French, Japanese, Spanish, and German.

**Anna Erzsebet Szucs** is a researcher and learning designer at Tomorrow University of Applied Sciences. She received her Master's degree in Hungarian literature at the University of Szeged, Hungary, and her PhD degree in Foreign languages and literature at the National Sun Yat-sen University, Taiwan. Her PhD research focused on Indigenous Pacific Islander literature with special attention to activism in poetry. Currently, her work concentrates on sustainability and sustainable development in interdisciplinary fields. She is interested in Indigenous eco-literatures and contemporary Indigenous cultural studies.

**Rob Wilson** is Professor of American literature, creative writing, and poetics at the University of California at Santa Cruz. His books of poetry and cultural criticism include *Waking in Seoul; American Sublime; Asia/Pacific as Space of Cultural Production; Global/Local: Cultural Production and the Transnational Imaginary; Inside Out: Literature, Cultural Politics and the New Pacific*; and *Reimagining the American Pacific: From "South Pacific" to Bamboo Ridge and Beyond. Be Always Converting, Be Always Converted: An American Poetics* was selected by *Choice* as an Outstanding Academic Publication in 2010. *Beat Attitudes: On the Roads to Beatitude for Post-Beat Writers, Dharma Bums, and Cultural-Political Activists* was published by New Pacific Press in 2010 and reissued on Kindle Books in 2020. His poems have appeared in various journals from *Poetry, Ploughshares, New Republic, Jacket,* and the *Berkeley Poetry Review* to *Bamboo Ridge, Tinfish, Segue Munhak, Good Times,* and *Korean Culture*. A dual-language poetry collection in English and Chinese called *When the Nikita Moon Rose* appeared in the Transpacific Archipelagic Poetry Series at National Sun Yat-sen University in Kaohsiung, Taiwan, in fall 2021. He administers two social groups on Facebook called "Beat Attitudes: World Becoming" and "Rethinking World Literature."

# Index

A'atsika 196–97, 206–08
Aberley, Doug 164
A-bomb Dome 118–19, 124, 127, 129
Abon, Limeyo 125–26
Aboriginal people
    of Australia 185, 191–92
    of Taiwan 51, 53, 56, 58–59, 59 n.8, 64
Acapulco 67, 94
*An Account of Ancient Matters* (古事記)
    59 n.9
activism 11–12, 14, 41 n.6, 46, 72–73,
    79–80, 85, 87–90, 92, 96, 126,
    163, 197, 202, 205
activists 2, 11, 14–15, 29, 43, 45, 67, 85,
    87, 96–99, 163–64, 178–79, 188,
    200–05, 208
A-Da 177 n.12
Adams, John Luther, "Become Ocean" 155
Adamson, Joni 14, 103, 114, 172, 174–75,
    197–99
    *American Indian Literature* 172,
    198–99, 202–04
Adorno, Rolena, *The Polemics of Possession*
    *in Spanish American Narrative*
    35 n.1
Adorno, Theodor 28
aesthetics x n.1, 6, 11, 45, 57–58, 61–63,
    80, 155, 172–73
    sabi (さび), Japanese aesthetics 11,
    61–64
Agate, Alfred 24
agent 89, 200
'āina (land) 12, 101, 103, 105–11, 113–14
Ainu 12–13, 135–37, 142–43
    Ainu Association of Hokkaido 135 n.2
    Ainu Law (1997) 135 n.1
    divine songs 12, 136–40, 143
    god/goddess 136–43
    hunting (respect for prey) 137, 140
    *inau* (ritual wood stick) 143
    racial discrimination 135, 135 n.2
    respect for soul 138–39

Air and Missile Defense Task Force 74
Alaimo, Stacy 153 n.20, 169
Alaska 139
Alcoff, Linda Martin 174
Allen, Chadwick 9, 16, 195, 197, 201, 204
    *Trans-Indigenous: Methodologies for*
    *Global Native Literary Studies* 9
American Indians 198, 201
Americanization 25
American Lake 3, 6, 21, 148
American Pacific 10, 14, 24, 29–31, 148
    n.4, 151–53
Anglo-American literature 190
Anglo-European 117, 185
animal rights 188
animal studies 189, 192
Anthropocene 12–13, 15, 118, 120–21,
    130, 150, 156, 178–79
anthropocentric/anthropocentrism 8, 12,
    63, 101–02, 106, 114, 144, 166,
    175
anthropology/anthropological 22, 51–52,
    57, 196, 200
anti-ethnic absolutism 39
anti-imperialism 21
anti-Japanese sentiments 72
anti-Kuokuang campaign 13, 163–64,
    166–69, 171–72, 174–79,
    176 n.11
anti-whaling protest 188
Aotearoa (New Zealand) 7, 195–96, 200,
    204
Appiah, Anthony, "Cosmopolitan
    Patriotism" 39, 48
Armbruster, Karla 175
Armstrong, Philip 189
    "Cetaceans and Sentiment" 189–91
Asia/Asian 1, 6, 14, 24, 31, 37, 37 n.4, 95,
    148–49, 186. *See also specific*
    *countries*
Asia-America 9
East Asia 15, 68

Asia Pacific 2–3, 7, 37 n.4, 46–47, 69, 74, 149, 149 n.10, 153 n.18, 155
Asia-Pacific Economic Cooperation (APEC) 41 n.6, 46
Astley, Thea 192
Athanasiou, Athena 43, 43 n.9
Atlantic 1, 148, 156–57
Australia 1, 9, 13, 47, 57, 153, 155, 183–88, 192
  Albany 187–88
  Australian literature 183, 192–93
  First Nations 184–86, 191–92
  land rights movement 192
  New South Wales 185–87
  Queensland 184–86, 191–92
  SSI community 183, 186–87
  sugarcane/sugarcane industry 183–87
  Sydney 187
  Western Australia 187–88
Australian Marine Conservation Society 192
Australia Pacific 9, 13, 193
Austronesia 67, 209
autobiography 27, 69, 136, 139–40
autoethnographic 198, 202
'auwai system (traditional Hawaiian irrigation ditch) 111

Bal, Mieke 40
Bamba, Cecilia 73–74
Banaba 46
Banivanua Mar, Tracey 7
barbaric/barbarism 27, 59–60, 63–64
Barnett, David, *Independent* 158
Bashō, sabi 11, 61–64
Beamer, Nona 38
Beavis, William 129
*Behind the Scenes* (of Whale Rider) 197, 201, 203
Benjamin, Walter 27
Berg, Peter, bioregionalism 164
Bergthaller, Hannes, *The Anthropocene: Key Issues for the Humanities* 179
Bernes, Jasper, *Starsdown* 154
Bevacqua, Michael Lujan 31, 86, 96
Bhabha, Homi, unhomely 130–31
Biden, Joe 23, 32

Bikini (Atoll) 13, 119, 121–22, 124, 130, 147. *See also* nuclear testing
Bikini Islanders 31, 46
bioregion/bioregionalism 1, 13, 38, 147–48, 163–68, 165 n.2, 170–71, 174
Black Arts Movement 48
blackbirding 14, 183, 185–87, 193
blue poetics/ecopoetics 153, 156
Bonn, Moritz Julius, decolonization 184
Borja-Quichocho-Calvo, Kisha 67, 77
  "Re-Occupation Day ('Liberation Day')" 77–79
Bowman, I. K. 96
Boyer, Dominic 131
Bravo bomb 122, 124–26
Britain/British Empire 2, 15, 26, 192
Buell, Lawrence 164–66, 196, 199
Bunun tribe 53, 62
Burroughs, William 157
Butler, Judith 43, 43 n.9
Buttimer, Anna 120

Calder, Kent E. 21
Camacho, Keith L. 3, 31
Canada/Canadian 139, 188
capitalism 3, 37 n.4, 55, 101, 108, 153, 156, 190, 203
capitalist ideology 12, 101–02, 106
Caribbean 148, 154, 157, 186
Caro, Niki, *Whale Rider* (film) 14, 195, 197, 203–05
Carson, Rachel 159
Cashman, Edward 102
Cawthorn, M. W. 195, 201, 203
Chamorro/Chamoru (CHamoru) 11, 31, 41, 67–79, 85–92, 93, 96–99. *See also* Guåhan (Guam)
  language 71, 78, 90–91
  self-determination 11, 72, 79–80
Chan, Chang-chuan 169 n.7
Changhua Environmental Protection Union 166, 177
Chappell, David A. 26, 30
Chaudhuri, Una, theater of species 167
Cheju Island 155
Chen, Bao-lang 166–68

Chen, Bobby, "My Grandmother is a Matsu Fish" 177
Chen, Ding-nan 168, 179
Chen, Kuan-Hsing 31
Chen, Ming-chang 177 n.12
Chen, Rui-bin 177
Chen, Zhao-lun 175
Cheynes Beach Whaling Company 187
Chief Deskaheh, Haudenosaunee 202
Child, Ben 153 n.18
China/Chinese xi, 6, 10, 21–23, 32, 57, 67, 147, 147 n.2, 153, 156 n.26, 160
    Diaoyu island 154
    Shanghai 148–49
Chinese Petroleum Corporation (CPC) 163, 168
Chinese white dolphin (CWD) 176 n.11, 177
Ching, Kou Chou, "Gray Coastlines" 177 n.12
Chiri, Yukie 12, 135–36, 140
    *Ainu Shin-yo-shu, the Anthology of Ainu Divine Songs* 135
    "the Song the Owl God Sang" 136–39, 143
Chou, Chiu-long (mother of the dolphins) 176 n.11
*The Chronicles of Japan* (日本書記) 59 n.9
Clifford, James 39 n.5, 48 n.13
climate change 15, 42 n.8, 121, 172
Clinton, Hillary 149 n.9
*Cloud Atlas* 150
Cochabamba 202, 205
code-switching 89
Cold War 5, 13, 15, 23, 31–32, 147, 149, 152
Cole, Luke W. 174, 178
    "Transformation" 174
colonial discourse 3, 58, 64, 152
colonialism (colonial power) 1–4, 6–7, 9–11, 15, 28–31, 43, 54–55, 57, 67, 72–73, 75, 78–79, 85–86, 88, 92, 97–98, 101, 117, 119 n.2, 122 n.3, 183
colonization 8, 12, 14, 30–31, 43 n.9, 51, 56, 86–87, 92, 95, 97–98, 135, 193

commerce/commercial 14, 21, 23–24, 26–27, 39, 55, 149, 154, 158, 187, 190
Commission on Water Resource Management 103
commodity/commodification 101–02, 105–06, 108, 114
commons 14, 45, 149, 154, 154 n.23, 155, 165 n.2, 177–78
Commonwealth of the Northern Mariana Islands 68
community/communities 2–3, 5, 8–9, 11–15, 45, 75, 79–80, 85, 88–89, 91–92, 94–95, 98–99, 107, 113, 125, 129, 163–65, 174–75, 178, 186–87, 205–06, 209
concrete 119–20
Connery, Christopher Leigh 2, 28, 147 n.2, 148 n.3
    "Pacific Rim Discourse" 2, 147, 153
connotations/connotative 88, 90, 173
consciousness 6, 8, 47 n.12, 55, 74, 120, 154, 158–60, 164, 183, 185
Cook, James 23–24
cosmopolitan patriotism 39
cosmopolitical pluriverse 208–09
cosmos 13–14, 41, 195, 197–98, 200–01, 204–05, 207–09
counter-conversion 8, 16, 152
Cousteau, Jean Michel 205 n.3
cracker/cracking 163 n.1
Crutzen, Paul 118
culture/cultural x, x n.1, 1–5, 7–9, 11–12, 14–15, 22–23, 30, 36, 38–39, 41, 47, 56, 61, 71, 85, 89, 98, 120, 125, 127, 135, 165, 172
    cultural artifacts 87
    cultural genocide 12, 135
    cultural hunt 207, 207 n.5
    cultural knowledge 41, 57, 88
    cultural memory 35, 70, 119, 127
    cultural possessions 36–37
    cultural significance 89, 102, 107
Cumings, Bruce, *Dominion from Sea to Sea: Pacific Ascendancy and American Power* 148 n.4

Damrosch, David, *What Is World Literature?* 7
Dangerous Islands/Dangerous Archipelago. *See* French Polynesia
D'Arcy, Paul 28
Dasmann, Raymond, bioregionalism 164
de Austria, María Ana 67–68
de Buffon, Comte 55
de Certeau, Michel 23, 29, 127
decolonial/decoloniality 2, 4–8, 11–12, 15, 129, 132
decolonial genealogy 5–7
decolonial solidarity 132
decolonization 3, 7, 10–11, 30–31, 67, 74, 98, 183–84, 191–92
Def, Mos (Yasiin Bey)
  *Black on Both Sides* 156 n.27
  "New World Water" 156, 160
De la Cadena, Marisol 199–200, 207
Delahunt, Michael 175
Deleuze, Gilles 89, 158
DeLong, Ed 149
Deloria, Philip 131
Deloria, Vine 37 n.3
DeLoughrey, Elizabeth 118, 122 n.3, 128, 147
del Toro, Guillermo, *Pacific Rim* 153
Demick, Barbara 153
Democratic Progressive Party political party (DPP) 171
Dening, Greg 37
Derrida, Jacques 118–19
DeSilva, Craig 114
diaspora 3–4, 14, 43 n.10, 92
Diaz, Vicente, M. 3, 29, 35, 35 n.1
dignity 10, 88, 117, 169
Dimock, Wai Chee 151
dioxin 168
Dirlik, Arif 2, 148 n.5
displacement 14, 31, 40, 43–44, 121, 124, 126, 129, 202
dispossession 10–11, 14, 35–37, 40–44, 43 n.9, 46
Doherty, Ben, "'Full Truth': Descendants of Australia's 'Blackbirded' Islanders Want Pioneer Statues Amended" 185–86
draft environmental impact statement (DEIS) 74–76, 93
Drayton, James 24
Driver, Felix 55
d'Urville, Dumont 152
Dylan, Bob 158

earth beings 200, 202, 205–08
East China Sea 148 n.5
East India Company 55
ecocide/ecocidal 154, 192, 196
ecocriticism 14, 54, 189, 192, 196, 198
ecofeminist 173
ecological collapse 122
ecological/ecology 1, 8, 12–13, 15–16, 45–46, 119 n.2, 120–21, 122 n.3, 123, 127, 136, 142–43, 151, 153, 156, 159, 164, 166 n.4, 171–78, 196, 199
Ecological Indians 196–98, 201–05
ecopoetics/eco-poetry 7–8, 12–13, 117, 121, 148–50, 153 n.20, 155–56.
  *See also* poetics/poetry
ecoscape 152
ecosystems 8, 12–13, 15, 60, 111, 117, 122, 122 n.3, 166 n.4, 170–71, 197, 199, 202
Elder, John 165
Elliot, Michael 114
Ellison, Ralph, *Invisible Man* 44
Enewetak Atoll 119, 124, 127
English 8, 26, 40, 43 n.10, 71, 78–79, 89–90, 101 n.1, 106, 150, 159
environmental degradation 15, 118, 186, 202
environmental humanities 12–13, 164, 171–78
environmental imagination 164, 166, 168, 179
environmental justice 169, 172–74, 179, 198
epistemology 6–7, 12, 39, 56, 121
Equinor (Norwegian oil company) 188
Erdrich, Louise 199
Esaki, Teizō 52
ethics 37, 45, 110, 174, 179, 206
ethnic/ethnicity x n.1, 8–9, 14, 22, 111, 135, 198–99, 202–03, 205–06
ethnic nationalism 39

ethnography 22, 53, 197, 201, 205. *See also* multispecies ethnography
Euro-American 4, 6, 8, 14, 29, 43 n.10, 103, 119 n.2, 121
Eurocentric 4–5, 97
Europe/European 1–2, 15, 23, 25, 27, 54–55, 67, 95, 185, 192, 196, 201, 203, 209. *See also specific countries*
Exclusive Economic Zones (EEZs) 154, 154 n.21

Farber, Paul Lawrence 55
Fergusson, Erna, *Our Hawaii* 40
Fiji Islands 7, 24, 26–27, 69, 149, 185
Finland 139
fishing tradition of Tao people x n.1
flourishing 15, 127, 131
Formosa Petrochemical Mailiao Plant 168
Formosa Plastics Corporation 168–70
Fortom-Gouin, Jean-Paul 187
fossil fuels 42, 154
Foster, Sheila R. 178
 "Transformation" 174
Foucault, Michel 5
 governmentality 51, 51 n.1, 56
France 15, 160
French Polynesia 27
Frost, Robert, "The Gift Outright" 150
Fujikane, Candace 7, 41 n.6, 101–02, 106 n.5, 114
 "Kanaka Maoli cartographies" 105
 on land divisions 102

Gaard, Greta 207
Gapps, Stephen 185
Garrard, Greg 196
gender 37–38, 40, 202
genealogy 5–7, 41, 130, 154 n.22, 195, 204
*Genji Monogatari* (源氏物語) 61 n.12
genocides 12, 121–22, 125, 135, 202
geopolitics/geopolitical 3, 6, 9, 14–15, 46, 76, 148, 183
Germany 26, 68, 149, 203
 Berlin 148
Ghosh, Amitav, *The Hungry Tide* 191

Giardin, Christia 109
 "Embracing the Sacred: An Indigenous Framework for Tomorrow's Sustainability Science" 105
Ginsberg, Allen 157–58, 160 n.28
glaciers 130
global capital/capitalism 2–3, 13, 45, 153
global environmental crisis 110, 113, 117
globalization 2, 15, 45, 48, 121, 147, 152
God/Goddess 55, 58–60, 62, 107, 128, 136–44, 157, 176–77, 190
Goodyear-Kaʻōpua, Noelani, "We are Islanders" 41, 41 n.7
Graham, Bill 125
Great Australian Bight 189, 192
*Great Pacific Garbage Patch* 152, 155
Great Shrine Island (Omiya Jima) 68, 86
Greenland 130
Greenpeace 187
Gregory, Regina, *The EcoTipping Points Project* 106–07
Guåhan (Guam) 2, 6–7, 11, 21, 26, 30–31, 42, 67–69, 80, 85, 90, 92–96, 151–52, 155. *See also* Chamorro/Chamoru (CHamoru)
 draft environmental impact statement (DEIS) 74–76, 93
 Guam Reparations Commission 73
 Japan's occupation of 69–72, 86
 Lens Aquifer 79
 Litekyan (Ritidian) 79
 Mangilao 74, 77
 military buildup 74–79, 93–95
 Pågat 74, 77, 79, 87, 93–94
 power of colonized 86
 reparation 73
 Santa Rita 75
 Sumay 75, 78
 Tomhom (Tumon) 78
 unincorporated territory 11, 68, 77, 85–86, 151
Guam Insular Arts Council 69
Guam Meritorious Claims Act (1945) 73
Guattari, Félix 89

*haikai* (俳諧) 61
Hāloa 106, 108

Hālona 108
Haraway, Donna 121, 130, 199–200
　making kin 129–32
Harris, Stephen 173
Hauʻofa, Epeli 3–5, 8, 10–11, 13, 15, 29, 149, 152
　"The Future of Our Past" 36
　"The Ocean in Us" 36
　*Our Crowded Islands* 36
　"Our Places Within" 36, 47
　"Our Sea of Islands" 35–38, 41, 46
　"Pasts to Remember" 47
　plural possessive pronouns 10, 35–38, 40
　pronominal poetics 35–40
　*We Are the Ocean: Selected Works* 36, 36 n.2, 38–39, 43, 45–48
Hawaiʻi 2, 7, 11–12, 21, 27, 30–31, 41 n.7, 47, 68, 75, 85, 91–92, 95, 101–03, 101 n.2, 103, 106–08, 111, 113, 148–50, 155, 195
　Hawaiian sovereignty movement 30
　Honolulu 107, 111, 148, 151, 157
　irrigation system 103, 106, 111–12
　Pearl Harbor (Puʻuloa) 26, 28, 94, 148, 148 n.4, 151
Hawaiian Islands 24, 104 n.3, 105, 108
Hayton, Bill, *The South China Sea: The Struggle for Power in Asia* 154 n.22
heat island effect 166 n.4
hegemony/hegemonic 2, 5, 9, 21, 36, 78–79, 127, 129, 148 n.5, 149, 149 n.7, 152–53
　colonial hegemony 6, 8, 193
　hegemonic oppression 7–8
Helmreich, Stefan 200
　*Alien Ocean* 149 n. 12, 155
Henderson, David, *Cranial Guitar: Selected Poems by Bob Kaufman* 160 n.29
Hofrichter, Richard 174
Hogan, Linda 205 n.3
　*People of the Whale* 14, 191, 195–99, 205–09, 206 n.4
　*Sightings* 205 n.3
*hoʻi wai* 111
holism 45

Hong Kong 153
Hood's Canal 26
Horkheimer, Max 28
Horn, Eva, *The Anthropocene* 179
*The Host* (film) 153
Howard, Edward 69, 71
Hsu, Hsuan L. 14
Huang, Hsinya x n.1, 6 n.2, 183
Huang, Vicky 176
human-cetacean cultures 14, 189–91
humanity 8–9, 36, 45–46, 88, 118–19, 153, 176, 199
humility 40, 54, 58, 63, 121
Hunters Point Naval Shipyard, San Francisco 26
Hurley, Jessica 130
hydrography (hydrographic survey) 10, 22–25, 28–29, 31

Ihimaera, Witi 203–04, 208–09
　*The Whale Rider* (novel) 14, 191, 195, 197
imaginations 8–9, 13, 29, 59, 70, 130, 148, 163–71, 179, 199
immigrants 15, 47. *See also* migrancy/migration
Immigration Restriction Act of 1901 185
imperialism (imperial power) 1–4, 6–7, 9–11, 14–15, 22, 31, 42, 55, 63, 72, 79, 117, 119 n.2, 121, 122 n.3, 127, 149
Imperial Literature (王朝文学) 61 n.12
Indian Ocean 14, 148, 153, 184, 187, 192
Indigenous 2–4, 9, 11–12, 14–15, 27–28, 31, 36, 38, 41, 43, 43 n.9, 47, 67, 70, 73–74, 80, 85, 94, 98–99, 102, 107, 109, 114, 120–21, 123, 125–27, 130–31, 196–99, 201, 204, 207
　Indigenous body 122–23
　Indigenous communities 15, 88, 92, 99, 206
　Indigenous cosmopolitics 8, 14, 198, 200–03
　Indigenous Fijian regime (racist constitution) 39
　Indigenous homing 12, 117, 129
　Indigenous language x–xi

Indigenous literatures 15, 85, 87–88, 199
Indigenous Oceanians 43
Indigenous Pacific 3–9, 12, 38–39, 117, 120–21
Indigenous resistance 4–7, 12, 15, 127, 196
Indigenous subjects 3, 121, 130–32
Indochina 57
indo-Fijians 39
Indonesia 57
industrialization 54, 170–71, 179
inhabitants 4, 9, 25, 27, 122, 174
inheritance 36
Insular Cases (1901–1922) 68, 77
international trade 86, 172
International Whaling Commission (IWC) 196, 207 n.5
Iraq war 76

Jacksonian America 10, 22
Japan 2, 6–7, 22, 51, 55–56, 59 n.9, 69, 74, 94–95, 140, 147, 149, 153, 155, 207, 207 n.5
   academic works in Taiwan 52
   Co-prosperity Sphere of Greater East Asia 68, 72
   Hiroshima 119, 121–22, 124, 127, 129
   Hokkaido 135, 140
   imperialist government 51
   the inland (imperial metropole) 57 n.7
   Japanese Archipelago 12, 135
   Japanese Empire/imperialism 6, 11, 21, 55, 57 n.7
   Nagasaki 122, 124, 160
   natural history writings 54–56
   nuclear disaster in Fukushima 13, 147
   occupation of Guam 69–72, 86
   Okinawa 7, 31, 74, 77, 79, 149
   Senkakus island 154
Japanese Alpine Club 53
Japanese Classic Literature 59 n.9
Jeju Island, South Korea 149, 149 n.10
Jennings, Ralph 178
Jetñil-Kijiner, Kathy 10, 12, 117, 120, 130
   "Dear Matafele Peinem" 42 n.8, 121
   Dome poem 119–20, 124–29
   "Part I: The Voyage" 124
   "Part II: Of Islands and Elders," 124–27
   "Part III: Anointed" 127–29
   "Fishbone Hair" 122
   *Iep Jāltok: Poems from a Marshallese Daughter* 121–22
   "island home" 121–31
   "Monster" 129
   and Niviâna 130
   "Rise" 130
   at UN Climate Leader's Summit 42 n.8, 121
Jidirah whale sculpture 192
*jinen* (naturalness/spontaneous practices) 56 n.6
Johnson, Chalmers 21–22, 31
Jolly, Margaret 29–30
Joyce, Barry Alan 22, 24, 26–27
Juan de Fuca, Pacific Northwest 23, 25–27
Judeo-Christianity 55

*kai* (sea/area near sea) 111
*kalo* (taro) 103, 105–09, 111, 113–14
Kamakakūokalani Center for Hawaiian Studies of UHM 106–07
*Kamui yukar* (divine songs) 136
Kānaka Maoli (Native Hawaiians) 12, 101–11, 106 n.5, 113, 115
   *kalo* (taro) 105–09, 112–14
   values of
   *aloha ʻāina* (love the land) 105, 114
   *laulima* (many hands working together) 107, 113
   *mālama ʻāina* (care for the land) 105, 107
   *puʻu honua* 107, 113
Kanaloa (god) 107, 107 n.6
Kan, Chen-yi 178
Kāne (god) 107, 107 n.6
Kānewai 107, 107 n.6, 114
Kano, Tadao
   and colonial mountains of Taiwan 52–54, 56–63, 59 n.8
   the god of mountains (山神) 58–59
   *With Mountains, Cloud and Savages: Travel in the Mountains of Taiwan* (*WMCS*) 11, 52–54, 61–64

travel experience and writings of
  56–58, 62
on Wulameng Mountain 60, 60 n.10
Xiuguluan Mountain (Mabolasi
  Mountain) 60 n.11
Ka Papa Loʻi O Kānewai 103, 111, 114
  cultivation 113
  restoration of 12, 101, 106–09, 106 n.5,
    108 n.7
  wood carving at 108, 110
Kaplan, Robert D. 148, 154
Kauanui, J. Kēhaulani 3, 29
Kaufman, Bob 160
Kealiikanakaoleohaililani, Kekuhi 105,
  109
Keever, Beverly, *News Zero: The New York
  Times and the Bomb* 46
Keown, Michelle 3, 89, 119, 129
Kerouac, Jack 13, 154, 156–57
  *Atop an Underwood* 158
  *Big Sur* 159–60, 160 n.28
  *Lonesome Traveler* 159
  *On the Road* 154, 157
  *The Sea Is My Brother: The Lost Novel*
    157–59
Kim, Myung Mi 23
Kindaichi, Kyosuke 139
King Car Corporation 168 n.6
King Kamehameha I 104 n.3
kinship 12, 39, 90, 105–06, 117, 130
Kirksey, S. Eben 200
Kissinger, Henry 149 n.8
Knopf-Newman, Marcy Jane 169
Knott, Bill 154
knowledge production 3, 5 n.1, 51 n.1,
  52, 164
*Kokin Wakashū* (古今和歌集) 61
Kolodny, Annette 201
Korea 2, 147
Krech, Shepherd 196, 209
Kubodera, Itsuhiko, *The Song Sung by the
  Goddess of the Old Boat* 140–42
*kuleana* (right and responsibility) 105,
  107, 109, 111
*Kumulipo* (Hawaiian creation chant) 105
Kuokuang project 167, 170–72, 174–78,
  176 n.11. *See also* anti-
  Kuokuang campaign

*kūpuna* (elders/ancestors) 103, 105–06,
  108, 111, 114

Lai, Paul 90, 96
land 2, 11–13, 15, 24, 27, 29–30, 36,
  43–45, 51, 56, 57 n.7, 59, 78,
  85–87, 89, 93, 96–98, 101–06,
  108, 111, 114, 127, 130, 135,
  140, 150–51, 154, 156–57, 159,
  164, 167–68, 170–75, 177–79,
  184, 192, 200–02
Lane-Kamahele, Melia 109, 115
language x–xi, 7–8, 26, 30, 35, 37, 39–40,
  43 n.10, 46, 53, 60 n.10, 71–72,
  77–78, 88–91, 101 n.1, 135–36,
  151, 185, 204
las Islas Marianas archipelago (the
  Mariana Islands) 67
Latour, Bruno 199
latte 78–79, 93–94, 98
Lawler, Ray, *Summer of the Seventeenth
  Doll* 13–14, 183–87, 192–93
Leclerc, Georges Louis 55
Lévi-Strauss, Claude 199
Lewis, Jonny 187
liberalization 172, 203
lifeworld (*lebenswelt*) 120–23, 125, 127
Linnaeus, Carl 55
literary activism 11, 80, 88–89
Liu, Ka-hsiang, "After the Eighth Naphtha
  Cracker Industrial Park" 177
*loʻi kalo* (water taro field) 12, 103, 106,
  108, 111, 113
Lyons, Paul 10–11, 16, 23–24
  *American Pacificism* 3
lyricism 124–25, 129, 131

Madsen, Deborah 37 n.3
Magellan, Ferdinand 67, 86
Mahan, Alfred Thayer 26, 28, 30
  wide commons 154
Makah tribe 196, 205, 205 n.3, 207–09,
  207 n.5
Malacca Strait 148
Malaysia 147
Malolo Island 27
Manhattan Project 118
manifest destiny 22, 76, 150

man-made objects 89, 94
Mānoa Valley 103–05, 107–08, 114
Maori tradition 195–98, 200–01, 203–04, 209
Mariana archipelago 67–68
Mariana Islands 11, 23, 31, 67–68, 151
Marine Corps Base Camp Blaz 31
marine environments 186, 192
maritime geography 154 n.23
Marshall Islands/Islanders 7, 12, 30–31, 42–43, 117, 119–22, 124, 128–30
Marti, José 45
mathesis universalis 28–29
Matsu (sea goddess) 177
Matsu Fish Conservation Union of Taiwan 175–76, 175 n.10
McDougall, Brandy Nālani 12–13, 101, 103, 149, 151
　"He Mele Aloha no Albert Wendt a me Reina Whaitiri" 105
　"Papatuanuku" 106
　"Pō" (*Kumulipo*) 151
　*The Salt-Wind: Ka Makani Paʻakai* 105, 151
McGinnis, Michael Vincent 176
McGlashan, Don 189
McGregor, Davianna Pōmaikaʻi 30
Mda, Zakes, *The Whale Caller* 191
Meander, Jerry 149 n.10
melting glaciers 130
Melville, Herman, *Moby-Dick* 147, 153, 191 n.2, 199
Mentz, Steve 153 n.19
Merrill, Lynn L. 58
Mexico 67, 157, 205 n.3
Micronesia 4, 11, 67, 152
migrancy/migration 3–4, 8, 29, 202, 205 n.3
militarism 6–7, 10–12, 28–29, 55, 67, 71–72, 74–79, 86, 88, 91, 95, 97–98, 102, 117–18, 120–22, 122 n.3, 125, 129
militarization 10–11, 14, 21, 25, 30, 85, 96, 98, 117
Mishra, Sudesh 37
Miyajima, Toshimitsu 140
Mizuno, Hiromi, scientific nationalism 56

Moana Nui 35–36, 41, 41 n.6, 46–47, 149, 149 n.10
Moana Nui Statement 41
modernity 3, 5, 15, 39, 46, 55, 119 n.2, 120–22, 122 n.3, 147
modernization 52, 96, 164, 172
Momaday, N. Scott 199
Monnig, Laurel A. 31
Monroe Doctrine 148–49
*moʻolelo* (hi/story, myth, legend) 101–03, 105, 107–09, 108 n.7, 115
　of Hāloanaka 105, 108
　of kalo 106–07, 109
　of Kānaka Maoli 114
　of Kānewai 109
more-than-human beings 8, 102, 105, 124, 130. *See also* other-than-human beings
Mortimer-Sandilands, Catriona 170
Morton, Timothy 131
Mother Earth 14, 198, 201–04
multispecies ethnography 8, 14, 198, 200, 204–06. *See also* ethnography
myth 8, 10, 29, 39, 59–62, 88–89, 96–98, 101, 118–19, 121, 176, 184

*nā akua* (deities) 105–06
Nam island 125
Naʻputi, T. R. 86
National Diet of Japan (国会, Japan's bicameral legislature) 51
nation-states 7–9, 38, 106, 184
Native America/Native American 7, 9, 28, 92
Native Hawaiians 30, 44, 101–03, 105–09, 111, 114, 150. *See also* Kānaka Maoli
Native Pacific 8, 41
　Native Pacific Islanders 28–29, 31
natural science 55–56
nature 8, 12–13, 26, 54–61, 64, 136, 142–44, 200, 208
　as aesthetic and literary appreciation 61–63
　natural resources 47, 51, 55–56, 60, 101, 105, 154 n.21, 200, 204
navigation x n.1, 26, 28, 95, 140, 142
Nelson, Chris 167, 177

neocolonial/neocolonialism 8, 10, 14, 38, 41, 43, 108, 129, 184
neoliberal/neoliberalism 37 n.4, 46, 149–50
neo-Mahanian 154 n.23
Ngati Porou, Maori subgroup 195–96, 201, 203, 209
Nicolar, Joseph, *The Life and Traditions of the Red Man* 201–02
Niviâna, Aka 130–31
  "Rise" 130
Nixon, Rob 149–50
*Nō Play* (能劇) 61 n.12
North America 2, 15, 188, 196–97, 201–02, 209
Norway 207, 207 n.5
nuclear colonialism 31, 120
nuclear detonations 119–20, 122, 125–26, 128, 189
nuclearism 120
nuclearization 117, 122, 122 n.3, 127
nuclear militarism 12, 117, 120–22, 125, 129
nuclear Pacific 119–23, 126–27
nuclear regime 118, 120
nuclear testing 13, 15, 46, 75, 122, 124, 128–30
nuclear toxicity 122–23
nuclear uncanny 130
nuclear waste 124, 127–28, 155

Obama, Barack 47
  Asia-Pacific Pivot 23, 32, 149
  "Remarks to the Australian Parliament" 47
Obayashi, Taryo 139
objectification 102
ocean-based ecopoetics 13, 148
ocean commons 13, 148, 155
Oceania 3–5, 8–10, 15–16, 24, 27–28, 35–36, 38–39, 117, 119, 121, 151–52, 184
Oceania Centre for Arts and Culture 48, 152 n.14
Oceanians 36–41, 41 n.6, 43, 45–48, 104
oceanic becoming 153, 155–56, 160
oceanic consciousness 154, 158, 160

oceanic feedback system 153
oceanic imaginaries 3–4, 7–9, 13–14, 147 n.2, 183, 192
oceanic multitude 28–32
Oki-kurumi (human god) 140, 142
ʻŌlelo Hawaiʻi (Hawaiian language) 101 n.1
Ōnishi, Yoshinori 62
ordinary objects 11, 88–90, 98
Organic Act of Guam (1950) 68, 86, 98
Organization of People for Indigenous Rights (OPI-R) 74
Osorio, Jonathan Kamakawiwoʻole 28
other/otherness 2–3, 9, 22, 121, 139
other-than-human beings 102, 106, 108, 111, 113–14, 143, 200, 204, 206. See also more-than-human beings

Pacific Basin 152
Pacific Century 47
Pacific Island Labourer Act of 1901 185
Pacific Islands/Islanders 1, 3–4, 6–7, 8, 10–11, 14–15, 22–23, 28–31, 42 n.8, 45–46, 67, 87, 89, 117, 120–22, 130, 152, 183, 185
Pacific Northwest 6–7, 14, 23, 26–27, 31, 149
Pacific Rim 2, 5, 7, 13, 147–49, 147 n.2, 153
paddling 92, 197, 209
Pago Pago harbor, Sāmoa 23, 25–26, 30
Paik, Koohan 149 n.10
Palmer, Jane 155 n.24
Paulding, James K. 23, 27
Penobscots 201–02
Perez, Craig Santos 4, 6–7, 10–11, 13, 42, 45, 87, 94, 149, 151
  *from unincorporated territory* (*guma*) 41, 45, 85, 91, 93–94
  *from unincorporated territory* (*hacha*) 33, 41, 85, 94–95, 151
  *from unincorporated territory* (*lukao*) 85, 91, 95
  *from unincorporated territory* (*saina*) 41, 85, 90–93, 97, 151
  interview with Lantern Review 94

"Poet to Poet Interview" 88, 98
"Transterritorial Currents and the Imperial Terripelago" 86–87, 94–95
Perez Howard, Chris
  *Mariquita, a Tragedy of Guam* 67, 69–74
  "Thoughts and Confessions of a Chamorro Advocate" 72
Peterson, Benjamin 136 n.3
Peterson, Brenda, *Sightings* 205 n.3
Philbrick, Nathaniel 24
Philippines 21, 26, 30–31, 67–68, 147
  Philippine-American War 23, 30
  Philippine archipelagos 23, 148
planetary belonging 1, 13, 150
planetary boundaries (PB) 15, 117–21
planetary imaginary/imaginaries 117–21, 123
Plant, Judith 120
Poblete-Cross, JoAnna 30
poetics/poetry 2–4, 11–12, 25, 29, 37, 85, 87–99, 120–21. *See also* ecopoetics/eco-poetry
Polynesia/Polynesian 4, 25, 27, 37, 40, 47, 152
*Pongso no Tao* (Orchid Island/Lanyu) xi, 16
Porter, David 22 n.1
positionalities 38–39, 43 n.10
postcolonial/postcolonialism 2–3, 39, 85, 151, 183–86, 189, 192–93
power relations 7, 10, 199, 204
Pratt, Mary Louise, *Planetary Longings* 131
prismatic ecology 153
protests 11, 30, 75, 79, 87–88, 173, 187–88, 192, 197, 202
Proust, Marcel 139
Puget Sound, Pacific Northwest 23, 26
Puleloa, William 111
Pustling, Des 188

race/racial/racism 22, 37 n.4, 72, 126, 135–36, 135 n.2, 152
  racist constitution 39
radiation ecologies 121, 122 n.3

radiative colonialism 120
radioactive debris 119–20
radioactive militarism 118
radioactive toxicity 118
radionuclides 119
Rapongan, Syaman x n.1, 16
  *Eyes of the Sky* xi
Ratana, T. W. 202
reciprocal relationship 109–10
reciprocity 4–5, 7, 29, 39, 117
Reeds, T.V. 101
regional identity 29, 35, 38
regionalism 165
regional literature 4, 8
Reid, Whitelaw 148, 148 n.4
relationality 3, 5, 102, 105, 121, 150
repossession 36, 38, 42, 151
resilience x n.1, 11–12, 15, 71, 87, 103, 106, 108–09, 114, 130
resistance 1–2, 8, 11, 15, 30–31, 46–47, 92, 96, 98, 117, 121, 127, 131, 137, 149, 152, 196, 201
  literature as 87–88
resource extraction 147, 150
reverence 38, 54–55, 63, 206
Rim of the Pacific (RIMPAC) 149
rising sea-levels 43, 91, 119, 124, 128, 130, 150, 155
Rockström, Johan
  planetary boundaries 117–18
  safe operating space for humanity 118, 118 n.1
Rogers, Robert 69
Roghozhkin, Aleksandr, *Kukushka (The Cuckoo)* film 139, 139 n.4
Roosevelt, Theodore 26
Ross, Peter S. 176
ROTC (Reserve Officers' Training Corps) programs 76
Runit Dome on Enewetak Atoll 119, 124, 127, 129
Runit Island 127, 129
Russia 207 n.5
Ryden, Kent C. 102

*sabi* (さび), Japanese aesthetics 11, 61–64
Sacks, Sam 158–59

Said, Edward, *Orientalism* 2
Sakano, Tōru 51
*sakman* (canoe) 92, 98
Sale, Kirkpatrick, on bioregionalism 164–65
Salesa, Damon, "The Pacific in Indigenous Time" 39
Samai-un-kur (human goddess) 141, 143
Sami 139, 198
Sāmoa 7, 21, 24–27
　American 26, 30
　Eastern Sāmoa 25, 30
　Mau movement 30
　Pago Pago harbor 23, 25–26, 30
Sampas, Sebastian 157
Sampas, Stella 157
San Francisco, California 25–27, 68, 148, 153
　Hunters Point Naval Shipyard 26
Schmitt, Carl 147 n.2
Schuler, Timothy A. 103, 111
Schultz, Susan 43 n.10
Schumacher, E. F., free goods 178
science and technology 55–56
scientific knowledge 23, 57–59, 63
scientific nationalism 56
Sea World Marine Park, Queensland 191
Second World War 6, 22, 52, 69–74, 86, 149, 187
Sekula, Allan
　*Fish Story* 152
　*The Forgotten Space* 152–53
sentiment 55, 72, 189–90
settler colonialism 3, 101
Shadbolt, Maurice
　*Love and Legend* 190
　*This Summer's Dolphin* 189–90
Sharrad, Paul 3, 5 n.1, 69, 73
Shiels, Maggie 155 n.24
Shigematsu, Setsu 3
Shimada, Kinji 61
Shiva, Vandana 171
*shizen* (environments/nature) 56 n.6
Siberia 139
Silko, Leslie Marmon 199
Singapore 156
Sinophone xi
Sloterdijk, Peter, *Neither Sun nor Death* 154

slow violence 12, 117, 123
Smith, Russell 37
Snyder, Gary 149, 159
socialism 21
social movement 21, 31, 87, 164, 172
solidarity 1, 13, 30, 41 n.7, 132, 148, 155
Somerville, Alice Te Punga 14
Sörlin, Sverker 55
Souder, Laura Torres, *Chamorro Self-Determination: The Right of a People / I Derechon i Taotao* 72, 80
South China Sea 147–48, 148 n.5, 153–54, 153 n.18
South Korea 31, 149, 149 n.10
South Sea Islanders (SSI) community 183, 186–87
sovereignty 7, 11, 29–30, 38–39, 43, 72, 74–76, 97–98, 147, 154 n.21
Soyinka, Wole, *Of Africa* 36
Spahr, Juliana 10, 13, 150–51
　"Connected Disconnection in Pacific Multicultural Literature" 43 n.10
　*Fuck-You-Aloha-I-Love-You* 43
　"Gathering: Palolo Stream" 43–44
　"Transitory, Momentary" 150 n.13
　*Well Then There Now* 150
Spain/Spanish 23, 30, 67–68, 70–71, 78, 86–87, 90, 95, 148, 151, 157, 159
　Spanish-American War (1898) 68, 86
　Spanish-Chamorro Wars (1668–1695) 68
Spence, Mark 165 n.2, 171
Spicer, Jack 157
spiritual/spirituality 58, 60, 62, 67, 77, 96, 102, 105, 108, 130, 136, 172, 196, 198, 201
Spivak, Gayatri Chakravorty 2, 121
*SS Dorchester* transport ship 157–58
Steinwand, Jonathan 191 n.2, 198–99
Stengers, Isabelle 199–200, 207
Sterling, Elspeth P., *Sites of Oahu* 103
Stillman, Amy Kuʻulealoha 3, 25
Stoermer, Eugene 118
Stokrocki, Mary L. 175
storytelling 37, 40, 70, 74, 111
Straits of San Juan de Fuca 26
Subramani 8, 29
　"The Oceanic Imaginary" 8, 183, 192
Sudo, Naoto 72

sugarcane/sugarcane industry 183–87
Summers, Catherine C., *Sites of Oahu* 103
survival 11, 38, 44–48, 56, 72, 87–88, 98–99, 118–21, 129, 174, 197, 206, 209
survivance 47, 47 n.12, 88, 92, 131
sustainability 110, 131, 167, 172, 175
Suzuki, Erin 2, 9, 15
Swinhoe, Robert 53 n.4

Tahiti Island 26–27
Taicho 72
Taiwan 2, 6–7, 11, 51, 155, 163, 166–68
    Aboriginal people of 51, 53, 56, 58–59, 59 n.8, 64
    bioregion/bioregionalism 1, 13, 38, 147–48, 163–68, 165 n.2, 170–71, 174
    colonial mountains of 52–54, 56–63, 59 n.8 (*see also* Kano, Tadao)
    environmental awareness 177
    environmental pollution 168–71, 174, 179
    Jade Mountain (Niitaka Mountain, 新高山) 53, 53 n.4, 58
    Japan's colonial base in 51
    natural history of 52, 54–56
    petrochemical industries, impacts of 163–71, 179
    pink dolphins 13, 167, 175–76
    nature writing 11, 52, 57–59, 63
Tao people x n.1, xi
*tatala* (Tao canoe) x, x n.1
Teaiwa, Teresia K. 4–5, 31, 124
    "AmneSIA" 5
    *A New Oceania* 37–38
    *Sweat and Salt Water* 5
*Te Waka: Building the Canoe* 197, 197 n.1, 204, 209
Thayer, Robert L. 165 n.2, 171
Thomashow, Mitchell 170
Thomas, Julia Adeney 55–56
Torres, Robert Tenorio 71
Torres Strait Island people (First Nations Australians) 185
tourism/tourist 10, 30–31, 36, 78, 86, 88, 95, 151
trade/traders 1, 6, 10, 22, 25, 27, 67, 86, 94, 96, 147, 154 n.22, 171–72, 203

traditional knowledge x n.1, 92, 113
transformational animals 199, 202, 205–08
trans-Indigenous 4, 6, 6 n.2, 9, 131
translation 88, 90, 130, 136 n.3, 141 n.5, 151, 177 n.13
transnational/transnationalism 2, 4, 6, 6 n.2, 9, 13, 37 n.4, 39, 75, 147, 152–53, 202
trans-oceanic 147, 152, 155, 160
transpacific 1–3, 5–9, 13–16, 41 n.6, 67, 151, 153
Trans-Pacific Partnership (TPP) 41 n.6, 86
Travis, Charles 120
Truman, Harry 86
tsunami 147, 155
Tuamotu Island 24, 27
Tu, Karen Kan-Lun x n.1
Turner, Fredric Jackson 26
Tutuila Island 25
Tuvalu island 155, 185

Underwood, Robert, *Chamorro Self-Determination: The Right of a People / I Derechon i Taotao* 72, 80
United Nations Conference on Sustainable Development 172
United Nations Convention on the Law of the Sea (UNCLOS) 154, 154 n.21
United Nations Declaration on the Rights of Indigenous Peoples (UNDRIP) 198, 202
United Nations Trust Territory of the Pacific Islands 68
United Nations Working Group on Indigenous Populations (WGIP) 202
The United States 1, 6, 11, 15, 21, 26–27, 30–31, 41–43, 46, 68, 74, 119, 121, 128–29, 147 n.2, 148–50, 153, 155
    detonation of nuclear bombs (1946–1958) 119
    expansionism 22–23, 22 n.1
    and Guåhan 72–74, 85–86, 95
    labor strikes in 21
    military bases 21, 26, 76, 79, 85–87, 93, 95

nuclear legacies in the Marshall Islands 121–22, 124
Treaty of Peace with Japan (1951) 73
United States Exploring Expedition (Ex. Ex.) 22
US empire 10, 21–32
Universal Declaration on the Rights of Mother Earth (UDRME) 198, 202, 208
University of Hawai'i at Mānoa (UHM) 12, 101, 103–04, 106, 106 n.5
UN Permanent Forum on Indigenous Issues (UNPFII) 202

Vietnam War 76, 206
violence 6, 12, 39, 42, 68, 70, 72, 74, 88, 117–18, 120–21, 123–25, 127, 206
Vizenor, Gerald, on survivance 47 n.12, 88, 92

*wai* (water) 12, 101, 107, 109
*waiwai* (wealth) 101 n.2
*waka* (canoes) 195, 197–98, 197 n.1, 198 n.2, 204–05, 209
Wākea (sky father) 105–06, 108
Wang, Hsiang-hua x n.1
Wendt, Albert 5 n. 1, 12, 35, 101, 103–05, 152
  "Mānoa Valley" 104–05
  "Toward a New Oceania" 35
Westernization 55, 172
Western maps/mapping 12, 101–03, 105–07, 111, 114
Western science 11, 56, 63–64, 208
whakapapa (genealogy) 195–96
Whale and Dolphin Coalition 187
whale hunting/slaughter 14, 183–84, 187–88, 196–97, 203, 206–07, 209
Whangara, New Zealand 195, 200, 203, 209
White Australia policy 185
White, Geoff 45
White, Gilbert 58
  *The Natural History of Selborne* 54–55
White, Lynn Jr. 55
White settlers 12, 101–03, 107, 111, 114
Wilkes, Charles 22–24

*Narrative of the U.S. Exploring Expedition* 24–25
Wilkes Expedition (1838–1842) 10, 22–32
Wilson, Rob 1–3, 16
  *Be Always Converting, Be Always Converted* 8, 37 n.4, 152
  *Reimagining the American Pacific* 3
  *When the Nikita Moon Rose* 3
Winduo, Steven Edmund 45
Winton, Timothy
  *Dirt Music* 192
  *Shallows* 14, 183, 187–93
Wolfe, Thomas 158
Won Pat-Borja, Melvin 67, 75–76
  on Insular Cases 77
  "No Deal" 75, 77
Wood, Houston 29
Woodward, Valerie 72
worlding/re-worlding, Pacific literature 1–4, 6, 8, 12, 15
World Wildlife Fund (WWF) 166 n.4
Worster, Donald, *Nature's Economy* 54
Wu, Mingyi 166–70, 172–75, 177–79
  *The Man with the Compound Eyes* 164, 171
  *The Stolen Bicycle* 164
  *Wetlands, Petrochemicals, and Imagining an Island* 13, 163–64, 172
Wu, Sheng 164, 166–67, 169–70, 172–73, 175, 177
  *Guarding River of Mother: Notes on the Jhuoshuei River* 164
  *Wetlands, Petrochemicals, and Imagining an Island* 13, 163–64, 172
  "Write You a Poem" 167, 176

Yamasaki, Tsukane, *A Life of Tadao Kano: A Naturalist Who Loved Taiwan* 52–53, 53 n.3
Yamashiro, Aiko, "We are Islanders" 41, 41 n.7
Yao, Jento 51, 51 n.1
Yardley, William 209
Yeh, Yi-chun 165–66
Yeo, George 156 n.26
Yoneyama, Lisa 5–6

www.ingramcontent.com/pod-product-compliance
Lightning Source LLC
Chambersburg PA
CBHW052035300426
44117CB00012B/1836